THE TERROR OF NATURAL RIGHT

THE TERROR *of*
NATURAL RIGHT

Republicanism, the Cult of Nature,
and the French Revolution

DAN EDELSTEIN

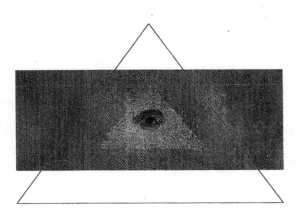

THE UNIVERSITY OF CHICAGO PRESS
Chicago & London

The University of Chicago Press, Chicago 60637
The University of Chicago Press, Ltd., London
© 2009 by The University of Chicago
All rights reserved. Published 2009
Paperback edition 2010
Printed in the United States of America
18 17 16 15 14 13 12 11 10   2 3 4 5 6

ISBN-13: 978-0-226-18438-8 (cloth)
ISBN-13: 978-0-226-18439-5 (paper)
ISBN-10: 0-226-18438-2 (cloth)
ISBN-10: 0-226-18439-0 (paper)

The University of Chicago Press gratefully acknowledges the generous
support of Stanford University toward the publication of this book.
Illustration on p. iii: Jean-Jacques Lebarbier, *The Declaration of Human Rights . . .
August 20–26, 1789* (detail). Musée de la Ville de Paris, Musée Carnavalet, Paris,
France. Photograph copyright Erich Lessing / Art Resource, New York.

Library of Congress Cataloging-in-Publication Data

Edelstein, Dan.
The terror of natural right : republicanism, the cult of nature, and the French
Revolution / Dan Edelstein.
p. cm.
Includes bibliographical references and index.
ISBN-13: 978-0-226-18438-8 (cloth : alk. paper)
ISBN-10: 0-226-18438-2 (cloth : alk. paper) 1. France—History—Reign of Terror,
1793–1794. 2. France—History—Revolution, 1789–1799. 3. France—Politics
and government—1789–1799. 4. Republicanism—France—History—18th century.
5. Political violence—France—History—18th century. I. Title.
DC183.5.E445 2009
944.04′4—dc22
2009001654

To my parents, Lynn Mahoney Edelstein and Stuart J. Edelstein

CONTENTS

❧ ACKNOWLEDGMENTS ❧

I DO NOT THINK I could have written this book anywhere besides Stanford. The garden campus and *ver aeternum* played no small part, to be sure, but it is the people that truly make Stanford a paradise of learning. Like a patient gardener, Robert Harrison transplanted me here and saw that I flourished: To his scholarly model and unparalleled support I am forever indebted. Sepp Gumbrecht and Josh Landy have been the best mentors, friends, and critics one could hope for. And this book would simply not have been the same without the intellectual generosity of Keith Baker. He truly was *il miglior fabbro*, revealing my own arguments to me, sharing his interpretations, and sharpening mine. I have also benefited tremendously from the invaluable advice of my Stanford colleagues Jean-Marie Apostolidès, John Bender, Russell Berman, Elisabeth Boyi, Philippe Buc, Joshua Cohen, J. P. Daughton, Jean-Pierre Dupuy, Paula Findlen, Grisha Friedin, Roland Greene, Josh Ober, Aron Rodrigue, and the Stanford Bungee Lunch group. I owe a special thanks to Sarah Sussman, curator for French and Italian Studies at Stanford Libraries, for her great assistance with securing primary and secondary sources. I am also grateful for a grant from the vice-provost for Undergraduate Education, supporting research assistants; to the Research Unit of the Division of Literatures, Cultures, and Languages; and to the president for the generous research funds made available to humanities faculty.

There are, of course, many wonderful people elsewhere, and I am particularly fortunate to work in a field that boasts such an array of brilliant and generous scholars. At an early stage of this project, and then at every subsequent turn, David A. Bell has provided crucial and decisive input and support. His incredibly attentive reading of my book manuscript transformed it in more ways than I could have imagined. I learned more in my dear friend Jake Soll's study than in most classes I've taken. Elena Russo has been a wonderful reader and colleague. As many other junior scholars, I benefited from Colin Jones's legendary support and suggestions. My understanding of republicanism and political thought owes much to conversations with David Bates, Andrew Jainchill, Jimmy Swenson, and Kent Wright. Carolina Armenteros, Göran Blix, Howard Brown, Hannah Dawson, Steven Englund, Nina Gelbart, Anthony Grafton, Carla Hesse, Marie-Hélène Huet, Eddie Kolla, Larry Kritzman, Antoine Lilti, Ted Margadant, Sarah Maza, John Merriman, Mary Ashburn Miller, Pernille Røge, Pierre Saint-Amand, Maurice Samuels, Anne Simonin, Jonathan Smyth, Malina Stefanovska, and Jessica Wardhaugh all offered most helpful comments. I received invaluable comments on my manuscript from Paul Friedland; raised eyebrows from Jean-Clément Martin and Tim Tackett moved this project in directions they could not have foreseen. I am especially grateful to Robert Morrissey, Paul Cheney, Charly Coleman, and the Modern France Workshop at the University of Chicago, as well as to Mark Olsen, Glenn Roe, and Robert Voyer of the ARTFL project. Also at Chicago, I am most obliged to my editor, Alan Thomas, as well as to Randy Petilos, and my copy editor, Lisa A. Wehrle. I'd also like to thank the undergraduate and graduate students who suffered through much of this material with me in class (especially the dreaded two-hour PowerPoint presentation!), and more particularly my research assistants, Samantha Kuok Leese, Emily Dalton, and Caitlin Crandell.

Before arriving at Stanford, I received excellent mentorship at Penn, where I did my graduate studies. Many thanks to my advisors, now friends, Philippe Met, Jean-Michel Rabaté, Maurie Samuels, and Caroline Weber. I am also grateful to Asif Agha, Kevin Brownlee, Joan DeJean, Gerry Prince, and Greg Urban. Early research for my dissertation was made possible by a Fulbright grant to Paris. Prior to coming to Penn, I was trained at the University of Geneva, where Antoine Raybaud, Michel Jeanneret, Laurent Jenny, and Guy Poitry taught me what it meant to be a scholar. Without André Della Santa's early encouragement, at the Collège Calvin, I might never have aspired to become one.

My first teachers are still the ones from whom I learn the most: My mother, Lynn, and my father, Stuart, inculcated in me the crucial virtues for both life and learning. Their unconditional support for my various ambitions (even when they involved lugging around guitar amplifiers) has been my greatest blessing. It is with a profound sense of gratitude that I dedicate this book to them. My sister Jenny has been unfailing in her support and friendship, now supplemented by my niece, Yaelle, and nephews, Liam and Gabriel. To my wife, Zoë, I owe what no number of scholarly accomplishments can ever provide: happiness.

Much of this book was written with our beloved cat Fang on my lap; sitting at the computer has never been the same since he passed away. Having our keeshond Teddy curled up under the desk has been an unabiding source of comfort since.

Parts of the prologue and chapter 5 appeared, respectively, in "*Hostis Humani Generis:* Devils, Natural Right, Terror, and the French Revolution," and "The Law of 22 Prairial: Introduction," *Telos: A Quarterly Journal of Critical Thought* 141 (2007): 57–81 and 82–91. I am grateful to the publisher for the permission to use this material. Parts of chapter 3 appeared in "War and Terror: The Law of Nations from Grotius to the French Revolution," *French Historical Studies* 31, no. 2, special issue on "War, Culture, and Society," ed. David A. Bell and Martha Hanna (2008): 229–62. I thank Duke University Press for permission to republish these sections.

TO LIVE AND DIE BY NATURE'S LAWS

UPON LEARNING that the National Constituent Assembly had finally drafted the Constitution that it had solemnly sworn to produce two years earlier, the journalist, poet, and radical *philosophe* Sylvain Maréchal addressed an anonymous pamphlet to the attention of the Assembly. Through the voice of "Lady Nature," he reproached the constituents for having mistaken their purpose and produced the wrong document:

> Twenty-five million men, spoiled by their interactions, unhappy and unable to stand each other, cry out to you for a new code, and you had the courage to promise them one. But why didn't you have the good sense to send them back to me, telling them: brothers, do you not have the laws of nature? Could we ever do better than those?[1]

This attack sounds oddly misguided. It would have been one thing to criticize the specific contents of the Constitution, but to call its very existence into question? Only a devout monarchist or utopian schemer could criticize the Assembly for its constitutional endeavors in their entirety. Admittedly, there was a utopian streak in Maréchal: a pastoral poet and freethinker before the Revolution, he would later become the ideological mastermind of the Conspiracy of Equals, a communist, insurrectionary group led by Gracchus Babeuf in 1795.[2] But in 1791, as in 1789, Maréchal was first and foremost a fervent republican: He had rejected monarchy as "an impractical machine [*rouage*] / A superfluous spring" as early as 1781, arguing that states "without kings only need their magistrates."[3]

---

1. *Dame Nature à la barre de l'Assemblée nationale* (Paris: Chez les Marchands de Nouveautés, 1791), 1; available online at http://humanities.uchicago.edu/images/DN/contents. html. Unless otherwise indicated, all translations in this book are my own.

2. See especially Maurice Dommanget, *Sylvain Maréchal, l'égalitaire* (Paris: Spartacus, 1950). Maréchal's politics and career are discussed in chapter 2.

3. *Dieu et les prêtres: fragments d'un poème moral sur Dieu* (1781; Paris: Patris, an II [1793]), 35; available online at http://gallica.bnf.fr/ark:/12148/bpt6k20581k.

From Livy to Machiavelli and from Milton to Madison, however, republicanism was always centered around a constitution: "For the maintenance of good customs laws are required," Machiavelli observed.[4] It was thanks to great lawgivers—men such as Moses, Minos, Confucius, Lycurgus, Solon, or Numa—that states could survive (be they republics or principalities, for that matter). The idea that unwritten, natural laws alone might provide the basis for a viable republic was inconceivable. Natural right might constitute a foundation for civil laws, but it was never seen as sufficient.

How, then, are we to interpret Maréchal's strangely anticonstitutional, yet republican declarations? Do they merely reflect the musings of a confused pamphleteer? Before rejecting them outright, we would do well to consider that these same ideas also appeared in the unpublished writings of a key leader of the first French Republic, Louis-Antoine Saint-Just. "The social state is not the product of a convention," Saint-Just argued, adding that "the art of establishing . . . society by a pact or by forced transformations is the selfsame art of destroying society."[5] For Saint-Just, as for Maréchal before him, natural right offered laws enough: "Since there can be no society that is not founded on nature, the state [*la cité*] can accept no other laws besides those of nature. . . . Law is thus not the expression of will but of nature."[6] Constitutions and civil legislation that did not content itself with echoing the laws of nature were pernicious to society.

This was not the republicanism of the ancients, which is what Jacobinism has commonly been branded ever since Benjamin Constant: Sparta, Athens, and even Rome were known for their elaborate constitutions, the gifts of godlike lawgivers. Nor was this classical republicanism: Machiavelli had little or nothing to say about natural law. He perceived the republic and its constitution as the most artfully crafted of political systems.[7] Saint-Just's statements

---

4. Machiavelli, *The Discourses*, trans. L. J. Walker and B. Richardson (London: Penguin, 2003), 1.18; 160. In *The Prince*, Machiavelli had famously pointed to the need for "good laws and good arms" to hold on to a state (chap. 12). On the place of the constitution in classical republicanism, see Quentin Skinner's observation on how "the laws relating to the constitution . . . served to ensure that the common good was promoted at all times," in "The Republican Idea of Political Liberty," in *Machiavelli and Republicanism*, ed. Gisele Bock, Quentin Skinner, and Maurizio Viroli (Cambridge: Cambridge University Press, 1990), 306; see also J. G. A. Pocock, *The Machiavellian Moment: Florentine Political Thought and the Atlantic Republican Tradition* (1975; Princeton: Princeton University Press, 2003), 169 and *passim*.

5. *Œuvres complètes*, ed. Michèle Duval (Paris: Lebovici, 1984), 922 (hereafter cited as *SJ*).

6. Ibid., 950–51.

7. On the distinction between republicanism of the ancients and "classical republicanism," see Paul A. Rahe, *Republics Ancient and Modern: Classical Republicanism and the American Revolution* (Chapel Hill: University of North Carolina Press, 1992), and Wilfried Nippel, "Ancient and Modern Republicanism: 'Mixed Constitution' and 'Ephors,'" in *The Invention*

may call to mind the modern republicanism of the American revolutionaries, but here as well appearances are deceptive: Whether one emphasizes a "liberal" or "republican" genealogy of this political enterprise, it would be senseless to suggest that the American case does not display traces of both. The Declaration of Independence may have begun by proclaiming Congress's (or at least Jefferson's) faith in "the Laws of Nature and Nature's God," but the rest of the document and its list of grievances clearly demonstrate how "Congress sailed into its conflict with England, securely guided by English stars,"[8] in the form of British constitutionalism and its republican tradition. The Jacobin variant, which sought to govern by nature's laws alone, seems to constitute a mutant strain, one that I call "natural republicanism." As it incorporated a number of traditional republican features, it may be considered one of the "transformations of classical republicanism" that occurred in eighteenth-century France,[9] even if it differed fundamentally from earlier theories by positing that natural right alone should furnish the legal framework of society.

The claim that the laws of nature were also the laws of the republic, however, led to a conflation between nature and nation that had grave consequences for anyone misfortunate enough to break (or to appear to break) the law. Indeed, it was a widely held assumption in liberal natural right theory that whoever violated the laws of nature could be killed with impunity. This situation was meant to prevail only in the state of nature, yet there were a few exceptions: Tyrants, savages, brigands, pirates, and other *hostes humani generis* ("enemies of the human race") could be executed by the proper authorities without due process or legal formalities. Since the Jacobins equated the republic and its goals with nature itself, almost any potentially subversive

of the Modern Republic, ed. Biancamaria Fontana (Cambridge: Cambridge University Press, 1994), 6–26. For Constant, see "The Liberty of Ancients Compared with That of Moderns," in *The Political Writings of Benjamin Constant*, trans. and ed. Biancamaria Fontana (Cambridge: Cambridge University Press, 1988).

8. Garry Wills, *Inventing America: Jefferson's Declaration of Independence* (Garden City, NJ: Doubleday, 1978), 63; see also Bernard Bailyn, *The Ideological Origins of the American Revolution* (Cambridge: Belknap Press of Harvard University Press, 1967); and Gordon Wood, *The Creation of the American Republic, 1776–1787* (Chapel Hill: University of North Carolina Press, 1969). For the "liberal" interpretation, see notably Louis Hartz, *The Liberal Tradition in America: An Interpretation of American Political Thought Since the Revolution* (New York: Harcourt, Brace, 1955); and Joyce Appleby, *Liberalism and Republicanism in the Historical Imagination* (Cambridge: Harvard University Press, 1992). For a review of these different currents, see Daniel T. Rodgers, "Republicanism: The Career of a Concept," *Journal of American History* 79, no. 1 (1992): 11–38.

9. See Keith Baker, "Transformations of Classical Republicanism in Eighteenth-Century France," *Journal of Modern History* 73 (2001): 32–53.

activity could be prosecuted as a crime against nature. The exceptional became terrifyingly normal.

The thesis of this book, therefore, is not just that Jacobin political leaders championed an unusual variant of republican thought, but that they drew on natural right to authorize and draft the laws underpinning the Terror. The *hostis humani generis* category lay at the heart of the Montagnard prosecution of the king, but subsequently provided a template for other categories of hostility, from the notorious *hors-la-loi* (outlaw) up to the "enemy of the people." In the context of a natural-republican legal system, in which natural right was perceived as the supreme body of law, this radical concept of hostility was unchecked by any civil guarantees. The *conventionnels* could exercise terror while appearing faithful to the principles of the 1789 Declaration of Rights.

This interpretation of the Terror rests largely on legal arguments and political theories, as opposed to much of the scholarship in the last fifteen years.[10] Most of this recent work is excellent, and I draw from it extensively in the following chapters. But it does not, to my mind, provide convincing answers to the fundamental questions of the Terror. How and why did it come about? How did it relate to Jacobin political thought? Was the Convention forced down the road to terror, or did it choose its own way? I have turned to legal traditions and political thought to answer these questions, not because I deem these areas more important than, say, social practices or the history of emotions, but because I found that they played more decisive roles in the establishment and development of the Terror.

The basic methodological approach I have adopted, then, owes greatly to such historians as Keith Baker, J. G. A. Pocock, and Quentin Skinner, as well as to earlier scholars such as Hannah Arendt, although my disparate corpus has also obliged me to be somewhat eclectic. Along with legal and political texts, this corpus includes literary, ethnographic, antiquarian, and even theological works, as well as cultural representations (either "imaginary," such as myths, or printed images) and revolutionary festivals. I have accordingly been ecumenical in my methodology, analyzing some documents as a cultural historian, others as a literary scholar, some as a social scientist, and yet others as a political theorist. Occasionally I have worn all four hats at once.[11] This book is not intended as a discourse

---

10. I discuss the current historiography of the Terror and its opposition to the "political culture approach" in chapter 3.

11. The disparity of my corpus has also led me to adopt a more "semiotic" rather than strictly linguistic approach to historical analysis, as well as, in some instances, a quantitative one.

on method; I have simply chased my arguments down every path they took.

This book does, however, propose a few methodological innovations. First, perhaps due to my own training as a literary scholar and to the fact that many examples of natural republicanism are found in literature, I chose to study political theories from a more narrative perspective. Political historians tend to analyze these theories in terms of their grammar, keywords, or discourse, often in an explicit analogy to Saussure's theory of *langue* and *parole*.[12] But there is also a temporal dimension to political theory, a dimension perhaps more evident in Greek and early-modern political philosophy than in its contemporary incarnations. Machiavelli's theory of republicanism, for instance, can conveniently be told as a story. A prince or strongman seizes power and gives the city laws. These laws are meant to inspire virtue in a people, and they are sustained by institutions such as religion and the military. Eventually, however, corruption sets in, in the form of luxury or moral laxity. Virtue soon slumps, and the republic dies.[13] As simplistic as this version may sound, it has the advantage of highlighting resemblances with other narratives, for instance, the natural right narrative of how civil society comes into being and eventually dissolves.[14] Considering political theories in narrative form may thus offer a better model for understanding

---

This combination of methods is much indebted to William H. Sewell Jr.'s *Logics of History: Social Theory and Social Transformation* (Chicago: University of Chicago Press, 2005).

12. See notably J. G. A. Pocock, "The Concept of a Language and the *Métier d'Historien*: Some Considerations on Practice," in *The Languages of Political Theory in Early-Modern Europe*, ed. Anthony Pagden (Cambridge: Cambridge University Press, 1987). In his more recent work, however, Pocock has himself emphasized the central importance of narratives, suggesting, for instance, that the history of eighteenth-century philosophy "is the history of the narratives which historians have been impelled to put together"; see *Narratives of Civil Government*, vol. 2 of *Barbarism and Religion* (Cambridge: Cambridge University Press, 2001), 6. On the use of keywords in historiography, see also David A. Bell, *The Cult of the Nation in France: Inventing Nationalism, 1680–1800* (Cambridge: Harvard University Press, 2001), 24–35. On the concept of discourse, see Keith Baker, *Inventing the French Revolution* (Cambridge: Cambridge University Press, 1990), 5–27.

13. This narrative, of course, is highlighted in the title and argument of Pocock's *Machiavellian Moment*. One could take this narrative analysis one step further and ask whether Hayden White's "tropological" theory of historiography, famously outlined in *Metahistory: The Historical Imagination in Nineteenth-Century Europe* (Baltimore: Johns Hopkins University Press, 1975), may not be better suited for political thought. Both Machiavelli's republicanism and *The Prince*, for instance, seem to adhere to the tragicomic genre: Fortune is always meddling with our affairs, but intelligence and daring (*virtù*) can overcome her—until a certain point, when fate wins out in the end. Rousseau's second *Discourse*, by contrast, recounts a classic tragedy of human society, which is fated to descend into iniquity and corruption. Obviously, not every political narrative will obey the rules of literary genre, but the parallel seems promising.

14. I compare these two narratives in chapter 1, with respect to Mably.

how these theories can transform and even combine—precisely the question at the heart of natural republicanism.

Second, I have sought to pay greater attention to the role that myths occupy in political thought. While it is commonplace in studies of twentieth-century political thought to acknowledge the shaping power of myths, political histories of earlier periods rarely consider their influence, despite their undeniable presence. To some extent, this neglect is due to the deeply ahistoricized manner in which some scholars have analyzed the significance of myths in modern settings. All too often myths are interpreted as archetypes, whose meanings never change and whose value for understanding the specificity of a historical moment is accordingly slight.[15] In the case of the golden age myth, which lies at the heart of natural republicanism, this timeless invariability could not be further from the truth. There was a wide assortment of variants for the myth, some royalist and others republican, some primitivist and others highly civilized. Moreover, the myth acquired a powerful hold on political thinkers only once it had been "naturalized" by anthropological and historical research.[16] Its force did not depend on unconscious yearnings but on clearly articulated visions of a "real" and truly possible Age of Gold.[17] Only by tending to the philological variants of myths can we hope to assess their specific influence on political thought.

Natural Right and Republicanism in France

A reader versed in early-modern European history might wonder why the "mutation" of natural right and republicanism occurred in a country that is not strongly identified with either of these traditions. I suggest that the relative marginalization of these traditions in France is precisely what made such

---

15. For instance, André Delaporte, in *L'idée d'égalité en France au XVIIIe siècle* (Paris: PUF, 1987), reads a number of eighteenth-century authors through the prism of the golden age myth; like many French scholars, however, his methodology is derived from the work of Mircea Eliade and Carl Jung, and his observations are much more oriented toward ancient wisdom than toward political theory or history. For a similar effort, see Raoul Girardet, *Mythes et mythologies politiques* (Paris: Seuil, 1986). I propose a different approach to the study of modern myths in "Editors' Preface: Mythomanies," with Bettina Lerner, *Yale French Studies* 111 (2007): 1–4.

16. I am borrowing the concept of a "naturalized" myth from Roland Barthes, *Mythologies*, trans. Annette Lavers (1957; New York: Hill and Wang, 1984), 129.

17. This pragmatic understanding of myth is deeply indebted to Georges Sorel's *Reflections on Violence*, ed. and trans. Jeremy Jennings (Cambridge: Cambridge University Press, 1999), esp. 20–29. I discuss Sorel's definition in greater detail in "The Birth of Ideology from the Spirit of Myth: Georges Sorel among the *Idéologues*," in *The Re-enchantment of the World: Secular Magic in a Rational Age*, ed. Joshua Landy and Michael Saler (Stanford: Stanford University Press, 2009).

a radical mutation possible. Natural right was not part of French law school curricula, as it was in England, Switzerland, Germany, or the Netherlands. Mably may not have been greatly exaggerating when he claimed that "our judges [*gens de robe*], who no doubt know a great deal . . . could not be more ignorant of the most common principles of natural right."[18] Indeed, until the "patriotic" reactions to the Maupeou reform of the parliaments, natural right hardly featured in French legal thought.[19] Though drawing, as did all European jurists, on the legacy of Roman law, the French jurists paid lip service to *ius naturale*, as politico-legal works focused instead on adapting the concept of *imperium* to the Bourbon monarchy.[20] By picking and choosing in this manner from the Justinian code, French jurists could present the sovereign as the sole source of law, by virtue of his position above the law (*princeps legibus solutus*). What this definition effaced was Roman law's dependency on the authoritative principles of natural right, a point on which English jurists and philosophers, such as Locke and Blackstone (as well as their continental counterparts, notably Christian Wolff and Jean-Jacques Burlamaqui), would insist.

Though all but banished from juridical theory, natural right nonetheless remained an accessible and commonly employed discourse in eighteenth-century France. Budding lawyers or philosophes could study Burlamaqui's textbooks, written for his students at the *Académie* of Geneva, or read Jean Barbeyrac's translations of, and commentaries on, Grotius and Pufendorf.[21] By the end of the century, a young lawyer from Arras

18. Gabriel Bonnot de Mably, *Des droits et des devoirs du citoyen* (Paris: Kell, 1789), 73.

19. See Durand Echeverria, *The Maupeou Revolution: A Study in the History of Libertarianism (France, 1770–1774)* (Baton Rouge: Louisiana State University Press, 1985), 67–69.

20. For a helpful overview of the concept of *imperium* in early-modern political thought, see Anthony Pagden, *Lords of All the World: Ideologies of Empire in Spain, Britain and France, c. 1500–c. 1800* (New Haven: Yale University Press, 1995). On France more specifically, see Donald R. Kelley, *Foundations of Modern Historical Scholarship: Language, Law, and History in the French Renaissance* (New York: Columbia University Press, 1970); by the same author, see also "Law"; and by Julian H. Franklin, "Sovereignty and the Mixed Constitution: Bodin and His Critics," in *The Cambridge History of Political Thought, 1450–1700*, ed. J. H. Burns and Mark Goldie (Cambridge: Cambridge University Press, 1991). Bodin, for instance, always spoke in one breath of "la loy de Dieu et de nature" in *Les Six livres de la république*, but did not elaborate on the potential conflict between this divine natural law and the will of the sovereign. For the relevant passages, see *On Sovereignty*, trans. Julian H. Franklin (Cambridge: Cambridge University Press, 1992). For an overview of French-language natural right theories in eighteenth-century France, see Robert Derathé, *Jean-Jacques Rousseau et la science politique de son temps* (1950; Paris: Vrin, 1970); on French legal training, see David A. Bell, *Lawyers and Citizens: The Making of a Political Elite in Old Regime France* (Oxford: Oxford University Press, 1994).

21. Barbeyrac's best-known translations are his editions of Pufendorf's *Le droit de la nature*

could even invoke the law of nations as a legal authority in his court case.[22] As we will see, natural right was the dominant language of political reform for a wide range of eighteenth-century writers, who criticized the variegated and seemingly arbitrary legal codes of France and other nations in the name of the universal and unchanging laws of nature.[23] The language and concepts of natural right were thus in open circulation throughout France; the *Déclaration des droits de l'homme et du citoyen* did not emerge *ex nihilo*. So detached were these concepts from actual legal practices, however, that their meaning and relations could be easily redefined. Their political value could also be freely determined since natural right outside of France was often identified with specific parties in political struggles.[24]

Republicanism was similarly a faint discourse in eighteenth-century France, though not nearly as absent as has sometimes been claimed.[25] If

---

et des gens (Amsterdam: n.p., 1706) and *Les devoirs de l'homme et du citoyen* (Amsterdam: H. Schelte, 1707), and his later edition of Grotius's *Le droit de la guerre et de la paix* (Amsterdam: P. de Coup, 1724). Barbeyrac's extensive, often critical, footnotes presented to his readers a much more liberal version of natural right, derived from Locke, whose ideas his commentaries contributed to disseminate in France. Burlamaqui's (equally Lockean) textbooks were published beginning in 1747; see in particular his *Principes du droit naturel* (Geneva: Barrillot, 1747) and his *Principes du droit politique* (Amsterdam: Zacharie Chatelain, 1751). On both these authors, see Derathé, *Jean-Jacques Rousseau et la science politique*, and, on Burlamaqui's meddling in Genevan politics, Helena Rosenblatt, *Rousseau and Geneva: From the First Discourse to The Social Contract, 1749–1762* (Cambridge: Cambridge University Press, 1997).

22. Maximilien Robespierre, "Pour Marie Somerville," in *Œuvres de Maximilien Robespierre*, ed. Société des études robespierristes (1913; Ivry: Phénix éditions, 2000), 2:344 (hereafter cited as *Rob.*). The law of nations was brandished here against the "barbarous people" (338) living in a "savage land" (343) of France who had imprisoned a widow for debts: clearly a case of "indignant humanity" (339)! Thankfully, "Europe is not populated by savage hordes" (388). On the relation between the *droit des gens*, or law of nations, and natural right, see the prologue.

23. This reformist current could also be described as neo-Stoic: Michael Sonenscher, in *Before the Deluge: Public Debt, Inequality, and the Intellectual Origins of the French Revolution* (Princeton: Princeton University Press, 2007), noted the importance of Stoic principles in Physiocratic thought. Robespierre similarly declared, in his own "study" of the Revolution's origins, that "stoicism preserved the honor of human nature"; see "Sur les rapports des idées religieuses et morales avec les principes républicaines, et sur les fêtes nationales," 18 floréal an II (May 7, 1794), *Rob.*, 10:454.

24. Rosenblatt, *Rousseau and Geneva*, demonstrates, for instance, how natural right (in the figure of no less than Burlamaqui) was closely associated with patrician arguments against the bourgeoisie.

25. There is a growing bibliography on French republicanism in the Old Regime. See notably Franco Venturi, *Utopia and Reform in the Enlightenment* (Cambridge: Cambridge University Press, 1971); Luciano Guerci, *Libertà degli antichi e libertà dei moderni: Sparta, Atene e i "philosophes" nella Francia del Settecento* (Naples: Guida, 1979); Claude Nicolet, *L'idée républicaine en France* (Paris: Gallimard, 1982); Blandine Barret-Kriegel, *La république incertaine* (Paris: PUF, 1988); Keith Michael Baker, *Inventing the French Revolution*, and, by the same author,

there were only a handful of homegrown republican theorists in France, various translations of English republican texts were available, as was Machiavelli's foundational work, the *Discourses* on Livy.[26] Many of the lessons (and the lexicon) of classical republicanism—the importance of good laws and even better morals, the dangers of corruption for civic virtue, the delicate timing of political change, the need to preserve and promote institutions, and so on—were also found in Montesquieu's discussion of republics in *De l'Esprit des lois*, which in turn was publicized in numerous articles in the *Encyclopédie*, such as "Démocratie," "Aristocratie," or "République." Mably's *Des Droits et devoirs du citoyen* and Rousseau's *Du Contrat social* similarly disseminated numerous republican themes (see below). Finally, as Elena Russo has recently argued, the prized aesthetic of the second half of the eighteenth century, *le grand goût*, or neoclassicism, infused the cultural imagery and imaginary of the arts with a "republican ideal."[27]

"Transformations of Classical Republicanism"; François Furet and Mona Ozouf, eds., *Le siècle de l'avènement républicain* (Paris: Gallimard, 1993); Fontana, ed., *Invention of the Modern Republic*; Mark Hulliung, *The Autocritique of the Enlightenment* (Cambridge: Harvard University Press, 1994); Eric Gojosso, *Le concept de la république en France (XVIe–XVIIIe siècle)* (Marseilles: Presses Universitaires d'Aix-Marseille, 1998); Johnson Kent Wright, *A Classical Republican in Eighteenth-Century France: The Political Thought of Mably* (Stanford: Stanford University Press, 1997), and "Républicanisme et lumières," in *Dictionnaire critique de la République*, ed. Vincent Duclert and Christophe Prochasson (Paris: Flammarion, 2002); Richard Whatmore, *Republicanism and the French Revolution: An Intellectual History of Jean-Baptiste Say's Political Economy* (Oxford: Oxford University Press, 2000); David A. Bell, "National Character and Republican Imagination," in *Cult of the Nation*; and various articles in *Republicanism: A Shared European Heritage*, ed. Martin van Gelderen and Quentin Skinner (Cambridge: Cambridge University Press, 2002).

26. On French translations of English republicanism, see especially Baker, "Transformations of Classical Republicanism," and Rachel Hammersley, *French Revolutionaries and English Republicans: The Cordeliers Club, 1790–1794* (Rochester, NY: Boydell Press, 2005); see also Michael Sonenscher, *Work and Wages: Natural Law, Politics, and the Eighteenth-Century French Trades* (Cambridge: Cambridge University Press, 1989), 337 and *passim*. In a subsequent article, Sonenscher quotes an illuminating passage from Burke's *Letters on a Regicide* describing French "diplomatic politicians": "They had continually in their hands the *Observations* of Machiavel on Livy. They had Montesquieu's *Grandeur et Décadence des Romains* as a manual"; see "Republicanism, State Finances and the Emergence of Commercial Society in Eighteenth-Century France—or from Royal to Ancient Republicanism and Back," in *Republicanism: A Shared European Heritage*, 2:277. On Machiavelli's influence in eighteenth-century France, see Albert Chérel's (rather dated) *La pensée de Machiavel en France* (Paris: L'Artisan du livre, 1935); Robert Shackleton, "Montesquieu and Machiavelli: A Reappraisal," *Comparative Literature Studies* 1 (1964): 1–13; and Jacob Soll, *Publishing "The Prince": History, Reading, and the Birth of Political Criticism* (Ann Arbor: University of Michigan Press, 2005).

27. Elena Russo, *Styles of Enlightenment: Taste, Politics, and Authorship in Eighteenth-Century France* (Baltimore: Johns Hopkins University Press, 2007), esp. 16–26. On neoclassicism in painting, see notably Thomas Crow, *Emulation: David, Drouais, and Girodet in the Art of Revolutionary France* (New Haven: Yale University Press, 2006).

As Keith Baker points out, historians of France have nevertheless long been oblivious to many other political aspects of republicanism.[28] Few authors may have openly advocated the creation of a French republic, but republicanism is much more than a belief in, or a desire for, a republican mode of government: It also constitutes a "diagnostic" that sees "disorder and vicissitude as the natural state of human existence" and seeks to identify "individual interests . . . with the common good through inculcation of civic virtue."[29] In this respect, a republican discourse can be wholly compatible with monarchy: Kant's definition of republicanism as a form not of sovereignty, but of government, would have been perfectly acceptable to many French revolutionaries before 1792 (not the least since Rousseau had proposed a very similar definition).[30] During the old regime, "patriotic" authors strived to create good citizens, who might still be subjects of a king.[31] Isaac Kramnick has shown how advocates of la thèse nobiliaire, such as the comte de Boulainvilliers, could espouse English republican principles just as easily as defenders of la thèse royale, such as the marquis d'Argenson.[32] Conversely, certain antimonarchists did not fully embrace republicanism: the curé Meslier's tirades against tyranny and superstition, for instance, include a few

---

28. Baker, "Transformations of Classical Republicanism," 34.

29. Ibid., 36.

30. For Kant, see "Perpetual Peace," trans. Lewis White Beck, in *On History*, ed. Beck (Upper Saddle River, NJ: Prentice Hall, 2001), 95–96. In *The Social Contract* (2.6), Rousseau defined the republic as "tout Etat régi par des loix, sous quelque forme d'administration que ce puisse être" ("any state governed by laws, regardless of its administration") (*Œuvres complètes*, ed. Bernard Gagnebin and Marcel Raymond [Paris: Gallimard/Pléiade, 1959–95], 3:379). For examples of this distinction in revolutionary France, see Raymonde Monnier, "Républicanisme et révolution française," *French Historical Studies* 26, no. 1 (2003): 104–5. Gareth Stedman Jones suggests that another source for Kant was a 1791 article by Sieyès; see "Kant, the French Revolution, and the Republic," in *Invention of the Modern Republic*, 155.

31. See Bell, *Cult of the Nation*, 140–68; Marisa Linton, *The Politics of Virtue in Enlightenment France* (New York: Palgrave, 2001); Jay M. Smith, *Nobility Reimagined: The Patriotic Nation in Eighteenth-Century France* (Ithaca: Cornell University Press, 2005); and John Shovlin, *The Political Economy of Virtue: Luxury, Patriotism, and the Origins of the French Revolution* (Ithaca: Cornell University Press, 2006).

32. Both of whom were in contact with Bolingbroke and echoed the sentiments of his "country" ideology; see Isaac Kramnick, *Bolingbroke and His Circle: The Politics of Nostalgia in the Age of Walpole* (Cambridge: Harvard University Press, 1968), 150–52; see also Harold Ellis, *Boulainvilliers and the French Monarchy: Aristocratic Politics in Early Eighteenth-Century France* (Ithaca: Cornell University Press, 1988); and Kent Wright, "The Idea of a Republican Constitution in Old Regime France," *Republicanism: A Shared European Heritage*. On Bolingbroke and "country" ideology, see Pocock, *Machiavellian Moment*, 478–86 and *passim*. On the "Real Whig" current of republicanism, see Caroline Robbins, *The Eighteenth-Century Commonwealthman* (Cambridge: Harvard University Press, 1959).

passing references to "public liberty" but do not develop any specifically republican ideas.[33]

Even accounting for these neglected traces of republican discourse, it must be acknowledged that republicanism was not nearly as predominant in France as it was in other European countries. One would have to wait until the first revolutionary stirrings for English republicanism to garner sustained interest among French politicians.[34] In the meantime, republicanism thrived in the imagination of students and novelists, of antiquarians and philosophers; and in those unbridled spaces, it was much freer to adapt and even to transform completely.

Natural Republicanism and the Golden Age

The fusion of natural right and republicanism into a single new political language did not originate in works of political theory but of literature (understood widely as *belles lettres*).[35] The most radical transformation that these imaginative (and often imaginary) retellings introduced was the elimination of contractualism—that is, the doctrine that humans pass from a state of nature into civil society as the result of an implicit or explicit contract.[36] Instead, works such as Fénelon's *Télémaque* and Montesquieu's *Lettres persanes* depicted societies (those of the Boeticans and the good Troglodytes, respectively) that existed in a revised state of nature, in which individuals were social and equal, no one ruled over anyone else, and virtue came naturally. The only laws that they recognized were the unchanging laws of nature, which lie within us; by extension, there was no need to write them down or to inscribe them in a constitution. Natural right alone, however, was incapable of *preserving* these virtuous societies over time; even if men were naturally good, they could be corrupted. In the absence of laws, it took

---

33. See, for instance, the "Conclusion" to his *Mémoire des pensées et sentiments*, in *Œuvres complètes*, ed. Jean Deprun, Roland Desné, and Albert Soboul (Paris: Anthropos, 1970–72), 3:127–70.

34. See notably Hammersley, *French Revolutionaries and English Republicans*; and Monnier, "Républicanisme et révolution française."

35. The following paragraphs outline the argument developed in chapter 1.

36. Contractualism was a core element in natural right theories going back to Grotius; see most recently Victoria Kahn, *Wayward Contracts: The Crisis of Political Obligation in England, 1640–1674* (Princeton: Princeton University Press, 2004). It was not antithetical to the theory of natural sociability (as Pufendorf demonstrated), but the two are generally found separately (as with Hobbes and Rousseau). In a different mode, contractualism also featured centrally in French constitutionalist discourse; see, for instance, Colin Jones, *The Great Nation: France from Louis XV to Napoleon* (London: Penguin, 2002), 10, 105.

republican institutions, such as education, censorship, and citizen armies, to ensure that natural right be continuously observed. This combination of natural right (as the source of virtue) and institutions is what formed the "natural republic."

One of the reasons this political ideal was both believable and highly attractive was its similarity with one of the most pervasive and long-lasting myths in Western culture, the myth of the golden age. This myth was first recorded by Hesiod, who provided its basic narrative: At the beginning of human history, "a golden generation" of men lived on Earth; they did not need to work, but were fed by a cornucopian nature and lived "free from all sorrow."[37] These fortunate mortals were followed by silver, bronze, and iron generations, each of which was progressively more violent and unjust. Given that the ancients perceived themselves as currently living in the age of iron, the natural innocence and virtue of the golden age appeared all the greater. It was developed and celebrated by later Latin poets, most notably Ovid. In *The Metamorphoses*—one of the prime early-modern sources for the myth since it figured on almost every *collège* syllabus—Ovid described it as a time when individuals "cultivated loyalty and rectitude on their own, without laws."[38] Not only did this society not need or have any written laws; it also thrived without rulers or any political structure at all.

Although in its traditional version, the golden age was a lost time of innocence, the myth was given new life by Virgil. In his famous fourth *Eclogue*, he prophesized that a divine child would soon "restore the reign of Saturn" (the god who, for the Romans, had presided over the first age), and recall Astraea, the goddess of justice, who had fled to the constellation Virgo at the close of the golden age.[39] Virgil returned to this theme in *The Aeneid*,

---

37. Hesiod, *The Works and Days*, trans. Richard Lattimore (Ann Arbor: University of Michigan Press, 1970), 31. On Hesiod's version of the myth (which interrupts the steady decline with a heroic age, between those of bronze and iron), see Jean-Pierre Vernant, *Mythe et pensée chez les Grecs* (Paris: Maspero, 1965). On the golden age myth in classical antiquity, see notably Harry Levin, *The Myth of the Golden Age in the Renaissance* (Bloomington: Indiana University Press, 1969), 3–31; Jean-Paul Brisson, *Rome et l'âge d'or: de Catulle à Ovide, vie et mort d'un mythe* (Paris: La Découverte, 1992); and Jacques Poirier, ed., *L'âge d'or* (Dijon: Figures libres, 1996).

38. Ovid, "Aurea prima sata est aetas, quae vindice nullo, / sponte sua, sine lege fidem rectumque colebat," *Metamorphoses*, I, lines 89–90. For the syllabus used in most *collèges*, see Harold Parker, *The Cult of Antiquity and the French Revolutionaries: A Study in the Development of the Revolutionary Spirit* (Chicago: University of Chicago Press, 1937); and L. W. B. Brockliss, *French Higher Education in the Seventeenth and Eighteenth Centuries: A Cultural History* (Oxford: Clarendon Press, 1987).

39. The oft-quoted line in Virgil is *iam redit et Virgo, redeunt Saturnia regna*. On this *Eclogue*, which was later interpreted as a Christian prophecy, see notably H. Mattingly, "Virgil's Golden Age: Sixth *Aeneid* and Fourth *Eclogue*," *Classical Review* 48, no. 5 (1934): 161–65.

book 6, where the return of the golden age was associated with the coming of Augustus.[40] In this forward-looking version of the myth, the golden age became both thoroughly civilized (it marked the apogee of the arts), as well as politicized, albeit on an imperial, "absolutist" model; accordingly, it became a set-piece in royalist propaganda from the Renaissance onward.[41] But the egalitarian, pastoral version of the myth never disappeared from the European imagination either. It was a common topos in the Middle Ages, when it was generally identified with free love (*liber amor*), whereas early-modern writers tended to associate the myth with gallant courtship of Arcadian shepherds.[42] Both of these interpretations of the myth continued to surface up through the eighteenth century.

The myth of golden age became in this way an equally powerful political, as literary, representation. Where the Virgilian version served the interests of monarchs and princes, political writers from Montaigne onward turned to Ovid's description as a lens through which to view the newly discovered societies in the New World. The emergent concept of a "state of nature" thus became tinged with the mythical attributes of the Age of Gold. Although many political philosophers, Hobbes in chief, resisted this assimilation, it gained traction with the rise of more "liberal" natural right theories in the eighteenth century (as opposed to the more "absolutist" theories of Gentili, Grotius, Hobbes, and Pufendorf). It was in this context that the myth came to underwrite the natural-republican theories described in the following chapters.

Even when they invoked natural right as the foundation of all political and legal theory, many philosophes rejected the myth of a golden age as just that, a myth. For natural republicanism to acquire genuine political legitimacy, therefore, the golden age had to become more than a poetic device. As it happened, the late Enlightenment experienced a series of cultural tremors

---

40. See, for instance, Chester G. Starr, "Virgil's Acceptance of Octavian," *American Journal of Philology* 76, no. 1 (1955): 34–46. Both of these Virgilian texts also figured on nearly every *collège* syllabus.

41. See Levin, *Myth of the Golden Age*; and Frances A. Yates, *Astraea: The Imperial Theme in the Sixteenth Century* (London: Routledge & K. Paul, 1975).

42. See Ernst Curtius, *European Literature and the Latin Middle Ages*, trans. Willard R. Trask (Princeton: Princeton University Press, 1990). For a canonical example, see Guillaume de Lorris and Jean de Meun, *Le roman de la rose*, ed. Armand Struebel (Paris: Libraire Générale Française, 1992), notably vv. 13879–970. This romance was republished in the eighteenth century by N. Lenglet du Fresnoy: *Le Roman de la Rose . . .* (Paris: Vve Pissot, 1735). For the early-modern period, see Levin, *Myth of the Golden Age*; and Jean-Pierre van Elslande, *L'imaginaire pastoral du XVIIe siècle* (Paris: PUF, 1999). The chief example of this Arcadian mode is Honoré d'Urfé's multivolume novel *L'Astrée* (1607–25).

that brought historical and anthropological validity to the myth. Voltaire's pioneering studies of ancient India, both in his *Essai sur les mœurs et l'esprit des nations* and in his Oriental *contes*, portrayed the original state of humanity as sophisticated, rational, and republican, closer to Atlantis than Arcadia. The "discovery" of Tahiti by Bougainville convinced many of his readers, amongst whom were Diderot, Sylvain Maréchal, and Saint-Just, that civil legislation should be strictly restricted to natural right and that political power was an unnecessary evil. By the time of the French Revolution, the myth of the golden age no longer appeared to many as a myth; it had become the ideal and natural template on whose basis all of society could be reorganized.[43]

It was a group of economists known as the Physiocrats, however, who provided the key philosophical framework for natural republicanism. By proclaiming that the regeneration of society depended on the restoration of a "natural and essential order," they both blurred the distinction between the state of nature and civil society, and argued for the sufficiency of natural laws. Even though it was devised as a defense of monarchy, Physiocracy offered a theoretical structure that could support a wide variety of political projects, even republicanism. The Physiocrats also made it possible to imagine a society in which political power was asymptotically reduced to zero, as the natural order eliminated the need for sovereignty. This emancipation of society from the state—a central Enlightenment project, as Keith Baker has suggested—would reach its high-water mark at the end of the eighteenth century, both in the political thought of Thomas Paine, whose point of departure in *Common Sense* is the distinction between society ("a state of blessing") and government ("a necessary evil"), and in the natural-republican theory of Saint-Just, whose political thought centered on the belief that "one cannot rule innocently," and who proclaimed that nature, not the general will, was the source of all law.[44]

---

43. For further details and references pertaining to this paragraph, see chapter 2.

44. Keith Baker, "Enlightenment and the Institution of Society: Notes for a Conceptual History," *Main Trends in Cultural History*, ed. Willem Melching and Wyger Velema (Amsterdam: Rodopi, 1994), esp. 119–20; see also Brian Singer, *Society, Theory, and the French Revolution: Studies in the Revolutionary Imaginary* (Basingstoke: Macmillan, 1986); Margaret C. Jacob, *Living the Enlightenment: Freemasonry and Politics in Eighteenth-Century Europe* (Oxford: Oxford University Press, 1991); and Daniel Gordon, *Citizens without Sovereignty: Equality and Sociability in French Thought, 1670–1789* (Princeton: Princeton University Press, 1994). As Pierre Manent argued in *An Intellectual History of Liberalism*, trans. Rebecca Balinski (Princeton: Princeton University Press, 1994), the separation of society from the state in the eighteenth century was also the founding act of liberalism. As such, this depoliticization also provides the ground for Carl Schmitt's critique of liberalism; see *Political Theology: Four Chapters*

"Enemies of the Human Race":
Transgressing the Laws of Nature

If natural republicanism allowed certain reform-minded writers to imagine if not a heavenly city, then a golden age of justice, their commitment to natural right alone came at a price. Indeed, this paradise was not without its serpent—a devil, in fact. What was one to do with those individuals who transgressed the laws of nature, which natural society demanded that everyone respect? How should they be brought into line or punished, and who should do it?

These questions were raised, of course, only by theorists who considered natural right to be a foundational and inviolable legal code in its entirety.[45] Hobbes took it for granted, for instance, that the natural *rights* of men (most famously, their "right to every thing, even to one another's body") would conflict with natural *laws*.[46] A primary role of the sovereign was precisely to limit natural rights and to enforce the laws of nature, as well as civil laws.[47] In the state of nature, however, it was to be expected that men would violate these laws; accordingly, such violations were not viewed as particularly troublesome.[48] For Locke, by contrast, natural rights did not extend nearly so far as for Hobbes, merely to one's individual body and to property acquired through labor. In this respect, there was no inevitable conflict between natural laws and natural rights; as Pufendorf before him, Locke

---

on the Concept of Sovereignty, trans. George Schwab (Chicago: University of Chicago Press, 2005). For Paine, see *Common Sense* (Mineola: Dover, 1997), 2–3. For Saint-Just, see chapter 4.

45. Throughout this book, I use the expression "natural right" (without a definite article) to refer to the corpus and theory of both natural laws and rights. The two principal components of this corpus are natural laws and natural rights—the latter not to be confused with "natural right" as a whole.

46. See, for instance, "For the Lawes of Nature . . . (in summe, *doing to others as wee would be done to*), of themselves, without the terrour of some Power to cause them to be observed, are contrary to our naturall Passions . . . And Covenants, without the Sword, are but Words and of no strength to secure a man at all. Therefore, notwithstanding the Lawes of Nature (which every one hath then kept, when he has the will to keep them, when he can do it safely), if there be no Power erected . . . every man will and may lawfully rely on his own strength and art, for caution against all other men," *Leviathan*, ed. C. B. Macpherson (London: Penguin, 1985), chap. 17; 223–24. The other quote is from chap. 14.

47. As Hobbes remarks, "The Right of Nature, that is, the naturall Liberty of Man, may by the Civill Law be abridged, and restrained: nay, the end of making Lawes, is no other, but such Restraint . . . Law was brought into the world for nothing else, but to limit the naturall liberty of particular men," *Leviathan*, 26, 315.

48. As we will see, Hobbes was following here the Spanish jurist Francisco de Vitoria; see Richard Tuck, *The Rights of War and Peace: Political Thought and the International Order from Grotius to Kant* (Oxford: Oxford University Press, 1999).

believed that even in the state of nature, men should obey the laws of nature.[49] In fact, violating natural law constituted, in his eyes, the highest possible offense: Such an offender "declares himself to live by another Rule, than that of *reason* and common Equity . . . and so he becomes dangerous to Mankind," and "every man . . . may restrain, or where it is necessary, destroy" him.[50] An equivalent case in civil society would be the "Absolute Ruler," or tyrant, who transgresses the natural rights of his people, thus "deserv[ing] to be thought a declared Enemy to Society and Mankind" (§93), or as "the common Enemy and Pest of Mankind" (§230).

Locke's repeated use of this phrase—"enemy of mankind"—to define the individual who has violated the laws of nature was no doubt intentional since its Latin equivalent, *hostis humani generis*, had a very long, complex, and yet untold history, which I survey in the prologue. First employed in antiquity by Pliny as a designation for tyrannical emperors, it rose to discursive prominence in medieval theology, where it was used as a common epithet for the devil. During the Renaissance, the term was applied to pirates, but more important, was used by humanist jurists to "demonize" (quite literally) the inhabitants of the New World. Since the latter violated the laws of nature on a constant basis, these jurists argued, they not only could be punished and destroyed as "enemies of the human race," but they also forfeited their own natural rights. While a few philosophers used the doctrine of natural rights to constrain Spanish imperialism, most early-modern jurists invoked precisely this theory to authorize the conquest and ravaging of the New World.[51] From a theological expression, the *hostis humani generis* had become a secularized, legalistic concept whose principal embodiment henceforth was the "savage."

The logic by which Locke justified the "destruction" of an individual in the state of nature can thus be traced back to the colonial debates that sparked the revival of natural right theory.[52] Once early-modern jurists had

---

49. John Dunn remarks that for Locke, "The state of nature . . . is a jural condition and the law which covers it is the theologically based law of nature," *The Political Thought of John Locke* (Cambridge: Cambridge University Press, 1969), 106.

50. *Second Treatise*, in *Two Treatises of Government* (1690), ed. Peter Laslett (Cambridge: Cambridge University Press, 1988), §8. As Dunn notes, for Locke, such offenders "no longer have any *rights* at all against other men," *Political Thought of John Locke*, 108.

51. See especially Anthony Pagden, *The Fall of Natural Man: The American Indian and the Origins of Comparative Ethnology* (Cambridge: Cambridge University Press, 1987); see also Richard Waswo, "The Formation of Natural Law to Justify Colonialism, 1539–1689," *New Literary History* 27, no. 4 (1996): 743–59.

52. On Locke's own entanglement in colonial matters, see, for instance, Barbara Arneil, "Trade, Plantations, and Property: John Locke and the Economic Defense of Colonialism," *Journal of the History of Ideas* 55, no. 4 (1994): 591–609. On the transition from medieval to

declared that the violation of natural law was grounds for radical punishment, however, their reasoning was applied to other figures besides the savage. "Brigands" were often identified as the equivalents of savages in civil society, but perhaps the most important transgressor of natural right in the Old World was the tyrant, who was, in fact, the original *hostis humani generis*. Throughout the seventeenth and eighteenth centuries, justifications of tyrannicide were consistently couched in terms of natural right, and the "unjust and perverse sovereign" increasingly identified as "the enemy of the human race [*l'ennemi du genre humain*]."[53] These injunctions received a more authoritative legal form in works on the "law of nations," that is, the body of laws and customs recognized (according to Roman jurists) by all reasonable peoples and, increasingly, equated in the eighteenth century with natural right. It was under the cover of the law of nations that the violent exceptions allowed for in natural right came to inform real legal categories during the French Revolution.

Natural Right and Terror Laws in the French Revolution

The second part of this book examines how natural right underpinned the Jacobin theory of republicanism, as well as the legal infrastructure of the Terror, both of which took shape, I argue, during the trial of the king. The trial was a painful, protracted affair; it constituted a political point of no return, but it also presented the deputies of the National Convention with a legal dilemma. Louis XVI, onward from September 1791, enjoyed constitutional inviolability. For the vast majority of the deputies, the question was thus how to punish Louis—his guilt was not in doubt—in a legally (and formally) acceptable fashion. But the inviolability clause was a major stumbling block.[54]

Very early on in the debates, however, a loophole was discovered. The king may be protected from prosecution by the Constitution, but was there not a higher law that condemned tyrants? Shared by all peoples at all times, this law had been dictated by nature herself. It was in fact by another name that the youngest deputy in the Convention, Saint-Just, identified this supreme authority in his riveting maiden speech: "The laws we must follow

---

early-modern natural right theories, see Brian Tierney, *The Idea of Natural Rights: Studies on Natural Rights, Natural Law, and Church Law, 1150–1625* (Atlanta: Scholars Press, 1997).

53. *Correspondance Politique de l'Europe: Ouvrage Périodique par une Société de Gens de Lettres*, 3 (Brussels: n.p., 1780), 52.

54. I discuss the place of the king's trial in the evolution of Jacobin thought in chapter 3.

are in the law of nations [*droit des gens*]."[55] Over two-thirds of his colleagues seem to have agreed with him: Louis XVI could be tried according to the law of nations.

The king's trial may well constitute the first attempt to prosecute a deposed ruler as a "criminal against humanity," which is in fact how Robespierre described him. But the deputies did not have a modern corpus of international law to work with. They used what was available to them, and the more radical deputies (known as the Montagnards) attacked Louis in the terms that tyrants and brigands had become known, as an *ennemi du genre humain*. This designation also determined the punishment—death— the Montagnards demanded be meted out, even though many of them argued concurrently for the abolition of the death penalty in ordinary cases. Given that the king had violated the laws of nature, some deputies (including Saint-Just and Robespierre) went even further and demanded that the proceedings be stopped short and Louis simply killed. Their argument was not symptomatic of a penchant for rough justice or lawlessness, but rather a logical consequence of the exceptional treatment reserved for individuals who transgressed natural right: They could lawfully be executed without a trial. As Saint-Just reminded his colleagues, "the courts are only instituted for citizens [*les membres de la cité*]."[56] Due process was a right that one could forfeit like any other.

The Convention was not swayed by this part of the Montagnard argument, nor did it ultimately convict Louis XVI of being an enemy of the human race. Dragging on as it did over two months, however, the trial provided the Jacobins with the time and perfect target against whom to refine their jusnaturalist prosecution. A legal category began to take shape around the figure of the king, with some deputies even devising a new name for this extraordinary criminal: He was an outlaw, *hors-la-loi*. While familiar to Anglo-Saxon ears, this term and concept were thoroughly foreign to French jurisprudence; the expression itself had entered the language less than twenty years before. To a considerable extent, then, the *conventionnels* could and did make it mean what they wanted. Once released into the highly charged arena of revolutionary politics, moreover, it could easily be appropriated for other ends. This is precisely what happened. Initially devised as an attack on the king's constitutional sovereignty (the inviolability clause was "a law that declares him to be beyond the law [*une loi qui le déclare hors de la loi*],"

55."Discours sur le jugement de Louis XVI," November 13, 1792; *SJ*, 378.
56. *SJ*, 379.

one deputy alleged),[57] the outlaw category was next extended to designate *anyone* who had usurped authority, before encompassing individuals who rebelled or showed signs of rebellion against the national government.[58] This last group suffered the fate that the Montagnards had unsuccessfully wished upon the king: Outlaws were to be brought before military commissions to have their identity verified and then summarily executed, without a chance to plead or appeal their cases. This law ultimately authorized 78 percent of the deaths throughout France during the Terror.[59]

The *hors-la-loi* decree was directed primarily against insurgents in the Vendée, whom the national deputies regularly denounced as brigands. Underpinning both the Montagnard prosecution of Louis XVI and the Convention's response to the troubles in the West were thus two traditional types of the *hostis humani generis*. Soon after the Convention outlawed rebels in armed insurrection, however, it approved Danton's motion that *all* "counterrevolutionaries" be declared *hors-la-loi*.[60] This incredibly vague designation—what qualifies someone as a "counterrevolutionary"?—is highly revealing of both the republican philosophy espoused by many Montagnards and the expansive nature of exceptional legal categories. With respect to the former, first, Danton's motion essentially equated any opposition to the Revolution with a violation of natural right. The establishment of a republican government (the goal of the Revolution) was reinterpreted as a law of nature. This identification of nature and nation, I argue, lay at the heart of Jacobin republicanism. From a legal perspective, second, the blanket outlawing of all "counterrevolutionaries" illustrates how criminal categories, once created, tend to grow in an outwardly direction, absorbing an increasing number of groups and individuals.[61] This phenomenon was particularly visible in the case of the 22 prairial law, which targeted "enemies of the people." Rather than identify specific offenders, however, the law functioned as a dragnet, given the open-ended definition of this new category.[62]

---

57. Didier Thirion, speech against the king, in *Archives parlementaires de 1787 à 1860*, ed. M. J. Mavidal et al. (Paris: Librairie administrative de P. Dupont, 1862–1913), 54:334.

58. See, respectively, Jean Debry's December 24, 1792, draft bill (*AP*, 55:384) and the March 19 decree (*AP*, 60:331), and the discussion in chapter 3.

59. Marc Bouloiseau, *The Jacobin Republic, 1792–1794*, trans. Jonathan Mandelbaum (Cambridge and Paris: Cambridge University Press/Maison des sciences de l'homme, 1983), 211.

60.Speech to the Convention on March 27, 1793; *AP*, 60:605.

61. In a different context, see Bruce Ackerman, *Before the Next Attack: Preserving Civil Liberties in an Age of Terrorism* (New Haven: Yale University Press, 2007).

62. On this law and the "Great Terror" more generally, see chapter 5.

The expanding scope of these extraordinary criminal categories cannot be interpreted in isolation. It was propelled forward by strong political dynamics, which led deputies on both sides to prove their toughness—it was the more "moderate" Girondins who were responsible for the first extensions of the outlaw category—and which encouraged them to exploit these categories for political gain. There is certainly no denying that sheer political ambition and the desire to hold on to power motivated many legal and political decisions during the Terror, most strikingly, perhaps, the Jacobin decision to suspend the 1793 Constitution. But the widespread evidence of political manipulation does not entail that the revolutionary groups and their leaders were ruthless cynics. On the contrary, radical political agendas can encourage people to bend, if not break, the rules—a phenomenon certainly not unknown in our own time. Where the legal categories of the Terror are concerned, natural right appears to have played an enabling role up until the end: It was in the name of the law of nations that Barère convinced the Convention that "no British or Hanoverian prisoners of war should be taken," while Couthon presented the draconian law of 22 prairial in opposition to the "ferocious and cowardly enemies of humanity."[63]

The Terror legislation therefore was not a matter of suspending the law but of substituting one body of law for another—natural right for the penal code—under certain extraordinary circumstances.[64] This distinction is crucial, as it allows us to comprehend how hundreds of *conventionnels*, nurtured in the late eighteenth-century culture of *sensibilité* and judicial reform, could approve draconian laws that stripped individuals of legal protections. Arguments rooted in natural right theory had special clout: Not only was prerevolutionary liberal philosophy often couched in this language, but the Revolution itself drew much of its political authority from "the natural, inalienable, and sacred rights of man," as stated in the 1789 Declaration of Rights. This, of course, is not to say that the Terror was a necessary consequence of this founding document. But it does point to how the deputies of

---

63. For Barère's decree, see his 7 prairial an II (26/5/94) speech, *Histoire parlementaire de la Révolution française, ou Journal des assemblées nationales depuis 1789 jusqu'en 1815*, ed. P. J. B. Buchez and P. C. Roux (Paris: Paulin, 1834–38), 30:91–127; see also Sophie Wahnich and Marc Belissa, "Les crimes des Anglais: trahir le droit," *AHRF* 300 (1995): 233–48; and my "War and Terror: The Law of Nations from Grotius to the French Revolution," *French Historical Studies* 31, no. 2 (2008): 229–62. This law was generally ignored by military commanders. For Couthon, see the report in *Réimpression de l'ancien Moniteur . . .* (Paris: Plon, 1861), 20:694–97, and chapter 5.

64. In this regard, attempts to analyze the Terror in terms of Giorgio Agamben's concept of *homo sacer* are unfounded, as I argue in chapter 3.

the Convention did not need to stray very far from their original principles to justify exceptional laws against "denatured" individuals.

Restoring the Republic of Nature: The Jacobin Project

There was also, to be sure, more to the Jacobin republic than the Terror. The Jacobins aimed at nothing less, after all, than a complete transformation of society. The new regime had to redress everything that was wrong with *l'ancien*, from education and the economy down to the calendar.[65] As with the repressive justice system of the Terror, the impetus for these transformations came predominantly from the central government, even if this impetus would be interpreted differently from place to place—again, similarly to the Terror. The co-presence of these two apparently heterogeneous imperatives (repressing political dissidents and insurgents versus transforming civic society) nonetheless begs the question of their relation. Was there a unifying vision behind both the creative and oppressive measures of the Jacobins? Was the Terror a self-contained aspect, an excrescence of their political agenda? Or did it constitute a fundamental part of their program for regenerating the nation and of natural republicanism?

All aspects of Jacobin legislative activity, be they penal, civil, or institutional, seem to have been grounded in the same authorizing referent: nature. While the meaning and dictates of nature are obviously vague and open to interpretation (not to mention exploitation), this persistent dedication did have tangible political consequences. For instance, it afforded the Jacobins considerable leeway in their debates with the Girondins over the republican Constitution. This debate would ultimately be resolved by the "purge" of the Convention on May 31–June 2, 1793, but it reveals the extent to which the Montagnard deputies were wary of enthroning the general will as the source of legitimacy, and even shied away from direct popular sovereignty: "Do not tire the people with their sovereignty," declared François Chabot.[66] Instead, these deputies pointed to nature as a more secure and august authority for refounding the French nation. Addressing the Egyptian goddess of nature on display at the festival celebrating the new Constitution, Héraut de Séchelles proclaimed that this document simply expressed "your laws."[67]

---

65. See notably Isser Woloch, *The New Regime: Transformations of the French Civic Order, 1789–1815* (New York: Norton, 1994).

66. *AP*, 64:163.

67. On this festival and the 1793 Constitution, see chapter 4.

Of course, the Convention would soon decide not to enact this constitution—indeed, the Jacobins had probably even decided on this course of action before its ratification on August 10, 1793. Once the Constitution went into effect, new elections would have to be held, and there was no guarantee that the Montagnards could maintain their majority. The decision to suspend it was an act of political expediency, a flagrant abuse of power. But it was also, and at the same time, more than that. A number of Jacobins, particularly Saint-Just in his unpublished manuscripts, had questioned the necessity of a constitution per se. Did France not already have the Declaration of Rights, that "Constitution of all peoples," as Chénier and Robespierre called it? Tellingly, *this* particular document was not suspended: It remained affixed in public places and was still considered the law of land (except for those unfortunate individuals who forfeited even their natural rights).[68] Since the Declaration already expressed the laws of nature, what need was there for a constitution? France had been in a political "state of nature" since August 1792, or so claimed Robespierre and many others, but was not the republic itself "the form of government that is closest to nature"?[69] If nature, and not the general will, was the source of all law, the existing Convention could proclaim and enforce natural right just as well as—some would say better than—any other assembly.

The argument retraced above was not spelled out in so many words by any one deputy, even if Saint-Just came close to saying as much in his political works. It is a speculative reconstruction, pieced together from a variety of texts, known influences (including a Physiocratic treatise in Saint-Just's possession), and the natural-republican theory that had taken shape in eighteenth-century France. We seem obliged, however, to have recourse to such speculation, since the Committee of Public Safety, after October 1793, was clearly in no rush to implement the Constitution, but did genuinely appear to want to establish some sort of republic and not just to rule dictatorially. What the Jacobin leaders projected to create, as difficult as this may be to determine, is a central piece in the puzzle of the Terror.

The final chapter of this book is an attempt to put this and other pieces back together, but also to suggest that "the Terror" may itself have been only a small piece in the puzzle of Jacobin republicanism. Onward from the

---

68. See Bronislaw Bazcko, "The Terror before the Terror?" in *The Terror*, ed. Keith Baker, vol. 4 of *The French Revolution and the Creation of Modern Political Culture* (Oxford: Pergamon Press, 1987–94).

69. Siméon Bonnescœur-Bourginière, speech to the Convention, December 6, 1792; *AP*, 54:118.

end of February 1794, the reports from the Committee of Public Safety insisted on the same message: The time for Terror was over; now *justice* was "the order of the day." There were obvious political advantages to this strategy, as it allowed the Committee both to deflect the criticism of the *indulgents* (who called for an end to the Terror) and to attack the hard-line demands of the Hébertistes (who sought to extend the Terror to economic domains). But it also underscores how what we think of as "the Terror" may have been related only marginally to the actual discourse of terror that rose to prominence between the summer of 1793 and February 1794.[70] Institutionally, the foundations of "the Terror" were almost entirely laid in the spring of 1793, often with the widespread approval of the Convention; the declaration of Terror as "the order of the day" in September 1793 was not accompanied by any major legislative transformations. The new institutions introduced by the Committee of Public Safety in the spring and summer of 1794, for their part, were presented as antitheses to the arbitrary measures of "the Terror." What we consider under this designation may simply be a facet of Jacobin natural republicanism.

But was the Committee of Public Safety even intent on founding a republic? Judging by the pronouncements of its members, one is entitled to have doubts. Although they initially declared the revolutionary government instituted on October 10, 1793, to be "provisional," subsequent reports gave no hint as to *when* it would cease; by March 1794, talk of restoring the Constitution had essentially disappeared. There are at least two reasons, however, to place a degree of faith in the Committee's stated intentions. The first is that republican theorists from Livy to Rousseau had constantly stressed the importance of choosing the appropriate moment for founding a republic. Precisely because the task at hand was so daunting and delicate, one had to proceed with extreme caution. Above all, the citizenry had to be prepared to take an active role in preserving the republic. To this end, and this is the second reason to accept the Committee's claims, the founders had to create or reinforce public institutions. Institutions were the backbone of the classical republic and played an even greater role in natural republicanism, where they did not have positive laws to support them: "There are too many laws, too few civil institutions," Saint-Just lamented.[71] Throughout

---

70. On this discourse, see Jacques Guilhaumou, "'La terreur à l'ordre du jour': un parcours en révolution (1793–1794)," Révolution Française.net, Mots (January 2007), http://revolution-francaise.net/2007/01/06/94-la-terreur-a-lordre-du-jour-un-parcours-en-revolution-juillet-1793-mars-1794.

71. *Fragments des Institutions républicaines*, in *SJ*, 976.

the winter and spring of 1794, the Committee obsessively promoted and created institutions that sought both to sustain civic virtue and to usher in an age of justice, in which the laws of nature were to be the only law of the land. Although the Jacobin theory of justice was "terrible" in every sense of the word, the fact that the Committee did press forward with an ambitious program of judicial institutions and reform suggests that its rhetoric was not all hot air. We may give some credence to its aspirations to found a French republic.

Two of the most important institutions introduced by the Committee in Year II are the cult of the Supreme Being and the reformed revolutionary tribunal. Though obvious in the latter case, both of these institutions were in fact concerned with justice, as Robespierre made clear in his 18 floréal (May 7, 1794) speech. The cult of the Supreme Being was to guarantee that French citizens obey the dictates of natural right "engraved in their hearts" by instilling in them the sense that all their actions were observed. This theory of an internalized surveillance mechanism is most apparent in the iconography and descriptions of the festival, where the Supreme Being (as in earlier revolutionary and Christian representations) is symbolized primarily as a disembodied *eye*. This divine eye that could "read in our hearts" may best be conceived of as a "metaphysical panopticon."

This revolutionary institution differed, however, from its Christian antecedents in that the eye of the Supreme Being was not only an abstract metaphysical concept, but was also "incarnated" in the most sublime of natural bodies, the sun. Strange indications of a "solar cult" indeed appear in both David's script for the Parisian festival and in its iconography. Here as well, an identification of the Supreme Being with the sun can already be found in earlier revolutionary representations and was common in late-eighteenth-century illuminism. As a republican institution, however, this solar symbolism enhanced the panoptic power of the Supreme Being and reinforced the golden age narrative of natural republicanism. According to the leading antiquarians of the day (one of whom, Charles-François Dupuis, was a member of the Convention and sat on the committee that reformed the calendar), solar worshipping had been the religion of the earliest humans, who also lived peacefully without other laws than their inner moral sense.

The Committee was certainly not going to wager the fate of the republic on a religious institution, even if republican theorists did consider a fear of the divine to be a crucial ingredient in the preservation of public virtue. Justice had to be meted out on Earth, as well: There is nothing to surprise us, then, in the presentation of a law, two days after the Festival of the Supreme Being was celebrated, radically streamlining the legal procedures of the revolutionary tribunal. The law of 22 prairial (June 20, 1794) is often considered to mark the bloody climax of Jacobin paranoia (the "Great Terror"), but it did not represent a fundamental shift or crescendo in the punitive legislation of the Terror. For the most part, it merely recapitulated the judicial theory defended by Montagnard deputies ever since the trial of Louis XVI. It can thus be seen, along with the cult of the Supreme Being, as laying down the foundations for the justice system of the republic-to-come.

Placing the guillotine in the heart of Arcadia undoubtedly perverted the myth of the golden age, but it was required by the explosive fusion of republicanism and natural right that characterizes the political discourse of the Terror and of the Jacobin Republic. Saint-Just was foreboding when he claimed that "the spirit with which the king is to be judged will be identical to the spirit with which the republic is to be founded."[72] From this perspective, the cult of the Supreme Being and the reformed tribunal truly appear as mirror images of one another: Where the first sought to force citizens to heed the precepts of natural right in our hearts, the second imposed the penalty reserved for those who violated nature's laws—death after few, if any, legal obstacles—on those who threatened the state, just as the Montagnards had demanded for the king. The alleged crimes by which one became an "enemy of the people," while for the most part treasonous, were hardly the stuff of natural law. Yet preserving the republic had become a new law of nature. The laws of the state had been thoroughly naturalized: Astraea had returned to Earth under the guise of Marianne, with a vengeance.

---

72. *SJ*, 380.

HOSTIS HUMANI GENERIS

AT THE HEART of this story lies a radical kind of enemy. Describing this enemy is daunting since its definition depends on (and in turn defines) legal principles, political theories, cultural representations, religious dogma and rituals, and anthropological considerations.[1] The conceptual content of this enemy, moreover, is continuously shifting—and not necessarily at a uniform pace. Its different incarnations do not follow neatly in succession but overlap and coexist, sometimes disappearing for centuries before reemerging. What its history ultimately uncovers is the richly populated imagination that lurks beneath this extreme expression of hostility. Five main characters emerge at the forefront of this "novel of the law," each associated with a different historical context.[2] The enemy appears as the *savage* in early-modern natural right theory and colonial debates; the savage in turn morphs into the *brigand*, his Old World cousin. In medieval theology, however, we could already find this inimical figure in the *devil*; in Renaissance jurisprudence, the same enemy reappears as the *pirate*. Finally (but also, from a chronological perspective, first), it is the *tyrant* who incarnates the *hostis humani generis*. In the eighteenth century, many of these different types acquired sounder legal footing in works that dealt with international law, or what was known as the law of nations (*ius gentium*). At all times, however, it was the reverence paid to nature that turned its offenders into inhuman monsters.

---

1. For some helpful benchmarks in the history of this enemy, see Carl Schmitt, *The* Nomos *of the Earth in the International Law of the* Jus Publicum Europaeum, trans. and ed. G. L. Ulmen (New York: Telos Press, 2003); and, on Schmitt's definition of the enemy, George Schwab, "Enemy or Foe: A Conflict of Modern Politics," *Telos* 72 (1987): 194–201; see also Gil Anidjar, *The Jew, the Arab: A History of the Enemy* (Stanford: Stanford University Press, 2003); and, by the same author, "Terror Right," *CR: The New Centennial Review* 4, no. 3 (2004): 35–69. This section draws on my article "*Hostis Humani Generis:* Devils, Natural Right, Terror, and the French Revolution," *Telos* 141 (2007): 57–71.

2. I borrow this analogy of the law with the novel from Annie Stora-Lamarre, *La république des faibles: les origines intellectuelles du droit républicain, 1870–1914* (Paris: Armand Colin, 2005).

Natural Man and Natural Right: New World Controversies

As noted in the introduction, natural right theory emerged as an essential political and philosophical language at the turn of the seventeenth century in direct response to the pressing legal questions raised by European imperialism in the New World.[3] Jurists in the Old World did not always agree on the appropriate answers to these questions. On the one hand, certain Spanish Thomists, such as Francisco de Vitoria, contested official claims that the Indians had no natural rights (and, most critically for the colonialist venture, no property rights).[4] Philosophers and jurists working in a more humanist vein, on the other hand, argued that because the "barbaric" practices of the "savages" violated the laws of nature, European sovereigns had a natural right and duty to punish them.[5] As Alberico Gentili, a famed Italian jurist who became Regius professor at Oxford, remarked in *De Jure Belli Libri Tres* (1598), "inasmuch as such men [savages] are the enemies of all mankind [*omnium hostem*] and spare absolutely no one . . . they cannot as I have remarked, enjoy the common law of all."[6] To designate both their unsavory

---

3. For a general overview, see especially Richard Tuck, *Natural Right Theories: Their Origin and Development* (Cambridge: Cambridge University Press, 1979), and *The Rights of War and Peace: Political Thought and the International Order from Grotius to Kant* (Oxford: Oxford University Press, 1999); Anthony Pagden, *The Fall of Natural Man: The American Indian and the Origins of Comparative Ethnology* (Cambridge: Cambridge University Press, 1987), and *Lords of all the World: Ideologies of Empire in Spain, Britain and France, c. 1500–c. 1800* (New Haven: Yale University Press, 1995); and Knud Haakonssen, *Natural Law and Moral Philosophy: From Grotius to the Scottish Enlightenment* (Cambridge: Cambridge University Press, 1996). The intellectual origins of natural right theory, of course, stretch much further back; on its medieval development, see Brian Tierney, *The Idea of Natural Rights: Studies on Natural Rights, Natural Law, and Church Law, 1150–1625* (Atlanta: Scholars Press, 1997).

4. See Francisco de Vitoria, *Political Writings*, ed. and trans. Anthony Pagden and Jeremy Lawrance (Cambridge: Cambridge University Press, 1991), as well as Anthony Pagden, "Dispossessing the Barbarian: The Language of Spanish Thomism and the Debate over the Property Rights of the American Indians," in *The Languages of Political Theory in Early-Modern Europe*, ed. Pagden (Cambridge: Cambridge University Press, 1987); Annabel S. Brett, *Liberty, Right, and Nature: Individual Rights in Later Scholastic Thought* (Cambridge: Cambridge University Press, 1997), 123–64; and Tuck, *Rights of War and Peace*.

5. See, for instance, Hugo Grotius's conclusion: "Kings . . . have a Right to exact Punishments, not only for Injuries committed against themselves, or their Subjects, but likewise, for those which do not peculiarly concern them, but which are, in any Persons whatsoever, grievous Violations of the Law of Nature or Nations," Grotius, *The Rights of War and Peace* [*De Jure Belli ac Pacis*], trans. from Barbeyrac's 1724 edition, ed. Richard Tuck (Indianapolis: Liberty Fund, 2005), 2.20.40; 1021; and for a discussion of this passage, see Tuck, *Rights of War and Peace*, 103. This right to punish was known as *ius gladii*.

6. Gentili, *De Jure Belli Libri Tres*, trans. John C. Rolfe (1612; New York: Oceana, 1964), 22–23; for the Latin, see the edition by Thomas Erskine Holland (Oxford: Clarendon, 1877), 21.

customs and fallen legal status, humanist jurists adopted specific titles of hostility for them, one of which was *humani generis hostes*.[7]

As men of the law, however, they also developed this concept in more general terms. In his *Advertisement Touching a Holy War* (1622), Francis Bacon recognized the legal similarities between the Incas, whose "abominable" customs "make it lawful for the Spaniards to invade their territory, forfeited by the law of nature"; pirates, whom he also described as "*communes humani generis hostes*"; "rovers by land," or what later authors would call "brigands"; and even kings who rule "*de facto*, and not *de jure*, in respect of the nullity of their title."[8] Finally, Bacon revealed how it was precisely (if perversely) the humanist faith in "the supreme and indissoluble consanguinity and society between men in general" (490) that authorized the violent destruction of those who strayed from the church of *humanitas*:

> Now if there be such a tacit league or confederation, sure it is not idle: it is against somewhat, or somebody: who should they be? . . . it is against such routs and shoals of people, as have utterly degenerated from the laws of nature; as have in their very body and frame of estate a monstrosity; and may be truly accounted . . . common enemies and grievances of mankind [*communes humani generis hostes et gravamina*]; or disgraces and reproaches to human nature. Such people, all nations are interested, and ought to be resenting, to suppress. (491)

Juridical responses to the colonial ventures in the New World thus did much more than paint an ugly portrait of the denatured savage: They provided a general theory of natural right violations that could be applied to a wide cast of characters. The high regard in which these authors placed the laws of nature, and which conversely led them to fall down so hard on anyone who violated them, foreshadows the celebration of natural right by liberal reformers in the eighteenth century, who would also wind up demanding

---

7. See Francis Bacon, *Advertisement Touching a Holy War*, in *The Works of Francis Bacon* (London: Baynes, 1824), 3:491; for the Latin translation of this text, *De Bello Sacro*, see vol. 10 (318 for quote). See also François Dollier de Casson's description of the Iroquois as *ennemis du genre humain* in his *History of Montreal, 1640–1672*, trans. and ed. Ralph Flenley (London: J. M. Dent and Sons, 1928), 179. My thanks to Richard Weyhing for supplying this last reference.

8. *Advertisement Touching a Holy War*, 3:487–90. Philip II, in fact, had already proscribed William of Orange, leader of the Dutch rebellion against the Spaniards, as an "enemie of mankinde," in 1580; the ban is reprinted in William's *Apologie or defence of the most noble Prince William* (Delft, 1581), 64. See Herbert H. Rowen, *The Princes of Orange: The Stadholders in the Dutch Republic* (Cambridge: Cambridge University Press, 1990), 25. My thanks to Noah Millstone for calling this text to my attention.

the harshest punishments for transgressors. It was in the name of the *humani generis* that less fortunate *humani* must be killed—a dark irony that would persist throughout the French Revolution and well beyond.

The different incarnations of the *hostis humani generis* were always perceived as sharing certain "family resemblances," chief amongst which were bestiality and inhumanity: "The justest War is that which is undertaken against wild rapacious Beasts, and next to it is that against Men who are *like* Beasts," Hugo Grotius declared in *De Jure Belli ac Pacis* (1625).[9] These monstrous qualities facilitated the incorporation of other offenders into this inimical family. Jean-Louis Guez de Balzac, for instance, added another set of barbarians:

> when the Goths, the Vandals, the Gepids, the Alains, the Huns . . .
> and those other enemies of the human race left their miserable home-
> land . . . when with their extraordinary faces, inarticulate speech, and
> wild-beast skins that hid even their eyes, they brought death and en-
> slavement all about them . . . an almost universal change in laws, cus-
> toms, government, and language ensued.[10]

The "extraordinary faces, inarticulate speech, and wild-beast skins" of the barbarian hordes underscore their hostility to civilization as a whole. This threat of incivility and anarchy ("an almost universal change in laws, customs, government") gave the savage/barbarian a lasting place in the imagination of natural right theory, even after the colonialist ventures in the New World receded from the spotlight. Eighteenth-century treatises on mendicity, for instance, warned of the savages within, namely, brigands. As the French Physiocrat Guillaume-François Le Trosne argued, these vagabonds "live in society without belonging to it; they live in that state where men would be if they had no laws, no police, no authority; in that state which is supposed to have existed before the establishment of civil societies."[11]

---

9. Grotius, *Rights of War and Peace*, 2.20.40.3 (emphasis added).

10. Guez de Balzac, *Le Prince* (Paris: Du Bray, 1631), 242.

11. Le Trosne, *Mémoire sur les vagabonds et sur les mendiants* (Paris: P. G. Simon, 1764), 8. My thanks to Colin Jones for this reference. The German jurist and philosopher Christian Wolff would describe brigands as the "enemies of the whole human race [*totius generis humani hostes*]," *Law of Nations Treated According to a Scientific Method [Jus Gentium Methodo Scientifica Pertractatum*], trans. Joseph Drake (1749; New York: Oceana/Carnegie Endowment for International Peace, 1964), §627. On representations of, and laws against, brigandry in eighteenth-century France, see Alan Forrest, "The Ubiquitous Brigand: The Politics and Language of Repression," in *Popular Resistance in the French Wars: Patriots, Partisans and Land Pirates*, ed. Charles J. Esdaile (London: Palgrave Macmillan, 2005).

Le Trosne pushed the analogy further, suggesting a racial difference between the "civilized" citizen and the "natural" vagabond: The latter is "a ferocious beast who cannot be tamed [*apprivoisé*]."[12] The Swiss diplomat and jurist Emmerich de Vattel extended the analogy with savages to belligerent nations, those who "delight in the ravages of war" but are really "monsters, unworthy of the name of men," and "should be considered as enemies to the human race [*ennemis du Genre-humain*]." Accordingly, he concluded in a Baconian vein that "all nations have a right to join in a confederacy for the purpose of punishing and even exterminating those savage nations."[13]

If the savage embodied the monstrosity of the *hostis humani generis*, he was not the first to be branded with this shameful phrase. It is often attributed to Cicero, who allegedly used it as a descriptive tag for pirates.[14] As Alfred Rubin pointed out, however, Cicero's expression was *communis hostis omnium*, or common enemy of all. "The source of the paraphrase '*hostes humani generis*,'" Rubin regretted, "has not been found."[15] But scholars may have been looking in the wrong places. Although the pirate was indeed another important personification of the "enemy of the human race" in early-modern jurisprudence, Renaissance jurists appear to have lifted this expression from the pages of a different kind of book: medieval theological and demonological treatises.

The "True Ancient Enemy of the Human Race": Theology and the Devil

Hostis humani generis was in fact one of the devil's epithets, appearing very early on in Christian writings. It can already be found in a hymn attributed to Saint Ambrose (d. 397).[16] Gregory the Great (d. 604) introduced

---

12. Le Trosne, *Mémoire sur les vagabonds et sur les mendiants*, 46.

13. Vattel, in *The Law of Nations, or Principles of the Law of Nature Applied to the Conduct and Affairs of Nations and Sovereigns*, trans. and ed. Joseph Chitty (Philadelphia: T. & J. W. Johnson, 1883), bk. 3, §34 (translation of *Le droit des gens, ou Principes de la loi naturelle appliqués à la conduite et aux affaires des nations et des souverains* [London: n.p., 1758]). On this work, see below.

14. See notably Douglas R. Burgess Jr.'s widely discussed article, "The Dread Pirate Bin Laden," *Legal Affairs* (July–August 2005), http://www.legalaffairs.org/issues/July–August-2005/feature_burgess_julaug05.msp.

15. Alfred Rubin, *The Law of Piracy* (Newport: Naval War College Press, 1989), 10–12 and 55n61. For Cicero, see *On Duties*, III, 107.

16. "Hymnus (paschalis) matutinus," in *Patrologia Latina*, ed. Jacques-Paul Migne, vol. 17 (online edition).

the phrasing that the Catholic Church would maintain, with few variations, calling the devil the *Antiquus vero hostis humani generis*.[17] As database searches of the *Patrologia Latina* and *Acta Sanctorum* reveal, this expression became a widespread designation for the devil in the medieval period; it was also found commonly in demonology treatises.[18] The fact that the Spaniards viewed the New World itself as a place where the devil had ruled unchallenged for fifteen hundred years may also explain why they would have applied this diabolical label to the "savages" whom they encountered there.[19] The term even became part of the official exorcism ritual of the Counter-Reformation Church, where the devil was summoned by all his names:

> Audi ergo, et time satana, inimice fidei, hostis generis humani, mortis adductor, vitæ raptor, justitiæ declinator, malorum radix, fomes vitiorum, seductor hominum, proditor gentium, incitator invidiæ, origo avaritæ, causa discordiæ, excitator dolorum.[20]

For the history of this phrase, the theological identification of the *hostis humani generis* with the devil is crucial. As opposed to the brigands or savages who threatened the *salus populi*, the diabolical *hostis* was a menace to each and every soul; no one was safe from the devil's temptations. This meant that the bar for determining absolute hostility was drastically lowered. Civil society need not be imperiled for severe measures to be required. Whosoever revealed a diabolical nature posed an immediate and constant danger. Accordingly, the imperative for extermination was all the greater.

The theological signification of this phrase was also available in other languages than Latin. The early-modern French equivalent, *ennemi du genre*

---

17. *Sancti Gregorii Magni Romani Pontificis Moralium Libri*, 6.3.7, in *Patrologia Latina*, vol. 76.

18. Accounting for case differences and word order, this expression appears over 230 times in a combined search of both databases. For demonology treatises, see, for instance, *Fratris Alfonsi a Castro, Zamorensis, Ordinis Minorvm, Regvlaris Obseruantiæ prouinciæ sancti Iacobi* (Venice: Spei, 1549), 679; and for more examples, see the Cornell Witchcraft Collection at http://historical.library.cornell.edu/witchcraft/about.html.

19. See Jorge Cañizares-Esguerra, *Puritan Conquistadors: Iberianizing the Atlantic, 1550–1700* (Stanford: Stanford University Press, 2006).

20. From the *Rituale Romanum* (the seventeenth-century Vatican service manual): "Hear then and obey, Satan, attacker of the faith, enemy of the human race, messenger of death, robber of life, destroyer of justice, root of all evils, spark of vices, seducer of men, merchant of peoples, rouser of hatred, origin of avarice, cause of discord, instigator of deceit"; reproduced in *Manuel d'exorcismes de l'Eglise* (1626; Charenton: G. V. P., 2000), 47.

humain, had the same diabolical referent.[21] This periphrase was moreover quite common, as a sample database search reveals: It appears in 45 texts (out of a corpus of 546) published between 1684 and 1805.[22] Only 30 percent of these instances, however, are references to the devil. The remaining two-thirds have either a figurative meaning or designate one of the other types.[23] While obviously incomplete, these numbers tell an interesting story. The humanist identification of the *hostis humani generis* with the savage or brigand was gaining ground in the eighteenth century over the theological signification, yet this older meaning was not forgotten. The earlier referent lurked, as in a palimpsest, beneath the new. The devil was in fact to remain an important incarnation of the *ennemi du genre humain* well into the nineteenth century.

Killing No Murder: Tyranny and Natural Right

Although the doctors of the church can take credit for having made this diabolical concept available to natural right theorists, they did not invent it. The earliest usage of the term that I discovered is in Pliny's *Natural History* (c. AD 77). In a chapter on unnatural births (*nascentem contra natura*), Nero, whose violent rule had recently ended, is there described as an "*hostem generis humani.*"[24] The emperor appears to have merited this title both for his inhuman actions (which included assassinating his own mother) and his monstrous birth (feet first). According to the fourth-century Roman historian Eutropius, this designation was later applied to another vicious emperor, Commodus, after his death in AD 192.[25] The

---

21. See, for instance, Corneille's *Polyeucte Martyr* (1643): "*Ainsi du Genre humain l'ennemi vous abuse: / Ce qu'il ne peut de force, il l'entreprend de ruse* [Hence you are abused by the enemy of the human race / What he cannot achieve by force, he attempts by ruse]" in *Œuvres complètes*, ed. Georges Couthon (Paris: Pléiade, 1980), 984.

22. Results acquired through proximity searches for "ennemi(e)(s) genre humain" in the FRANTEXT database, operated by ARTFL, at the University of Chicago. The proximity search includes very similar expressions such as *l'ennemi de tout le genre-humain* or *ennemi commun du genre humain*.

23. Of the forty-five recorded uses in the long eighteenth century, only fourteen are literally theological, whereas the remaining thirty-one (70 percent) are figurative. If one considers cases from only the second half of the century (1745–1805), the numbers are even more striking. Out of a total thirty-four cases, eight (24 percent) are theological, versus twenty-six (76 percent) that are metaphorical. Among these eight theological uses, furthermore, one is in jest (Mercier's *Tableau de Paris*), another is from a non-Christian context (Florian's *Numa Pompilius*), and a third is a quotation from a Catholic priest (the abbé Calmet, in Voltaire's *La Bible enfin expliquée*). Readjusted for these statistics, the percentages are 15 and 85, respectively.

24. *Historia Naturalis*, 7.8.46.

25. *Breviarium historiae romanae*, 8.15.

"tyrant" thus appears to have been the first incarnation of the *hostis humani generis*.[26]

This political, Roman meaning of this expression may have been forgotten during the Middle Ages, but was remembered in early-modern times. Richard Cumberland, in *De legibus naturae* (1672), embroidered Pliny's comments to claim that Nero was declared a *hostem humani generis* by the Roman Senate.[27] It is no coincidence that this work was a forceful defense of natural right *contra* Hobbes, as natural right was precisely the legal code commonly invoked in defense of tyrannicide. Applying the logic of colonialist jurists to Old World politics, the Spanish Jesuit Juan de Mariana appealed to "the natural law" in his famous justification of tyrannicide, found in *De rege et regis institutione* (1599), while also emphasizing the similarity between the tyrant and the "wild and monstrous . . . beast."[28] Even Grotius recognized that it was just to wage war against "Tyrants" and "Insolent Princes," albeit safely choosing his examples of such rulers from classical mythology, at the furthest possible remove from current sovereigns.[29]

These arguments were put to the test during and after the English civil war. The 1657 republican (but anti-Cromwellian) pamphlet, *Killing No Murder*, asserted, for instance, that a tyrant is someone "over whom every man is naturally a Judge and an Executioner; and whom the Laws of God, of Nature, and of Nations expose, like Beasts of prey, to be destroyed as they are met."[30] Algernon Sidney, who fought against Charles I and would

---

26. Carl Schmitt discusses the tyrant as an early incarnation of the *hostis humani generis*, in *The Nomos of the Earth*, but describes him as a subsequent land-based equivalent of the pirate. Cicero provides an interesting (and, judging by modern dictionaries, plausible) etymology of *hostis* as "stranger" in *De Officiis*, 1.37.

27. *De legibus naturæ disquisitio philosophica* . . . (London: Flesher, 1672), 7.19; 406. This work was better known through Barbeyrac's translation, *Traité philosophique des loix naturelles* (Amsterdam, 1744), 410 for the quote.

28. See *The King and the Education of the King*, trans. George Albert Moore (Washington, DC: Country Dollar Press, 1948), bk. 1, chaps. 6–7 (153 and 146). The classic reference for this defense of tyrannicide is Cicero, *De Officiis*, 3.32: "There can be no fellowship between us and tyrants . . . and it is not contrary to nature to rob a man, if you are able, to whom it is honorable to kill. Indeed, the whole pestilential and irreverent class ought to be expelled from the community of mankind," *On Duties*, trans. M. T. Griffin and E. M. Atkins (Cambridge: Cambridge University Press, 1991), 111.

29. *Rights of War and Peace*, 2.20.40.3.

30. See Olivier Lutaud, *Des révolutions d'Angleterre à la Révolution française: le tyrannicide et 'Killing No Murder'* (The Hague: Nijhoff, 1973), 376; the authors drew among others on Grotius's authority for their argument, referring to the justification in *Rights of War and Peace*, 1.15.1, that a usurper may be "lawfully" killed (*Des révolutions d'Angleterre*, 387n46). See more generally Franklin L. Ford, *Political Murder: From Tyrannicide to Terrorism* (Cambridge: Harvard University Press, 1985); and Mario Turchetti, *Tyrannie et tyrannicide de l'Antiquité à nos jours* (Paris: PUF, 2001).

be executed for allegedly plotting against Charles II, similarly invoked the law of nations to justify the assassination of tyrants: "By an established Law among the most virtuous Nations, every man might kill a Tyrant; and no Names are recorded in History with more honour, than of those who did it."[31] Even a moderate defender of the monarchy recognized that "monstrous unnatural tyranny" should be resisted if the ruler "were truly what the Senate pronounced to be [referring to Nero], *humani generis hostis*."[32] These justifications bear witness to both a lasting memory of, and in some cases strong nostalgia for, the ancient defenders of "public liberty," as may be seen in the radical curé Jean Meslier's impassioned plea:

> Where are the Jacques Cléments? And the Ravaillacs of our France? Why are they not of our century? And of all centuries? To topple or murder all these detestable monsters and enemies of the human race [*ennemis du genre humain*]? And to deliver in this fashion all the peoples of the world from their tyrannical domination? Why are these worthy and generous defenders of public liberty no longer with us![33]

While indebted to a Greco-Roman past (as well as, of course, to recent French history), the emphasis on monstrosity in these claims suggests that neither the savage nor the theological genealogy of the *hostis humani generis* had been forgotten. The tyrant was a secularized incarnation of the Prince of Darkness, whose hellish underworld resembled the former's ravaged state. In Ambrogio Lorenzetti's "Allegory of Bad Government" (1338–40) in Siena's Palazzo Pubblico, for instance, the *tyrannos* wears diabolical horns. This association, we shall see, was still evident during the French Revolution.

Pirates and the Law of the Land

The figure most closely associated with the *hostis humani generis* today, the pirate, seems to have received this title in the fourteenth century, in the

---

31. *Discourses Concerning Government* (London: n.p., 1698), 2.24; 175. On the relation between the law of nations and natural right, see below.

32. Philip Hunton, *A Treatise of Monarchy, Containing Two Parts* . . . (1643), in *Divine Right and Democracy: An Anthology of Political Writing in Stuart England*, ed. David Wooton (Indianapolis: Hackett, 2003), 181.

33. *Mémoire des pensées et sentiments de Jean Meslier*, in *Œuvres complètes*, ed. R. Desne (1729; Paris: Anthropos, 1972), 3:134. See also the baron d'Holbach, *La morale universelle* (Amsterdam: M.-M. Rey, 1776), 227.

writings of the Italian jurist Bartolus de Saxoferrato.[34] In the seventeenth century, this referent subsisted alongside the identification with savages. In his 1652 response to John Selden's *Mare Clausum*, Theodor Graswinckel defined pirates as *generis humani publicos hostes*, an expression that he could have found in Bacon or in the English jurist Edward Coke's famous *Institutes of the Lawes of England* (1628).[35] The reference to pirates also obtained in vernacular languages: Jean Bodin described pirates as "*ennemis du genre humain*" at the beginning of his 1576 *Six livres de la république*, as did Pierre-Daniel Huet over a century later.[36] This designation continued to be justified, in the eighteenth century, in terms of natural right. In his influential *Commentaries on the Laws of England*, William Blackstone defined the pirate as

> *hostis humani generis*. As therefore he has renounced all the benefits of society and government, and has reduced himself afresh to the savage state of nature, by declaring war against all mankind, all mankind must declare war against him: so that every community has a right, by the rule of self-defense, to inflict that punishment upon him, which every individual would in a state of nature have been otherwise entitled to do, any invasion of his person or personal property.[37]

While bearing traces of Locke's "very strange doctrine" (*Second Treatise*, §9), Blackstone's gloss perpetuates the humanist legal argument that "offences against the law of nations" (the title of the chapter in which piracy is discussed) turn the offender into a *hostis humani generis* and strip him of

---

34. See Emily Sohmer Tai, "Marking Water: Piracy and Property in the Pre-Modern West" (paper presented at Seascapes, Littoral Cultures, and Trans-Oceanic Exchanges, Library of Congress, Washington DC, February 12–15, 2003), available at http://www.historycooperative.org/proceedings/seascapes/tai.html, n9.

35. Theodor Graswinckel, *Maris liberi vindiciæ: Adversus Petrum baptistam burgum ligustici maritimi dominii assertorem* (The Hague, 1652), 4. Graswinckel, in fact, had collaborated with Grotius on the work that launched this controversy, *Mare Liberum* (1608). On this controversy, see Tuck, *Rights of War and Peace*. On Graswinckel, see E. Haitsma Mulier, *The Myth of Venice and Dutch Republican Thought in the Seventeenth Century*, trans. Gerard T. Moran (Assen: Van Gorcum, 1980). For Bacon, see above. For Coke, see *The Selected Writings and Speeches of Sir Edward Coke*, ed. Steve Sheppard (Indianapolis: Liberty Fund, 2003), 3.1; 2:965.

36. Bodin, *Les six livres de la république* (Paris: Fayard, 1986), 1.1; 27. For Huet, see *Histoire du commerce et de la navigation des anciens* (Bruxelles, 1716), 184–85.

37. *Commentaries on the Laws of England* (Oxford: Clarendon Press, 1765–68), 4.5.3. Blackstone's commentaries were translated into French by the abbé Gabriel-François Coyer; see the *Commentaire sur le code criminel d'Angleterre, traduit de l'anglois de Guillaume Blackstone* (Paris: Knapen, 1776). This translation renders the Latin term as *l'ennemi commun du genre humain*, 1:79.

any legal protection. If the pirate provided a sense of continuity in the history of the law, his presence is nonetheless felt less strongly in eighteenth-century legal and philosophical works. With the widespread use of privateers by European powers, the concept of piracy became rather diffuse, particularly in France, where economic pressures and military setbacks forced the state to settle for a navy suited only for commercial raiding (*guerre de course*).[38] Natural right theory, like many of its great continental practitioners, became mostly "landlocked." But it was in law books about war waged on solid ground that the "enemy of the human race" came closest to acquiring an actual legal status.

The Law of Nations and the Law of Nature

With the exception of the devil, the other principal incarnations of the *hostis humani generis* were both cultural representations and legal categories. As legal entities, however, they existed at some degrees removed from the law and usually were encountered only in works of political philosophy. The destruction of "savages" in the New World may have been encouraged by philosophical justifications, but no one, not even Charles I (or Commodus, for that matter), was tried in court as a *hostis humani generis*.[39] This label was applied either post facto or in the abstract; it was not brandished as an accusation.

There was, of course, a good reason that law books made no mention of such an enemy: Whether a brigand or a tyrant, a pirate or a savage, his crime was precisely to reject the rules of civil society altogether. But there was another body of law, more codified than the laws of nature, that was thought to govern all human relations, within and without societies, and under which these figures could indeed be prosecuted. This was the law of nations. Etymologically and conceptually descended from the Roman *ius*

38. See Geoffrey Symcox, *The Crisis of French Sea Power: From the* Guerre d'Escadre *to the* Guerre de Course (The Hague: Nijhoff, 1974); and *Pirates and Privateers: New Perspectives on the War on Trade in the Eighteenth and Nineteenth Centuries*, ed. David J. Starkey, Els van Eyck van Heslinga, and J. A. de Moor (Exeter: Exeter University Press, 1997). I am grateful to Christy Pichichero for enlightening me on this development in early-modern naval warfare.

39. On the trial of Charles I, see Geoffrey Robertson, *The Tyrannicide Brief: The Story of the Man Who Sent Charles I to the Scaffold* (New York: Anchor, 2005). Although the prosecutor, John Cooke, ultimately accused the king of being "a public and implacable enemy to the Commonwealth of England," his written commentaries reveal his familiarity with both *ius gentium* and current natural right theories; see, for instance, his comment, "This law—*if the King become a tyrant he shall die for it*—is the law of nature and the law of God, written in the fleshly tablets of men's hearts," *King Charles, His Case*, qtd. in Robertson, *Tyrannicide Brief*, 149 and 192.

gentium, this "law of peoples" (*droit des gens* in French) consisted of the established customs and practices common to all humanity.[40] These customs were universally recognized as just, or so it was argued, because all humans shared the same "natural reason";[41] the law of nations was thus already related in Roman times to natural right (*ius naturale*; *Institutes*, 1.2.1). In this respect, it was immutable and commanded the highest respect, having been established by divine providence, as opposed to civil laws, which were variable and differed from city to city (*Institutes*, 1.2.11). For the Romans, *ius gentium* even took precedence over *ius naturale* in matters where custom had departed from natural right (although this rapport would be inversed by medieval scholars).[42]

In the eighteenth century, by contrast, the law of nations and that of nature were widely considered to be identical. In a footnote to a passage in Grotius, Jean Barbeyrac (his translator) scoffed, "This Positive *Law of Nations*, distinct from *the Law of Nature*, is a mere Chimera."[43] As the noted jurist Antoine-Gaspard Boucher d'Argis summarized in the *Encyclopédie*,

> natural right is the same thing as the law of nations, both being founded on the natural powers [*lumières naturelles*] of reason: hence most authors who have written on this matter have conflated these two objects, such as the baron von Pufendorf, who entitled his work *The Law of Nature and Nations*.[44]

In practice, the law of nations tended to pertain more specifically to international conflicts, that is, a sphere over which no civil authority

---

40. *Ius autem gentium omni humano generi commune est* ("the law of the nations is common to the entire human race"), *Institutes*, 1.2.2. On the *ius gentium*, see Stephen C. Neff, *War and the Law of Nations: A General History* (Cambridge: Cambridge University Press, 2005). I develop the relation between natural right and the law of nations in greater detail in "War and Terror: The Law of Nations from Grotius to the French Revolution," *French Historical Studies* 31, no. 2, special issue on "War, Culture, and Society," ed. David A. Bell and Martha Hanna (2008), 229–62.

41. See again *Institutes*, 1.2.1: *naturalis ratio inter omnes homines constituit* ("Natural reason establishes [this law] among all men").

42. See, for instance, Gratian's *Decretum*, 8.2, which stated that "whatever has been recognized by custom or set down in writing must be held null and void if it conflicts with natural law"; qtd. and discussed in David Johnston, "The Jurists," in *The Cambridge History of Greek and Roman Political Thought* (Cambridge: Cambridge University Press, 2000), 621–22.

43. *Rights of War and Peace*, note 3 to 1.1.14.

44. *Encyclopédie, ou Dictionnaire raisonné des sciences, des arts et des métiers*, ed. Denis Diderot and Jean-le-Rond d'Alembert (Paris: Briasson, David, Le Breton, 1755), s.v. "droit des gens," 5:127. The reference here is to *De jure naturae et gentium* (1672). See also Robert Derathé, *Jean-Jacques Rousseau et la science politique de son temps* (1950; Paris: Vrin, 1992), 386–90.

could claim jurisdiction, but in which the laws of nature could still be said to hold.[45] The most influential eighteenth-century treatise to deal with these matters was Emmerich de Vattel's *The Law of Nations*, whose subtitle clearly indicated its jusnaturalist framework. A brief examination of this text reveals how this Enlightenment jurist came close to codifying natural right in such a way that the "enemy of the human race" could become an effective legal category, liable of being used in courts and introduced into legislation.

While recognizing with Grotius that war formed an inevitable part of international affairs, Vattel sought in a more Fénelonian vein to proscribe those practices that had resulted in "bloody wars."[46] His legal philosophy was premised on the liberal tenet that individuals have fundamental rights, derived from nature: "Let us never forget that our enemies are men . . . let us not divest ourselves of that charity which connects us with all mankind. Thus shall we courageously defend our country's rights without violating those of human nature" (bk. 3, §158). Accordingly, in the *Law of Nations*, he sought to establish the clear limits of acceptable conduct in warfare.

If an enemy happened to transgress these limits, however, then Vattel's appeals for moderation abruptly ceased. Indeed, the enemy who violated the law of nations de facto (and de jure) forfeited all rights: "Whoever therefore takes up arms without a lawful cause, can absolutely have no right whatever: every act of hostility that he commits is an act of injustice . . . he is guilty of a crime against mankind in general" (bk. 3, §§183–84). The nonrespect of

---

45. As Rousseau remarked: "The law of nature only persisted [*n'eut plus lieu*] between different societies . . . under the name of the law of nations," *Discours sur l'origine de l'inégalité*, in *Œuvres complètes*, ed. Bernard Gagnebin and Marcel Raymond (Paris: Gallimard/Pléiade, 1959–95), 3:178 (hereafter cited as *JJR*). This did not imply that nations obeyed this law in practice. In a fragment on the state of war, Rousseau calls the laws of *droit des gens* "only illusions even weaker than the law of nature," *Plan for Perpetual Peace*, in *The Plan for Perpetual Peace . . .*, vol. 2 of *The Collected Writings of Rousseau*, trans. Christopher Kelly and Judith Bush (Hanover, NH: Dartmouth College Press, 2005), 62. Though weak, it is mistaken to characterize the law of nations in Rousseau as merely "the law of corrupted nature, the law of *amour-propre* and competition," as Stanley Hoffmann does in *The State of War* (New York: Praeger, 1965), 66, since it is glossed in the second *Discourse* as "a few tacit conventions to enable commerce and to supplement natural pity [*suppléer à la commisération naturelle*]" (*JJR*, 3:178).

46. From the title of a volume of essays by Vattel, *Mémoires pour servir à l'histoire de notre tems, où l'on déduit historiquement le droit et le fait de la guerre sanglante qui trouble actuellement toute l'Europe . . .* (Frankfurt/Leipzig, 1758). On Fénelon's pacifism, see especially David A. Bell, *The First Total War: Napoleon's Europe and the Birth of Warfare as We Know It* (Boston: Houghton Mifflin, 2007). On Vattel, see also Reinhart Koselleck, *Critique and Crisis: Enlightenment and the Pathogenesis of Modern Society* (Cambridge: MIT Press, 1988), 43–48.

the laws of war was so serious that it freed the opposite side from respecting them as well: "We are no longer bound to observe them towards an enemy who has himself been the first to violate them" (bk. 3, §176); "when [an] enemy has been guilty of some enormous breach of the law of nations, and particularly when he has violated the laws of war," then "refusal of quarter" is permissible (bk. 3, §141). The appearance or interpretation of a viola-tion of natural right could thus lead to a vicious cycle of reprisals: "If the hostile general has, without any just reason, caused some prisoners to be hanged, we hang an equal number of his people, and of the same rank," Vattel asserted. The fundamental rights of noncombatants were voided if one was dealing with a nonlawful enemy.[47] This apparently justified form of retribution was paradoxically intended to restore respect due to the laws of nations: "We will continue thus to retaliate, for the purpose of obliging him to observe the laws of war."[48]

The logic on display in Vattel's *Law of Nations* is a frightening demon-stration of how the best intentions can themselves result in "bloody wars." As Bacon before him, Vattel authorized and encouraged the temporary sus-pension of lofty liberal principles in the name of these very principles.[49] This logic also highlights the difficult, and all too relevant, challenge that liberal-ism constantly faces: Are there certain circumstances under which the in-alienable rights of individuals become alienable? Do we possess fundamental rights, only so long as we do not commit actions that deprive us of them? Natural right theorists were generally willing to draw a line past which only "inhuman" enemies would cross, thus clearly indicating that their rights as "humans" were rescinded.[50]

As did his predecessors, Vattel considered two main types of inhuman enemy. The first was the brigand, who in war corresponded to the unlaw-ful troops and who could be summarily executed even after being made

---

47. Since Vattel is often accused of merely copying Wolff, it should be noted that he com-pletely departs from his mentor on this account. Wolff does not admit any such exceptions: "The law of nature is everywhere consistent with itself [and] does not allow anything contrary to what it enjoins or forbids. . . . The right against persons in war is not the right of the promiscuous slaughter of those who are in the category of enemies," *Law of Nations Treated According to a Scientific Method*, §792. On the treatment of prisoners and the (rare) right to kill in battle, see §§790–807. On Vattel and Wolff, see T. J. Hochstrasser, *Natural Law Theories in the Early Enlightenment* (Cambridge: Cambridge University Press, 2000).

48. See also the mention of an "inhuman enemy" in the rest of this paragraph (bk. 3, §142).

49. This argument owes much to the thesis developed by David Bell in *The First Total War*.

50. See Reinhart Koselleck, "The Historical-Political Semantics of Asymmetric Counter-concepts," in *Future Past: On the Semantics of Historical Time*, trans. Keith Tribe (New York: Columbia University Press, 2004), 192–93, in reference to Saint-Just's speech against Louis.

prisoner.[51] The other type was the leader of such troops, or any "sovereign" who waged war without respecting the laws of nations. Vattel characterized this offender as the now-familiar "enemy of the human race":

> Assassination and poisoning are therefore contrary to the laws of war, and equally condemned by the law of nature and the consent of all civilized nations. The sovereign who has recourse to such execrable means should be regarded as the enemy of the human race [*l'ennemi du Genre-humain*]; and the common safety of mankind calls on all nations to unite against him and join their forces to punish him. His conduct particularly authorizes the enemy, whom he has attacked by such odious means, to refuse him any quarter. . . . Whoever, by setting the example, contributes to the introduction of so destructive a practice, declares himself the enemy of mankind [*l'ennemi du Genre-humain*], and deserves the execration of all ages.[52]

The specific characterization and condemnation of the tyrannical sovereign—who brings to mind Adrastus, the evil king of the Daunians and "scourge of the human race," in Fénelon's *Télémaque*—is not particularly original to Vattel. As we have seen, it was commonplace by the mid-eighteenth century to castigate tyrants as enemies of the human race. The innovative quality of Vattel's work seems rather to lie in its systematic analysis of legal concepts and actual situations that had previously either been treated in more philosophical and/or polemical works, or else by less liberal authors, such as Grotius (or by authors whose success did not exceed their country's borders, such as Wolff). By treating a variety of traditional questions under the heading of "the law of nations," Vattel helped turn theoretical notions about natural right into concrete legal matters. If they could still be distinguished at all, the law of nations now bore a greater resemblance to a real code of law than did the laws of nature (over which philosophers were still wrangling). No longer was it simply a law of nature that anyone could kill a tyrant: now the specific actions that constituted tyranny, at least in warfare, were spelled out with great precision.

---

51. "A nation attacked by such sort of enemies is not under any obligation to observe towards them the rules prescribed in formal warfare. She may treat them as robbers [*brigands*]. The inhabitants of Geneva, after defeating the famous attempt to take their city by escalade, caused all the prisoners whom they took from the Savoyards on that occasion to be hanged up as robbers [*voleurs*], who had come to attack them without cause and without a declaration of war," *Law of Nations*, bk. 3, §68.

52. *Law of Nations*, bk. 3, §155; see also §§167 and 168. For a similar assessment, see d'Holbach, *La morale universelle*, 7.

It was indeed under the name of *le droit des gens* that the king would be prosecuted as an *ennemi du genre humain* during the French Revolution (see chapter 3). By that time, of course, the entire institution of monarchy was being attacked in the terms previously reserved for tyranny: Thomas Paine denounced "monarchical sovereignty" as "the enemy of mankind" in the *Rights of Man*, while William Godwin argued that "every king is by unavoidable necessity enemy of the human race."[53] As with tyrants, kings were reviled for their monstrosity: "To reign, is that not to be the most mortal enemy of humanity?" wrote Jacques Hébert in his journal, *Le Père Duchesne*; "Kings and their race are born to harm us; they are destined to crime from birth, as some plants are destined to poison us."[54] The "race" of kings was "*destined* to crime"; their once sacred body and blood were now proof of their "poisonous" nature.[55] But the *hostis humani generis* construction had also become an actionable legal category: Although unsuccessful in their prosecution of the king, the Jacobins would pass legislation against other "counterrevolutionaries" who adopted the violent logic demanded by natural right theory. Two hundred years of jurisprudence had finally made it into the courtroom.

Conclusion: Enlightenment and Hostility

The strange history of the "enemy of the human race" stretches back across centuries, but it is revealing that important episodes in this history, in particular its judicial role in the French revolutionary Terror, took place in a century that elevated nature to a rung previously occupied by God alone.[56] To an even greater extent than in Bacon's time, philosophers and jurists in the Enlightenment placed a boundless faith in nature as the foundation of all laws, science, and even aesthetics. But the age that pioneered human rights had difficultly imagining salvation outside the church of *la belle nature*.[57] Rousseau

---

53. For Paine, see his *Collected Writings* (New York: Library of America, 1995), 538. For Godwin, see *An Enquiry Concerning Political Justice* (Dublin: n.p., 1793), 5.3; 1:372.

54. *Père Duchesne*, issue 280 ([Sept.?] 1793), 3–4. See also Jean-Baptiste Chemin-Dupontès, *Morality of the Sans-Culottes of Every Age, Sex, Country, and Condition; or, The Republican Gospel* (Philadelphia: n.p., 1794; translation of *Morale des sans-culottes* . . . [Paris, 1793]): "Who is a Tyrant? It is the enemy of equality, that most darling right of man. It is therefore the enemy of the human race. Shew no favour to a monster of this sort" (35).

55. See Antoine de Baecque, *The Body Politic: Corporeal Metaphor in Revolutionary France, 1770–1800*, trans. Charlotte Mandell (Stanford: Stanford University Press, 1997), 157–82.

56. See especially Jean Ehrard, *L'idée de la nature en France dans la première moitié du XVIIIᵉ siècle* (Paris: S.E.V.P.E.N., 1963).

57. Lynn Hunt, *Inventing Human Rights: A History* (New York: Norton, 2007).

railed against "those low-born men, deaf to the gentle voice of nature, inside of whom no true feeling of justice and humanity ever sprouts. . . ."[58] An individual who was not sensible to the plight of others was simply an *homme à étouffer* (a man to be choked), he concluded on the last page of his *Confessions*. These sentiments were not unique to *âmes sensibles* such as Jean-Jacques. In an article that Rousseau admired greatly, Diderot had similarly denounced as an *ennemi du genre humain* whoever violated the laws of nature, claiming that "he should be choked."[59] To be sure, such harsh condemnations were intended only for exceptionally vicious and immoral offenders. But "nature" is a dangerous standard against which to measure departures from the norm. If the Terror could be established on the basis of natural right, it was only because such polymorphous, violent categories as the *hostis humani generis* existed there already.

---

58. *The Confessions*, in *The Collected Writings of Rousseau*, ed. Christopher Kelly, Roger D. Masters, and Peter G. Stillman (Hanover, NH: University Press of New England, 1995), 5:277. For the French, see *Les confessions* (Paris: Gallimard, 1973), 436; he later speaks of "*ces gens bien nés* [well-born men]" (496). In a similar vein, Carla Hesse has argued that "it is not unfounded to suggest that, in the end, of all Rousseau's works, the most revolutionary was the story of Julie"; see "La preuve par la lettre: pratiques juridiques au tribunal révolutionnaire de Paris (1793–1794)," *Annales HSS* 3 (1996): 642.

59. See the *Encyclopédie*, s.v. "Droit naturel," 5:116. On this article, see chapter 1. See more generally Pierre Saint-Amand, *The Laws of Hostility: Politics, Violence, and the Enlightenment*, trans. Jennifer Curtiss Gage (Minneapolis: University of Minnesota Press, 1996).

PART I

❖c ɔ❖

A SECRET HISTORY OF
NATURAL REPUBLICANISM
IN FRANCE (1699–1791)

CHAPTER ONE

IMAGINARY REPUBLICS

IN THE EIGHTEENTH CENTURY, republics existed primarily in books. To be sure, there was Casanova's Venice and Rousseau's Geneva, along with Bayle's United Provinces and a few others (the Swiss cantons, San Marino, and various northern Italian states), but to most observers, these governments were mostly aristocratic and, moreover, were increasingly sidelined to "the fringe of history."[1] The vibrant republics that had inspired Renaissance theorists—Florence in particular—had either disappeared from the political scene or fallen into politico-economic slumber. When eighteenth-century authors wrote about republicanism, it was from a very different perspective than Machiavelli or Harrington: They were describing less a reality than an imagined past or future.

Even as imaginary entities, however, republics had a very real existence. Livy's *Early History of Rome* was taught in nearly all French *collèges*—those "nurseries [*pépinières*] of republicans," as Robespierre later called them—lighting up the minds of students with heroic scenes from a bygone world.[2] "Everyone knows the history of this republic by heart," Jaucourt began his *Encyclopédie* article on the Roman Republic.[3] Relegated to books, republics

1. Franco Venturi, *Utopia and Reform in the Enlightment* (Cambridge: Cambridge University Press, 1971), 70. Madison's assessment of European republics was commonplace: "No satisfactory one [is to] be found" in Europe. *The Federalist Papers* (London: Penguin, 1987), no. 39, p. 254. On Geneva, see in particular Helana Rosenblatt, *Rousseau and Geneva: From the First Discourse to the Social Contract, 1749–1762* (Cambridge: Cambridge University Press, 1997).

2. Maximilien Robespierre, *Œuvres de Maximilien Robespierre*, ed. Société des études robespierristes (Ivry: Phénix éditions, 2000), 9:581 (hereafter cited as *Rob.*). On the instruction received in an old regime French *collèges*, see Harold Parker, *The Cult of Antiquity and the French Revolutionaries: A Study in the Development of the Revolutionary Spirit* (Chicago: University of Chicago Press, 1937); Peter France, *Rhetoric and Truth in France: Descartes to Diderot* (Oxford: Clarendon Press, 1972); Roger Chartier, Dominique Julia, and Marie-Madeleine Compère, *L'éducation en France du XVIe au XVIIIe siècle* (Paris: SEDES, 1976); and L. W. B. Brockliss, *French Higher Education in the Seventeenth and Eighteenth Centuries: A Cultural History* (Oxford: Clarendon Press, 1987).

3. *Encyclopédie, ou Dictionnaire raisonné des sciences, des arts et des métiers*, ed. Denis Diderot and Jean-le-Rond d'Alembert (Paris: Briasson, David, Le Breton, 1751–66), 14:154.

and their glorious citizens obtained a fantastical and alluring hue: Plutarch's generals and statesmen became imaginary models for adolescents.[4] This romancing of republicanism had long worried defenders of monarchy: In *Leviathan*, Hobbes had expressly warned against "the Reading of the books of Policy, and Histories of the antient Greeks, and Romans; from which . . . men have undertaken to kill their Kings, because the Greek and Latine writers . . . make it lawfull, and laudable, for any man so to do."[5] So concerned were the authorities of the University of Cambridge in 1627 that the new professor of classical history, Isaac Dorislaus, was corrupting the youth with his rousing discussions of Tacitus and the fall of the Roman Republic, they suspended him after only two lectures. Dorislaus would later eat his plate of vengeance cold, assisting the prosecution during the trial of Charles I.[6]

If nothing new, these attachments to ancient republics became only exaggerated in the age of *sensibilité*. Where Don Quixote's aristocratic delusions stemmed from an overdose of chivalric romances, eighteenth-century readers seem to have experienced similar republican fantasies. While undoubtedly more *bovaryiste* than his contemporaries, Rousseau's republicanism derived much more, by his own account, from classical sources than his native city's traditions: "Ceaselessly occupied with Rome and Athens; living, so to speak, with their great men . . . I believed myself to be Greek or Roman; I became the character whose life I read." Once over dinner he reenacted the famous gesture that earned Gaius Mucius his nickname of Scaevola—and

---

4. As Jean-Marie Goulemot observed, "Roman history is the province of . . . naive adolescent dreams," "Du républicanisme et de l'idée républicaine," in *Le siècle de l'avènement républicain*, ed. François Furet and Mona Ozouf (Paris: Gallimard, 1993), 39. On the "republican imagination" in eighteenth-century France, see also Jacques Bouineau, *Les toges du pouvoir, ou la révolution de droit antique, 1789–1799* (Toulouse: Editions Eché, 1986); Mouza Raskolnikoff, "L'adoration' des Romains sous la Révolution française et la réaction de Volney et des Idéologues," in *Des anciens et des modernes* (Paris: Publications de la Sorbonne, 1990); Chantal Grell, *Le dix-huitième siècle et l'antiquité en France, 1680–1789* (Oxford: SVEC/Voltaire Foundation, 1995); Henri Morel, "Le poids de l'antiquité sur la Révolution française," *L'influence de l'antiquité sur la pensée politique européenne* (Aix: Presses universitaires d'Aix-Marseille, 1996); and David Bell, *The Cult of the Nation in France: Inventing Nationalism, 1680–1800* (Cambridge: Harvard University Press, 2001).

5. Thomas Hobbes, *Leviathan*, ed. C. B. Macpherson (London: Penguin, 1985), 2.29 (369); see also 1.2 (89), and 2.21 (266).

6. On Dorislaus, see Mark H. Curtis, "The Alienated Intellectuals of Early Stuart England," *Past and Present* 23 (1962): 26–27; see also Ronald Mellor, "Tacitus, Academic Politics, and Regicide in the Reign of Charles I: The Tragedy of Dr. Isaac Dorislaus," *International Journal of the Classical Tradition* 11, no. 2 (2004): 153–93. My thanks to Anthony Grafton for bringing this episode to my attention. On the trial itself, see Geoffrey Robertson, *The Tyrannicide Brief: The Story of the Man Who Sent Charles I to the Scaffold* (New York: Pantheon, 2006).

nearly burnt his right hand in the process.[7] After his revelation on the road to Vincennes to visit Diderot, Rousseau "converted" to a life of republican virtue, with a rapturous enthusiasm reminiscent of his earlier (and later) flights of fancy into the *pays des chimères*.[8]

The regal splendor of eighteenth-century courts served only to accentuate the delusive nature of these republican fantasies. Louis-Sébastien Mercier depicted in exquisite and humorous detail how confusing it was to come of age in a world centered around a king but enamored with ancient republics:

> The name of Rome is the first that caught my attention. As soon as I could grasp rudimentary ideas, I was told the story of Romulus and his she-wolf, and had the Capitol and Tiber described to me. The names of Brutus, Cato, and Scipio pursued me in my sleep; Cicero's familiar epistles were piled into my memory . . . in such a manner that I was far away from Paris, a foreigner in her walls, living in Rome, which I have never seen, and probably never will.[9]

As with Rousseau, it was primarily in Livy's airbrushed portrait of preimperial Rome that Mercier discovered the heroic world of republicanism.[10] The spellbinding power of this lost Roman world led Mercier (as Hobbes

---

7. *The Confessions*, trans. Christopher Kelly, in *The Collected Writings of Rousseau*, ed. Christopher Kelly, Roger D. Masters, and Peter G. Stillman (Hanover, NH: University Press of New England, 1995), 5:8 (hereafter cited as *CWR*). For the French, see *Les confessions* (Paris: Gallimard, 1973), 38. See also Livy, *The Early History of Rome*, trans. Aubrey de Sélincourt (London: Penguin, 1960), 2.12.1–13.5. Mucius was demonstrating the bravery of Roman citizens to King Porsena, who was besieging the city at the time. On Rousseau's classical imagination, see Peter Gay, *The Enlightenment*, vol. 1 of *The Rise of Modern Paganism* (New York: Knopf, 1966), 46–58.

8. "All my little passions were stifled by enthusiasm for truth, for freedom, for virtue, and what is most surprising is that this effervescence maintained itself in my heart during more than four or five years to as high a degree perhaps as it has ever been in the heart of any other man," *CWR*, 5:295; *Confessions*, 431. This "effervescence" is later tied to his juvenile reading of Plutarch: *Confessions*, 436. The religious dimension of Rousseau's "conversion" is made even clearer in *Les rêveries d'un promeneur solitaire* (Paris: Poche, 1983): "I left the world and its pomp, I renounced all appearances. . . . I uprooted from my heart all cupidity and coveting. . . . I did not limit my reform to exterior matters. . . . I sought to submit my inner thoughts to a severe exam." Ibid., 45–46. On the land of chimeras, see, for instance, *Confessions*, 216.

9. *Tableau de Paris* (Amsterdam: n.p., 1783), chap. 81, 1:254–55. On Mercier, see notably Robert Darnton, "The High Enlightenment and the Low-Life of Literature," in *The Literary Underground of the Old Regime* (Cambridge: Harvard University Press, 1982); and Enrico Rufi, *Le rêve laïque de Louis-Sébastien Mercier entre littérature et politique*, in *SVEC* 326 (Oxford: Voltaire Foundation, 1995).

10. *Tableau de Paris*, 1:255–56.

before him) to ponder why, in an absolutist monarchy, students are not only permitted but encouraged to spend their formative years with republican authors who celebrate tyrannicidal acts:

> It is certain that the study of Latin imparts a certain taste for republics, and that one wishes to restore the one whose great and long history one reads. . . . It is nonetheless in a monarchy that young people perpetually entertain these strange ideas, which they must quickly lose and forget, for their safety, success, and happiness; and it is an absolute king who pays professors to expound in all seriousness on the eloquent declamations against the power of kings; in such a way that a university student, when he finds himself in Versailles, and has some sense, cannot help but to think of Tarquin, of Brutus, of all the proud enemies of royalty. Then he nearly loses his head . . . and it takes a while for him to acquaint himself with a country that has no tribunes, no decemvirs, no senators, and no consuls.[11]

Republican fantasies, in Mercier's account, reveal themselves to be just that—the illusory dreams of an adolescent boy, who, in Mably's words, "ruined his mind reading the beloved history of the Greeks and Romans, who now only make good novel or theater heroes."[12] These dreams were not restricted to boys: adolescent girls, most notably Manon Phlipon, the future Mme Roland, and Charlotte Corday, also indulged in Roman republican fantasies.[13] Whether or not it was thought possible to create a republic in

---

11. Ibid., 1:256–57. For similar analyses of the "bizarre contradiction of our education under the Old Regime," see Pierre-Louis Ginguené's article in *La Décade philosophique, littéraire et politique*, 20 Vendémiaire an II (October 12, 1794), 104; qtd. Andrew Jainchill, *Rethinking Politics after the Terror: The Republican Origins of French Liberalism* (Ithaca: Cornell University Press, 2008), 72; and the quotations by Talleyrand and Desmoulins cited in Raskolnikoff, *Anciens et modernes*, 199–200.

12. Mably, *Des droits et des devoirs du citoyen* (Paris: Kell, 1789), 51. The narrator is complaining that his ardent love for liberty will make his friends believe he is crazy.

13. See Mme Roland's *Mémoires particuliers*: "[*The Parallel Lives* of] Plutarch seemed to be the ideal pasture for me; I will never forget the carem of 1763 . . . when I took it to Church instead of my missle [*Semaine-sainte*]. It is from that moment that date the impressions and ideas that turned me into a republican without my realization," in *Mémoires de Mme Roland* (Paris: Plon, 1905), 2:22; see Marilyn Yalom, *Blood Sisters: The French Revolution in Women's Memory* (New York: Basic Books, 1993). For Corday, see Nina Gelbart, "Last Letters and Revolutionary Self-Fashioning" (paper presented at the annual meeting of the Western Society for French History, Long Beach, CA, October 19–21, 2006). For a very insightful related study, see Caroline Winterer, *The Mirror of Antiquity: American Women and the Classical Tradition, 1750–1900* (Ithaca: Cornell University Press, 2007).

France, "the heroism of nascent republics" (to borrow Helvétius's phrase) did not cease to enchant.[14] The few French subjects who would rather have been citizens of a French Republic even before 1789 also seem to have acquired their political views from books on Roman history: Camille Demoulins allegedly carried a copy of the abbé Vertot's *Histoire des révolutions arrivées dans le gouvernement de la République romaine*, a bastardized version of Livy, in his pocket as a schoolboy.[15] As his later speeches and writings reveal, Desmoulins was very familiar with the classical-republican tradition: He was one of few Jacobins not to use "Machiavellian" as a synonym for "deceitful," but instead cited the Machiavelli of the *Discorsi*.[16] Even revolutionaries, such as Saint-Just, who had revealed few republican feelings before August 10, 1792, burst into austere Roman discourse as soon as they made the switch.[17]

While there may not have been a "republican party" in prerevolutionary France, there certainly seems to have been a republican cultural imagination that would be fired up by revolutionary events, even if it did not contribute to their advent. But what are we to make of the fact that republicanism occupied the same *lieu de mémoire* as romanced, and often fanciful, histories

---

14. Helvétius, *De l'homme, de ses facultés intellectuelles et de son éducation* (London: Société typographique, 1773), 5.5 (2:23).

15. M. Mallon, ed., *Le Vieux Cordelier* (Paris: Ébrard, 1834), vi. Mallon refers only to Vertot's "*Révolutions romaines*"; this text, undoubtedly the *Histoire des revolutions . . .* (Paris: F. Barois, 1719), went through at least fifteen editions in the eighteenth century. Goulemot claims that for Vertot, "the so-celebrated Roman republic is from the onset presented as a transitory moment in the history of Rome, and not as a long awaited perfection" (39), but this overlooks the strongly antipatrician and antimonarchic tone prevalent throughout the book. Vertot writes, for example, that "Royalty . . . seemed to Servius [Tullus] as an excessive piece, useless in a state that was nearly republican" (40). For another instance of his plebian sympathies, see 56–57, and his assessment of the Roman *populus* after the death of Caesar: "It was no longer those ancient Romans who preferred liberty to life" (771).

16. The epigraph to *Le Vieux Cordelier*, "Once those in government are despised, their competitors will soon be admired," was borrowed from the *Discourses on Livy*; see Michael Sonenscher, *Work and Wages: Natural Law, Politics, and the Eighteenth-Century French Trades* (Cambridge: Cambridge University Press, 1989), 333; see also Keith Baker, "Political Languages of the French Revolution," in *The Cambridge History of Eighteenth-Century Political Thought*, ed. Mark Goldie and Robert Wolker (Cambridge: Cambridge University Press, 2006) (hereafter cited as *CHECPT*). Gabriel Riquetti, comte de Mirabeau, also refers to Machiavelli as a republican authority in his *Considérations sur l'ordre de Cincinnatus, ou Imitation d'un pamphlet anglo-américain . . .* (London: J. Johnson, 1784), 75–76. Compare with Robespierre's disparaging reference to Machiavelli in his "Rapport sur les principes de morale politique," *Rob.*, 10:351.

17. See, for instance, Saint-Just's challenge that the Convention dispose of Louis XVI as the Roman senators had silenced Caesar, "without any other formalities than twenty-three dagger thrusts," Louis-Antoine Saint-Just, *Œuvres complètes*, ed. Michèle Duval (Paris: Lebovici, 1984), 377 (hereafter cited as *SJ*).

of antiquity? To begin with, this close proximity obliges us to look at works of the imagination if we are to complete the eighteenth-century history of republicanism. This fictional context, however, also affects the way we study it: The "imaginary" life of republicanism was certainly much looser and freer than the traditional grammar and narrative of political thought demanded.

These imaginative reworkings of republicanism did not necessarily constitute "utopian" projections. The essential republican keywords (for example, virtue, corruption, *mœurs*, equality, liberty) remained present, as did the central institutions (notably religious festivals, pedagogical institutions, and citizen armies). The parts stayed the same: It was their relations that changed, and with them, the shape of the republican discourse and story. If the distinction between imaginary republics and utopian representations sometimes appears slim, as in the case of Fénelon's Boetica, the label "utopian" does not confer any advantages, at least for the present study: Not only does it trivialize the republican dimension of these political projects, but it also implies that contemporary readers could not have distinguished the clearly fantastical traits from the more relevant and familiar. As Dena Goodman emphasized, literature in the Enlightenment participated in the wider empirical trend of "experimentation."[18] Under the cover of utopian states, authors could express ideas that were more subversive than fantastic. Fiction, for the philosophes, offered an opportunity to explore "possible worlds"—a Leibnizian notion that has recently regained favor in literary theory—that rested on certain fundamentally different premises, but that nonetheless obeyed logic and causality.[19] This experimental strategy was famously employed in one of the most widely read works of the eighteenth century, Fénelon's *Aventures de Télémaque*, analyzed below. Through such literary, political, and philosophical texts, a cultural and legal imagination emerged that would

---

18. Dena Goodman, *Criticism in Action: Enlightenment Experiments in Political Writing* (Ithaca: Cornell University Press, 1989), 4; see also Erica Harth, *Ideology and Culture in Seventeenth-Century France* (Ithaca: Cornell University Press, 1983). Literary theorists have written volumes on the relations between literature and the political order; see notably Frederick Jameson, *The Political Unconscious: Narrative as Socially Symbolic Act* (Ithaca: Cornell University Press, 1981); and, more recently, Jean-Marie Schaeffer, *Pourquoi la fiction?* (Paris: Seuil, 1999); see also Lynn Hunt's study of literature and the law, *Inventing Human Rights: A History* (New York: Norton, 2007).

19. On the concept of "possible worlds," which is not, to my knowledge, employed in political theory, see notably Umberto Eco, *Lector in Fabula*, trans. Myriem Bouzaher (1979; Paris: Grasset, 1985); Raymond Bradley and Norman Swartz, *Possible Worlds: An Introduction to Logic and Its Philosophy* (Oxford: Blackwell, 1979); Thomas Pavel, *Fictional Worlds* (Cambridge: Harvard University Press, 1986); and Ruth Ronen, *Possible Worlds in Literary Theory* (Cambridge: Cambridge University Press, 1994).

inform the institutions and laws of the new French state, once the Revolution had made it possible to imagine the state anew.[20]

The State of Nature and the Golden Age: From Montaigne to Fénelon

Where ancient Rome and the Peloponnesian city-states generally provided both the fodder and backdrop for eighteenth-century debates on political theory, a different classical referent lay at the heart of the more experimental and imaginative Enlightenment reworkings of classical republicanism: the myth of the golden age.[21] A fixture of various cultural discourses in the early-modern period, this myth had also become associated with the condition in which the New World "savages" lived.[22] Montaigne's essay "On Cannibals" was only the most famous text to invoke this Greek myth in reference to their "state of nature."[23] Although this specific expression became current only with Hobbes, American societies were certainly perceived in Montaigne's time as living in a condition ruled by nature alone: The *cannibales* "are still in that happy state of desiring only as much as their natural needs demand."[24] But unlike the Hobbesian version of the state of nature (discussed in the introduction), the inhabitants of this "*âge doré*" obeyed the laws of nature: "Natural laws, not yet bowdlerized by our own, command

---

20. For an analogous study of how literary representations shaped Third Republic legislation, see Annie Stora-Lamarre, *La république des faibles: les origines intellectuelles du droit républicain, 1870–1914* (Paris: Armand Colin, 2005).

21. On the classical sources for the golden age, with which eighteenth-century readers would have been familiar, see the introduction and, more generally, Harry Levin, *The Myth of the Golden Age in the Renaissance* (Bloomington: Indiana University Press, 1969).

22. For other examples, see Levin, *Myth of the Golden Age*, 58–83; see notably Shakespeare's *Tempest* (London: Arden, 1999), 2.1.

23. Montaigne wrote that "what we actually see in these nations surpassees not only all the pictures in which poets have idealized the golden age [*l'âge doré*] and all their inventions in imagining a happy state of man," *The Complete Essays*, trans. Donald M. Frame (Stanford: Stanford University Press, 1958), 153; *Essais* (Paris: Gallimard, 1965), bk. 1, chap. 21; 1:304–5. This essay has been extensively discussed; see notably Edwin Duval, "Lessons of the New World: Design and Meaning in Montaigne's 'Des Cannibales' (I:31) and 'Des coches' (III:6)," *Yale French Studies* 64 (1983): 95–112; Dudley M. Marchi, "Montaigne and the New World: The Cannibalism of Cultural Production," *Modern Language Studies* 23, no. 4 (1993): 35–54; Philippe Desan, *Montaigne, les Cannibales et les Conquistadores* (Paris: Nizet, 1994); Tom Conley, "The *Essays* and the New World," and, in the same volume, André Tournon, "Justice and the Law: On the Reverse Side of the Essays," in *The Cambridge Companion to Montaigne*, ed. Ullrich Langer (Cambridge: Cambridge University Press, 2005).

24. *Complete Essays*, 156.

them."[25] Montaigne was so impressed by their "primitive rules given by Nature" (in Virgil's words, which he quotes) that he compared the entirety of his *Essais* to their natural condition, in a prefatory text: "Had I been placed among those nations which are said to live still in the sweet freedom of nature's first laws, I assure you I should very gladly have portrayed myself here entire and wholly naked."[26]

As in Ovid's celebrated description of the golden age, the state of nature that Montaigne perceived in Brazil is defined primarily by negation: It knows neither writing nor arithmetic, riches nor poverty, contracts nor inheritances, agriculture nor metallurgy, wine nor wheat. Certain important differences with the classical referent do stand out: The inhabitants of the golden age were vegetarians, whereas the *cannibales*, of course, were not. They digested their enemies after vanquishing them in *war*, another unknown activity during the Age of Gold. Other differences are more subtle. Where Ovid had underscored the absence of laws and judges in the golden age,[27] Montaigne added a more pointed political commentary: The *cannibales* had "no name for a magistrate or for political superiority."[28] This insistence on the fact that sovereignty—a key political issue after the publication of Jean Bodin's *Les Six livres de la République* in 1572, eight years before the first edition of the *Essais*—was missing from the state of nature is reinforced at the end of the essay, when Montaigne relates two observations allegedly made by the *cannibales* who had been brought to France in 1562. Both concern the status of the sovereign: First, the visitors cannot understand why adult French men pay such homage to a mere boy (Charles IX, who was twelve at the time), and, second, they explain that the only power of command that exists in their society pertains to military expeditions and ceases entirely once the hostilities are over. While Montaigne does not comment on their remarks, they do not exactly paint a flattering portrait of French royal power.[29]

The themes and arguments developed in "Des Cannibales" would be elaborated much more explicitly in the eighteenth century, yet already in

---

25. *Essais*, 304. I have given a literal translation of this passage, as Frame's loses the reference to natural laws.

26. *Complete Essays*, 2.

27. Ovid: "No punishment they knew, no fear; they read / No penalties engraved on plates of bronze; / No suppliant throng with dread beheld their judge; / No judges had they then, but lived secure," *Metamorphoses*, trans. A. D. Melville (Oxford: Oxford University Press, 1998), 4.

28. *Complete Essays*, 153.

29. This point is underscored by David Lewis Schaefer in "Of Cannibals and Kings: Montaigne's Egalitarianism," *Review of Politics* 43, no. 1 (1981): 43–74.

Montaigne we may detect the antipolitical bent that would come to inform natural republicanism. Since individuals in this golden age–like state of nature respect natural laws, they have no need for a *princeps legibus solutus* (or "ruler above the laws," the juristic definition of a sovereign). At worst, sovereignty is reduced to law enforcement, in which case, it can be redefined as (and restricted to) a monopoly on violence, as it would be by the Physiocrats. At best, individuals can police themselves and others by appeals to "right reason" and virtue, as we will see with Fénelon's Boetica. Political power, in this case, would ideally vanish altogether. While the opposition between sovereignty and natural right could be used to argue against monarchic rule, as it would be by Montaigne's friend Etienne de la Boétie, in his *Discours de la servitude volontaire*, the more republican concepts of equality and liberty emerged here not so much in opposition to monarchical rule as in its absence.[30] Since there is no need to pass laws or judgments, the citizens of a natural republic are not called on to participate in the expression of popular will ("positive liberty"). They would become "republicanized" only in a positive sense in response to the demythologizing of the state of nature by seventeenth-century theorists.

The State of Nature in Seventeenth-Century Natural Right Theory

By the time of Rousseau, it would once again become commonplace to describe the state of nature as "another universe, a real golden age"[31] and to perceive Montaigne's "cannibals" as models of natural virtue. For many seventeenth-century authors, however, the New World did not appear in such a happy light. Indeed, given the complicated relations between natural right theory and European colonialism (discussed in the prologue), it was in the interest of the imperial powers to quite literally demonize indigenous peoples and to deny that they obeyed the laws of nature. This negative depiction of the New World "savages" did not necessarily lead theorists to recast the state of nature per se as violent and unvirtuous: Grotius, for instance, calls the American "*Aborigenes* . . . a wild and savage People, without Laws, without Government, loose and dissolute," but still claims that "the first Men were created in a State of Simplicity. . . . They were rather ignorant

---

30. See Murray Rothbard, "The Political Thought of Etienne de la Boétie," introduction to la Boétie, *The Politics of Obedience: The Discourse of Voluntary Servitude*, trans. Harry Kurz (New York: Free Editions, 1975).

31. *Dialogues: Rousseau juge de Jean-Jacques*, in Jean-Jacques Rousseau, *Œuvres complètes*, ed. Bernard Gagnebin and Marcel Raymond (Paris: Gallimard/Pléiade, 1959–95) (hereafter cited as *JJR*), 1:828. Rousseau is referring here to his "illumination" on the road to Vincennes. I shall return to Rousseau at the end of this chapter.

of the Nature of Vice, than versed in the Knowledge of what was virtuous."[32] While less rhapsodic than Montaigne's "Des Cannibales," this description nonetheless perpetuates the golden age topos of a naturally good, primitive human society, which may have been lawless but was not disorderly. But others found it only logical to identify these "first Men" with the "Aborigenes" discovered in the New World. Hobbes, most famously, invokes "the savage people in many places of America," who "have no government at all, and live at this day in that brutish manner," as evidence that the state of nature was in fact a state of war and not a golden age at all.[33]

Although it would be with *Leviathan* (1651) that the term and concept of a "state of nature" fully entered natural right theory, Hobbes's own definition tended to be greeted with skepticism. It was challenged notably by Pufendorf, who recognized the limitations of the state of nature, but nonetheless argued that in that state, "all Men are inclined to perform . . . all those Duties which the *Law of Nature directs*."[34] Only civil society could guarantee that men would actually perform their duties, but the insecurity characterizing Pufendorf's state of nature was still a far cry from the violence of Hobbes's state of war. Writing within a Christian theological framework, Pufendorf also considered the "Primitive State of Nature, before the Fall"[35] to be a state of moral perfection, as opposed to the "Deprav'd

---

32. Hugo Grotius, *The Rights of War and Peace*, ed. Richard Tuck (1625; Indianapolis: Liberty Fund, 2005), 1.4.2; 1:340–1 and 2.2.1; 2:422. Grotius also quotes Tacitus as saying that "the first Men . . . being free from vicious Inclinations, lived in Innocence, without committing any Crime or dishonest Action; and therefore there was no Need to keep them to their Duty through the Fear of Punishment" (2.2.1). See more generally Richard Tuck, *Natural Rights Theories: Their Origins and Development* (Cambridge: Cambridge University Press, 1981), and *The Rights of War and Peace: Political Thought and the International Order from Grotius to Kant* (Oxford: Oxford University Press, 1999).

33. *Leviathan*, 1.13; 187. See notably Noel Malcolm, *Aspects of Hobbes* (Oxford: Oxford University Press, 2002), esp. chaps. 2 and 13. Locke agreed that "in the beginning all the world was America," *Second Treatise*, §49. For a comparison between Hobbes's and Locke's views on the state of nature, see the introduction.

34. The full quote reads: "Altho' every one, under that Independence in which all Men are supposed to be in a *State of Nature,* may and ought to presume, that all Men are inclined to perform towards him all those Duties which the *Law of Nature directs,* until he has evident Proof to the contrary: Nevertheless, since Men have *natural Inclinations* to that which is ill, no one ought to rely so securely on the Integrity of another, as to neglect taking all necessary Precautions to render himself secure, and placed, as far as may be, out of the Reach of other Men's ill Designs," *The Whole Duty of Man According to the Law of Nature [De Officio Hominis et Civis Juxta Legem Naturalem]*, trans. Andrew Tooke, ed. Ian Hunter and David Saunders (1673; Indianapolis: Liberty Fund, 2003), 1.3.17; 84. On Pufendorf, see notably T. J. Hochstrasser, *Natural Law Theories in the Early Enlightenment* (Cambridge: Cambridge University Press, 2000); and Alfred Dufour, "Pufendorf," in *CHECPT*.

35. *Whole Duty of Man*, 24.

State of Man," which followed. This reinscription of a perfect primitive state, where human society was determined purely by the laws of nature, would in turn facilitate the return to a golden age interpretation of the state of nature.

An important step in this direction was taken by Locke, whose *Second Treatise of Government* (1690) emphasized the similarities between the state of nature and the golden age, while acknowledging, as Pufendorf before him, the insufficiency of this natural condition:

> The *Golden Age* (before vain ambition, and *amor sceleratus habendi*, evil Concupiscence, had corrupted Mens minds into a Mistake of true Power and Honour) had more Virtue, and consequently better Governours, as well as less vicious Subjects, and there was then *no stretching Prerogative* on the one side to oppress the People; nor consequently on the other any *Dispute about Privilege*, to lessen or restrain the Power of the Magistrate, and so no contest betwixt Rulers and People about Governours or Government. (§111)

The distinction between "governors" and "subjects" in this passage would imply that Locke is not, in fact, referring here to the state of nature, but to an early stage of government, even if the reference to the golden age myth (reinforced by the Latin quote from the relevant passage in *The Metamorphoses*) suggests otherwise.[36] In fact, the difference may not be so great: Were the "golden age" to designate the state of nature, the "governors" could be construed simply as fathers exercising a natural authority over their families (§105), whereas if it referred to a nascent society, they would be father *figures* who had been chosen to exercise a similar authority (§110). This difference is certainly important from a contractualist perspective, but Locke himself seemed to view the two states as organically related, blurring the distinction with his use of a mythical tag traditionally associated with

---

36. The first interpretation is strengthened by the discussion in the previous paragraph of the "poor but vertuous Age," in which "are almost all those which begin Governments, that ever come to last in the World." See Peter Laslett's footnote, *Two Treatises of Government*, ed. Laslett (Cambridge: Cambridge University Press, 1988), 342; Martin Seliger, "Locke's Natural Law and the Foundation of Politics," *Journal of the History of Ideas* 24, no. 3 (1963): 349–51; John Dunn, *Political Thought of John Locke* (Cambridge: Cambridge University Press, 1969), 96–119; and Robert Markley, "'Land enough in the World': Locke's Golden Age and the Infinite Extension of 'Use,'" *South Atlantic Quarterly* 98, no. 4 (1999): 817–37. On the state of nature in Locke, see also William G. Batz, "The Historical Anthropology of John Locke," *Journal of the History of Ideas* 35, no. 4 (1974): 663–70.

the state of nature.[37] Moreover, in neither case was this golden age to last, as the remainder of the above quote indicates: *amor sceleratus habendi* ("a wicked love of wealth," Ovid) would lead to excesses of power that obliged members of civil society to construct more careful and sophisticated models of government.

Whether referring to a pre- or early-political state, Locke's "golden age" is particularly striking for its quasi elimination of political power. As with Montaigne's *cannibales*, there is "no contest betwixt Rulers and People" because the role of the fathers (and later father figures) is limited to leading the way into war (§107) and to punishing violations of the laws of nature (§105). Apart from these functions, "they exercise very little Dominion, and have but a very moderate Sovereignty" (§108). They have no part, in fact, in perhaps the most important and defining feature of sovereignty, namely, lawgiving: The only laws to which the inhabitants of this golden age abide are those of nature.[38] The "magistrates" ensure that these laws are respected, hence ameliorating the condition of individuals who had been in a complete state of nature, but the latter become aware of the laws of nature only through reason and natural virtue. A century after Montaigne, the golden age had thus once again emerged as a semipolitical ideal state (without a State), that was, if not identical to the state of nature, then at least largely modeled on the "natural" New World societies.[39]

Apart from deep in the forests of the Amazon, however, this golden age without rulers or positive laws could last only for a fleeting moment in the inevitable progression toward civil society. Its instability was due less to external factors (war between rival groups, population increase, property conflicts, and so forth), but to the decline of our natural virtue, as Martin Seliger observed: "Moral deterioration is not the consequence, but the cause, of the

---

37. An earlier paragraph describes how it was possible that "*a Family* by degrees *grew up into a Commonwealth*, and the Fatherly Authority being continued on to the elder Son, every one in his turn growing up under it, tacitly submitted to it," §110.

38. The introduction of positive laws occurred only "in future ages" (that is, well after the golden age was over), as the footnote attached to this expression (and quote from Hooker) make clear; see §111n.

39. Locke's chief model for this golden age was, in fact, the same as Montaigne's: the Brazilian tribes described by Jean de Léry in his *Histoire d'un voyage faict en la terre du Brésil* (1578). Locke owned this book and commented on it in his journal in 1678, right around the time he was most likely writing the *Second Treatise*; see his *Political Essays*, ed. Mark Goldie (Cambridge: Cambridge University Press, 1997), 270–71. Montaigne's description of the *cannibales* was also largely influenced by this same work; see Frank Lestringant, "The Philosopher's Breviary: Jean de Léry in the Enlightenment," *Representations* 33 (1991): 210. Locke also drew on José de Acosta, whom he cites in §102, and a number of other ethnographic works.

institution and intensification of government."[40] Unless this fated corruption of virtue could be halted, Locke's golden age offered no viable model for political reformers.

The corruption of virtue, however, was a well-known problem in another area of political inquiry, republican thought, where theorists since Machiavelli (and well before) had considered a range of possibilities for preventing moral decay. Some of these, such as the mixed form of government, would figure centrally in Locke's own prescription for civil society (although for Locke, a virtuous people was not a sine qua non for sustaining government). These constitutional solutions, however, were incompatible with the absence of political power in the golden age. Other republican solutions aimed at preserving moral rectitude through social rather than political institutions, which could conceivably coexist with the extremely limited form of government found in Locke's golden age. It was to them that another writer interested in the golden age, Fénelon, would turn in his literary depiction of a people governed by natural right alone.

Republicanizing the Golden Age: Fénelon's Boetica

Fénelon's literary masterpiece, *Télémaque*, has long been recognized for its "republican" qualities, precisely in the sense that it encouraged republican values, while not openly advocating a republican form of government.[41] The book was written, after all, to teach the Duke of Burgundy, dauphin of France, how to rule in a virtuous yet kingly manner. The hero of the novel is a young prince who will one day assume the throne of his father, Ulysses; the rulers he meets during his voyages are either exceptionally good, like the Egyptian Sesotris, or exceptionally bad, like the Phoenician Pygmalion. The longest episode in the book concerns the Cretan Idomeneus, a "corrupt" king who is striving, under the guidance of Telemachus's own

---

40. Seliger, "Locke's Natural Law," 350.

41. On Fénelon's politics, see notably Lionel Rothkrug, *Opposition to Louis XIV: The Political and Social Origins of the French Enlightenment* (Princeton: Princeton University Press, 1965); Nannerl O. Keohane, *Philosophy and the State in France: From the Renaissance to the Enlightenment* (Princeton: Princeton University Press, 1980), 332–46; and Patrick Riley, "Fénelon's 'Republican' Monarchism in *Telemachus*," in *Monarchisms in the Age of Enlightenment: Liberty, Patriotism, and the Common Good*, ed. Hans Blom, John Christian Laursen, and Luisa Simonutti (Toronto: University of Toronto Press, 2007), 78–100. On Fénelon's eighteenth-century influence, see Albert Chérel, *Fénelon au 18ᵉ siècle en France (1715–1820): son prestige, son influence* (1917; Geneva: Slatkine Reprints, 1970). On *Télémaque* in particular, see Volker Kapp, *Télémaque de Fénelon: la signification d'une œuvre littéraire à la fin du siècle classique* (Tübingen/Paris: G. Narr & J.-M. Place, 1982); and Marguerite Haillant, *Culture et imagination dans les œuvres de Fénelon 'ad usum Delphini'* (Paris: Belles Lettres, 1983).

teacher, Mentor, to become virtuous. The book thus seems to adhere to the traditional calling of *prudentia*: It exhibits "fine things to take as models, base things, rotten through and through, to avoid."[42]

The most exemplary land of the novel is not, however, a monarchy. This is the fabled land of *la Bétique*, or Boetica: "In this country the golden age seems still to exist," proclaims Adoam, the Phoenician captain who visited the land and provides Telemachus with a description.[43] Its resemblance with the golden age, as described most famously by Ovid, is indeed striking, yet it has also led scholars astray.[44] Boetica is almost always categorized by commentators as "utopian," even though Fénelon clearly anticipated and countered this criticism. The episode closes with Telemachus's reflection on how "we regard the morals of such a people as entertaining fables," but he inverts this judgment, claiming that "they, on their part, must regard ours as a monstrous dream" (114). Moreover, unlike More's Utopia or Bacon's New Atlantis, Boetica does not exist in complete isolation: It benefits from natural barriers but has relations with neighboring nations and is often chosen by them as arbitrators of their differences. Fénelon seems to be suggesting, through these international contacts, that the Boetican model could spread to other states. Their probity and virtue not only make their own happiness, but also raise the prospect of "perpetual peace" between peoples: "This is what brings about a profound peace between them and their neighbors."[45]

---

42. Livy, *Early History of Rome*, 1.1; 34. From the medieval princely "mirror" authors to Machiavelli (see, for instance, the preface to his *Discourses*), this definition would remain at the heart of historical prudence; see Victoria Kahn, *Rhetoric, Prudence, and Skepticism in the Renaissance* (Ithaca: Cornell University Press, 1985); Timothy Hampton, *Writing from History: The Rhetoric of Exemplarity in Renaissance Literature* (Ithaca: Cornell University Press, 1990); and Jacob Soll, *Publishing "The Prince": History, Reading, and the Birth of Political Criticism* (Ann Arbor: University of Michigan Press, 2005).

43. *Telemachus, son of Ulysses*, trans. and ed. Patrick Riley (Cambridge: Cambridge University Press, 1994), 109.

44. The inhabitants make no use of gold or precious metals (109; as in Voltaire's later *El Dorado*, "they yield them up to us without the least hesitation," 113); they are vegetarian, following Pythagoras's lessons (109); and their land produces goods in natural abundance (111). They do not recognize private property, do not wage war (110–11)—although we will see one important exception to this rule—and have no knowledge of navigation (114), all features of the Age of Gold. Most importantly, they apparently benefit from a "natural" justice system, without magistrates or laws: They have, Adoam claims, "no need of judges, being judged by their own consciences," concluding, "It would seem that Astraea . . . is still in this lower world" (111). Only at the end of the golden age had Astraea, goddess of justice, exiled herself in the constellation Virgo (the mistranslated "virgin" of Virgil's fourth *Eclogue*).

45. *Telemachus*, 113. On Fénelon's pacifism, see David A. Bell, *The First Total War: Napoleon's Europe and the Birth of Warfare as We Know It* (Boston: Houghton Mifflin, 2007), 54–65.

Some object that because of Boetica's mythical appearance, it does not constitute a state, or that, if it does, it is only a state of nature.[46] Its inhabitants may well be "indebted to simple nature alone for their wisdom" (110) and may base their conduct only on "nature and right reason" (114, *recta ratio* being a Roman law definition of natural right). But they are not completely uncivilized. As opposed to Ovid's golden age, the Boeticans have knowledge of both agriculture and metallurgy; they even have mines and highways (109). More important, their society is organized around a basic political structure: "Every family is governed by its head, who is in reality its king" (110). In this respect, Boeticans seem to have remained at the village stage described by Aristotle, as a society in which "every household is ruled by its senior member, as by a king."[47] Although this formulation might seem to imply a proto-monarchic, patriarchal order (in the spirit of Robert Filmer's *Patriarcha*), these heads of households do not wield anything like absolute power: They always consult with the rest of the family before deciding on a form of punishment, when needed (110–11). Their political organization thus appears to resemble more closely Locke's golden age, when fathers similarly monopolized executive right in the family but did not lay down any positive laws.[48]

Although Boetica exhibits only limited signs of political organization, its people nonetheless share a strong sense of national identity and pride. These patriarchs are patriots; using republican (if also jusnaturalist) language, Fénelon describes the Boeticans as "all free and all equal" (111). More important, they are fully aware of the fragility and exceptionality of their situation, preferring to "submit to the loss of their lives or their country, rather than be made slaves" (113). Their liberties are thus not only negative; this peaceful society is willing to arm itself and defend its freedom, if threatened: "War ought never to be thought of *but for the defense of liberty*" (112, emphasis added). This commitment to the defense of the country is the centerpiece of what was known in republican theory as public liberty: "Let us die rather than change: that is his [the republican's] motto," the revolutionary Mirabeau would write at the end of the century.[49]

---

46. Istvan Hont, "The Early Enlightenment Debate on Commerce and Luxury," in *CHECPT*, 384.

47. *The Politics*, trans. T. A. Sinclair and Trevor J. Saunders (Harmondsworth: Penguin, 1981), 1.2; 1252b15 (58).

48. Hont comments on this parallel in "Early Enlightenment Debate," 385–86.

49. Mirabeau, *Considérations sur l'ordre de Cincinnatus*, 22. It is this kind of liberty—an unconditional freedom from political domination—that Quentin Skinner has described as a "third," specifically republican, yet "negative" concept of liberty; see his "A Third Concept of Liberty," *Proceedings of the British Academy* 117 (2002): 237–68.

In another sign of their republican spirit, the Boeticans shun luxury and corrupting activities: "No other arts *are allowed* but such as serve the true necessities of men" (109, emphasis added). The rationale for this censorship— a traditional republican institution, famously introduced by Lycurgus[50]—is their great fear that they may some day "abandon the path of virtue" (114). They reveal through such acts and statements their awareness that the graced land of Boetica is no enchanted world of godlike men but the product of a delicate balance: "It is to their contempt for vain riches and delusive pleasures that they are indebted for this union, peace, and liberty" (111). This was precisely the sort of "contempt" that characterized republican prudence: For fear that it would become corrupt, virtuous citizens must constantly keep watch over their state. Natural virtue alone is wholly insufficient to maintain their peaceful way of life; republican institutions are needed to see to its preservation. The Boeticans are thus not as foreign to Telemachus as most commentators suggest. Just as the young prince must learn to forgo "vain riches" and erotic passions in order to recognize the natural *recta ratio* within him, so too the Boeticans can obey "simple nature" only by dominating the other, dark side of nature, their passions.

Rather than a pure state of nature, the "wise nation" (113) of Boetica appears perched between total freedom, on the one hand, and civil society, on the other, as was Locke's golden age. Where this virtuous society had only a fleeting existence in Locke, however, Fénelon prolongs its life with a series of republican institutions. But do republican institutions a republic make? While resembling in some respects past republics, Boetica nonetheless contradicts many other precepts of classical republicanism. If the Boeticans must constantly fend off the danger of corruption, there is no sense that their republic will eventually lapse. On the contrary, it appears everlasting, constantly perpetuating itself according to natural cycles.[51] Even more unusually, it does not require a good constitution or even good laws to ensure that its inhabitants remain virtuous. So long as they steer clear of "delusive pleasures," virtue will continue to come to them naturally.

---

50. Plutarch recounts how Lycurgus "declared an outlawry of all needless and superfluous arts," *Plutarch's Lives*, trans. John Dryden, ed. Arthur Hugh Clough (New York: Modern Library, 2001), 1:60. On Fénelon's fusion of the Spartan and golden age myths, see Patrick Riley, "Rousseau, Fénelon, and the Quarrel between the Ancients and the Moderns," in *The Cambridge Companion to Rousseau*, ed. Riley (Cambridge: Cambridge University Press, 2001), 82.

51. The time-bound dimension of classical republicanism is emphasized in the title (and thesis) of J. G. A. Pocock's *Machiavellian Moment: Florentine Political Thought and the Atlantic Republican Tradition*, 2nd ed. (Princeton: Princeton University Press, 2003).

Monarchical Republicanism:
The Fénelonian Model in Enlightenment France

The people of Boetica are republican only by default: They live in equality, without a king, but do not have anything resembling a participatory democracy. This absence of popular or representative assemblies in Boetica is not surprising: Because the people obey and respect natural law, they have no need for legislators. It is telling, in this regard, that the Boeticans are not viscerally antimonarchic. They could have accepted kingship, albeit in certain forms.[52] Their golden age reappears under monarchic guises elsewhere in the novel: Idomeneus learns to govern his new city of Salente in such a way that a similar golden age returns (171–72), and Telemachus himself is destined to "revive the golden age" (232) on the island of Ithaca. It is sometimes argued that these other exemplary states in *Télémaque* are incompatible, if not opposed, to the blessed order of Boetica.[53] But what has become of sovereignty in these ideal monarchies? A wise king simply ensures that the laws of the state correspond as closely as possible to the laws of nature and that his people remain virtuous. In both Salente and Boetica, political power is reduced to its bare minimum: enforcing the laws (of nature).

The myth of the golden age thus enabled Fénelon to propose a model of society in which virtue came naturally to all, but was preserved through institutions. This society could be construed equally well as a republic or a monarchy since sovereignty (for legislative matters, at least) was replaced by natural right. This model anticipates the Physiocratic "natural order" where the king's role as "legal despot" is similarly limited to the declaration of natural laws and their enforcement. More generally, it highlights how republicanism could serve throughout the eighteenth century as a depoliticized language of criticism and contestation, focusing not on existing political institutions (such as the monarchy, the courts, or state bureaucracy), but on moral, familial, and cultural values.[54] David Bell has shown how old-regime

---

52. "It is all a wise man can be supposed to do, to claim to govern a docile people over whom the gods have sent him; or a people who *ask him* to be their father and ruler" (111, emphasis added).

53. Judith Shklar, *Men and Citizens: A Study of Rousseau's Social Theory* (Cambridge: Cambridge University Press, 1969), 5; Hont, "Early Enlightenment Debate," 385.

54. See Keith Baker, "Transformations of Classical Republicanism," *Journal of Modern History* 73 (2001): 34. Charles Rollin's *Histoire ancienne* provides a classic example of how the paternal model of royalty was invoked to indirectly counter theories of absolute monarchy; see *Histoire ancienne des Égyptiens, des Carthaginois, des Assyriens, des Babyloniens, des Mèdes et des Perses, des Macédoniens, des Grecs*, vols. 1–12 of *Œuvres complètes de Rollin* (Paris: Firmin Didot, 1821–1825), esp. 1:1–2, 1:50, and 2:359.

lawyers commonly appealed to republican concepts of virtue that did not challenge established political norms; Jay Smith and John Shovlin have similarly examined how proposals for reforming the nobility and commerce, respectively, were couched in nonpolitical, republican terms.[55] So long as the king fulfilled the natural duties of a father (that is, acted as a Boetican head of household), there was no need, so many thought, for any real "political" change.[56]

This belief in natural models of governance, however, came at a price. A king who disobeyed the laws of nature (as Adrastus in *Telemachus* or Louis XIV in real life) became an exceptionally diabolical character: "To desire to be a ruler of men, purely for one's own sake, to get authority, grandeur, and pleasure, is to desire to be a tyrant, a miscreant, and the scourge of mankind [*fléau du genre humain*]."[57] This parallel insistence on the great dangers presented by such "scourges of mankind" uncovers the double-edged sword of natural republicanism. Just as obedience to the laws of nature becomes a higher moral duty, so too does their disobedience become a much graver violation.

Troglodytes and Romans: Montesquieu's Two Republicanisms

One reader who fell under the spell of *Télémaque* and the land of Boetica was Montesquieu, who proposed in his *Lettres persanes* (1721) another version of this golden age in the story of the Troglodytes. This account has attracted a great deal of commentary, yet it is often read independently from the rest of the novel or with an eye toward Montesquieu's more mature theory of republicanism, expressed in *The Spirit of the Laws* (1748). Resituated in its original context, the Troglodyte society, in fact, may be seen as the first fully developed model of a "natural republic," albeit one that Montesquieu would later reject.[58]

---

55. David Bell, *Lawyers and Citizens: The Making of a Political Elite in Old Regime France* (New York: Oxford University Press, 1994); Jay M. Smith, *Nobility Reimagined: The Patriotic Nation in Eighteenth-Century France* (Ithaca: Cornell University Press, 2005); and John Shovlin, *Political Economy of Virtue: Luxury, Patriotism, and the Origins of the French Revolution* (Ithaca: Cornell University Press, 2006). See more generally Marisa Linton, *The Politics of Virtue in Enlightenment France* (New York: Palgrave, 2001).

56. See in this respect Lynn Hunt, *The Family Romance of the French Revolution* (Berkeley: University of California Press, 1992), 17–21. On the importance of seemingly apolitical affairs in eighteenth-century politics, see also Sarah Maza, *Private Lives and Public Affairs: The Causes Célèbres of Prerevolutionary France* (Berkeley: University of California Press, 1993).

57. *Telemachus*, 286. *Fléau du genre humain* appears to be a conflation of *fléau de Dieu* (Attila's famous epithet) and *ennemi du genre humain*.

58. See Alessandro S. Crisafulli, "Montesquieu's Story of the Troglodytes: Its Background, Meaning and Significance," *PMLA* 58, no. 2 (1943): 379–92, who also discusses Montesquieu's

The Good Troglodytes of the Persian Letters

After a brief prologue concerning the plight of their nasty ancestors, Usbek tells the story of two naturally virtuous Troglodytes who "were humane; they understood what justice was; they loved virtue."[59] No climactic or cultural reasons are given for these qualities, which seem merely to stem from a source within. Just as the first Troglodytes were innately vicious, this generation is innately good.[60] They even find the exercise of virtue to be a pleasurable affair: "Virtue is not such as to cost us anything, and should not be considered as a wearisome exercise," the good Troglodytes tell their children (57). This definition contains the answer to the question that had originally prompted Usbek to tell the Troglodytes' story: His friend Mizra has asked him whether "pleasure and satisfaction of the senses" were contrary to "the practice of virtue" (53). Usbek's answer, clearly, was no: Virtue can be both natural and pleasurable.[61]

---

indebtedness to Fénelon in these letters (as elsewhere: the satirical allegory concerning John Law, in letter 142, is situated in "Bétique"); Sergio Cotta, *Montesquieu e la scienza della società* (1953; New York: Arno Press, 1979), 139–54; Goodman, *Criticism in Action*, 7–15; Donald Desserud, "Virtue, Commerce and Moderation in the 'Tale of the Troglodytes': Montesquieu's *Persian Letters*," *History of Political Thought* 12 (1991): 605–26; Elizabeth Heckendorn Cook, *Epistolary Bodies: Gender and Genre in the Eighteenth-Century Republic of Letters* (Stanford: Stanford University Press, 1996), 52–55; and C. P. Courtney, "Montesquieu and Natural Law," in *Montesquieu's Science of Politics: Essays on the Spirit of Laws*, ed. David W. Carrithers, Michael A. Mosher, and Paul A. Rahe (Lanham: Rowman and Littlefield, 2001), 41–68. Both Eric Nelson, in *The Greek Tradition in Republican Thought* (Cambridge: Cambridge University Press, 2004), 155–58, and Michael Sonenscher, in *Before the Deluge: Public Debt, Inequality, and the Intellectual Origins of the French Revolution* (Princeton: Princeton University Press, 2007), 95–108, interpret this tale in light of the unpublished sequel that Montesquieu composed at a later date. As I argue below, however, this reading is not compatible with the other observations on republicanism found in the novel.

59. *Persian Letters*, trans. C. J. Betts (Middlesex, England: Penguin Books, 1973), 56; for the French, see *Lettres persanes*, ed. Laurent Versini (Paris: Flammarion, 1995), 56.

60. As for Rousseau's noble savages (in the second *Discourse*), their goodness seems to derive from a natural sense of compassion (56). Throughout the *Persian Letters*, Montesquieu depicts moral virtue as resting on an innate principle. In letter 83, for instance, Usbek proclaims, "What peace of mind it is for us to know that all these men have in their hearts an inner principle [of justice] which is on our side, and protects us from an action that they might undertake against us!" (162–63). For an interesting discussion of natural law in the Troglodyte society, see Goodman, *Criticism in Action*, 70–72, 80.

61. Montesquieu would further develop this idea that we are naturally predisposed toward moral conduct in *Traité des devoirs* (1725); see Robert Shackleton, "Montesquieu and Machiavelli: A Reappraisal," *Comparative Literature Studies* 1 (1964): 4–5; and Crisafulli, "Montesquieu's Story of the Troglodytes." On the rapprochement between pleasure and virtue during the Enlightenment, see Jean Ehrard, *L'idée de la nature en France dans la première moitié du XVIIIe siècle* (Paris: S.E.V.P.E.N., 1963), chap. 6; and Robert Mauzi, *L'idée du bonheur au XVIIIe siècle* (Paris: Armand Colin, 1960).

Usbek's tale evolves into little pastoral vignette, foreshadowing Montesquieu's later *Temple de Gnide*. Once again, the referent underpinning this description is the Age of Gold. As in that time, the Troglodytes practice a sort of agrarian communism; they also institute religious festivals to celebrate the pleasures of their Arcadian life. The role of these ceremonies "in the honour of the gods" is to reinforce virtuous practices: "Religion appeared to soften any roughness of manner left over from nature" (57).

Though mirroring the mythical model of perfect society, the good Troglodytes are not so naturally good as to dispense with social institutions altogether. This reliance on institutions reveals the other political discourse informing this story—republicanism. Indeed, Montesquieu exhibits a fascination with republics throughout the novel. He describes them as the most natural, if not the original, form of human government—a distinction that may explain why the story of the good, "republican" Troglodytes is prefaced by a brief history of their tyrannical predecessors.[62] Michael Sonenscher has argued that Montesquieu considered republican virtue to be antithetical to commerce and wealth, yet other letters in the novel clearly demonstrate that republicanism and commerce are compatible.[63] The Roman Republic did not succumb to Caesar's tyranny because it was unable to accommodate riches, Usbek claims, but primarily because provincial governors were granted too much power and could unjustly acquire excessive treasure (letter 131). In a discussion of the Swiss and Dutch republics (letter 122), Usbek also states unambiguously that "nothing encourages immigration more than freedom, together with prosperity [*l'opulence*], *which always accompanies it*" (219, emphasis added). Even in the unpublished sequel to the Troglodyte letters, luxury is portrayed, in fact, not so much as a threat to republicanism but to monarchy itself.[64]

---

62. "The first governments of which we have any knowledge were monarchies: it was only chance, and through the passage of hundreds of years, that republics come into being" (233, letter 131). In letter 136, Rica speaks of "the sweetness of freedom, which is in such close concord with reason, humanity and nature" (241), in opposition to monarchy, defined in letter 102, by Usbek, as "a state of tension [*état violent*], which always degenerates into despotism or republicanism" (187); see also the very flattering discussion of republics in letters 80, 89, and 131.

63. Sonenscher, *Before the Deluge*, 97–102.

64. "Troglodytes, said the king, you shall acquire riches, but I tell you that if you are not virtuous you will be one of the most unhappy peoples on earth," *Lettres persanes*, vol. 1 of *Œuvres complètes de Montesquieu*, ed. Jean Ehrard (Oxford: Voltaire Foundation, 1998–),1:602–3; it is not known when this extra letter was composed. Montesquieu would later express a very different opinion: "The laws [in a monarchy] replace all these virtues, for which there is no need," *The Spirit of the Laws*, trans. Anne M. Cohler, Basia C. Miller, and Harold Stone (Cambridge: Cambridge University Press, 1989), 25; for the French, see *De l'Esprit des lois*, ed. Robert Derathé (Paris: Garnier, 1973), 3.5; 30.

The Troglodyte society may accordingly be perceived as a model republic, which need not necessarily give way to a commercial monarchy. In addition to religious practices (without which, as Machiavelli repeatedly warned, no republican state can long exist), the Troglodytes place enormous weight on civic education as the foundation of virtue:[65]

> Their only concern was to bring up their children to be virtuous. They constantly described to them the distress of their fellow-countrymen, letting their wretchedness serve as an example to them. Above all they made them realize that the individual's self-interest is always to be found in the common interest. (57)

What the first good Troglodytes experienced naturally is expressed and transmitted in the terms of republican theory ("the common interest") and through the exemplary use of historical precedent. They also practice a form of censorship, as the Boeticans before them: "One day, when a number of Troglodytes were together, one of the older ones mentioned a young man whom he suspected of having committed a crime, and reproached him for it" (57). If they do not assemble for democratic deliberation, they do not live in anarchy. They enjoy a social order most similar to Fénelon's patriarchal code.[66]

Their republican spirit is most apparent, however, in light of their opposition to monarchy. This opposition first appears retrospectively: The first generations of Troglodytes, who had been closer to beasts than men, were ruled by a "king of foreign origin" (53). Whether the bad Troglodytes were naturally "corrupt" (57) or whether their corruption came from the rule of this foreign king is not clear. In either case, however, ridding themselves of the king does not improve their situation: They kill the successor that they had chosen for him and then degenerate into anarchy—although, tellingly, Montesquieu still refers to their land as a "small *kingdom*" (58, emphasis added).

A more affirmative celebration of republicanism is to be found in the last two letters, which are brimming with a republican imagination. First the good Troglodytes are attacked by their jealous neighbors and defend

---

65. See also Shackleton, *Montesquieu*, 38.

66. Elsewhere in the *Persian Letters*, Montesquieu singles out the *paterfamilias*, who was granted "great authority" over his family, as the only worthy legislation in all of Roman law (letter 129). In the second *Discourse*, Rousseau would similarly describe paternal authority as contrary to despotism (*JJR*, 3:182).

themselves like Livy's Romans.[67] Although this military campaign shores up their sense of community, a political crisis then ensues, and the Troglodytes decide to give themselves a king. As good Aristotelians, they select the eldest, wisest, and most virtuous among them. This venerable Troglodyte, however, shames them with his refusal, in terms that echo the book of Samuel:[68] "You would prefer to be subject to a king, and obey his laws, which would be less rigid than your own customs [*mœurs*]" (60). The election of a king is tied to the imminent corruption of the polity and to the fall from natural virtue: "Would you want him to perform a virtuous action," the wise Troglodyte laments, referring to one of his kin, "because I tell him to, when he would have done just the same without me, by natural inclination alone?" (61). Rather than mark Montesquieu's resignation to the eventual need, in commercial societies, for monarchy, this concluding oration seems rather to signal his belief that natural virtue can be preserved by republican institutions, even in the absence of positive laws. As Usbek summarized in letter 129, "morality always produces better citizens than laws."[69]

The theory of republicanism developed in the context of the Troglodyte story resonates throughout the rest of the novel. It is not authentic virtue that Usbek demands of his wives, the last and most cherished of them, Roxane, tells him in the final letter of the book: She has "profaned the name of virtue by permitting it to be applied to my acceptance of your whims" (281). Her secret life of pleasure in the seraglio was ultimately more virtuous than his unnatural rule of chastity: "I have amended your laws according to the laws of nature," she confesses while expiring (280).[70] This model of "reformation" would become a rallying cry of the Enlightenment: Repeal arbitrary laws, the "*plaisante justice qu'une rivière borne*" (in Pascal's memorable phrase), and all other legislation that violated the

---

67. For a similar celebration of military patriotism, see Rica's celebration of the Invalides in letter 84: "I would like the names of soldiers who die for their country to be preserved in churches [*temples*]" (164).

68. 1 Sam. 8:7–18 (New Oxford Annotated Bible). Rousseau also refers to this biblical injunction in *Du Contrat social* (3.6), as does Thomas Paine in *Common Sense*.

69. *Persian Letters*, 230; I have revised the translation to render it more literal.

70. On the connections between this final episode and the Troglodyte sequence, see Mark Hulliung, *Montesquieu and the Old Regime* (Berkeley: University of California Press, 1976), 137; see also Aram Vartanian, "Eroticism and Politics in the *Lettres persanes*," *Romanic Review* 60 (1969): 23–33; Alain Grosrichard, *La structure du sérail: la fiction du despotisme asiatique dans l'Occident classique* (Paris: Seuil, 1979); Diana Schaub, *Erotic Liberalism: Women and Revolution in Montesquieu's "Persian Letters"* (Lanham: Rowman and Littlefield, 1995); and Ruth Bernard Yeazell, *Harems of the Mind: Passages of Western Art and Literature* (New Haven: Yale University Press, 2000), 66–73.

laws of nature, and equity and justice would be restored, or so clamored many philosophes.[71]

But from an intellectual-historical perspective, this theory of republicanism remains strikingly unusual. The opposition between virtue and the law contradicts a fundamental tenet of classical-republican theory: In Machiavelli's words, "just as for the maintenance of good customs laws are required, so if laws are to be observed, there is need of good customs" (*Discourses*, 1.18). The laws referred to here are not only particular acts of legislation, but also the fundamental laws of a state. Yet such laws are missing from the Troglodyte nation as well. Their morals may be transmitted through instruction but are dictated by nature. Finally, classical-republican authors did not subscribe at all to the idea of natural virtue: When Madison quipped that "if men were angels, there would be no need for government," he summarized the deep republican skepticism regarding the natural goodness of man.[72] The crooked timber of humanity was precisely the reason why republican institutions such as laws and government were needed in the first place. Of course, the ancestors of the good Troglodytes had been far from natural goodness; but then again, they lived under a king and were in a state of corruption. Without any corrupting influences, the good Troglodytes, like the Boeticans, came much closer to becoming angels.

Once angels reemerge in the picture, moreover, the likelihood of finding devils also increases, and Montesquieu's natural republicanism does include a fundamental exclusionary principle. In a letter on justice, Usbek rhapsodizes about the joys of the man who knows his heart is good, tellingly contrasting him to much less admirable beings:

> When a man takes stock of himself, how satisfying it is for him to conclude that he has justice in his heart!—it may be an austere pleasure, but it is bound to cause him delight, as he realized that his state is as far above those without justice as he is above tigers and bears. (letter 83, 163)

Those who are *not* naturally just, in other words, are as dangerous and naturally violent as savage animals. This comparison echoes earlier jusnaturalist attacks on the "Men who are like Beasts," whom the sovereign has a

---

71. See, for instance, Voltaire's retort, "The laws that we pass are fragile, inconstant, / The work of a moment, are everywhere different." *Poème sur la loi naturelle*, II, in *Voltaire électronique*, http://efts.lib.uchicago.edu/efts/VOLTAIRE/restricted/search.form.html.

72. Machiavelli was customarily blunter in his *Discourses*: "All men are wicked and they will always give vent to the malignity that is in their minds when opportunity offers" (1.3).

natural right, even duty, to exterminate (see the prologue). As it turns out, the natural-republican theory of virtue inevitably offers a parallel account of the origin of evil. Some individuals have a "natural wickedness" (53), which no laws or institutions can curb. Such poor devils must simply be destroyed.

Montesquieu's Classical Republicanism

Literature allowed Enlightenment authors to imagine radical political change, but this liberty came at a cost: Readers *expected* playfulness and fantasy from literary works, particularly those written in *le goût moderne*.[73] "Republics of letters" could be more outlandish than historical descriptions or political theories of republicanism since they were not assumed to be (or presented as) real in the first place. Destined for the worldly audience of the French salons, novels such as *Persian Letters* had to be equal parts *dulce et utile*.[74] While some historians have argued that a distinctively republican attitude infused the salons, Antoine Lilti has cast doubt on these assertions, reaffirming instead the "curial" structure of the salon and its inseparability from court culture.[75] The natural republicanism of Montesquieu's Troglodytes appears all the more playful when compared with his more "serious" *Spirit of the Laws*, published nearly thirty years later. Here, the language of natural republicanism has been chastised by the hard lessons of historical prudence.[76]

As its opening chapters make clear, natural laws do not enjoy anything close to the same privileged status in *The Spirit of the Laws* as they had in *Persian Letters*.[77] To be sure, Montesquieu recognizes that a more abstract version of natural *right* always presides over human legislative efforts: "Before laws were made, there were possible relations of justice . . . therefore, one must admit that there are relations of fairness prior to the positive law that establishes them" (1.1.1; 4). As a "spirit of the laws," this structural definition of natural right in terms of "relations of fairness [*rapports d'équité*]" is

---

73. On the tension between modern and classical taste among philosophes, see Elena Russo, *Styles of Enlightenment: Taste, Politics, and Authorship in Eighteenth-Century France* (Baltimore: Johns Hopkins University Press, 2007).

74. Montesquieu sent passages from his novel to the marquise de Lambert as his (literal) letters of introduction; see Shackleton, *Montesquieu*, 57.

75. See in particular Dena Goodman, *The Republic of Letters: A Cultural History of the French Enlightenment* (Ithaca: Cornell University Press, 1994). For Lilti, see *Le Monde des salons: sociabilité et mondanité à Paris au XVIIIᵉ siècle* (Paris: Fayard, 2005).

76. On prudence, see Montesquieu's repeated claims that "*ce que je dis est confirmé par le corps entier de l'histoire*" (3.3; 1:26), or that "*je parle après toutes les histoires*" (3.5; 1:30).

77. See in general Mark H. Waddicor, *Montesquieu and the Philosophy of Natural Law* (The Hague: Nijhoff, 1970); and Melvin Richter, *The Political Theory of Montesquieu* (Cambridge: Cambridge University Press, 1977). My own ideas about the *Spirit of the Laws* have been considerably shaped by conversations with Kent Wright.

what explains that positive laws will necessarily vary from place to place, and that no one form of government can be considered "natural." "The government most in conformity with nature is the one whose particular arrangement best relates to the disposition of the people for whom it is established," he argues instead (1.1.3; 8).

To the specific *laws* of nature, however, Montesquieu no longer attributes much direct moral function, with the possible exception of the law of nonaggression (but this stems from a feeling of weakness that disappears in civil society).[78] In the state of nature, man "constantly violates the laws god has established," making it impossible to imagine the sufficiency of natural virtue; if it took philosophers to provide him with "the laws of morality," even this moral supplement was not enough, as it was only "legislators [who] have returned him to his duties by political and civil laws" (1.1.1; 5).

In the absence of a moral code directly accessible in nature, Montesquieu's theory of republicanism in *The Spirit of the Laws* falls back on the classical reliance on "fundamental laws" and constitutions.[79] Without such laws, no republic could exist: "The laws establishing the right to vote are fundamental in this government" (1.2.2; 10–11), Montesquieu concludes.

---

78. See the four natural laws defined in chapter 1.1.2; Montesquieu even defines the law of nations (*droit des gens*) in such a way that ignores its traditional relation to natural law (1:11–12). There are a few exceptions to this general effacement of natural right; see Montesquieu's claims that positive laws should be reformed on the basis of natural laws, in the case of master-slave relations (3.15.17) and sexual profilagcy (3.16.12); see also the sections on "civil laws that are contrary to the natural law" (5.26.3), on "cases concerning marriage between family members, when the laws of nature or civil laws should hold" (5.26.14), and on how "one should decide according to religious precepts when it is a matter of the natural law" (5.26.7).

79. On the importance of, and differences between, these two notions in *De l'esprit des lois*, see Jean Ehrard, "La notion de 'loi(s) fondamentale(s)' dans l'œuvre et la pensée de Montesquieu," *Montesquieu en 2005*, ed. Catherine Volpilhac-Auger, *SVEC* 5 (2005): 267–86. On Montesquieu's republicanism, see Shackleton, *Montesquieu*, 265–301; Judith Shklar, "Montesquieu and the New Republicanism," *Machiavelli and Republicanism*, ed. Gisele Bock, Quentin Skinner, and Maurizio Viroli (Cambridge: Cambridge University Press, 1990); Hulliung, *Montesquieu and the Old Regime*; and, with certain reservations, David Lowenthal, "Montesquieu and the Classics: Republican Government in the *Spirit of the Laws*," in *Ancients and Moderns: Essays on the Tradition of Political Philosophy in Honor of Leo Strauss*, ed. Joseph Crospey (New York: Basic Books, 1964), 258–87. J. G. A. Pocock touches on Montesquieu's place in the classical-republican tradition in *The Machiavellian Moment*; more recently, a number of essays in the *Cambridge History of Eighteenth-Century Political Thought* also deal with this topic. Michael Sonenscher has noted how Jean-Jacques Rutledge already called attention to Montesquieu's republican genealogy (*Work and Wages*, 336): "Machiavel, Harrington, genies immortels! . . . avoient ouverts d'autres sources plus profondes & plus pures," *Eloge de Montesquieu* (London, 1786), 19; see also 33–34. On Rutledge's later career with the Cordeliers, see Rachel Hammersley, "English Republicanism in Revolutionary France: The Case of the Cordelier Club," *Journal of British Studies* 43 (2004): 474–75.

He repeatedly admires "the constitutions of Rome and Athens" (1.2.2) for their insight that only the people could ratify laws.[80] Elections and referenda replace the nonpolitical order of the naturally virtuous Troglodytes. This was the well-worn language of classical republicanism, which Montesquieu spoke with a distinct Florentine accent. As Machiavelli ("this great man"),[81] he stresses the importance of ancient laws and institutions in a republic: "The senate must, above all, be attached to the old institutions . . . With regard to mores, much is to be gained by keeping the old customs."[82] He similarly warns against the inevitable dissolution of a republic that had been corrupted by money or through territorial growth.[83] To prevent these dangers, the republic must fortify itself with virtue, which Montesquieu again defines in classical-republican terms: "One must note that what I call *virtue* in a republic is love of the homeland, that is, love of equality."[84] This love,

---

80. In his 1734 *Considérations sur les causes de la grandeur des Romains et de leur décadence*, Montesquieu had already adopted a Machiavellian theory of republicanism: "There is nothing so powerful as a republic in which laws are observed, not from fear, not from reason, but from passion," *Considerations on the Causes of the Grandeur and Decadence of the Romans*, trans. Jehu Baker (New York: D. Appleton, 1889), 80; for the French, see *Considérations*, ed. G. Truc (Paris: Garnier, 1954), 17. On Montesquieu's debts to Machiavelli in this text, see Ettore Levi-Malvano, *Montesquieu e Machiavelli* (Paris: Honoré Champion, 1912), 59–96, and Shackleton, "Montesquieu and Machiavelli," 5–6.

81. *Spirit of the Laws*, 6.5; 77; a footnote in this chapter refers to the *Discourses*. According-ing to Shackleton, Montesquieu exhibited familiarity with Machiavelli as early as 1716; see "Montesquieu and Machiavelli," 3; see also Levi-Malvano, *Montesquieu e Machiavelli*. Shklar overstates Montesquieu's differences with Machiavelli, on the unfounded basis that "the young were taught as part of the classical curriculum" that Louis XIV "is the republic now" (266). As we saw earlier, the *collèges* in fact imparted a very different message, and republicanism was less used by courtiers to praise the king than by critics (such as Fénelon) to reprimand him.

82. *Spirit of the Laws*, 1.5.7; 49. Montesquieu had already made similar comments in his *Persian Letters*, notably in letter 129: "It is sometimes necessary to change certain laws. But this situation is uncommon, and when it occurs they should be amended only in fear and trembling. There should be so much solemnity about it, and so many precautions should be taken, that the people should naturally conclude that laws are deeply sacred, since so many formalities are required in order to repeal them" (229).

83. On venal corruption, see 1.2.2 and 1.8.2. On the dangers brought about by conquest, see 1.8.16. Machiavelli discussed how territorial enlargement had brought about the downfall of Sparta and Venice in *Discourses*, 1.6 and 2.1–5; he cautions against financial corruption through-out this work. On the need to maintain old institutions, see, e.g., 1.25 (as well as *The Prince*).

84. *Spirit of the Laws*, xli. This passage from the *Avertissement de l'auteur* was first published in the posthumous edition of 1757. Montesquieu further defines this term by calling it "political virtue," and, in a chapter on republican education, describes virtue as "love of the laws and homeland" (1.4.5; 36). For a reading of "virtue" in Montesquieu that stresses the resemblance between the Troglodytes and the Romans, see Elena Russo, "The Youth of Moral Life: The Virtue of the Ancients," in *Montesquieu and the Spirit of Modernity*, ed. David W. Carrithers and Patrick Coleman, *SVEC 9* (Oxford: Voltaire Foundation, 2002): 101–23; and, also by Russo, *Styles of Enlightenment*.

both of the fatherland and its laws, does not naturally arise in the republican citizen but must be inculcated through educational institutions, as it had been in Sparta (1.4.6).

A number of "modern" traits are found in Montesquieu's mature republicanism: The Machiavellian anxiety regarding the ultimate demise of the republic, for instance, is missing, as is the traditional celebration of republicanism as a form of mixed government.[85] But do any traces remain of the natural republicanism evident in his earlier work? On a few occasions, Montesquieu does part company with his Florentine predecessor and recovers the voice of the wise Troglodyte in Usbek's tale. In a discussion of republican Rome, for instance, Montesquieu claims that "often the legislator need only to show them [the people] the good to have them follow it" (1.6.11; 84), contradicting the classical-republican premise that Rome's "laws kept it so rich in virtue that there has never been any other city or any other republic so well adorned" (Machiavelli, *Discourses*, 1.1; 104). This difference may be small, but is not insignificant. The implication that virtue *could* be distinct from laws opened a wedge that the Jacobins would later turn into a gaping hole, with Saint-Just arguing, for instance, that "there are too many laws, too few institutions."[86] On the whole, however, these differences were drowned out by the loud classical-republican refrains that *De l'esprit des lois* intoned, chapter after chapter—a political mantra that seemed unlikely to undergo significant change from within.

Classical Republicanism and Natural Right: Mably and Rousseau

Ironically, natural right theory was probably the one political language that classical republicanism could accommodate without disturbing its inner coherence.[87] In the antiauthoritarian, Lockean formulation through which it became primarily known in France, natural right meshed almost seamlessly with republicanism, as it brought to the fundamental laws of the city

---

85. I owe this last point to Kent Wright; see his "The Montesquieuian Moment: Republicanism in *De l'Esprit des lois*" (paper presented at the Western Society for French History, Albuquerque, NM, November 7–10, 2007). On Montesquieu's modern traits, see Sklar, "Montesquieu and the New Republicanism."

86. *SJ*, 976.

87. Keith Baker already called attention to how "the classical-republican tradition became entwined in [eighteenth-century] France with a radicalization of natural rights theory," "Transformations of Classical Republicanism," 40. See also Johnson Kent Wright, *A Classical Republican in Eighteenth-Century France: The Political Thought of Mably* (Stanford: Stanford University Press, 1997), 70–90.

a suprahuman authority.[88] This combination of natural right theory and republicanism can be clearly observed in the case of Mably.[89] His most classical-republican work, *Des droits et des devoirs du citoyen*, insists on the need for "good laws" to counter human passions and to delay the inevitable demise of the state—all standard republican themes—but also celebrates the natural order that all political systems must obey.[90] As milord Stanhope tells the narrator, "One can never depart from the order prescribed by Nature with impunity; it is right that we should be punished when we seek to be wiser than she, or do not consult her."[91]

Despite a superficial resemblance, this inscription of natural right as the basis of a political system is far removed from the cult of natural law found in the imaginary societies of Fénelon and Montesquieu. Mably never suggests that the citizens of a good republic can be governed by natural laws alone; on the contrary, he insists on the need for good *positive* laws, dictated by human lawgivers.[92] Following Locke and his liberal commentators, Mably merely argues that "political laws must never contradict the law of Nature" (110–11). His political model thus resembles what Michael Zuckert has termed the "natural rights republic": To the classical-republican theory of a time-bound, humanly constituted state, a natural right foundation for its laws is joined.[93] This foundation did not replace positive law but guided it. As Guillaume-Joseph Saige later wrote, in his otherwise classical-republican (and arch-Rousseauist) *Catéchisme du citoyen*, "the law of nature . . . is the

---

88. On the French reception of Locke, see Ross Hutchinson, *Locke in France, 1688–1734* (Oxford: SVEC/Voltaire Foundation, 1991).

89. On Mably, see notably Keith Baker, *Inventing the French Revolution: Essays on French Political Culture in the Eighteenth Century* (Cambridge: Cambridge University Press, 1990), 86–106; Kent Wright, *Classical Republican in Eighteenth-Century France*; Michael Sonenscher, "Republicanism, State Finances, and the Emergence of Commercial Society in Eighteenth-Century France—or from Royal to Ancient Republicanism and Back," in *Republicanism: A Shared European Heritage*, ed. Martin van Gelderen and Quentin Skinner (Cambridge: Cambridge University Press, 2002), 2:278–82, and, by the same author, "Property, Community, and Citizenship," in *CHECPT*.

90. For the "good laws," see *Des droits et des devoirs du citoyen*, 350; see also "Everything becomes disfigured, everything changes, everything is corrupted; Nature has condemned us to this" (352), which echoes Machiavelli's *panta rei* philosophy in the *Discourses*: "All human affairs are ever in a state of flux and cannot stand still" (1.6; 123).

91. *Des droits et des devoirs du citoyen*, 24.

92. This difference also explains why Mably was highly critical of the Physiocrats ; see his *Doutes proposés aux philosophes économistes sur l'ordre naturel et essentiel des sociétés politiques* (The Hague and Paris: Nyon, 1768), an attack on Le Mercier de la Rivière's treatise (see chapter 2).

93. See Michael P. Zukert, *Natural Rights and the New Republicanism* (Princeton: Princeton University Press, 1994), and *The Natural Rights Republic: Studies in the Foundation of the American Political Tradition* (Notre Dame: University of Notre Dame Press, 1996). On Locke and Mably, see Wright, *Classical Republican*, 78–79.

essential foundation of all compacts."[94] If these two political languages could be so easily enmeshed, it was because they told a similar tale about conventions. Just as in natural right theory, civil society (and positive law) emerged after a people contracted to form a political union, so too in classical republicanism it took a constitution to create the republic and its citizens.[95] The point of intersection between these two narratives of natural rights republicanism is thus precisely the one political institution—the social contract—that is missing from natural republicanism.

Given their complementarity, the introduction of natural right theory into the discourse of classical republicanism left the latter relatively unchanged; yet this entwinement did not come without a certain amount of tension. Contemporary political theorists often point to the potential conflict between, in John Rawls's terms, the republican emphasis on the good and the liberal emphasis on the right.[96] But in the context of eighteenth-century utilitarianism, this distinction does not seem to have presented much of a problem for Enlightenment theorists. The issue that did preoccupy them lay rather in the ambiguous ties between natural right and the state of nature, on the one hand, and positive law and civil society, on the other. Within the Lockean framework that Mably and most other French political authors adopted, these ties formed a Gordian knot. In some instances, for Locke, natural laws continue to operate in civil society, alongside positive laws, thereby setting up a possible conflict between them. He also suggested that politically constituted states may still find themselves, in some respects, in

94. *Catéchisme du citoyen* (Geneva, 1787), 7. On Saige, see Baker, *Inventing the French Revolution*, 128–52. In his republican treatise, Helvétius similarly stressed that in order to "provide clear ideas of fairness," we need to be "well versed in natural right, the law of nations, and the principal laws of every empire," *De l'homme*, 10.8 (2:432).

95. This parallel becomes explicit when one considers the following narrative in Machiavelli's *Discourses*: "Many people having retired to those sandbanks on which the city [Venice] now stands . . . when their numbers grew to such an extent that it became necessary for them to make laws if they were to live together, they devised a form of government. They had frequently met together to discuss the city's affairs, so, when it seemed to them that the population was sufficient to form a body politic, they decided that all newcomers who meant to reside there, should not take part in the government. . . . Such a form of government could arise and be maintained without tumult because, when it came into being, whoever then dwelt in Venice was admitted to the government" (1.6; 119). Had Machiavelli been writing a century later, he could very well have formulated this passage in the jusnaturalist terms of Grotius's *De Jure Belli ac Pacis*.

96. John Rawls, *A Theory of Justice*, rev. ed. (Cambridge: Belknap Press of Harvard University Press, 1999); for a "republican" restatement of this tension, see Michael Sandel, *Democracy's Discontent: America in Search of a Public Philosophy* (Cambridge: Belknap Press of Harvard University Press, 1996). As Quentin Skinner has observed, these two political objectives may just as often be complementary as contradictory: see "Republican Idea of Political Liberty."

a state of nature.[97] These claims, which overtly contradict the arguments of earlier natural right theorists, rest on Locke's much more favorable impression of the state of nature, an impression passed on to his eighteenth-century emulators: For Mably's Stanhope, as Kent Wright notes, "the error of the great natural law writers . . . was to conceive of the state of nature as a condition to be ended or canceled rather than secured and perfected."[98] The problem with this upwardly revision of the state of nature, however, is that it diminished the importance of contractualism for the formation and preservation of civil society. Once positive law is defined merely as the "perfection" of natural law, it loses its absolute necessity in the narrative of civil constitution. Its fallibility is also highlighted, transforming natural right into the gold standard against which to measure every "political [i.e., positive] law."

The way that Mably found to get around this problem was to reemphasize the insecurities of a pure state of nature and to reject its identification with the golden age. Some writers, he acknowledged, may have depicted our primitive forefathers as "wise men who lived a tranquil and innocent life, while the earth looked after their needs and brought forth fruits without cultivation." But this "golden age . . . should never have been more than a poetic dream" since we today know "what one should think of . . . that sweet carelessness that enchanted a society ignorant of passions." In reality, Mably concludes in a Hobbesian key, "violence determined everything among them, and the strongest oppressed the weakest; all of these peoples lived off raids; none of them cultivated the earth."[99]

This denial of the historical reality of a golden age was quite common in the eighteenth century, yet it, too, as the following chapter shows, was subject to change. New historical inquiries into the origins of Indian culture, the ethnographic discovery of peaceful "aborigines," and the pastoral style that infused the late eighteenth-century arts, all combined to redress the fallen image of an original Age of Gold. The continuous insistence by political reformers, chief amongst whom the Physiocrats, on the need for positive legislation to stick as closely as possible to natural laws, encouraged the identification of this golden age with a (quasi) state of nature, which knew and respected natural right alone. In this transformed context,

97. See, for instance, *Second Treatise*, §14. On these ambiguities, see Patrick Riley, "The Social Contract and Its Critics," in *CHECPT*.

98. *Classical Republican in Eighteenth-Century France*, 73.

99. *Observations sur la Grèce* (Geneva: Compagnie des Libraires, 1749), 2–3. See also his *Entretiens de Phocion* (first published in 1763), in *Œuvres complètes* (Paris: Bossange, Masson et Besson, 1797), 10:39.

the concept of a "natural rights republic" would be increasingly challenged by that of a natural republic *tout court*: If the dangers of the golden age could be checked by institutions rather than laws, then it no longer became necessary to find good *lois politiques*. Saint-Just would take this argument one step further, claiming that "the State [*la cité*] can admit *no other* laws than those of nature."[100] The distinction between the state of nature and a political state became blurred and, more important, inoperative: Neither a social contract nor constitution was required for individuals to live harmoniously in society. The flip side of this indistinction was that violations of the laws of nature now became the ultimate crime: "Not to conform to [natural law] is to cease being human [*cesser d'être homme*]," Mably coolly affirmed.[101]

But how could natural laws be known for certain? As Rousseau protested, the seventeenth-century theorists themselves were not always in agreement about what they were.[102] And even if they could be determined beyond doubt, none could ever be sufficiently specific to dictate the correct course of action in ambiguous situations. A society without abundant positive legislation would need its members to possess a special moral sensibility—"a rapid instinct," in Robespierre's words, that would lead citizens "to do good and avoid evil" without "the delayed assistance of reason."[103] Rousseau sought to recreate this moral instinct in political communities through a concept often regarded as central to Jacobin thought, the general will. Did the general will still relate to natural right? As I argue in the following section, while apparently insisting on the supremacy of civil legislation, Rousseau maintained a "principle" (his term) of natural right at the very heart of the general will. A close reading of his work reveals how his own politico-legal theory could easily be reassimilated into a natural right framework (from which, in fact, it was derived in the first place). Rousseau himself showed how this was possible, developing in parallel to his voluntaristic theory of political government, a depoliticized vision of society that closely resembles a natural republic, very similar, again, to the Age of Gold.

Rousseau: The General Will or the Order of Nature?

The tension that natural right introduced into classical-republican discourse can be said to characterize the entire œuvre of Rousseau.[104] Readers

---

100. *SJ*, 950, emphasis added.

101. *Des droits et des devoirs du citoyen*, 28–29.

102. See the preface to the second *Discourse*, in *JJR*, 3:125.

103. 18 floréal speech; *Rob.*, 10:453; see chapter 5.

104. Amidst the voluminous bibliography on Rousseau's political thought, I found the following works particularly helpful: Robert Derathé, *Jean-Jacques Rousseau et la science politique*

familiar with his two *Discourses*, his *Emile*, his *Julie*, and most of his other late works are predominantly struck by the consistent and relentless emphasis on the moral and philosophical value of nature: "View the spectacle of nature; hear the inner voice," the vicaire Savoyard tells Jean-Jacques, foreshadowing Kant's more famous injunction in the *Critique of Practical Reason*.[105] The myth of the golden age always seems to linger in the background of these representations of nature. In his third letter to M. de Malesherbes, Rousseau described how "I made myself a golden age at my whim. . . . I became tender to the point of tears over the true pleasures of humanity, pleasures so delightful, so pure, and which now are so far from men," an image that he also employed in his *Essay on the Origin of Languages*: "These barbarous times were the golden age; not because men lived together, but because they were separate."[106]

Readers of Rousseau's most complete and coherent political statement, however, *Du contrat social*, find that nature there has been all but banished: "The social order is a sacred right that serves as a basis for all others. However this right does not come from nature," Rousseau asserts straight off the bat, later adding, "Everything that is not in nature has its problems, and civil society more than all the rest."[107] There is virtually no discussion of natural laws (or principles) in the *Social Contract*; it no longer provides a basis or an authority for civil law, which is entirely dictated by the sovereign.

---

de son temps (1950; Paris: Vrin, 1992); Roger Masters, *The Political Philosophy of Rousseau* (Princeton: Princeton University Press, 1968); Shklar, *Men and Citizens*; Robert Wolker, ed., *Rousseau and Liberty* (Manchester: Manchester University Press, 1995); Jean-Fabien Spitz, *La liberté politique* (Paris: PUF, 1995), 311–466; Rosenblatt, *Rousseau and Geneva*; Luc Vicenti, *Jean-Jacques Rousseau: l'individu et la république* (Paris: Kimé, 2001); Patrick Riley, ed., *The Cambridge Companion to Rousseau* (Cambridge: Cambridge University Press, 2001); and Christopher Kelly, *Rousseau as Author: Consecrating One's Life to the Truth* (Chicago: University of Chicago, 2003).

105. *Emile: Or, on Education*, trans. Alan Bloom (New York: Basic Books, 1979), 295; *JJR*, 4:607. Kant would later refer to "the starry sky above me and the moral law within me." While the second *Discourse* takes natural right authors to task for failing to reach a consensus, Rousseau's two natural "principles," *amour de soi* and *compassion*, are remarkably similar to natural laws (in no small part because there was, in fact, a consensus among most authors on the subject that self-preservation constituted the first natural law).

106. See, respectively, the letter of January 26, 1762, in *CWR*, 5:578 (the French original is reprinted in *Les rêveries du promeneur solitaire*, 231), and the *Essay*, in *CWR*, 7:306; *JJR*, 5:396. The myth is not named in the second *Discourse*, although he did leave a number of commonplace signifiers for it; see, for instance, the quote from Saint-Jerome, mentioning "the reign of Saturn" (*JJR*, 3:199), or the telltale expression, "thine and mine [*le tien et le mien*]" (*JJR*, 3:207). On the golden age myth in Rousseau, see Marc Eigeldinger, *Jean-Jacques Rousseau: univers mythique et cohérence* (Neuchâtel: Baconnière, 1978); and Shklar, "Sparta and the Age of Gold," in *Men and Citizens*.

107. *Social Contract*, 1.1 and 3.15, in *CWR*, 4:131 and 3:193, or *JJR*, 3:352 and 3:431.

This apparent paradox, well known to Rousseau scholars, did not go unnoticed by his contemporaries either. Saint-Just complained that "Rousseau incessantly gazes toward nature, [yet] he seeks an independant society, but this cannot be reconciled with the vigorous government he envisages."[108] If Rousseau looked elsewhere to establish his vigorous government, it was because he had absorbed Montesquieu's lesson: It is nearly impossible to explain the variability of laws in different states when considering, in a Lockean manner, the laws of nature as an *active* body of law in civil society. With the general will, Rousseau was able to profess a legal philosophy that could account for precisely these differences.

It is somewhat surprising that Rousseau chose this concept to describe the legal principle of civil society since neither its earlier theological or political uses had been synonymous with legal variability—*au contraire*.[109] Borrowing the expression from Malebranche, for whom it designated the unchanging and universal way that God acted in the world, Diderot defined the general will, in the *Encyclopédie* article on "Droit naturel," as the unchanging and universal law that all humans must obey.[110] The general will did not change from place to place or society to society; it was simply another way of defining the laws of nature. Accordingly, anyone who violated the general will by obeying his particular will was denounced as "an enemy of the human race."

Diderot's article seems to have been Rousseau's direct source for this concept, which appears for the first time in his own *Encyclopédie* article on "Économie," later published as the *Discours sur l'économie politique* and probably written in 1754–55. Already in this early work, Rousseau amends his friend's definition, introducing a crucial distinction between the general will and natural right. Only in such instances where the whole of humanity is under consideration can the general will be identified with the law of nature.

---

108. *SJ*, 929. See also Masters, *Political Philosophy*, 275. The paradoxical appearance of Rousseau's thought is nowhere clearer than in book 1 of *Emile*: In the space of a few pages, Rousseau argues that "he who in the civil order wants to preserve the primacy of the sentiments of nature does not know what he wants" (*Emile*, 40; *JJR*, 4:249), but that the goal of his pedagogical treatise "is the very same as that of nature" (*Emile*, 38; *JJR*, 4:247). On the importance of reading Rousseau's literary works alongside his political treatises, see notably Thomas Kavanagh, "Rousseau's *The Levite of Ephrahim*," in *The Cambridge Companion to Rousseau*, 397–417; and, by the same author, *Writing the Truth: Authority and Desire in Rousseau* (Berkeley: University of California Press, 1987).

109. See Patrick Riley, *The General Will Before Rousseau: The Transformation of the Divine into the Civic* (Princeton: Princeton University Press, 1986); and, by the same author, "Rousseau's General Will," in *Cambridge Companion to Rousseau*, 124–53.

110. *Encyclopédie*, s.v. "Droit naturel," 5:116.

Otherwise, when the members of a given state are determining a course of action, their will may be "general" with respect to them, but not to the citizens of other states. In this regard, it can no longer be considered a law of nature, even if, as Rousseau says rather ambiguously, the will of a state "has its rule of justice in the law of nature."[111]

In the "Économie" article, it does not yet take a political assembly to determine the will of a state.[112] Rousseau would change his mind, however, when writing the *Social Contract*, where only a popular vote can determine when the particular and the general will are the same (2.7). Despite this insistence on the need for a democratic assembly, *deliberation* plays no role for Rousseau in the expression of the general will. Debate would only serve factional interests.[113] Voting itself, furthermore, is insufficient to determine the general will. Where Locke saw majority decision as the natural basis of civil government, Rousseau emphasized how even a unanimous vote ("the will of all") might not always express the true general will (2.3). Although a majority vote was required for an opinion to be considered "general," the *source* of this will cannot be found in popular assemblies.

From where, then, does the general will spring? The only other logical possibility is from within each individual citizen. Rousseau suggested as much: "Each individual can, as a man, have a private will contrary to or differing from *the general will he has as a Citizen*."[114] As a citizen, in other

---

111. *Encyclopédie*, s.v. "Économie ou Œconomie," 5:338; in *CWR*, 3:143. See in particular Masters, *Political Philosophy of Rousseau*, 257–65; Robert Wokler, "The Influence of Diderot on the Political Theory of Rousseau: Two Aspects of a Relationship," *Studies on Voltaire and the Eighteenth Century* 132 (Oxford: Voltaire Foundation, 1975): 55–113; Riley, *General Will Before Rousseau*; and Jean-Claude Bourdin, "L'effacement de Diderot par Rousseau dans l'article *économie politique* et le *Manuscrit de Genève*," in *Diderot et Rousseau: un entretien à distance*, ed. Franck Salaün (Paris: Desjonquères, 2006). Rousseau also addressed Diderot's article on natural right in his first draft of the *Social Contract* (the "Geneva manuscript"), book 1, chapter 2, but suppressed this passage in his final version.

112. Rousseau provides the following argument: "This means is impractical for a large people; and . . . it is rarely necessary when the government is well intentioned. For the leaders know very well that the general will is always for the side most favorable to the public interest—that is, for the most equitable; so that it is only necessary to be just and one is assured of following the general will," *CWR*, 3:148; *Encyclopédie*, 5:340.

113. *Social Contract*, 2.3. Plutarch writes that Lycurgus had similarly ruled out popular deliberation: "The people then being thus assembled in the open air, it was not allowed to any one of their order to give his advice, but only either to ratify or reject what should be propounded to them." *Plutarch's Lives*, 1:58. On the Spartan model in Rousseau's thought, see Shklar, *Men and Citizens*.

114. *Social Contract*, 1.7; in *CWR*, 4:140–1; *JJR*, 3:363, emphasis added. As Lester Crocker observed, "The general will is an abstract entity, *pre-existing* the collective vote," *Rousseau's Social Contract* (Cleveland: Case Western Reserve University Press, 1968), 70, author's emphasis; see also Kelly, *Rousseau as Author*, 125–30. While I am essentially in agreement with Crocker, I would argue that it is worth distinguishing between an interior moral and civic sense

words, each individual has the capacity to perceive what is in the common interest of the community. But why is this so? What makes the citizen capable of seeing beyond his own particular interest?

Rousseau never explicitly addresses this question in the *Social Contract*. At times, he seems to imply that the general will depends on reason (as in the case of the Lawgiver or of the citizen "who until that time only considered himself, finds himself forced to act upon other principles and to consult his reason before heeding his inclinations"),[115] yet elsewhere argues that reason alone is incapable of determining human, as opposed to universal, justice (2.6; *JJR*, 3:378). Rousseau's devastating critique, in the second *Discourse*, of the insensitive philosopher whose "reason" prevents him from identifying with a victim (*JJR*, 3:156) makes it particularly doubtful that he would claim the general will could be rationally deduced, as does his rejection of Diderot's universalist definition. Patrick Riley has suggested that it is the product of "civic education,"[116] but then how can the people desire the general will (if not "see" it) even *before* they have been given the laws that education teaches them to respect? And where does the Lawgiver himself find it?

Rousseau may not have provided a clear answer to these questions in the *Social Contract*, but he did offer a number of intriguing clues, some of which he would elaborate in later texts. In a key passage, for instance, Rousseau argues that a good citizen "cannot work for someone else without working for oneself," and that citizens will always want "the happiness of each," because "there is no one who does not appropriate this word *each* to himself, and does not think of himself as he votes for all."[117] The well-ordered republic, in other words, ensures that altruism (working for others, wishing them well) is also in the citizen's personal interest, even if the converse is not true. This formulation is very reminiscent of the discussion in the second *Discourse* of the two natural principles, self-preservation (*amour de soi*) and pity, that, rather than laws, guide man in the state of nature. The first of these principles "interests us ardently in our well-being and our self-preservation," whereas the other "inspires in us a natural repugnance to see any sensitive Being perish or suffer, principally those like ourselves."[118] It is the "combination" of these two principles, however, that creates our moral sensibility:

---

of "the common good" and "the general will" per se, which is the name given to this interior sentiment once it has been approved by vote.

115. *Social Contract*, 1.8; in *CWR*, 4:141; *JJR*, 3:364.

116. *General Will before Rousseau*, 207 and 212.

117. *Social Contract*, 2.4; in *CWR*, 4:148–49; *JJR*, 3:373.

118. Preface to the second *Discourse*, in *CWR*, 3:15; *JJR*, 3:126; subsequent quotations in this paragraph are also from this page. Rousseau repeats this argument later in the *Discourse*, in *JJR*, 3:154.

From this combination "all the rules of natural right appear [*découlent*]."
The role of society is "to reestablish [these laws] upon other foundations,"
namely, the foundation of reason. But this restoration on a higher plane can
take place only once reason itself "has succeeded in stifling Nature," that is,
once society has succumbed to the negative social contract described at the
end of the second *Discourse*.[119] It is this sort of chiasmatic logic that Jean
Starobinski aptly described, using one of Rousseau's own metaphors, as *le
remède dans le mal*.[120]

The connection between these natural principles and their degenera-
tion—the first into *amour propre*, the second into oblivion—and their re-
demption through a rational social order is thus already announced at the
very onset of the second *Discourse*.[121] As many commentators have noted,
the story of the *Social Contract* picks up where this *Discourse* ended, yet
the "genius" of the Legislator consists precisely in realigning, "upon other
foundations," the natural principles that had determined our conduct in
the state of nature. Since both of these principles must be incorporated, it
seems insufficient to claim that the general will is merely an *amour de soi*
of the people for themselves.[122] Without a preexisting capacity for pity, it
would be impossible for individuals in civil society to will anything other
than their own private good or to act in a virtuous manner.[123] In this respect,

---

119. This relation between natural right principles and the general will had been explicit in
earlier texts, including the first draft of the *Social Contract* (the "Geneva manuscript"), which
equates the laws dictated by the general will with a "reasonable natural right [*droit naturel raisonné*], different from literal natural right [*droit naturel proprement dit*]" (2.4; *JJR*, 3:329).

120. See the chapter on Rousseau in Jean Starobinski, *Le remède dans le mal: critique et
légitimation de l'artifice à l'âge des Lumières* (Paris: Gallimard, 1989). This concept appears in
Rousseau's work as early as his first *Discourse* (*JJR*, 3:26); see also the first version of the *Social
Contract* (*JJR*, 3:288). A passage at the beginning of *Emile* explains its rationale: "In the present state of things a man abandoned to himself in the midst of other men from birth would be
the most disfigured of all" (37; *JJR*, 4:245).

121. While my overall interpretation of Rousseau is greatly indebted to conversations with
Keith Baker, I owe this observation entirely to him; this section also benefited tremendously
from discussions with Jean-Pierre Dupuy and Joshua Cohen. Rousseau's theory of the general
will is also foreshadowed at the end of the second *Discourse*; see *JJR*, 3:184–85.

122. Cf. Lucien Scubla, "Est-il possible de mettre la loi au dessus de l'homme? Sur la
philosophie politique de Jean-Jacques Rousseau," *Introduction aux sciences sociales: logique des
phénomènes collectifs*, by Jean-Pierre Dupuy (Paris: Ellipses, 1992), 105–44; and Luc Vicenti,
Jean-Jacques Rousseau, 141–58.

123. Since all individuals ought to have a clear sense of moral virtue (which is not the case
with the general will), it may be more accurate to equate the latter with the classical-republican
notion of "civic virtue," as Keith Baker suggests in "Transformations of Classical Republicanism,"
41. The word "*vertu[s]*" is used only six times in the *Social Contract* (excluding the expression
"*en vertu de*," which appears once), including two times in one sentence referring back to Mon-

it would seem that pity is the more important of the two natural principles, as it is primarily pity that "in the state of Nature . . . takes the place of Laws, morals, and virtue" and dictates to natural man the fundamental maxim, "*Do what is good for you with the least possible harm to others.*"[124] The affinity and structural resemblances between pity and the general will are suggested more clearly in later texts, notably a passage of *Emile*: "To prevent pity from degenerating into weakness, it must, therefore, be *generalized* and extended to the whole of mankind."[125] And in one of his later *Rêveries du promeneur solitaire*, Rousseau was even more direct: "My expansive soul seeks . . . to extend its feelings . . . to other beings."[126] Pity cannot directly dictate to individuals what constitutes the common good of society, but it does provide the basic moral instinct that civic education can transform into sound political judgment.

The paradoxical banishment of nature from the *Social Contract* may therefore be more apparent than real.[127] Although this text proposes one of strongest contractualist arguments in eighteenth-century political theory, it ultimately reinscribes natural right at its very core. The general will may not apply to the whole of humanity, but it does depend on natural principles that already existed in the state of nature. Moreover, it must ultimately correspond to the laws of nature, however vague they may be. This second requirement is made clear in the sixth of his *Lettres écrites de la montagne*, which seeks to defend the *Social Contract* from the accusations made by Genevan magistrates: "It is no more permitted to infringe natural Laws by the Social Contract."[128] Positive laws, or the "acts" of the general will, must be

tesquieu. By contrast, the term appears thirty-five and thirty-one times, respectively, in the first and second *Discourses* (results obtained by means of ARTFL's online editions). What virtue was in the first two *Discourses* thus seems to be subsumed in civil society into the general will.

124. Second *Discourse*, in *CWR*, 3:37–38; *JJR*, 3:156. Here again, Rousseau points to the relation between the natural moral sensibility and "rational justice [*justice raisonnée*]," which transforms this maxim into the biblical imperative to "do unto others as you would have done to yourself."

125. *Emile*, 253, emphasis added.

126. *Rêveries du promeneur solitaire*, 113.

127. As Robert Derathé observed half a century ago, *contra* C. E. Vaughan and Alfred Cobban: "All of Rousseau's efforts are directed toward discovering a political system that conforms with the ideal of natural right," *Jean-Jacques Rousseau*, 171.

128. *CWR*, 6:231; *JJR*, 3:807; this letter is discussed by Masters, *Political Philosophy*, 318. A rather obtuse passage of the *Social Contract* had suggested as much: "considering things from a human point of view," as opposed to theologically, Rousseau argues that all laws are vain "*for want of a natural sanction*. . . . Therefore, there must be conventions and laws to combine rights with duties and to bring justice back to its object" (2.6; *CWR*, 4:152; *JJR*, 3:378, emphasis added). The "rights" in this passage refer to the "natural right" that Rousseau, following

in line with natural law in order to be deemed just. But since the general will itself has a "natural" righteousness (2.4), this sanction is always implicit, and by extension, invisible, further hinting at the secret bond between natural right and the general will.

Societies without Laws: The Golden Age of Conscience

There was another kind of society, however, that Rousseau imagined in the *Social Contract* and elsewhere, one in which the general will hardly needed to be consulted, democratic assemblies were superfluous, and natural right played a much more direct role in determining moral action.[129] In smaller communities, such as the "Montagnons" described in Rousseau's letter to d'Alembert; certain Swiss cantons and villages, such as that of Clarens in *Julie*; or in a more classical vein, Sparta, where "Lycurgus established morals which [almost] allowed him to dispense with adding Laws," each individual's sense of patriotism and moral rectitude was so strong that it could take the place of the general will.[130] Such societies needed hardly any laws (4.1); its citizens were governed principally by their *mœurs*, that "most important" of legal categories, "which is not engraved on marble or bronze, but in the hearts of the citizens."[131] This insistence on morals was of course a keystone of classical-republican theory, and Rousseau followed Machiavelli in stressing the need for a "civil religion" to preserve moral probity (4.8). But Rousseau departed from the classical-republican dictum that it took "good laws" to make good citizens since Rousseau's tightly knit societies ultimately required very few, if any, laws at all. In a short story set in biblical times, for instance, Rousseau depicted an age when

---

Locke, still considers active in civil society: "It is a matter, then, of making a clear distinction between the respective rights of the Citizens and the Sovereign, and between the duties that the former have to fulfill as subjects and the natural right which they ought to enjoy in their quality as men" (2.4; *CWR*, 4:148; *JJR*, 3:373).

129. See, for instance, the description of "a State . . . so small, . . . a people so simple and upright, that the execution of laws follows immediately from the public will, as is the case in a good Democracy" (3.5; *CWR*, 4:175; *JJR*, 3:407). I am again particularly grateful to Keith Baker for drawing my attention to this point.

130. For the description of the Montagnons, who lived in the vicinity of Neufchâtel (a Prussian territory at the time), see the *Lettre à d'Alembert*, in *JJR*, 5:55–59. For the ideal Swiss cantons, see notably the *Social Contract*, in *JJR*, 3:437. For the quotation about Sparta, see the second *Discourse*, in *CWR*, 3:62; *JJR*, 3:187–88.

131. *Social Contract*, 2.12, in *CWR*, 4:164; *JJR*, 3:394. It is through the process of becoming a citizen, here, that morals are engraved in one's heart, yet in other passages Rousseau claims that the natural law is *already* engraved there; see, for instance, the fragment known as *État de guerre*, in *JJR*, 3:602, and the passages quoted below.

no one reigned over the people of the Lord. . . . [E]ach, without recognizing either magistrate or judge, was alone his own master and did
all that seemed to him good. Israel, then scattered in the fields, had
few great cities, and the simplicity of its morals rendered superfluous
the empire of laws.[132]

If a people could live virtuously without laws, it followed that they would
not be in much need of government either: "A Country where no one eluded
the Laws and abused the Magistracy would need neither Magistracy nor
Laws," Rousseau acknowledged elsewhere.[133] Such peoples were not necessarily in a state of nature: The Montagnons may have lived in a bucolic
setting, but they were intimately familiar with both the mechanical and fine
arts. The absence of laws or government in these societies, however, did
ultimately make them (in what would soon come to be called a "dialectical"
manner) revived versions of humanity's lost golden age, "upon other foundations."[134] Rousseau could accordingly proclaim that "the golden age will
return for us [*L'âge d'or renaîtra pour nous*]," all the while defending himself
against the charge that he wished us to walk about on all fours.[135]

132. *Le lévite d'Ephraïm*, in *CWR*, 7:353; *JJR*, 2:1208.
133. Second *Discourse*, in *CWR*, 3:62; *JJR*, 3:187–88. See also one of Rousseau's *Fragments
politiques* on laws (§7): "The will to do what is good can take the place of everything, and one
who knows how to listen to the law of his conscience hardly needs any others" (*CWR*, 4:29;
JJR, 3:315); and the *Considérations sur le gouvernement de Pologne*: "as abuses were seen, a law
was made to remedy it. From that law were born other abuses that had to be corrected again.
This manner of operating has no end at all, and leads to the most terrible of all abuses, which
is to enervate all the laws by virtue of multiplying them" (*CWR*, 11:186; *JJR*, 3:975). This
suspicion of written laws calls to mind Lycurgus's refusal to "reduce his laws into writing," as
he believed that "being imprinted on the hearts of [Spartan] youth by a good discipline, would
be sure to remain, and would find a stronger security." *Plutarch's Lives*, 1:63. Plutarch's Solon is
similarly mocked by Anacharis for "imagining the dishonesty and covetousness of his country-
men could be restrained by written laws," 1:109.
134. For an example of how this logic foreshadows later, more self-consciously dialectical arguments, see, for instance, Pierre-Joseph Proudhon's claim that "if Providence placed the
first human beings in a condition of equality" (a condition that he identifies with "what the
ancient poets called golden age"), "it was an indication that it presented them with a model
that it wished them to realise in other areas [*sur d'autres dimensions*]," *What Is Property?* ed.
and trans. Donald R. Kelley and Bonnie G. Smith (Cambridge: Cambridge University Press,
1994), 45 and 202, for the parenthetical quote; *Qu'est-ce que la propriété?* (1840; Paris: GF,
1966), 97, 293. On Proudhon's debt to Rousseau, see G. D. H. Cole, *Socialist Thought: The
Forerunners (1789–1850)*, vol. 1 of *A History of Socialist Thought* (London: MacMillan, 1953),
216.
135. For the quotation, see *Le siècle pastoral*, in *JJR*, 2:1170. Rousseau put this idyll by
Jean-Baptiste Gresset to music, but amended the final stanzas, which had questioned the existence of the lost *siècle* ("It is but a pleasing fable; / Let us not envy our ancestors. / Man was
always guilty, / Always was he unhappy," in *JJR*, 2:1908). Rousseau made clear that he was not

For these societies in particular, morals had a lot of civic work to do, but it is also here that we can perceive the form in which natural right continuously presents itself to us, even after we have left the forests. This form is *conscience*, famously celebrated by Rousseau's Savoyard vicar, for whom it is a "divine instinct," which, what is more, can never be wrong: "He who follows conscience obeys nature and does not fear being led astray."[136] Even in larger societies, it ultimately falls on this natural moral principle to determine whether an act of law is truly just since the people may have been led astray and the general will abandoned: "Conscience persists in following the order of nature against all the laws of men."[137] It is in his discussion of conscience that the primary role given to natural right in Rousseau's political and moral philosophy becomes clearest. He leaves no doubt that should human and natural law conflict, the latter must always be obeyed: "The voices of nature and reason would never contradict each other if man had not imposed [social] duties upon himself, which he has since deemed necessary to prefer to the natural impulse."[138] But if the voice of nature is the final judge of all human laws and responsibilities, then in ideal circumstances—namely, the small, tightly knit societies discussed above—conscience can determine proper moral conduct on its own. Laws, in this case, become the redundant expressions of what the inner voice of conscience has already dictated.[139] As in Montesquieu's good Troglodytes' society, laws can thus present just as much of a threat as a solution to the preservation of virtue, since only they, and not conscience, can contradict the "order of nature."[140] (Of course, this staying power of conscience, which always judges in accordance with the natural order, can occur only in civil society—*le remède est dans le mal*, and

suggesting we should "go back to live in forests with bears" in note 9 to the second *Discourse*, in *CWR*, 3:79; *JJR*, 3:207.

136. *Emile*, 290, 286–88. Already in the first *Discourse*, Rousseau had described conscience as being "engraved in every heart," *JJR*, 3:30. See also the description of "the law of nature" in his *Considerations* on Poland as "that holy, indefeasible law, that speaks to man's heart and to his reason," *CWR*, 11:185; *JJR*, 3:973.

137. *Emile*, 267. On the difficult and complex relation between conscience and the general will, see Derathé, *Jean-Jacques Rousseau et la science politique*, 343.

138. Fragment §2 on the state of nature, in *JJR*, 3:475.

139. Rousseau hinted at this potential redundancy in the first draft of the *Social Contract* (1.2), albeit in the negative; see *JJR*, 3:285–86.

140. On the danger of conflicting legal dictates, see also Rousseau's discussion of religious laws in the *Social Contract*, 4.8. Diderot would similarly elaborate on this risk in the *Supplément au voyage de Bougainville* (Paris: Gallimard, 2002); see chapter 2.

there is no possible return to the forest.[141]) Robespierre would later single out conscience, that "rapid instinct . . . to do good," as the cornerstone of France's republican institutions.[142]

Rousseau recognized that society was rife with contradictions and sought to resolve them through a dialectical synthesis of natural right and republican good.[143] Many of his readers, however, would reject this complex, contractualist framework, proclaiming instead the natural sociability and virtue of man.[144] Since this framework did not impinge on Rousseau's theory of social justice, and was in fact supported by many of his examples, he could offer these readers the theoretical outlines of a society needing few laws, yet whose members were endowed with a natural moral sensibility. Others, of course, would read him in the opposite manner, as the defender of a society governed entirely by positive laws. These two readings would come to a head at various times during the French Revolution, most notably during the National Convention's discussion of the 1793 Constitution.[145] But both sets of readers would often take away Rousseau's stringent and austere notion of punishment, in which he conflated violations against the social order with those against natural law. As it would later be interpreted during the king's trial, this theory seemed to suggest that *any* legal infraction could be punished by death, if it appears threatening enough.[146] Nature and nation were fast becoming identical. Lord Bolingbroke had already argued that "he who breaks the laws of his country resists the ordinance of God, that is, the law of nature," given that "the law of nature is the law of all [the king's] subjects: the constitutions of particular governments are like the by-laws of

---

141. As Masters noted, "The precepts of natural law formulated by the Socratic thinker, and made possible to most men in the form of the Savoyard Vicar's natural religion, arise only in civil society," *Political Philosophy*, 269.

142. See the discussion of the cult of the Supreme Being in chapter 5.

143. Once again, *Emile* provides a clearer understanding of how these "contradictions" are resolved: "If the laws of nations could, like those of nature, have an inflexibility that no human force could ever conquer, dependence on men would then become dependence on things again; in the republic all of the advantages of the natural state would be united with those of the civil state, and freedom which keeps man exempt from vices would be joined to morality which raises him to virtue" (85; *JJR*, 4:311).

144. See, for instance, Maréchal, discussed in chapter 2, and Saint-Just, discussed in chapter 4.

145. See chapter 4, and more generally James Swenson, *On Jean-Jacques Rousseau Considered as One of the First Authors of the Revolution* (Stanford: Stanford University Press, 2000).

146. See the famous discussion of "the rights of life and death" in the *Social Contract*, 2.5, in *JJR*, 3:376–77; for the discussion of this passage during the trial of Louis XVI, see chapter 3.

cities."[147] Later in the century, the philosophe Marmontel would claim in a similar vein that military desertion should be treated as "a crime against nature."[148] As before, the specter of the *hostis humani generis* haunted Rousseau's natural republic.

If natural sociability and natural right were to provide the only foundations of the state, however, this meant that the original state of nature had to be favorably revalued by philosophers. Although the fortunes of this state had vastly improved, from Hobbes to Pufendorf and Locke to Rousseau, it remained for most political theorists fundamentally flawed and unstable, perfect in principle, perhaps, but impossible to maintain or to restore. So long as this golden age was viewed as having been inevitably corrupted by man's "vain ambition" and "evil concupiscence" (Locke, *Second Treatise,* §111), natural right would almost always need to be complemented by a social compact, a constitution, and civil laws. As the following chapter analyzes, the late eighteenth century experienced a number of cultural, historiographical, and economic changes that radically transformed "enlightened" ideas about the original state of humanity and made it a more suitable model to restore in the future, "upon other foundations."

---

147. Henry St. John Bolingbroke, *The Idea of a Patriot King* (1738), in *Political Writings,* ed. David Armitage (Cambridge: Cambridge University Press, 1997), 227.

148. *Bélisaire,* ed. Robert Granderoute (Paris: Société des textes français modernes, 1994), 168. In a footnote, Marmontel refers to Cicero's *De officio* for authority: *communis utilitatis derelictio contra naturam est,* which he translates as *"l'abandon de l'intérêt général va contre la nature."*

CHAPTER TWO

FINDING NATURE

DURING THE FIRST YEAR of the French Republic, it was common-place to compare the nascent government to "those days that can be called the true golden age [*le véritable âge d'or*]," as Billaud-Varenne suggested, a time "when each nation determined on its own its rights and duties" and when the people "shared more or less equally the advantages of a collective administration."[1] These comparisons insisted on the golden age not only as an ideal social model, but as a real (*véritable*) historical epoch. The myth of the golden age, in other words, had been *naturalized*, escaping from the confines of poetry and royalist rhetoric to enter the authoritative narratives of history and ethnography. Less than fifty years earlier, however, it was largely dismissed as little more than a "poet's dream."[2] How could its historical and political value transform in so little time?

The present chapter charts the rapid evolution of this myth across an array of anthropological, historical, geographical, religious, and even economic discourses. It examines three critical shifts in particular: (1) Orientalist studies, which provided proof to many Europeans that the golden age once existed in hitherto unknown parts of the world; (2) new voyages of discovery, in particular Bougainville's visit to Tahiti, which complemented this impression through descriptions of pristine and perfect societies in the present; (3) Physiocracy, which theorized these mythical representations of an ideal, an original, and, most importantly, a *natural* social order, arguing that a natural order should replace the cumbersome system of civil legislation.[3]

---

1. Jacques-Nicolas Billaud-Varenne, *Les éléments du républicanisme* (Paris: n. p., 1793), 19. For other examples, see the end of the present chapter and chapter 4.

2. Frank Manuel, *The Eighteenth Century Confronts the Gods* (Cambridge: Harvard University Press, 1959), 138. This rejection of the golden age myth can be seen as part of the wholesale rejection of mythology in the early Enlightenment; see in particular Pierre Bayle, *Pensées diverses sur la comète*, ed. A Prat (1683; Paris: Droz, 1939), §§31, 79, and 84–89; and Bernard le Bovier de Fontenelle's *De l'origine des fables*, ed. J.-R. Carré (1724; Paris: Libraire Félix Alcan, 1932).

3. These three lines of inquiry should be situated within the wider scope of research on nature in this period. For a study that examines the place of natural history both before and during the French Revolution, see Mary Ashburn Miller, "Violence and Nature in the French

The spreading belief in a past golden age thus fueled the hope that a new one was coming—*redeunt Saturnia regno*. This hope could now be expressed in republican terms, as it would be with Sylvain Maréchal, even if it was not always: Court de Gébelin, one of the main synthesizers of these late Enlightenment trends, would address himself to Louis XVI. But the golden age myth was sufficiently associated with republicanism for this egalitarian version to be available as well, alongside the more common Augustan-Virgilian version. Hence, if it was under this latter guise that the French Revolution would first be saluted, the myth came to connote, after the downfall of the monarchy, a very different ideal—the natural republic. When in the summer of 1794, Robespierre proclaimed that the French people had recalled Astraea, goddess of justice, back to Earth, he was not only embroidering on his *collège*-day rhetoric, but also expressing the strange dream of republican authors in an age of *sensibilité*.

Republican Orientalism (Voltaire)

The changing fortunes of the golden age myth in eighteenth-century France may best be measured by considering the conversion of Voltaire from his early worldly philosophy to the nostalgic charms of a bygone age. In a famous poem, *Le Mondain* (1736), Voltaire had mocked the pastoral simplicity elegized by Fénelon ("monsieur du Télémaque"), celebrating instead his own "age of iron":

> Regrettera qui veut le bon vieux temps,
> Et l'âge d'or et le règne d'Astrée,
> Et les beaux jours de Saturne et de Rhée,
> Et le jardin de nos premiers parents . . .
> Ce temps profane est tout fait pour mes moeurs . . .
> O le bon temps que ce siècle de fer![4]

At a time when *mondanité* was considered a necessary, if not defining, feature of intellectual, artistic, and political achievement, Voltaire's position

---

Revolutionary Imagination, 1789–94" (PhD diss., Johns Hopkins University, 2008). On the centrality of natural authority during the Enlightenment, see Lorraine Daston and Fernando Vidal, eds., *The Moral Authority of Nature* (Chicago: University of Chicago Press, 2004).

4. "Regret as you will the good old days / The Golden Age and the Astraea's reign / The sweet days of Saturn and Rhea / And the garden of our first parents . . . This profane age is fine by me / What a sweet time is this Age of Iron!" In *Mélanges*, ed. Jacques van den Heuvel (Paris: Pléiade, 1961), 203–6.

was very much the majority one.[5] Most philosophes rejected Rousseau's alleged primitivism and sought to demystify "the deceitful dream of a golden age."[6] According to d'Holbach, "Savage life or the state of nature, to which unhappy dreamers [*spéculateurs*] have sought to return mankind, that golden age so praised by the poets, is in truth only a state of misery, of stupidity, of unreason."[7] The comte de Volney argued that if one looked closely at ancient Greece, "one would see what we should really think about the alleged golden age, when men wandered naked through the forests of Hellas and Thessalonia, living off grasses and nuts: one would realize that the ancient Greeks were real savages, comparable to those in America."[8] Most other philosophes, from Diderot to Destutt de Tracy, concurred: The golden age was merely "the time of suffering and impoverishment; and the state of nature is that of stupidity and complete immaturity."[9]

What made it possible, then, for Voltaire, at the end of his life, to assert most enthusiastically that "there is still a great country nearby [Benares] where what is called the golden age has been preserved"?[10] What was this golden age that stood up to the comparison with Voltaire's own vaunted age of iron? We may perhaps catch a glimpse of what he had in mind in a short story, *La Princesse de Babylone* (1768), set in part on the banks of the Ganges.[11] Here we discover a shepherd's paradise, yet of a very different sort than that found in pastoral idylls:

> Do not imagine that these shepherds resembled yours, who, barely covered by ripped threads, keep watch over sheep that are better dressed

---

5. On *mondanité* and sociability in the Enlightenment, see in particular Antoine Lilti, *Le Monde des salons: sociabilité et mondanité à Paris au XVIIIe siècle* (Paris: Fayard, 2005); and Daniel Gordon, *Citizens without Sovereignty: Equality and Sociability in French Thought, 1670–1789* (Princeton: Princeton University Press, 1994).

6. Alexander Hamilton's expression, in *The Federalist Papers* (London: Penguin, 1987), no. 6.

7. *Système social ou principes naturels de la morale et de la politique avec un examen de l'influence du gouvernement sur les mœurs* (Paris: Fayard, 1994), 252.

8. *Eclaircissements sur divers ouvrages indiqués dans cet ouvrage* (Paris: Fayard, 1989), 125.

9. Antoine-Louis-Claude Destutt de Tracy, *Eléments d'idéologie. I, Idéologie* (Paris: Courcier, 1804), 307. See also Diderot's satire against the golden age and Rousseau in his *Salon de 1767*, ed. J. Seznec and J. Adhemar (Oxford: Clarendon Press, 1963), 121–22.

10. In Jean-Sylvain Bailly, *Lettres sur l'origine des sciences et sur celle des peuples d'Asie. Adressées à M. de Voltaire par M. Bailly & précédées de quelques lettres de M. de Voltaire à l'Auteur* (Paris: Debure, 1777), 6.

11. On this conte, see P. C. Mitchell, "An Underlying Theme in *La Princesse de Babylone*," *Studies on Voltaire and the Eighteenth Century* 137 (1975): 31–45.

than they; who groan under the yoke of poverty, and pay in excessive taxes half the meager wages they receive from their masters.[12]

Not only do these shepherds own their flocks; they possess "everything that can flatter man's desires," as the heroine, Formosante, learns when she visits the land.[13] These earthly pleasures, moreover, are not the invention of corrupt minds: "In everything it was nature pure and simple [*la belle et simple nature*]" (474). Far from being primitive brutes, then, the Gangarid shepherds are natural *mondains* who practice a sublime religion:

We assemble to pay homage to God when the moon is full; the men in a great cedar temple, and women in another for fear of distractions; all the birds gather in a grove, and the animals on a pretty lawn. We thank God for all the good he has done for us. (464)

There is no need for priests here: They have "parrots who preach wonderfully." In fact, instead of a shepherd, Amazan incarnates the Enlightenment ideal of an *homme de lettres*: He spends his time "doing good, cultivating the arts, penetrating the secrets of nature, perfecting his being." The Gangarids are the Indian equivalent of Voltaire's earlier *El Dorado* (which was situated, like Bacon's *New Atlantis*, in South America).

This celebration of a golden age on the Ganges in fact reflects the vast historiographical revision of universal history that reached its climax in the late eighteenth century and that was largely spearheaded by Voltaire himself.[14] Already in his *Essai sur les mœurs et l'esprit des nations*, Voltaire had emphasized the cultural and chronological primacy of the East, and more specifically, of *les Indes*: "Look towards the Orient, cradle of all arts, which gave the Occident everything."[15] This preference allotted to India over Israel

---

12. In *Romans et contes* (Paris: Flammarion, 1966), 463.

13. As in Pythagoras's golden age, the delicacies served are all vegetarian; see Ovid, *Metamorphoses*, trans. A. D. Melville (Oxford: Oxford University Press, 1998), bk. 15.

14. I discuss the arguments in this paragraph (and the related bibliographical material) in greater detail in "Hyperborean Atlantis: Jean-Sylvain Bailly, Madame Blavatsky, and the Nazi Myth," *Studies in Eighteenth-Century Culture* 35 (2006): 267–91; see also J. G. A. Pocock, *Barbarism and Religion, II: Narratives of Civil Government* (Cambridge: Cambridge University Press, 1999), 97–119.

15. *Essai sur les mœurs et l'esprit des nations*, ed. René Pommeau (Paris: Bordas, 1990), 1:197. On this Enlightenment version of Orientalism, which (*pace* Edward Said) often ran counter to European imperialism rather than condoned it, see in particular Raymond Schwab, *The Oriental Renaissance: Europe's Rediscovery of India and the East, 1680–1880*, trans. Gene Patterson-Black and Victor Reinking (New York: Columbia University Press, 1984); as well as, more recently, Madeleine Dobie, *Foreign Bodies: Gender, Language, and Culture in French Ori-*

(or Egypt, the traditional, antiquarian source of wisdom and science) went along with a winner-take-all theory of cultural diffusion. For Voltaire and many of his contemporaries, it was widely assumed that the arts and sciences could have been invented only once, possibly even by a single people. This latter, more radical theory of cultural diffusion was reinforced by a myth of its own, the myth of Atlantis. It was precisely in the context of a discussion about the truth-value of this myth—Jean-Sylvain Bailly's 1775 *Histoire de l'astronomie ancienne, depuis son origine jusqu'à l'établissement de l'école d'Alexandrie*—that Voltaire made his comment about the Eastern land where "the golden age has been preserved." The golden age myth had been made palatable to the worldly sage of Ferney through its "Atlanticization": Rather than portray wooded life in Arcadia, it conveyed the sophistication of Plato's (or Bacon's) Atlantis, conjoined with Socrates' Athens. As it turned out, the age of gold and the *siècle de fer* were not all that different.

Most interestingly, the Gangarids also exhibit a distinctly republican form of government. Its leading citizen, Amazan, "is not a king . . . he loves his compatriots too much: like them, he is a shepherd" (463). These wealthy shepherds are "all born equal"; and, as with Monsieur de Télémaque's Boeticans, they are naturally "*virtuous* and invincible" (463, emphasis added), no other laws or constitution being needed. Although the word *république* is not uttered, Voltaire's emphasis on a republican vocabulary and the absence of a king clearly indicate the form of government chosen by the Gangarids.[16] Or rather, as in Fénelon, this republican form of government is not so much chosen as it constitutes the natural social order of men: "Only the Gangarids had preserved the nature and dignity of man" (504). Instead of being the first incarnation of Oriental despotism, the golden age of the East was a natural republic.

What is the significance of this political dimension? Because of the fantastic nature of the Gangarids (who go into battle riding unicorns), their country is often dismissed as entirely "fabulous."[17] But there is nothing particularly fabulous about their political organization. In his *Poème sur la loi*

entalism (Stanford: Stanford University Press, 2001); and Sankar Muthu, *Enlightenment against Empire* (Princeton: Princeton University Press, 2003).

16. Voltaire disagreed with Montesquieu about the need for virtue in a republic; see, for instance, the discussion of *De l'esprit des lois* in the *Siècle de Louis XIV*, chap. 21; see also his *Pensées sur le gouvernement* and *Questions sur l'Encyclopédie* (s.v. "Honneur"); and, for a more lengthy critique, see his *Commentaire sur "l'Esprit des lois,"* and the wry conclusion, "On se met en république quand on le peut"; in *Voltaire électronique*, http://efts.lib.uchicago.edu/efts/VOLTAIRE/.

17. See, for instance, Roger Pearson, *The Fables of Reason: A Study of Voltaire's "Contes Philosophiques"* (Oxford: Oxford University Press, 1993), 199.

naturelle, Voltaire had defended a proto-Physiocratic theory of natural right, arguing against the addition of positive laws to the perfect corpus of natural ones: "*Aurons-nous bien l'audace, en nos faibles cervelles, / D'ajouter nos décrets à ces lois immortelles*," he proclaims, regretting in a later passage how "*C'est que de la nature on étouffa la voix; / C'est qu'à sa loi sacrée on ajouta des lois.*"[18] He was also a staunch defender of republicanism under the right circumstances: "The most tolerable of all [governments] is doubtlessly the republican," he asserted in his *Idées républicaines par un membre d'un corps*, "*parce que c'est celui qui rapproche le plus les hommes de l'égalité naturelle.*"[19] The narrator of this text, however, is meant to be a Genevan citizen, and as Peter Gay has admirably shown, Voltaire's republicanism seems largely to have depended on local context.[20] If the republic was the best, or most tolerable, form for a small state, Voltaire adhered to the common opinion that it was unsuited to large ones: "Small machines do not work when enlarged."[21] So long as monarchy respected the rule of law—which is what distinguished it, in his eyes, from despotism—it was an acceptable, perhaps even preferable, political system: England may be a "monarchic country," but its inhabitants "are freer than elsewhere because they are more enlightened."[22] His literary descriptions of ideal states often depicted monarchies in which the king was chosen through a series of exams. Zadig, for instance, in the eponymous tale, ascends to power by answering a series of riddles, before restoring an Augustan golden age to Babylon ("The Empire knew a time of peace, a time of glory, a time of plenty: it was the finest age [*le plus beau siècle*] the world had ever known. Justice and love ruled the Empire").[23]

---

18. "Are we so daring, with our weak minds / To add our decrees to these immortal laws . . . We are smothering the voice of nature / We are adding laws to the sacred law," *Poème sur la loi naturelle*, II and III, in *Voltaire électronique*.

19. In *Œuvres complètes de Voltaire* (Paris: Garnier, 1879), 24:424; see Franco Venturi, *Utopia and Reform in the Enlightenment* (Cambridge: Cambridge University Press, 1971), 86–88.

20. Peter Gay, *Voltaire's Politics: The Poet as Realist*, 2nd ed. (New Haven: Yale University Press, 1988), 214–19. See also, on Voltaire's favorable views on monarchy, Derek Beales, "Philosophical Kingship and Enlightened Despotism," and on Enlightenment comparativism and relativism, Melvin Richter, "The Comparative Study of Regimes and Societies," both in *The Cambridge History of Eighteenth-Century Political Thought*, ed. Mark Goldie and Robert Wolker (Cambridge: Cambridge University Press, 2006) (hereafter cited as *CHECPT*).

21. *Pensées sur le gouvernement*, in *Voltaire électronique*. A similar expression appears in the *Idées républicaines*, 418.

22. *Idées républicaines*, 418.

23. In *Candide and Other Stories*, trans. Roger Pearson (Oxford: Oxford University Press, 1990), 171; for the French, *Romans et contes* (Paris: Flammarion, 1966), 85. William Penn is similarly hailed, in the fourth of Voltaire's *Lettres philosophiques* (Paris: Flammarion, 1964), for having "brought to earth the golden age, about which so much is said, and which most likely only ever existed in Pennsylvania" (38).

What, then, are we to make of this golden age on the shores of the Ganges? Rather than interpret this state as a model for eighteenth-century politics, it is more fitting to describe it as an account of the original form of human society. Voltaire, in fact, consistently presented republicanism as the first political organization known to men: "There cannot be a state on earth which was not first governed as a republic: it is the normal course of human nature," he declared in the article "Patrie," in his 1764 *Dictionnaire philosophique*.[24] He pointed to the New World for further evidence: "When we discovered America we found all the tribes divided into republics."[25] This philosophy of history did not exclude Europe: "So it was in the ancient world. All was republican in Europe before the petty kings of Etruria and Rome," Voltaire argued, driving home a sarcastic wedge against the foundation of monarchy by "*roitelets*." The article concludes with an almost Rousseauist paean to the "Hottentots," who "live as men are said to have lived in the first ages of the world, free, equal among themselves, without masters, without subjects, without money, and almost without needs." These shepherds are not as worldly as the Gangarids: "The flesh of their sheep feeds them, their skins clothe them, huts of wood and earth are their shelters. They stink worse than any other men, but do not know it." For these reasons, Voltaire concludes, almost sentimentally, "they live and die more calmly [*plus doucement*] than we do." The article "Démocratie," in the *Questions sur l'Encyclopédie*, returns to this point, insisting on the naturalness of republicanism: "Everything that was not subjugated in this part of the [New] world is still republican. There were only two kingdoms on the continent when it was discovered," Voltaire summarizes, adding: "this could well prove that republican government is more natural." He coats this saucy observation with his signature wit: "It takes a great deal of refinement and many challenges to submit oneself to the government of a single person."[26]

If Voltaire's historical and Orientalist studies did not transform him into a hardened republican, they nonetheless produced a radical result, the belief

---

24. *Philosophical Dictionary*, trans. and ed. Theodore Besterman (Middlesex: Penguin Books, 1971), 328; *Dictionnaire philosophique* (Paris: Flammarion, 1993), 307. Subsequent quotes in this paragraph are from this same source.

25. Jaucourt made a similar claim in the *Encyclopédie* article on "République Romaine": "Before the Romans conquered all the *republics*, there were almost no kings anywhere, either in Italy, Gaul, Spain, or Germany; there were only small peoples or small republics. Even Africa was a large republic . . . only in Persia could one find a government of one" (14:150).

26. In *Voltaire électronique*.

that republicanism constituted the "most natural" form of government.[27] It is worth emphasizing the radicalness of this finding, which has not received much attention in the scholarship, as (1) it represented a U-turn from traditional patriarchal theories, even found in such liberal thinkers as Locke and Fénelon; (2) it constituted a major departure from the mature (and most authoritative) Montesquieu, for whom *no* political form was natural; (3) it placed republican government per se on a very solid foundation; and (4) it departed from the classical tradition in suggesting that republics need not be grounded in a constitution. While none of these revisions necessarily changed the value and relevance of republicanism in modern times, they nonetheless made it much easier to justify contemporary claims for a republican government.

As with the writers surveyed in the previous chapter, however, Voltaire's naturalization of republicanism had another result—the demonizing of those who went against the natural order. In a dialogue on natural law, Voltaire has "B," initially a skeptic, acknowledge the existence of natural law, only to remark that "it is even more natural for many to forget it"; to which "A" replies, "It is also natural to be blind, to have a humpback or a limp, to be ungainly or sick; but one prefers well built and healthy people."[28] The parallel could not have been clearer: Whosoever disregarded natural right was as morally monstrous as these physically imperfect creatures.

Ethnography of the Golden Age: Diderot and Tahiti

The fact that Voltaire himself stood behind these potentially subversive transformations of republicanism no doubt made them all the more subversive, but it did not take the authority of a philosophe to turn the ethnographic discoveries of the eighteenth century into wondrous and revolutionary events. A case in point was the (re)discovery of Tahiti, described by Bougainville in the 1771 account of his voyage, already much discussed in the press upon

---

27. Spinoza had similarly emphasized the naturalness of republics: "It seems to be the most natural and to be that which approaches most closely to the freedom nature bestows on every person," *Theological-Political Treatise*, trans. and ed. Jonathan Israel and Michael Silverthorne (Cambridge: Cambridge University Press, 2007), 16.11; 202. But Voltaire only ever refers to Spinoza as a dangerous materialist, and I have come across no indication that he considered Spinoza's political thought. On Spinoza's influence in eighteenth-century France, see Jonathan Israel, *Enlightenment Contested: Philosophy, Modernity, and the Emancipation of Man, 1670–1752* (Oxford: Oxford University Press, 2006).

28. *Dictionnaire philosophique*, s.v. "Loi naturelle." In this article, Voltaire also paraphrases Rousseau as having written in the second *Discourse* that "the first person to have dared enclose and cultivate a field was the enemy of the human race [*l'ennemi du genre humain*]."

his return in 1769.[29] Voltaire himself enthused about the natural Tahitian society in *Les oreilles du comte de Chesterfield et le chapelain Goudman* (1775): "It is in Tahiti that nature resides," asserts an English doctor who had visited there. "This island is much more civilized than Zeland . . . and, if I dare say, than our England."[30] Tahiti was a modern equivalent to Voltaire's long-lost Gangarids; it provided living proof that the golden age was not merely a poetic conceit, while this myth, conversely, confirmed the naturalness of Tahitian society.[31]

Where the historical Orient revealed its republican past only to astute and learned readers, Tahiti seemed to reveal the true order of nature to anyone curious enough to flip through Bougainville's little book. By and large, the reaction to his voyage (and to the Tahitian whom he brought back to France) emphasized a common theme, neatly summarized by Diderot: "The Tahitian is close to the origins of the world and the European near its old age."[32] The people of Tahiti were a time capsule that allowed Westerners to discover both their own pristine origins and to lament their present degenerate state.

Not everyone was content with drawing merely historical conclusions from Bougainville's discovery: In Diderot's reading, for instance, Tahiti also offered Europe a series of moral and political lessons. As Rousseau before him in his discussion of civil religion, Diderot laments the existence of contradictory legal codes (natural, civil, and religious) governing "civilized"

---

29. *Voyage autour du monde par la frégate du roi "la Boudeuse" et la flûte "l'Étoile" en 1766, 1767, 1768 et 1769* (Paris: Saillant and Nyon, 1771); for an excellent modern edition with a valuable introduction, see *Voyage autour du monde*, ed. Michel Bideaux and Sonia Faessel (Paris: Presses de l'Université de Paris-Sorbonne, 2001). On the Tahitian imaginary, see Sonia Faessel, *Vision des îles: Tahiti et l'imaginaire européen, du mythe à son exploitation littéraire (XVIIIᵉ–XXᵉ)* (Paris: L'Harmattan, 2005); and, more generally, Michèle Duchet, *Anthropologie et histoire au siècle des Lumières* (1971; Paris: Albin Michel, 1995); Chantal Grell and Christian Michel, eds., *Primitivisme et mythes des origines dans la France des Lumières, 1680–1820* (Paris: Presses de l'Université de Paris-Sorbonne, 1989); and Christian Marouby, *Utopie et primitivisme: Essai sur l'imaginaire anthropologique à l'âge classique* (Paris: Seuil, 1990).

30. In *Romans et contes*, 681.

31. In *Les oreilles du comte*, Tahiti is not depicted as a republican state since it has a "religious queen" who presides over "the undoubtedly most respectable" of "religious ceremonies" (682); but as this ceremony consists of public couplings by mature adolescents, one is entitled to treat this political indication with a grain or two of salt.

32. *A Supplement to the Voyage of Bougainville* (1772), in *Political Writings*, trans. and ed. John Hope Mason and Robert Wokler (New York: Cambridge University Press, 1992), 40; *Supplément au voyage de Bougainville* (Paris: Gallimard, 2002), 37. References to the French text are provided following a semicolon. On the numerous binary structures in this text, see Christie McDonald, *The Dialogue of Writing: Essays in Eighteenth-Century Literature* (Waterloo: Wilfrid Laurier University Press, 1984), 63–72.

Europeans, whereas "the Tahitians . . . have kept strictly to the law of nature" and are accordingly "nearer to having good laws than any civilized people."[33] To unravel the Gordian knot of civil legislation, Europeans must wield the sword of natural right: "Civil law should merely articulate the law of nature" (67, translation modified). Laws would then be sublimely simple and just: "How brief would be the codes of nations, if only they conformed rigorously to that of Nature!" (71).

For Diderot, Tahiti thus constituted the real-life example of a society governed by natural right. Of course, this example was itself mediated by another model of natural society, the golden age, as it had been for Bougainville (who dubbed the island "the new Cythera").[34] As in that mythical time, there are no private possessions in Tahiti: "Here, everything belongs to everyone, and you have preached I can't tell what distinction between 'yours' and 'mine'" (42), a reference to the terms—*meum et teum*—that traditionally were said to have put an end to the golden age. Particularly attractive for this unhappily married Frenchman was the fact that the Tahitians can change wives and husbands as they like (so long as each "marriage" lasts one lunar cycle), practicing the sort of *amor liber* that had given the golden age myth its captivating power on the minds of medieval Christians.[35] More than the freedom to change partners, or even to select partners from among one's family, it was the naturalness and openness of Tahitian sexuality that fascinated European commentators. Here no shame was found in "pleasure to which Nature, that sovereign mistress, invites every person" (47).[36]

---

33. See also Voltaire: "*Malheur aux nations dont les lois opposées / Embrouillent de l'État les rénes divisées!*" ("Misfortune to those nations whose conflicting laws / Entangle the divided reins of the State!"), *Poème sur la loi naturelle*, IV.

34. See Janet Whatley, "Un retour secret vers la forêt: The Problem of Privacy and Order in Diderot's Tahiti," *Kentucky Romance Quarterly* 24 (1977): 200–201.

35. See Harry Levin, *The Myth of the Golden Age in the Renaissance* (Bloomington: Indiana University Press, 1969), 24–37. In *Le Roman de la Rose*, one of the most popular medieval romances in the eighteenth century, the golden age is repeatedly defined in terms of what Ernst Robert Curtius has called "erotic communism"; see *European Literature and the Latin Middle Ages*, trans. Willard R. Trask (Princeton: Princeton University Press, 1990), 125; and, in particular, the speech by "la Vieille" (vv. 13879–970) and Genius's description of the *parc dou champ joli*.

36. This fascination with open sexuality echoes both Voltaire's description of the Tahitian "religious ceremony" and Montesquieu's story about the "Guèbres," or Zoroastrians, in *Persian Letters*. This brother and sister, who adhere to the world's oldest religion (so we are told), are also incestuous lovers, a relationship that is equated with primitive liberty (letter 67). See in general Georges Benrekassa, "Loi naturelle et loi civile: l'idéologie des Lumières et la prohibition de l'inceste," *Studies on Voltaire and the Eighteenth Century* 87 (1972): 115–44; and Marcel Hénaff, "Supplement to Diderot's Dream," in *The Libertine Reader,* ed. Michel Feher (New York: Zone Books, 1997), 52–75. Saint-Just would similarly defend incest as being natural; see *Œuvres complètes*, ed. Michèle Duval (Paris: Lebovici, 1984), 947.

The "natural" superiority of Tahitian morals was not limited to sexuality, but extended to all social behavior: "We follow the pure instincts of nature," the wise, elder Tahitian—reminiscent of the wise, elder Troglodyte of the *Persian Letters*—tells the intruding Frenchmen (42). As in the golden age, which they appear to perpetuate, the Tahitians live virtuously *sine lege* and, more importantly, without crimes: "It was you who first brought the idea of crime and the risk of illness to us" (44). There is no constitutional or traditional source for this probity; it derives entirely from nature.[37] But the Tahitians are not, for that matter, deprived of political sentiments; for each of them "the love of liberty is the deepest of all feelings" (41). This feeling of liberty may be natural, but it is not taken for granted. As the elder Tahitian tells Bougainville, "We are free. . . . Do you suppose, then, that a Tahitian cannot defend his own liberty and die" (42). To live free or die: The Tahitians, as the Boeticans before them, will defend their natural rights with republican zeal. And it is precisely this liberty that "B" most envies: "When I see how we plant trees round our palaces, or how a woman's bodice at once hides and exposes her breast, I seem to detect a secret wish to return to the forest, a recollected longing for the freedom [*liberté première*] of our first habitat" (69).[38] The opposition between Europe and Tahiti, around which the text is structured, pits not only culture versus nature, but also monarchic "palaces" and the republican "liberty" of the forests. The freedom of Tahiti is the freedom denied to European subjects.

Is Diderot's Tahiti a republic (a designation never used in the work)? The island fits the bill only in purely negative terms, in that it knows neither monarchy nor aristocracy; its wise elders appear have a consultative role in society. But does it have *any* political organization? While it differs greatly from the republics discussed by Machiavelli or Montesquieu, Tahiti nonetheless exhibits certain traits that distinctly evoke classical-republican theories. The islanders' reliance on natural law is mediated by their good morals—"our ways [*mœurs*] are better than yours" (48), Orou tells the chaplain—and these two modes of judgment are defined, in good classical-republican fashion, as interdependent: "If the laws are good, morality is good. If the laws are bad, morality is bad" (66). The power of law, even natural, is only as forceful as the morals that sustain it. The transformation of laws into morals, furthermore, is the result of "institutions," the most

---

37. See Dena Goodman, *Criticism in Action: Enlightenment Experiments in Political Writing* (Ithaca: Cornell University Press, 1989), 216 (and on the *Supplément* more generally, 186–224).

38. On the confusing implications of this phrase, see Whatley, "Un retour secret vers la forêt."

important of which is "domestic education" (through which "the most important item of public morality" is inculcated, 55). Though they obey the order of nature, the Tahitians still find it necessary to instruct their young in its ways, as in a republic.[39] Finally, the islanders themselves translate their natural social imperative into the patriotic language of classical republicanism: "Do you know a better [rule] than the general welfare [*le bien général*] and individual utility?" (61). The common good, in Tahiti as in republican Rome, is the *suprema lex* of the state.

Resembling from afar an apolitical state of nature, Tahiti thus proves itself on closer analysis to be a natural society; as already in Voltaire, this society is structured according to republican principles. Unlike Rome or other classical republics, however, there is hardly any political structure to Tahitian society. Public liberty is limited to military defense: Since the Tahitians obey the laws of nature, they have no need for deliberative, legislative assemblies. As with Boetica and the Gangarids, this ideal social order has been thoroughly depoliticized. However, where Voltaire's Oriental republic was chiefly relegated to the primitive stage of humanity, the historical immediacy (and alluring erotic charms) of Tahiti provide it with greater reality and relevance. If a natural social order can be shown to exist in the present time, then it inevitably becomes a measuring stick for all other forms of government and society. The apolitical order visible in Tahiti thus necessarily reflects back—and poorly, at that—on European states.

As noted above, the political systems of the Old World come under fire above all for their contradictory and arbitrary legal codes. Orou is astounded by the human whims that parade themselves as justice in France: "I don't know what you mean by 'magistrates' and 'priests' . . . but tell me, are they masters of good and evil? Can they make what is just unjust, and transform what is unjust into what is just?" (51). If you obey these competing masters, Orou warns the chapelain, "you'll have to abandon Nature" (51).

But the comparison between Europe and Tahiti is extended to political structures as well. When the chaplain exclaims that Tahitian morality "threatens the political order [*la constitution politique*]," Orou replies that "instead of one great society there would be fifty small ones, more happiness overall and one less crime" (61). The "crime" to which he is referring seems to be monarchy itself ("one great society" run by "a leader"). Europeans, Orou seems to be saying, would be better off if monarchies were broken up into

39. Georges Van Den Abbeele called attention to the Tahitian's "prescriptive morality" in "Utopian Sexuality and Its Discontents: Exoticism and Colonialism in the *Supplément au voyage de Bougainville*," *L'Esprit créateur* 24 (1984): 43–52.

smaller republics ("fifty small ones"). "B" picks up on this political criticism in a later, more overt passage: In Europe, "suspicious and jealous masters"—a clear jab at monarchy—"have been engaged in keeping man in what you call a state of brutishness" (73). Only Venice, which pays the least lip service to a "less artificial" morality and to "chimerical" vices and virtues, is excepted from this blanket judgment—only Venice, which, in name at least, is a republic.

Although the reconciliatory and reformist tone of Diderot's *Supplément* is often stressed—the characters fall back into line *in extremis*: "We must speak out against senseless laws until they're reformed and, in the meantime, abide by them" (74)—its revolutionary scope is no less ambitious: "I call to witness all political, civil, and religious institutions. Examine them closely, and I should be much mistaken if, throughout the ages, you didn't find the human race broken under the yoke which a handful of scoundrels had determined to place upon it" (72). Tahiti thus provided Diderot with a pretext for advancing a naturalistic theory of society and politics that extended to *all* political institutions. This was a radical message, one which would admittedly only be heard posthumously (the dialogue was published in 1796), but that Diderot would repeat loudly, if in a disguised voice, in the third edition of the abbé Raynal's *Histoire philosophique et politique des établissements et du commerce des Européens dans les deux Indes*.[40]

For all his criticism of, and hostility toward, European monarchy, however, Diderot did not turn into an unflinching republican. In his rebuttal of Helvétius, also written in 1771–73, he granted that the philosophe's energetic celebration of republicanism "seems entirely true," but subscribed to the commonplace Enlightenment belief that "there can only be small republics, and . . . the well-being of this only kind of society that can be happy will always be precarious."[41] Tahiti did not offer proof that republicanism was the sole natural and acceptable form of government, but rather confirmed a more general line of politico-legal inquiry that Diderot, among many

---

40. See, for instance, the Rousseauist argument that "the vices of morality and legislation . . . came from founders and legislators who, for the most part, had created social order for their own use." In *Political Writings*, 193. On Diderot's involvement in this enterprise, see notably Hans Wolpe, *Raynal et sa machine de guerre: 'L'Histoire des deux Indes' et ses perfectionnements* (Stanford: Stanford University Press, 1957) ; and Michèle Duchet, *Diderot et 'l'Histoire des deux Indes'* (Paris: Nizet, 1978).

41. *Réfutation suivie de l'ouvrage d'Helvétius intitulé "L'Homme,"* in *Œuvres Complètes*, ed. M. Assézat (Paris: Garnier, 1875), 1.4.11 (2:390). Helvétius had declared: "Let us not be surprised if this [republican] form of government has always been considered to be the best. Free and happy citizens only obey to laws that they have given themselves; they only perceive justice and the law above them," *De l'homme, de ses facultés intellectuelles et de son éducation* (London: Société typographique, 1773), 4.11 (1:314–15).

others, had pursued for some time. This inquiry concerned the relationship between natural and civil law, and the potential redundancy of the latter. Diderot had already advanced the central thesis of this radical jusnaturalist theory in the *Encyclopédie* article on "legislation" (published in 1765, six years before Bougainville's *Voyage*, but undoubtedly written even earlier): "The best possible legislation is that which is the simplest and most conforms with nature."[42] It obviously did not take the discovery (or invention) of Tahiti to reach the political conclusions of the *Supplément*; the Pacific island served rather to confirm preexisting theses that Diderot had formulated in other contexts. In this respect, it is misleading to categorize this work as utopian: "It's not a myth" (41), one of the characters insists. Bougainville's Tahiti was for Diderot an anthropological antidote to Galiani's biting criticism of Physiocracy, the political theory that had most fully developed the radical jusnaturalist thesis. Until reading Galiani's *Dialogues*, Diderot had been an enthusiastic admirer of Paul-Pierre Le Mercier de la Rivière's 1767 *L'ordre naturel et essentiel des sociétés politiques*, a work that constituted "the definitive statement of physiocracy," and was written under the strict supervision of the doctor Quesnay.[43] The Neapolitan *abbé* had shaken Diderot's faith in Le Mercier (an ex-*intendant* of Martinique, whom the philosophe nonetheless convinced Catherine II to call to Saint-Petersburg), but given the many echoes of Physiocracy that one can detect in the *Supplément*, Tahiti apparently rekindled Diderot's belief in its political, if not economic, message.

---

42. *Encyclopédie*, 9:363; qtd. in Gerolamo Imbruglia, "From Utopia to Republicanism: The Case of Diderot," in *The Invention of the Modern Republic*, ed. Biancamaria Fontana (Cambridge: Cambridge University Press, 1994), 72. See also the *Encyclopédie* article on "Droit naturel," discussed above. More generally, see Anthony Strugnell, *Diderot's Politics: A Study of the Evolution of Diderot's Political Thought after the "Encyclopédie"* (The Hague: Martinus Nijhoff, 1973); and Franco Venturi, *The End of the Old Regime in Europe, 1776–1789*, trans. R. Burr Litchfield (Princeton: Princeton University Press, 1991), 1:357–75.

43. Georges Weulersse, *Le mouvement physiocratique en France de 1756 à 1770* (Paris: Alcan, 1910), 1:127; Weulersse also notes how by 1770, Physiocracy as a school was dead (1:241). See also Thomas P. Neill, "Quesnay and Physiocracy," *Journal of the History of Ideas* 9, no. 2 (1948): 155, 173. On Diderot's infatuation with Le Mercier, see Strugnell, *Diderot's Politics*, 99–114. On Galiani's dampening effect, see Imbruglia, "From Utopia to Republicanism," 74–75. Galiani's *Dialogues sur le commerce des bleds* (London, 1770), which Diderot, Mme d'Épinay, and Grimm prepared for publication, had killed mostly with ridicule: "It appeared evident to the Economists that the evidence of their evidence would make it evident to all nations the evident advantage of free exportation" (301). To appreciate the sarcasm of this passage, one must recall that Quesnay had written the article on "évidence" for the *Encyclopédie*. Diderot composed an *Apologie de l'abbé Galiani* in 1770, in response to Morellet's fierce rebuttal of the *Dialogues*; for an account of this episode, see Gordon, *Citizens without Sovereignty*. As noted above, Le Mercier's work also drew harsh criticism from Mably; see his *Doutes proposés aux philosophes économistes sur l'ordre naturel et essentiel des sociétés politiques* (The Hague and Paris: Nyon, 1768).

As with most of Diderot's thought, however, this belief never ceased to waver; in his later *Observations sur le Nakaz*, he again emphasized the inherent problem with the Physiocratic doctrine: "When will such an order be discovered? Who will introduce it? How many interests will be opposed to its establishment?" (XIX).[44] Ultimately, political reform for Diderot seems to have boiled down to a paradox:

> Natural laws are eternal and universal; positive laws are only the corollaries of natural laws. Therefore, positive laws are eternal and universal. Nevertheless, a particular positive law is certainly good and useful in one circumstance, bad and harmful in another. And there is certainly no Code which does not need to be reformed in time. This difficulty is perhaps not insoluble; but it must be solved.[45]

Faced with this same problem in America, Jefferson would press for regular revisions of the Constitution;[46] from a classical-republican, "great Lawgiver" standpoint, however, this dynamic solution presented as many dangers as advantages. The other option was to make do, as Diderot's Tahitians and Montesquieu's Troglodytes, with natural laws alone. This was the solution recommended by the Physiocrats, which would also be championed by certain Jacobin leaders. How was it, though, that a political theory advocating "legal despotism" could feature so centrally in antimonarchic discourses? As the following section suggests, it was ironically in the Physiocrats' ambiguous defense of monarchy that the most complete theory of natural republicanism was to be found.

Physiocracy: Conceiving the Natural Republic

The Physiocrats have chiefly been treated by historians, and for good reason, as the precursors of modern economic theory.[47] Known to their

---

44. *Political Writings*, 96; see T. J. Hochstrasser, "Physiocracy and the Politics of *Laissez-Faire*," in *CHECPT*, 433–34.

45. *Observations sur le Nakaz*, V, in *Political Writings*, 88.

46. Hannah Arendt, *On Revolution* (London: Penguin, 2006), 227.

47. On Physiocracy, see Weulersse's *Mouvement physiocratique en France*; Neill, "Quesnay and Physiocracy," 153–73; *François Quesnay et la Physiocratie* (Paris: Institut national d'études démographiques, 1958); Elizabeth Fox-Genovese, *The Origins of Physiocracy: Economic Revolution and Social Order in Eighteenth-Century France* (Ithaca: Cornell University Press, 1976); Catherine Larrère, *L'Invention de l'économie au XVIIIe siècle: du droit naturel à la physiocratie* (Paris: PUF, 1992); Michael Sonenscher, "Physiocracy as Theodicy," *History of Political Thought* 23, no. 2 (2002): 326–39, and *Before the Deluge: Public Debt, Inequality, and the Intellectual Origins of the French Revolution* (Princeton: Princeton University Press, 2007), chap. 3; John Shovlin, *Political Economy of Virtue: Luxury, Patriotism, and the Origins of the French Revolution* (Ithaca: Cornell University Press, 2006); and Hochstrasser, "Physiocracy and the Politics of *Laissez-Faire*."

contemporaries as the *économistes*, it was their free market theories (emblematized in Quesnay's enigmatic *Tableau économique*) that attracted the
greatest attention, particularly in the context of France's perennial grain
shortages.[48] Adam Smith's celebrated tip-of-the-hat to Quesnay in *The
Wealth of Nations* (which was at one point to have been dedicated to the
French doctor) further helped ensure the Physiocrats their place in economic
history.[49] While their political views, particularly the notion of "legal despotism," have not been neglected, they tend to be considered in relation to their
economic theories, as part of their larger political economy. Removed from
the tradition of political theory, however, the radicalness of their political
ideas is not always fully appreciated. For in the process of buttressing their
economic proposals with a political foundation, the Physiocrats overthrew
the central tenets of the natural right tradition in which they were writing.[50]

The traditional narrative of natural right theory could be told as a three-
act play: In the first act, the state of nature is found to be insufficient for
human needs; in the second, individuals come together and agree on some
form of civil society; in the finale, new laws are passed to supplement the
natural laws of the earlier state. To be sure, there were disagreements about
the specificities of this narrative, but as a basic plot outline, it remained unchanged from Grotius to Rousseau.

The Physiocrats rewrote this script entirely. In their retelling, civil society
and the state of nature are no longer distinct entities: Apart from a few rare
cases, all humans cohabitate with others,[51] and the simplest social organization, the family, exhibits the same "natural order" as complex societies. "It is
part of the natural order that the strongest be the head of the family," Quesnay

---

48. For an overview of the economic context of this period, see Steven L. Kaplan, *Bread,
Politics, and Political Economy in the Reign of Louis XV* (The Hague: M. Nijhoff, 1976), and
"The Famine Plot Persuasion in Eighteenth-Century France," *Transactions of the American
Philosophical Society* 72, no. 3 (1992): 1–83.

49. See notably Emma Rothschild, *Economic Sentiments: Condorcet, Adam Smith, and the
Enlightenment* (Cambridge: Harvard University Press, 2001).

50. See Quesnay's programmatic statement, *Le droit naturel*, analyzed below, which serves
as an introduction to Dupont de Nemours's *Physiocratie ou Constitution naturelle du gouvernement le plus avantageux au genre humain* (Paris and Leiden: Merlin, 1768), 1:1–38. An earlier
version of this text was first published in the *Journal de l'agriculture, du commerce et des finances*
in September 1765 (Weulersse, *Mouvement physiocratique*, 1:98 and 129).

51. According to Le Mercier, "il subsiste naturellement entre les hommes une sorte de
société universelle et tacite," *L'ordre naturel et essentiel des sociétés politiques*, ed. Edgard Depitre
(1767; Paris: Paul Geuthner, 1910), 34; see also the *Traité de la monarchie*, ed. Gino Longhitano (Paris: L'Harmattan, 1999), 7. As Sonenscher notes, this claim "set what became Physiocracy apart from the two most usual eighteenth-century accounts of the fundamental principles
of every political society," "Physiocracy as Theodicy," 329.

affirms (*Le droit naturel* 24); in larger societies, this chief becomes the "tutelary authority" (28) who guarantees that property is respected. Whether alone, in small groups, or in populated nations, men are always governed by the same law: "Natural right, understood as part of the order of nature and the order of justice, extends to all states in which men can find themselves with respect to one another" (11–12). The only differences between these states are ones of scale.

At some point along this scale, however, a formal government and positive laws are needed. In this respect, Quesnay concurred that in the "state of pure nature," which he tellingly prefers to call "state of multitude" (versus the rarer "state of solitude"), our natural rights run the risk of being overrun. As in Locke, civil society is instituted to preserve our natural right to own the fruits of our labor. But the manner in which this transition occurs, and the resulting society, are described in a highly original fashion. To begin with, this transition is almost seamless. When families become aware of others, "they grow used to seeing each other, confidence grows between them, they help each other out, they become allied through marriages, and constitute in some way individual nations [*Nations particulières*], where all are in league for their common defense" (27). These nations make no demands on their constituents: "Everyone remains in a state of entire liberty and independence with respect to each other." They are all governed by natural right, which teaches them to work the land and to respect the property of others. Without government or positive laws, these naturally good men will lead "free" lives since liberty is only the rational faculty through which we recognize that this natural order is "evidently" the best (16–21). Rational men, in Quesnay's story, resemble the model individual in Diderot's "Droit naturel" article, choosing to obey the general will (here, the universal "natural order") rather than be swayed by their passions—except that for Quesnay, this freedom is already in nature. A closer comparison for this "state of pure nature" would thus be the society of good Troglodytes in the *Persian Letters*.

Ultimately a more formal government structure is needed to protect the natural rights of individuals. Although Quesnay dismisses the traditional argument that the state of nature tends toward (as in Locke and Rousseau) or is tantamount to (for Hobbes) war, the progressive accumulation of wealth in the "state of multitude" makes it a tantalizing target.[52] But missing from

---

52. Quesnay argues that "in the state of pure nature, men hurrying to satisfy their needs . . . will not waste time waging useless war" (11), but goes on to suggest, somewhat contradictorily, that violence is one of the reasons why individuals enter into civil society (14).

this transition-narrative is the keystone of modern natural right theories: the social contract.[53] Quesnay grants that men pass "conventions" to help secure their property and rights, but (a) these do not constitute social contracts, but rather pacts of nonaggression (27); and (b) these also exist among "savage peoples" (26) who have no civil government. The passage from "*Nation particulière*" to "society" does not require the consent of the governed because it does not represent a substantial change. The chief of the family is replaced by a "tutelary power" (30) and the natural laws are expressly formulated as positive laws. But the laws, which the civil authority, like the family head, merely enforces, stay the same. Indeed, Quesnay establishes a feedback loop between natural and positive legislation: "Positive legislation consists . . . in the declaration of natural laws" (35). There is no need for a lawgiver in this civil state. Positive laws should simply be copies of the "sovereign laws, decreed by the Supreme Being," which are "immutable and irrefutable, and the best possible laws" (32).

In a radical departure from tradition, the Physiocrats thus elaborated a political theory in which natural right alone was responsible for all civil legislation. They resolved Rousseau's famous legal conundrum—"One would need Gods to give men laws" (*Social Contract*, 2.7)—simply by claiming that God *had* given men laws; the "Author of Nature" was also "Author of laws and rules" (21). Rather than constituting "sublime," "godlike" creations, which supplement or replace natural right in civil society, positive laws are accordingly viewed with suspicion since "the laws of men are not as perfect as the laws of the Author of nature" (7). If natural right is a pristine source to be copied, it is only in the *traddutore* that the *traditore* can appear, as is evidenced by the "multitude of contradictory and absurd laws established successively among nations," which proves "that positive laws are liable to depart from the immutable rules of justice and from the most advantageous natural order for society" (8). To reform society thus becomes tantamount to restoring natural order, disturbed by "the transgressions of natural laws," which constitute "the most widespread and common causes of the physical ills plaguing man" (16).[54] Accordingly, some Physiocrats demanded that these violators be treated as enemies of the human race.[55]

---

53. Sonenscher, *Before the Deluge*, 214.

54. This idea had already been voiced by Mirabeau in *L'ami des hommes, ou traité de la population* (Avignon: n.p., 1756): "il est toujours nécessaire de déraciner dans l'intérieur de l'état tout ce qui y subsiste de contraire au droit naturel" (3:238).

55. See, for instance, Le Trosne, *Mémoire sur les vagabonds et sur les mendiants*, discussed in the prologue, and Nicolas Gabriel Clerc's *Yu le Grand et Confucius, histoire chinoise* (Soissons: Ponce Courtois, 1769), discussed in chapter 4.

But who had the power to revise positive laws on the model of natural right? It is here that the Physiocratic theory of "legal despotism" intervenes.[56] Only alluded to in Quesnay's *Droit naturel*, this theory is discussed more fully in Le Mercier's *Ordre naturel et essentiel*:

> Legislative power is ultimately nothing but the power to establish good positive laws: but *good* positive laws are laws that conform perfectly to the natural and essential order of societies; they are only *good* to the extent that they are taken from the evidence of this essential order; that they are, in a word, dictated by this very evidence to the Legislator. (86)

The tutelary power that guaranteed the natural right to property in civil society was thus also charged with ensuring that positive laws perfectly reflected their natural model. In this regard, the Physiocrats *did* incorporate a lawgiver into their political system; as in Rousseau, furthermore, Le Mercier argues that this function is best fulfilled by a single person, rather than an assembly, since it is more likely that one enlightened individual will hear the dictates of natural right more clearly. The "legal despot," as Le Mercier calls him (141), thus exercises a rule of one over positive laws—but never was a despot's rule more limited. There was no room in this theory for the *bon plaisir du roi*, Le Mercier adamantly affirmed: "It is absolutely necessary that full authority be granted to these [natural] laws, and that at no time their enforcement depend on any *arbitrary will*, since otherwise they would cease to be laws" (36, emphasis added). The limitations of sovereign power are equally clear in Quesnay: "It is against the order of justice that [the chief] encroach on the natural right of those who live with him in a community of interests" (24). Fathers may have a natural right to rule over others in the "state of pure nature," but the Physiocrats could not be more opposed to patriarchalism *à la* Robert Filmer: The fatherly chief, like the tutelary power, must distribute goods and wealth "according to the very order of distributive justice, following the duties prescribed by nature" (24). To paraphrase Frederick the Great, the legal despot was merely the servant of the natural state. His apparent "despotism," the marquis de Mirabeau assured Rousseau in 1767, "should not astound you any more than the despotism of arithmetic . . . the number appears, is despotically determined,

---

56. For an insightful discussion of this concept, see Weulersse, *Mouvement physiocratique*, 2:48–76.

without appeal, since, tell me, what counter-forces exist to addition and subtraction?"[57]

Even this "despotic" function was limited only to cases where positive law had gone awry. The Physiocratic lawgiver, in fact, was not nearly as sublime and unique as his Rousseauist equivalent since *all* rational individuals were supposed to recognize the "evident" advantages of the natural order: "The justice and necessity of these natural, essential, and universal laws, are so evident, that they appear so *to all men*, without the need for any written trace [*signe sensible*]," Le Mercier writes; "it is in the very code of nature that they are written, where we read them distinctly with the help of reason" (56, emphasis added). Instead of a superhuman legislator dictating laws to the community, the Physiocrats argued that universal education should be able to train everyone's rational faculties: "The first positive law, the fundamental law for all other positive laws, is *the institution of public and private instruction into the natural order*," stipulates Quesnay (34, emphasis in original), a requirement also stressed by Le Mercier (56). In the context of their own political system, where positive and natural law were identical and all citizens *already* observed the natural order, the despotic legislator thus played a superfluous role.

For a political theory that nominally supported absolute monarchy, Physiocracy offered a rather weak defense of royal power. If the legal despot's legislative function was ultimately redundant, he still fulfilled an executive role; but this policing role (in Le Mercier's words, "a physical and coercive force," 78) was not dependent on monarchic government and necessarily required the armed forces of many. Quesnay, in *Le Droit naturel*, went so far as to suggest that the "natural constitution" of government could equally well be aristocratic, democratic, or monarchic, so long as "the positive laws and the tutelary power" "guarantee . . . property and liberty" (30). Since all governments can theoretically ensure such benefits, monarchy constitutes only a mildly privileged form. All types of government, in any case, were variations on "the natural and immutable order, *archetype* of Governments" (31).

The relationship between Physiocracy and monarchy is a vexing one. One of the first texts that Quesnay and Mirabeau worked on together was a *Treatise on Monarchy*. Its justification of monarchic rule proved so feeble that they declined to publish it for fear of *embastillement*.[58] The ease with which Phys-

---

57. Letter of July 30, 1767, in *Jean-Jacques Rousseau, ses amis et ses ennemis*, ed. G. Streckeisen-Moultou (Paris: Calmann-Levy, 1865), 2:364. I thank Pernille Røge for providing me with this reference.

58. Fox-Genovese discussed this treatise in *Origins of Physiocracy*, 167–201; see also Sonenscher, "Physiocracy as Theodicy."

iocracy lent itself to a republican adaptation is also evident in Turgot's *Mémoire sur les municipalités*.[59] Even Le Mercier's *Ordre naturel et essentiel* expressed a range of views that can be characterized as republican. The legal despot resembles the founder of a republic, who, in Machiavelli's narrative, must grab the reins of society in order to institute good laws and institutions before abandoning absolute power.[60] Le Mercier was also an adamant supporter of an independent judiciary, and even cautioned against judicial misconduct in almost Whiggish terms: [61] "Is it not evident that the furious barbarian, who would pass judgments on the basis of a perverse law, would be complicit with its atrocity, and similarly murderous?" (74). The need for public instruction was answered by the creation of "social *institutions*" (53, emphasis added), which would foster, as in Machiavelli, Montesquieu, and Rousseau, an appreciation of the fundamental order (or laws) of society. Finally, Le Mercier's work concludes with a warning couched in terms highly reminiscent of republican theory: "Virtues can exist fleetingly without the [natural] order, whereas the order cannot exist without virtues. Indeed, this order is nothing but the practice of these same virtues, only established on the basis of their evident absolute necessity" (358). The necessary complementarity of laws and morals, so often discussed by republican authors, has here been rephrased in familiar Physiocratic terms, but the underlying idea remains unchanged. For a state to steer clear of the "monstrous chaos," from which arise "murders, robberies, thefts of all sort, crimes, all excesses," it must ensure that its fundamental laws—its natural and essential order— be recognized and respected; but this can occur only if "corruption" and "moral depravity" (61) have not blinded citizens to the evidence of the law's goodness.

The one facet of republicanism to which Physiocracy was least amenable was popular sovereignty. Even if municipal assemblies, in Turgot's model, were attributed deliberative functions, the sovereignty of the state always lay in its "sovereign laws" (Quesnay, *Droit naturel*, 32). Physiocracy

---

59. See Keith Baker, *Condorcet: From Natural Philosophy to Social Mathematics* (Chicago: University of Chicago Press, 1975), 305; and Hochstrasser, "Physiocracy and the Politics of *Laissez-Faire*," 437, who also notes the incompatibility, in other respects, between Physiocracy and republicanism (432–33).

60. See, for instance, *Discourses*, 1.9, 1.16, and 1.18.

61. Weulersse, *Mouvement physiocratique*, 2:62–64. As Baker points out, however, the Physiocrats were strongly opposed to any separation of powers; see "The Idea of a Declaration of Rights," in *The French Idea of Freedom: The Old Regime and the Declaration of Rights of 1789*, ed. Dale Van Kley (Stanford: Stanford University Press, 1994), 165–66, which also addresses the Physiocratic underpinnings of Condorecet's and Dupont de Nemours's perception of the Declaration.

did not incorporate any social contract, so the people were never called upon to give their willing consent to government. But since the king, or other executive power, was also subject to the rule of natural law, sovereignty was not a monarchic attribute either. Physiocracy thus offered the ultimate blueprint of a depoliticized society: *All* forms of sovereignty were brushed aside to make way for what might be called the "despotism of Nature."

Whether or not it covertly advanced a republican agenda, in any event, Physiocracy could, and would, be interpreted in republican terms, most notably during the French Revolution (see chapter 4). Developed in a series of synthetic presentations, embracing the *esprit de système* that the early Enlightenment had shunned, the Physiocratic doctrine formed a coherent totality; but the same pedagogical qualities that led its proponents to formulate each aspect of their doctrine clearly and succinctly also made these pieces easily detachable. The political, legal, economic, and institutional aspects of Physiocracy may have all held together, but it did not have to be swallowed whole; as Michael Sonenscher points out, even critics of Physiocracy often expressed their counterproposals in Physiocratic terms.[62] It had become commonplace, in any case, by the late eighteenth century, to insist on the fundamental centrality, and often uniqueness, of natural right in civil government. The abbé Raynal, in his *Histoire philosophique et politique des deux Indes*, celebrated Confucius (perhaps in an underhanded compliment to Quesnay, widely known as the "French Confucius") for having constructed a philosophy entirely on natural law, which, he added, "ought to be the ground-work of all the religions, the rule of society, and standard of all governments . . . the supreme law consist[s] in the harmony between nature and reason."[63] The baron d'Holbach similarly proclaimed, in the preface to his *Politique naturelle*, that "no people can be happy, if it is not governed according to the Laws of Nature, which always lead to virtue."[64] By reaffirming the natural sociability of mankind, and the clarity of natural laws, d'Holbach further promoted the idea of a mostly depoliticized society, in which the "social pact" is merely a tacit understanding, "renewed at every moment," between society and its members—nothing like the social contract of natural

---

62. Sonenscher, "Property, Community, and Citizenship," in *CHECPT*, 466–68.

63. Raynal, *Philosophical and Political History of the Settlements and Trade of the Europeans in the East and West Indies*, trans. J. O. Justamond (London: Strahan, 1783), 1:168. This passage is discussed in Alan Charles Kors, *D'Holbach's Coterie: An Enlightenment in Paris* (Princeton: Princeton University Press, 1976), 80.

64. *La politique naturelle, ou Discours sur les vrais principes du gouvernement* (London: n.p., 1773), 1:vii.

right theorists.[65] The revolutionary consequences of this concept of society can be seen in Thomas Paine's *Common Sense*, which opens a wide breach between society and government, all the better to damn the (royalist) latter.[66] In the French context, the political importance of this social theory would be felt during the constitutional crisis of 1793: If the Jacobins could so easily suspend their own Constitution, it was thanks in part to this alternative model of a society without formal government, regulated only by the laws of nature.[67]

With its central and constant emphasis on the natural right of property, the Physiocratic description of a perfect society would seem to move us away from the golden age myth, which was traditionally associated with the absence of private property, even of possessive pronouns. But it would be underestimating the great plasticity of this myth to presume it to be incompatible with the Physiocratic doctrine. In fact, thanks to Court de Gébelin's nine-volume "encyclopedia" of the ancient world, the *Monde primitif considéré dans son génie allégorique et dans les allégories auxquelles conduisit ce génie* . . . (1773–81), the golden age would be interpreted by most late-eighteenth-century Europeans as the time immediately following the advent of private property. This was not a coincidence: Court moved in devoutly Physiocratic circles.[68] More than anything, however, his work shows how Physiocracy found itself at the center of various interlocking, prerevolutionary discourses, which included Orientalism, ethnography, and Freemasonry.[69]

One could say that the overall effect of Court's work was to "historicize" the Physiocratic *ordre*—or rather, to "mythologize" it. In Court, Le Mercier's "natural and essential order" becomes an "ancient and eternal order," thrusting it into ancient history.[70] Proof that this *ordre* once really existed can be found in a variety of myths: The twelve labors of Hercules, for

---

65. *Politique naturelle*, 1.6; 13. See in general on this topic Keith Baker, "Enlightenment and the Institution of Society: Notes for a Conceptual History," in *Main Trends in Cultural History*, ed. Willem Melching and Wyger Velema (Amsterdam: Rodopi, 1994); Gordon, *Citizens without Sovereignty*; and the discussion of their work in the introduction.

66. See Thomas Paine, *Common Sense* (Mineola: Dover, 1997), 2–3.

67. See chapter 4.

68. See Anne-Marie Mercier-Faivre, *Un Supplément à l'"Encyclopédie": Le "Monde Primitif" d'Antoine Court de Gébelin* (Paris: Champion, 1999); see also the chapter dedicated to Court in Frank Manuel, *The Eighteenth Century Confronts the Gods* (Cambridge: Harvard University Press, 1959).

69. Venturi, *End of the Old Regime*, 424–25.

70. See, for instance, Court's directive to "bring [men] back, in a word, to the ancient and eternal Order, rather than offer them a new one," *Monde primitif*, 8:xviii. At times, Court also refers to this order as an *ordre naturel*; see, e.g., *Plan général et raisonné*, in *Monde primitif*, 1:80.

instance, clearly celebrate the inventor of agriculture.[71] More generally, the *ordre* was expressed in the myth of the golden age, when men obeyed nature and lived in perfect harmony:

> One sees in it [this myth] the skill with which the first legislators presented to Men the most essential lessons and most salutary doctrines . . . the origin of the Arts & human knowledge; the happiness enjoyed by peoples so long as they listened to the voice of the Order, and obeyed the Laws of Justice.[72]

Court's golden age, as with Voltaire's Gangarids, was not a brutish, simplistic society: It was both naturally just and conversant in the arts. As such, it was a plausible model for preindustrial France, whose legislators needed to "bring back this Order which the Ancients regarded so highly that they called it the age of Gold."[73]

Though adding little more than a mythological patina to this Physiocratic injunction, Court did introduce an interesting historical variation. The Lockean state of nature, which he equated with "American" savagery, came *later* for Court, once the principles of the golden age had been forgotten:

> The state of savage and ignorant nations is not the natural state of man, but rather a disorderly state, the product of depravation, of invasion, of the abandonment of the order, and of cessation of society; it is a state of brigands or of wasps who despise all work. (8:xvi)

This distinction between an *état naturel*, the golden age of humanity, and an *état des nations sauvages* would reappear under the pen of Saint-Just ten years later (see chapter 4). For Court, however, like Le Mercier, the only way to restore this natural and essential order was through monarchy: He ends a lengthy address to his reader (in volume eight) with a celebration of Louis XVI.[74] Given the Physiocratic terms of this *éloge*, however, Court's

---

71. Court's interpretation of the myth of Hercules can be found in book II; Vico, whom Court quotes on numerous occasions, had in fact already interpreted Hercules in this manner (without of course any Physiocratic intentions); see *New Science*, trans. David Marsh (London: Penguin, 1991), §371.

72. *Plan général et raisonné*, in *Monde primitif*, 1:68. See also *Allégories Orientales*, 1:85.

73. *Monde primitif*, 8:lxvii. See also the conclusion to the above quote, *Allégories Orientales*, 1:85.

74. "May the magnanimous empire of the Lilies [i.e., the Bourbon monarchy] to which this high destiny was reserved, be that happy nation" who would restore the Order (*Monde primitif*,

wish addressed itself to the Louis XVI of Turgot's ministry, who had claimed to "to reign only by justice and laws" and asserted his adherence to the "rights of humanity."[75] The *ordre* did not owe its existence to any king, even to this fresh-faced Bourbon, on whom so many hopes were riding.[76]

The Politics of *Sensibilité*: Sylvain Maréchal, Natural Republican

Although most admirers of the natural social order favored some version of monarchy, there were nonetheless other voices that condemned the institution of royalty altogether, both in the name of nature and of the myth of the golden age. Perhaps the most eloquent and intriguing natural republican of the prerevolutionary decades was Sylvain Maréchal. Not only would Maréchal go on to play a rich and eventful role during the Revolution, but he would also demonstrate how the belief in a society governed solely by natural right was wholly assimilated into the discourse of *sensibilité*.

Maréchal was born in the heart of Paris, but made his reputation as a pastoral poet.[77] He adopted his pen name from his first publication, *Bergeries* (1770), an imitation of Salomon Gessner's idylls. His pastoral tone and subjects, however, masked a more serious and seditious agenda, one for which he would lose his modest job at the Bibliothèque Mazarine (in 1784, after the publication of his *Lettre échappée au deluge*). While it was his "impious" views that got him into trouble with religious authorities, he was no less radical in his political opinions: "Kings, you must account to the meekest of humans," he exclaimed.[78]

8:LXVII). Court concludes his invocation to the reader by quoting (in its quasi entirety) Virgil's fourth *Eclogue* (8:lxix).

75. For a discussion of these statements, made during his 1776 *lit de justice*, see Rothschild, *Economic Sentiments*, 22–23.

76. Mme Campan, Marie-Antoinette's handmaiden, recorded how a sense of excitement and expectancy ran throughout the entire kingdom at the time of Louis XVI's coronation: "Never did a reign begin with such an outpouring of love and unanimous support," *Mémoires de Madame Campan, première femme de chambre de Marie-Antoinette* (Paris: Mercure, 1988), 83. The inscription on the pedestal of a statue of Justice at Louis's coronation read *les beaux jours*; see Simon Schama, *Citizens* (New York: Vintage, 1990), who also corroborates Mme Campan's entry: "[Louis XVI] began, in 1774, with the highest expectations, echoed throughout France, that the future would be blessed with a renewal of the Golden Age" (51).

77. In addition to Maurice Dommanget's *Sylvain Maréchal, l'égalitaire* (Paris: Spartacus, 1950), see notably Sanja Perovic, "Untamable Time: A Literary and Historical Panorama of the French Revolutionary Calendar (1792–1805)" (PhD diss., Stanford University, 2004).

78. *Dieu et les prêtres: fragments d'un poème moral sur Dieu* (1781; Paris: Patris, an II [1793]), XXXVI (hereafter referred to by its better-known subtitle).

Maréchal's early republican views tend to be overshadowed by his later involvement in the *Conspiration des égaux*.[79] This political insurrection is commonly identified as the first communist uprising (with the problematic consequence for scholars that many of Maréchal's works today can be found only in Moscow). Though led by Gracchus Babeuf, Maréchal was the ideological mastermind of this group, penning the *Manifeste des égaux* that announced its political agenda.[80] Many of the key notions and expressions found in this work (in particular, that of a "community of goods," and the "table of nature," to which all humans were summoned) can be traced back to Morelly's 1755 *Code de la nature*.[81] Since these same expressions were already found in Maréchal's prerevolutionary work (notably the 1784 *Apologues modernes à l'usage du Dauphin*), his political views are often assumed to be derivative of Morelly's "utopian" plans for an ideal state, *la Basiliade*.[82]

As in Diderot's case, however, viewing Maréchal through a utopian lens distorts the anthropological realism and political traditions that inform his thought. It was Tahiti that made the golden age appear true, not Ovid or Morelly: "*O! vous, qui de nos jours réalisez encor / Le fabuleux récit de*

---

79. Most of the documentary evidence concerning this conspiracy was published by Philippe Buonarotti in his *Conspiration pour l'égalité, dite de Babeuf, suivie du procès auquel elle donna lieu, et des pièces justicatives, etc., etc.* (Brussels: Libraire Romantique, 1828). On this conspiracy, see in particular Dommanget, *Sylvain Maréchal*; K. D. Tonnesson, "The Babouvists: From Utopian to Practical Socialism," *Past and Present* 22 (1962): 60–76; R. B. Rose, *Gracchus Babeuf: The First Revolutionary Communist* (Stanford: Stanford University Press, 1978); Albert Soboul, "Utopie et Révolution française," in *Histoire générale du socialisme*, ed. Jacques Droz (Paris: PUF, 1979); and James H. Billington, *Fire in the Minds of Men: Origins of the Revolutionary Tradition* (New York: Basic Books, 1980).

80. This text can be found in Buonarotti, *Conspiration pour l'égalité*, vol. 2. Dommanget convincingly argues that Maréchal was the "missing" leader at the subsequent trial, where Babeuf was sentenced to death.

81. On Morelly, see notably Nicolas Wagner, *Morelly, le méconnu des lumières* (Paris: Klincksieck, 1978); Venturi, *Utopia and Reform*, 95–100; and Sonenscher, "Property, Community, and Citizenship." On the long-standing attribution of this text to Diderot, see Pascale Pellerin, "Le *Code de la nature* ou l'histoire d'un procès intenté à Diderot," *SVEC* 1 (2003): 105–17.

82. In Morelly's case, the adjective "utopian" can serve as a generic designation; as in More's *Utopia*, his *Code de la nature* is a prescriptive description of a perfect society. It would nonetheless be worth further exploring the relations between Morelly and the Physiocrats, who in many respects were "mirror-images" (to borrow Sonenscher's expression; "Property, Community, and Citizenship," 468) of each other. Although Morelly wished to abolish private property, he, too, claimed that all social problems derived from our neglect of natural law: "Since I claim that the vulgar morality was founded on the ruins of the laws of Nature, the former must be entirely overthrown to re-establish the latter," *Code de la nature, ou Le véritable esprit de ses loix, de tout tems négligé ou méconnu* (Par-tout: Chez le vrai sage, 1755), 41. He also believed that only a sublime and heroic "Legislator" could achieve this regeneration. Sonenscher has drawn attention to the republican features of Morelly's Basiliade (which he himself calls a "République").

l'antique âge d'or, / Peuples d'Otaiti, fortunés insulaires!"[83] Maréchal may
have accepted Morelly's argument that private property was the source of all
ills, but that was a commonly voiced opinion in eighteenth-century France
(and of course in most pastoral literature). As the subject of an absolute
monarchy, Maréchal's views on property were no more utopian than his
republican dreams.

But did these dreams amount to republican*ism*? Maréchal was not content, in fact, with simply denouncing monarchy; he developed through his
works a distinct republican theory. And this theory ended up owing more to
Fénelon's *Télémaque* than to Machiavelli's *Discourses*. In a text modeled on
Montesquieu's *Temple de Gnide*, Maréchal announced the underlying equation on which natural republicanism depended: "Le Plaisir, dans ce Temple, /
Est devenu une Vertu; et / La Vertu un plaisir."[84] It was this naturalness
of virtue that made religion unnecessary, even harmful, in Maréchal's eyes:
"We already have virtue, why go in search of Gods?"[85] In the spirit of Bayle,
Maréchal defended the "true atheist," as "a sensible wise man. The love of
virtue makes everything possible, for him alone" (*Fragments d'un poème
moral*, XIX; 21).

Natural virtue not only removed the need for God and religion; it also
constituted the political bond in a perfect society: "Sans doute, il fut un
temps, appelé l'âge d'or / Où l'homme pour son Dieu n'avait que la Nature, / Et coulait une vie aussi douce que pure . . . / *Pour le sage éclairé,
ce temps existe encore*."[86] While the wise man could still relive this blessed
time, it was not solely reserved for a people of philosophers or gods. In a
collection of tales imitating Gessner's *Fables*, but revealingly entitled *L'Âge
d'or*, Maréchal described how a simple agrarian society could recreate it.
One of the stories, the *Tableau d'une matinée champêtre* ("Pastoral Morning Scene"), depicts this pastoral people whose sole occupation is "herding

---

83. "Oh you who still today bring to life / The fabled story of the ancient golden age /
Peoples of Tahiti, happy islanders!" *Fragments d'un poème moral sur Dieu*, XVII (18). For
Morelly, the golden age was also the historical time when humans had lived according to the
dictates of natural law: "Almost all peoples had, and still have, a notion of a golden age, which
would really be the time when the perfect sociability, whose laws I have retraced, existed among
men. Perhaps this original innocence was spontaneously put into practice for many centuries,
and was thus liable to be corrupted," *Code de la nature*, 141.

84. "Pleasure, in this Temple, / Has become a Virtue; and / Virtue, a pleasure," *Le Temple
de l'Hymen*, qtd. in Dommanget, *Sylvain Maréchal*, 23.

85. *Fragments d'un poème moral*, XL.

86. "No doubt there was time, called the golden age / When man's only god was Nature, /
And he lived a life as sweet as it was pure . . . / For the enlightened sage, this time lives on,"
Fragments d'un poème moral, XV; 16.

sheep and agriculture"; as the Physiocrats (and Fénelon) would have wanted it, "they had outlawed commerce and the arts that distance one from pastoral morals."[87] Also in line with Physiocratic precepts, this people lived according to "a patriarchal code, dictated by nature, that maintained them in the most perfect harmony. . . . They lived without ambition and, accordingly, without crimes." Although this code (possibly a reference to Morelly) was centered around natural virtue, it was not the Physiocratic "natural and essential order" since Maréchal's "people, proud of their simplicity, thought that man could not obey another man besides his father without degrading himself." Like Fénelon's Boeticans, this community of shepherds and farmers lived in a depoliticized society characteristic of the natural republic. They even had their own republican institutions: There is a "little senate" of older women who determine, "through a plurality of votes" (60), whether young girls are ready for marriage (in *Le Banquet des Vierges*). And every year, a virtuous shepherd—the one "who had exhibited the greatest sensibility" (78)—is chosen as minister for the Temple of Love, where he exercises "a sort of judicial power [*magistrature*] over lovers" (79). As in the Roman Republic, he is judged at the end of this term: "The village . . . asked the Pontiff to justify his actions. . . . Following the general agreement, the Pontiff was either removed from office or had his term renewed" (80). Interspersed in his sentimental tales, Maréchal offered lessons in republican government.

Virtue, of course, was not only a keyword of republicanism. In eighteenth-century literature, it also figured centrally in the language of *sensibilité*, and much of Maréchal's writing was inscribed within this moral, if amorous, discourse.[88] *L'Âge d'or*, for instance, was dedicated

to young men whom the pleasures of the capital have not yet jaded, to women who managed to preserve that flower of sensibility which life in large towns so quickly withers. The mother can safely put this

---

87. *L'Âge d'or, recueil de contes pastoraux; par le Berger Sylvain* (Mitylene [Paris]: Guillot, 1782), 23.

88. On the languages of virtue, see especially Marisa Linton, *The Politics of Virtue in Enlightenment France* (New York: Palgrave, 2001). On the discourse of sensibility in France, see David Denby, *Sentimental Narrative and the Social Order in France, 1760–1820* (Cambridge: Cambridge University Press, 1994); Anne Vila, *Enlightenment and Pathology: Sensibility in the Literature and Medicine of Eighteenth-Century France* (Baltimore: Johns Hopkins University Press, 1998); William Reddy, *The Navigation of Feeling: A Framework for the History of Emotions* (Cambridge: Cambridge University Press, 2001); and Jessica Riskin, *Science in the Age of Sensibility* (Chicago: University of Chicago Press, 2002). For an English comparison, see John Mullan, *Sentiment and Sociability: The Language of Feeling in the Eighteenth Century* (New York: Oxford University Press, 1988).

collection in the hands of her children. The most chaste virgin can let her eyes rest on the scenes it contains.

The "chaste virgin" who read Maréchal's tales may have found a series of challenges to her chastity, but therein lay the ambiguity of *sensibilité*: It celebrated the emotions while implicitly expecting the sort of self-sacrifice found only in a Julie. Although other fictional characters, such as the abbé Prévost's Manon Lescaut, reminded readers that such virtuous behavior was not a necessary outcome, moral and political works usually patched over the fault lines that literature exposed in the sentimental theory of virtue. Unlike his fictional sibling, Rousseau's Emile learns that sentiment is the true source of conscience—only to be undone by passion in the more narrative sequel, *Emile et Sophie*.[89] *Sensibilité* and virtue had become nearly interchangeable by the late eighteenth century: As the *encyclopédiste* and pastor Jean-Edme Romilly wrote in the *Encyclopédie*, "Reader, whoever you may be, if you ever tasted the sweetness of virtue, withdraw within yourself, its definition is in your heart."[90]

The natural-republican and Physiocratic ideals of "natural virtue" undoubtedly owed their widespread acceptance to this unquestioned place of *sensibilité* as the physiological origin of moral sentiments. That said, it would probably be extravagant to suggest that the discourse of *sensibilité* inevitably led to the political conclusions of natural republicanism. As with virtue, *sensibilité* could be assimilated into a wide range of political languages, aristocratic and monarchic, just as well as republican.[91] In its literary development, there may even have been an elitist, aristocratic structure to *sensibilité*. Not everyone could be an *âme sensible*: There was a *noblesse du cœur* just as there was a *noblesse de cour*.[92] This exclusionary principle also gave the discourse of

---

89. See, for instance, *Emile*, 100, 390; and the discussion of Rousseau in chapter 1.

90. *Encyclopédie*, s.v. "Vertu," 17:176. See also Jaucourt's article on "Sensibilité": "Sensibility is what makes man virtuous" and is "the mother of humanity, of generosity," 15:52. On the relation between physiological and literary/moral significations of *sensibilité*, see in particular Vila, *Enlightenment and Pathology*. On the "revolutionary" consequences of this equation, see Carla Hesse, "La preuve par la lettre: pratiques juridiques au tribunal révolutionnaire de Paris (1793–1794)," *Annales HSS* 3 (1996): 629–42.

91. See Chris Jones, *Radical Sensibility: Literature and Ideas in the 1790s* (London: Routledge, 1993); Denby, *Sentimental Narrative*; and Linton, *Politics of Virtue*.

92. Marivaux defines this *noblesse de cœur* in a passage of *La Vie de Marianne* (Paris: Garnier, 1966), which emphasizes its elitist qualities as well as its relation to *sensibilité*: "These instances of goodness are invaluable and, of all the obligations a great and noble soul can confer upon us, this secret politeness of sentiment, these tender regards, are the most moving. I call them secret because the heart that bestows them, does not put them to the score of the other's gratitude. It thinks they are only perceptible to itself. It conceals them from you, and, as it were, buries the whole merit of them in oblivion. This is a height of goodness, which is quite angelic. For my part I presently saw into her soul, for those persons who have a little of this nobleness of heart themselves are extremely quick-sighted in observing it and easily take notice of every instance of

sensibilité a violent subtext, which occasionally burst to the surface, notably on the last page of Rousseau's *Confessions*. Even Maréchal's pastoral universe could be the site of fierce retribution when its inhabitants violated the code of nature. One of the *Apologues* describes how all the monarchs ("tyrants") in the world were rounded up and left on a desert island, where they proceeded to kill each other.[93]

Within the narrower context of republicanism, however, *sensibilité* may well have favored a natural-republican discourse over its classical cousin. As Chris Jones remarks, "The ideas of sensibility were not radical in themselves, but they were capable of being applied in a radical way" (*Radical Sensibility*, 59). Although, as we saw with Mably, Rousseau, and Saige, classical republicanism was not itself incompatible with natural right, both *sensibilité* and natural republicanism elevated the laws of nature to a similar transcendental position. Ideally, the *âme sensible* would act virtuously and avoid immoral or illegal conduct even in the absence of threatening laws, as in the natural-republican and Physiocratic paradigms. Romilly had suggested as much in his *Encyclopédie* article: "A moral people is more likely to subsist without laws than a people without morals ever could, even with the most admirable ones. Virtue can replace anything, but is itself irreplaceable" (17:178). While such definitions would not necessarily lead good *âmes sensibles* to throw their law books into the fire, one can see how the sudden disappearance of a recognized legal framework—for example, France after August 1792—would not seem as alarming within this context. And there is no doubt that the language and pathos of *sensibilité* remained hugely prevalent during the period of Jacobin ascendancy.[94]

In Maréchal's case, the co-presence of these two discourses does seem to have radicalized his republican politics. More generally, Maréchal's work is a testimony to how natural republicanism extended, over the course of the

---

it," *The Virtuous Orphan, or The Life of Marianne, Countess of *****,* trans. Mary Mitchell Collyer (Carbondale: Southern Illinois University Press, 1965), 177; for the French, 154–55. On this novel and the "class-specific" qualities of *sensibilité*, see Vila, *Enlightenment and Pathology*, 127–40.

93. See *Apologues modernes*, XXVIII, "Vision de l'isle désert," 30–31. Maréchal would bring this idea to the stage at the height of the Terror, with his successful 1793 *Le Jugement dernier des rois*. On this play, see Jean-Marie Apostolidès, "La guillotine littéraire," *French Review* 62 (1989): 985–96.

94. Arendt, in *On Revolution*, noted how the revolutionaries' "passion for compassion" possessed "a greater capacity for cruelty than cruelty itself" (79, and 65–80). See also Denby, *Sentimental Narrative*, 139–65; and David Andress, "Popular Identification with the Convention in the Civil War Summer of 1793" (paper presented at the Society for the Study of French History Twentieth Annual Conference, University of Sussex, Brighton, UK, July 3, 2006).

eighteenth century, from works of the imagination into generically political texts. Indeed, it was not only in Maréchal's pastoral tales that naturally
republican societies can be found; in the last years of the old regime, he also
published political pamphlets that directly challenged the monarchy in the
name of natural equality and liberty:

> We would remind you that we were once all equal; that still in the
> time of Homer, Achilles cooked, and princesses, daughters of kings,
> did the laundry. Those days were called the *golden age* or the *heroic
> age.* . . . Our intention is to reestablish society forever on its ancient
> foundation, the primitive state; that is, on the most perfect and legiti-
> mate equality.[95]

As in his pastoral tales, the golden age is here marshaled to justify a
"primitive state" without rulers, or at least in which kings and princesses had
no political rights. The point of comparison is clearly France, and the ad-
dressee of this speech is the royal dauphin. This new Telemachus now learns
of a world in which kings are no different than shepherds; instead of Salente,
he is only shown la Bétique. At the time of his writing, Maréchal was still
aware that this republican ideal seemed more suited to novels: "All of this is
but a story [*conte*] at the time that I write it." But it was no longer restricted
to this imaginary world: "But I say, in truth, it will some day become history
[*une histoire*]" (35). The tale of natural republicanism was now a feasible political narrative; the literary story was poised to make history (the two meanings of *histoire*). This was the "story" that Maréchal attempted to impose in
his 1791 address to the National Assembly, *Dame Nature*:

> There is much talk about the golden age in the speeches addressed
> to you: but those who speak of it, and yourselves, do you remember
> exactly what the golden age was? It was a time when there were on
> earth no masters, no servants, no priests, no soldiers, no kings, no
> peoples, no poor, no rich; men were but naturally men. Is that indeed

---

95. *Apologues modernes à l'usage du Dauphin: premières leçons du fils aîné d'un roi* (Brussels,
1788), XXXI; 34 (emphasis in original). This passage seems directly inspired by Charles Rollin's
description of ancient Greek customs; see *De la manière d'enseigner et d'étudier les belles-lettres*
(Lyon: Rusand, 1819), 1:467–68. This passage is cited, without reference to Maréchal, in Bouineau, *Toges du pouvoir*, 307n6. Rollin goes on to cite Anne Dacier's preface to her translation of
Homer, where she describes the Greek custom of serving oneself at table "a precious remnant of
the golden age" (468).

the point toward which you wish to lead your representatives? If so, you are leading them astray.[96]

The Coming of the French Republic

By the end of the eighteenth century, an informed reader might thus have been well inclined to accept the golden age myth as a historical reality, and no longer even as a myth. The world of the golden age had opened up beyond the savage woods of Rousseau's *siècle d'or*: Orientalism, Physiocracy, Freemasonry, the discovery of the polite inhabitants of Tahiti, and the discourse of *sensibilité* had all contributed to civilize the state of nature. One need not wish to "walk around on all fours" to fantasize about regenerating humanity. The promise of sexual freedom, in a country that forbade divorce, certainly contributed to the appeal of this natural state, yet it was most likely the all-pervasive eighteenth-century cult vowed to nature that made it possible to imagine a state based entirely on nature's law.[97] The cultural changes that enabled this naturalistic imagination to permeate political thought were also greatly assisted by the revolution in the eighteenth-century perception of the past. Buffon had extended natural and human history by tens of thousands of years; his friend and colleague Bailly had written a prehistory for the great Oriental civilizations.[98] The six thousand years of Vatican-certified history had been blown apart, revealing strange chronological cavities into which the golden age could conceivably fit. Bailly surmised as much: "The golden age, that seductive myth, is thus but the memory of an abandoned, yet still dear, fatherland."[99]

It would be a mistake, however, to assume that the golden age myths of Rousseau, Voltaire, Diderot, Court de Gébelin, Bailly, or others were identical.[100] This mythical designation could denote considerably different

96. Maréchal, *Dame Nature à la barre de l'Assemblée nationale* (Paris: Chez les Marchands de Nouveautés, 1791), 3–4.

97. See Jean Ehrard, *L'idée de la nature en France dans la première moitié du XVIIIᵉ siècle* (Paris: S.E.V.P.E.N., 1963); see also Frank and Fritzie P. Manuel, *Utopian Thought in the Western World* (Cambridge: Harvard University Press, 1979), 535–77.

98. For Buffon, see his *Des époques de la nature* (Paris: Imprimerie Royale, 1778). For Bailly, see the following note. See also Hannah Arendt, *Between Past and Future* (London: Faber and Faber, 1961); and Anthony Kemp, *The Estrangement of the Past: A Study in the Origins of Modern Historical Consciousness* (New York: Oxford University Press, 1991).

99. *Lettres sur l'origine des sciences*, 103; see also 95.

100. It is this assumption that mires so many political studies of the golden age myth, such as André Delaporte's *L'idée d'égalité en France au XVIIIᵉ siècle* (Paris: PUF, 1987), and Raoul Girardet's *Mythes et mythologies politiques* (Paris: Seuil, 1986).

entities, from a sophisticated society resembling Plato's Atlantis to the Arcadian simplicity of Fénelon's Boetica. The golden age might be antithetical to worldly possessions or owe its existence to the advent of private property. It was a perfect, natural republic for some, and a perfect, natural monarchy for others. There was nothing new to this variability: Classical Rome had seen both Ovidian and Virgilian versions of the same myth; and Plato's description of the golden age (in *The Statesman*) is much closer to his own ideal republic than to the society of Hesiod's golden men. "Roughly speaking," Harry Levin once observed, "the golden age is all that the contemporary age is not."[101]

Despite these significantly divergent interpretations, this myth had nonetheless acquired a number of widely shared attributes by the end of the eighteenth century. The most important of these, as we just saw, was its identification as a possible historical period, still present in certain geographical areas. In this respect, the myth could not be dismissed outright as utopian or fanciful. Moreover, independent of its particular content, the golden age was invariably defined in terms of naturalness: Its government, laws, institutions, and morals were not the creation of a sublime legislator or a social contract, but the pure products of nature. The golden age, in other words, could difficultly accommodate a human constitution. If not always glossed in republican terms, it was wholly incompatible with juristic theories of absolute sovereignty, as best summarized, near the end of his reign, by Louis XVI's unfortunate *mot*: "It is legal because I want it to be [*c'est légal parce que je le veux*]."

Perhaps the strongest indication that the golden age was viewed as both a historical reality and a future possibility in the late eighteenth century was its repeated use as a representation of the momentous events of 1789.[102] Even before the Estates General assembled, the *cahiers de doléance* regularly referred to Louis XVI as "the new Augustus" who would "renew the Age of Gold."[103] The marquise de la Tour de Pin, daughter-in-law of the king's war

101. *Myth of the Golden Age*, 11.
102. On representations of the French Revolution, see notably Jean Starobinski, "Sur quelques symboles de la Révolution française," *NRF* 188, no. 16 (1968): 41–67; E. H. Gombrich, "The Dream of Reason: Symbolism in the French Revolution," *British Journal for Eighteenth-Century Studies* 2, no. 3 (1979): 188–204; Ronald Paulson, *Representations of Revolution (1789–1820)* (New Haven: Yale University Press, 1983); Lynn Hunt, *Politics, Culture, Class in the French Revolution* (Berkeley: University of California Press, 1984); Sandy Petrey, ed., *The French Revolution 1789–1989: Two Hundred Years of Rethinking* (Lubbock: Texas Tech University Press, 1989); James Heffernan, ed., *Representing the French Revolution* (Hanover, NH: University Press of New England, 1992).
103. Qtd. in Schama, *Citizens*, 345.

secretary, recalled how in the first half of 1789, "serious people [were say-
ing] that France . . . would be regenerated. . . . That explains why so many
honest and wholesome people, amongst whom the king, one of the first to
share their illusions, hoped at this time, that we were entering the golden
age."[104] When the Estates finally did meet, this mythical representation was
immediately adopted by reformist parties: Mirabeau chose a line echoing
Virgil's fourth *Eclogue*—"*Novus Rerum Nascitur Ordo*" (a new universal
order is born)—as the banner for his *Journal of the Estates-General*; Masonic
diplomas featured a similar phrase, "*Aurea Nunc Redeum Saecula*" (indeed,
the Golden Age returns), across the top.[105] This mythical representation was
even given "scientific" validity by Jean Delormel, who suggested that, due
to the earth's rotation on its axis, "perpetual spring" was now at hand.[106]
The myth was trotted out so routinely that it became a point of mockery:
A counterrevolutionary author in England, for example, published a spoof
of these revolutionary effusions, entitled *The Golden Age* (1794). Written
under the name of Erasmus Darwin (an admirer of the Revolution and
grandfather of Charles), its subject matter—"the renovation of the world
under the benign influence of French Freedom" (5)—was deemed so real-
istic that generations of librarians have catalogued it among Darwin's actual
works.[107]

The king seemed initially to profit from these mythical connotations,
as he was cast in the ready-made role of an Augustan savior. This Virgilian
identification is evident, for instance, in Dubois's 1790 print showing a bust
of the king, with the words "*L'Epoque de l'Âge d'Or*" engraved beneath it.[108]
But here and elsewhere, Louis XVI could not escape being celebrated as the
"*restorer* of French liberty" (the title bestowed upon him by the National
Assembly on August 4, 1789); his Augustan stature derived only from this

104. *Journal d'une femme de cinquante ans, 1778–1815*; qtd. in Paul Bénichou, *Le sacre de
l'écrivain, 1750–1830* (Paris: Corti, 1973), 58. On prerevolutionary millenarian currents, see
Clarke Garrett, *Respectable Folly: Millenarians and the French Revolution in France and England*
(Baltimore: Johns Hopkins Press, 1975).

105. For Mirabeau, see Schama, *Citizens*, 353. For an example of one such diploma, see the
Encyclopédie de la Franc-Maçonnerie, 726. The Latin is a quote from Virgil's fourth *Eclogue*.

106. See *La grande période ou le retour de l'âge d'or* (Paris: Blanchon, 1790). On Delormel,
see Jean Starobinski, "L'inclinaison de l'axe du globe," in Rousseau, *Essai sur l'origine des langues*, 165–89; and René Alleau, "Epistémologie du mythique et du symbolique dans les discours
politiques de la Terreur," *Mythe et Révolutions*, ed. Yves Chalas (Grenoble: PUG, 1990).

107. See Donald Reiman's introduction to Darwin, *The Golden Age: The Temple of Nature,
or the Origin of Society* (New York: Garland, 1978), xii–ix. For a sampling of its verse: "Behold,
behold, the Golden Age appears! / Skip, skip, ye Mountains! Forests, lend your Ears! / See red-
capt Liberty from heaven descend . . ."

108. A copy of this print is visible at the Musée Carnavalet in Paris.

bestowal of original, natural liberty onto his subjects.[109] The golden age that the French Revolution was celebrated for achieving was a "natural order" akin to that of the Physiocrats, an order in which the powers of the king were significantly curtailed.

Extracted from the specific discourses in which they are embedded, however, cultural representations can tell us only so much about political intent. In the case of the golden age myth, it had to compete with various other representations of the Revolution, some of which appeared only in counterrevolutionary contexts (such as the apocalypse), but others which were used interchangeably with the golden age (the "solar" representation, for instance). How much can one really deduce from a representation that was not seen as unique and essential? Furthermore, since the golden age myth itself knew a number of variants, each of which expressed different political ideals, there is often no way to determine to which variant a given representation alludes. Complicating matters even further, representations can have a figurative as well as literal sense. The golden age myth in particular could simply convey a sense of enthusiasm, or "possibilism" about the future.[110]

While the preponderant presence of this myth in representations of the French Revolution strongly suggests, then, that the late Enlightenment discourses of Physiocracy, Orientalism, ethnography, and *sensibilité* will have been "activated" and brought to bear on current events, an analysis of the precise political thought of the revolutionary groups is still required to assess their relevance and effect. This is the objective of the following chapters: to identify if, how, and why natural republicanism became a revolutionary discourse. The nature of the causal relationship at work here should not be misunderstood: I do not suggest that the latent republicanism found in the discourses studied above was in any way responsible for the "republican turn" of the French Revolution. Rather, I argue that once republicanism became an imaginable and acceptable political possibility for France, these discourses, already prominent in late Enlightenment political culture, offered ready-made models, arguments, and justifications for republican government in a

---

109. David Bell similarly emphasized how in eighteenth-century France, "new constructions . . . tend to be presented as acts of reconstruction, recovery, and regeneration," *The Cult of the Nation in France: Inventing Nationalism, 1680–1800* (Cambridge: Harvard University Press, 2001), 5. On the revolution as restoration and the Virgilian golden age myth, see Arendt, *On Revolution*; and Paulson, *Representations of Revolution*, 49–50.

110. "Possibilism" is the neologism that Robert Darnton coined to describe the boundless optimism of the French revolutionaries; see *The Kiss of Lamourette: Reflections in Cultural History* (New York: Norton, 1990), 17.

nation without a vibrant tradition of republicanism. More specifically, I submit that that natural republicanism became the dominant political language
of the Jacobins from August 1792 until 9 Thermidor Year II. It is only this
contingent fact, however, that in hindsight makes these prerevolutionary
discourses its genealogical precursors.[111]

Proof that these discourses may be described only retrospectively (as
opposed to teleologically) as the intellectual precursors of Jacobinism can
be found in the first forms of revolutionary republicanism, which owed
much more to the classical-republican tradition than to any French models.[112] Rachel Hammersley has recently detailed how Cordeliers and (future)
Girondin authors borrowed heavily from English republican theorist in
their formulation of a French variety.[113] There were, admittedly, natural-
republican traits to these French "adaptations": François Robert, for instance, in *Le républicanisme adapté à la France*, argues that republicanism
is the only natural form of government and that "every institution except
for republicanism is a crime of *lèze-nation*."[114] But his proposal for republican government does not assume that its laws will merely replicate those
of nature: It is a system of political representation that, thanks to print-
ing and an improved postal service, could base law on the general will
of the nation (89–96). The only lasting trace of natural right in Robert's
republicanism can be found in his violent hostility to any potential adversaries: "If anyone dares to condemn my system," he warns, "I could only
consider that person to be a enemy of humanity and of liberty" (103);
those who oppose the republic, he repeats in conclusion, are "enemies . . .
of justice and of humanity." This jusnaturalist condemnation of the *hostis
humani generis* would soon become a hallmark of Terrorist discourse; but

---

111. This argument mirrors the one made by James Swenson who, in *On Jean-Jacques Rousseau*, emphasizes the "invention" of Rousseau as a revolutionary author by the revolutionaries
themselves.

112. On early revolutionary republicanism, see Gary Kates, *The "Cercle Social," the Girondins,
and the French Revolution* (Princeton: Princeton University Press, 1985); Michel Vovelle, ed., *Révolution et république: l'excéption française* (Paris: Kimé, 1994); Patrice Gueniffey, "Cordeliers et
girondins: la préhistoire de la république?" in *Siècle de l'avènement républicain*, ed. François Furet
and Mona Ozouf (Paris: Gallimard, 1993); Raymonde Monnier, "Républicanisme et révolution
française," *French Historical Studies* 26, no. 1 (2003): 87–118, and *Républicanisme, patriotisme
et Révolution française* (Paris: L'Harmattan, 2005); Rachel Hammersley, "English Republicanism
in Revolutionary France: The Case of the Cordelier Club," *Journal of British Studies* 43 (2004):
464–81; Michael Sonenscher, *Work and Wages: Natural Law, Politics, and the Eighteenth-Century
French Trades* (Cambridge: Cambridge University Press, 1989).

113. See in particular *French Revolutionaries and English Republicans: The Cordeliers Club,
1790–1794* (Rochester, NY: Boydell Press, 2005).

114. In *Aux origines de la République, 1789–1792* (Paris: EDHIS, 1991), 2:1.

this discourse was no other than the natural-republican language of the Jacobins.[115]

It would indeed only be during the Terror that republican theories would be translated into actual institutions. By that time, however, the Girondins and Cordeliers had effectively been marginalized by the Jacobin Mountain, at least in the Convention. The first revolutionary advocates and theoreticians of republicanism thus did not get a chance to implement their ideas. This is not to say that this early republican moment had no effect on the course of the Revolution. As Keith Baker has shown, Marat's own terrorizing discourse was underpinned by a number of classical-republican themes, which "metastasized" over time.[116] It did not, of course, take a natural-right theory of hostility to justify state violence. In an infamous chapter of the *Discourses*, Machiavelli recommended killing off all the nobility before attempting to establish a republic (1.55).

It is somewhat ironic that it fell to the Jacobins to design the first French republic, as they had been among the last of the progressives to abandon constitutional monarchy. When Condorcet and Paine published *Le Républicain, ou Défenseur du gouvernement représentatif* (July 1791), Saint-Just was busy writing *L'Esprit de la Révolution et de la constitution*, in which he celebrated constitutional monarchy (and even the Salic law); the last issue of Robespierre's journal, *Le Défenseur de la constitution* (a reference to the 1791 monarchic Constitution), appeared after the August 10, 1792 insurrection.[117] Once they embraced republicanism, they never looked back, but their unusual political trajectory, as well the turbulent times during which they underwent their political conversion, did lead them to look beyond classical republicanism for the foundation of their ideas. As I will argue in chapter 4, the republican project that the Jacobins ultimately pursued owed more to Physiocracy and the language of *sensibilité* than to Rousseau or Paine. Similarly to Maréchal, they defended a republic without a constitution or social contract, legally grounded in natural right alone, as in the Age of Gold.

---

115. Robert himself would rally to Robespierre under the Convention ; see L. Antheunis, *Le conventionnel belge François Robert (1763–1826) et sa femme Louise de Keralio (1758–1882* [i.e., 1822]) (Wetteren: Bracke, 1955).

116. See Keith Baker, "Transformations of Classical Republicanism in Eighteenth-Century France," *Journal of Modern History* 73 (2001): 43–47.

117. See notably Pierre Nora, "Republic," in *A Critical Dictionary of the French Revolution*, ed. François Furet and Mona Ozouf, trans. Arthur Goldhammer (Cambridge: Belknap Press of Harvard University Press, 1989), 794. This last issue, however, contained a glowing account of the sack of the Tuileries, as well as a natural-republican interpretation of its portent.

The central and defining place of natural right in Jacobin republicanism, however, also brought the violent, jusnaturalist concept of hostility into the heart of the city, and the case made in the second half of this book is that Jacobin republicanism was inseparable from the Terror. The central question for the Terror, "How does a state justify the violent repression of its own citizens?", was intrinsically tied up in the revolutionaries' minds with the central question for the republic: "On what authority does the republic base its laws?" The answer to both of these questions, for the Jacobins, would be found in natural right. Their enshrinement of natural right as a transcendental political value took place during Louis XVI's trial, where it provided a much needed juridical loophole for judging the king. The following chapter describes how it was in the spirit of this trial that both the Jacobin republic and the Terror took shape.

PART II

THE REPUBLIC OF NATURE
(1792–94)

OFF WITH THEIR HEADS

Death and the Terror

IN ONE OF THE MORE BITTER ironies of history, Maximilien Robespierre, the politician most closely associated with the Terror, began his career as an outspoken opponent of the death penalty.[1] Were it not for his more notorious activities, this stance would not have been particularly surprising: The increasingly utilitarian considerations of justice in the eighteenth century, along with the general Enlightenment horror of "barbaric" executions à la Damiens, had led criminal justice reformers to demand the abolition of capital punishment.[2] At the time of the Revolution, these utilitarian and enlightened currents had become sufficiently mainstream to inform the penal code project presented to the Constituent Assembly by Lepeletier de Saint-Fargeau in 1791. Full of Beccarian insistences on the gradation and utility of punishments, his preliminary report also argued against the death penalty.[3] He was not to sway the Assembly: A majority of deputies rejected his arguments and voted to maintain it. But during the ensuing debate, Robespierre delivered a rousing speech in favor of abolition.[4]

---

1. For a discussion of this oft-noted (though only apparent) paradox, see Jacques Goulet, "Robespierre: la peine de mort et la Terreur," *AHRF* 244 (1981): 219–38, and, for part 2, *AHRF* 251 (1983): 38–64. Goulet does not address the place of natural right in Robespierre's theory of capital punishment.

2. Most notably Cesare Beccaria, in *De delitti e delle pene* (1764). On the state of judicial reform at the time of the French Revolution, see Barry Shapiro, "Introduction," in *Revolutionary Justice in Paris, 1789–90* (Cambridge: Cambridge University Press, 1993); and Jean-Marie Carbasse, *Histoire du droit pénal et de la justice criminelle* (Paris: PUF, 2000), 353–94. On Damiens's execution and its impact, see Dale Van Kley, *The Damiens Affair and the Unraveling of the Ancien Régime, 1750–70* (Princeton: Princeton University Press, 1984).

3. May 23, 1791; for full text of his report, see the *Archives parlementaires de 1787 à 1860*, ed. M. J. Mavidal and M. E. Laurent (Paris: Librairie administrative de P. Dupont, 1862–), 26:319–45 (hereafter cited as *AP*). On the 1791 penal code and Lepeletier's project, see Pierre Lascoumes, Pierrette Poncela, and Pierre Lenoël, *Au nom de l'ordre: Une histoire politique du code pénal* (Paris: Hachette, 1989), 65–151. On "abolitionism" during the Revolution, see Michel Pertué, "La Révolution française et l'abolition de la peine de mort," *AHRF* 251 (1983): 14–37.

4. See his May 30, 1791, speech to the Constituent Assembly, in *Œuvres de Maximilien Robespierre*, ed. Société des études robespierristes (1913; Ivry: Phénix éditions, 2000), 7:432–37 (hereafter cited as *Rob.*).

Delegates on the right heaped scorn on him: "Mr. Robespierre should be asked to go deliver his speech in the forest of Bondy," the abbé Maury interrupted.[5] There was some unintentional truth to Maury's derision: Capital punishment, Robespierre affirmed, could exist only in the state of nature, when men still lived in Rousseau's forests. Only in such a state, and if one's life were threatened, "the law of natural justice justifies and approves my action: but in society, when the force of all is gathered against one individual, where is the principle of justice that authorizes us to put him to death?"[6] No civil laws could authorize the death penalty; natural right approved it only in exceptional circumstances.

How would Robespierre go from being a leading humanitarian voice in the Constituent Assembly to become an arch-theorist of the Terror? Would he change his mind about the lawfulness of execution, or did his initial opinion contain a violent exception? Robespierre's trajectory may well be read as a synecdoche of the French Revolution. Was there something in Enlightenment thought that led the men of 1789 to adopt the measures of the Terror? Or were the latter imposed on them, either by "the Parisian street," the counterrevolutionary insurgency, paranoid bureaucratic practices, or some intrinsic (if illusive) logic of Revolution?

The genesis of the Terror is, and will no doubt long remain, an "enduring mystery."[7] So contested, in fact, are its origins that there is little agreement on what even constitutes "the Terror." When did it begin? What are its main characteristics? As a historical marker, it was imposed on the events of Year II by those who succeeded or (to borrow Sieyès's *mot*) survived it.[8]

---

5. *AP*, 26:622.

6. *Rob.*, 7:433. Lepeletier de Saint-Fargeau had argued on the contrary that society had the right to put individuals to death ("this right seems indisputable"), but he criticized this punishment in similar terms as Robespierre: "Society can only legitimately execute an individual if no other punishment can possibly repress his crime" (*AP*, 26:325). His final argument was purely utilitarian: "The death penalty . . . is a very ineffective punishment for crimes" (326).

7. Timothy Tackett, "Interpreting the Terror," *French Historical Studies* 24 (2001): 569. For some recent reviews of the historiographical approaches to this "mystery," see Suzanne Desan, "What's after Political Culture? Recent French Revolutionary Historiography," *French Historical Studies* 23 (2000): 163–96; Jeremy Popkin, "Not Over After All: The French Revolution's Third Century," *Journal of Modern History* 74 (2002): 801–21; Antoine de Baecque, "Apprivoiser une histoire déchaînée: Dix ans de travaux historiques sur la Terreur (1992–2002)," *Annales: Histoire, Sciences Sociales* 57, no. 4 (2002): 851–65; Rebecca L. Spang, "Paradigms and Paranoia: How Modern Is the French Revolution?" *American Historical Review* 108 (2003): 119–47; and Patrice Higonnet, "Terror, Trauma and the 'Young Marx' Explanation of Jacobin Politics," *Past and Present* 191 (2006): 121–64.

8. On the problem with dating the Terror, see Bronislaw Baczko, "The Terror before the Terror?" in *The Terror*, ed. Keith Baker, vol 4. of *The French Revolution and the Creation of Modern Political Culture* (Oxford: Pergamon Press, 1994), 19–38; hereafter referred to as *Ter-*

A number of historians have recently emphasized the emotional contents of this term, and there is no doubt that this period was emotionally super-charged.[9] The question is, however, how helpful is the word "terror" for unraveling the complex knot of fear, anxiety, but also intense excitement experienced by the revolutionaries, as well as by most of the French people, at this time?[10] The word "terror" may designate "a psychic state, more intense than fear, which affects anyone threatened by an extreme danger,"[11] but who exactly was terrorized during the Terror? The peasants who organized armed defenses during the *Grande Peur* of July 1789 may have acted out of terror, but the same cannot be said for the deputies who enacted the first Terrorist measures in March 1793. Though they often claimed to be facing an "extreme danger," they were hardly in a state "more intense than fear." Regardless of how the *conventionnels* felt, moreover, it is highly questionable whether emotions can translate into governmental actions without the mediating interference, at many levels, of political strategy, legal thought, and cultural or historical precedent.[12] The violence "on the ground" in the Vendée or during the so-called Federalist rebellion may at times have adopted a raw, almost instinctive form, yet it is far from clear that the same can be said about the decision making in Paris.

---

ror. On the role of the Thermidorians in defining the Terror, see Bronislaw Baczko, *Comment sortir de la Terreur: Thermidor et la Révolution* (Paris: Gallimard, 1989); and Mona Ozouf, "The Terror after the Terror: An Immediate History," in *Terror.*

9. See in particular Sophie Wahnich, *La liberté ou la mort: essai sur la Terreur et le terrorisme* (Paris: La Fabrique, 2003); and Higonnet, "Terror, Trauma and the 'Young Marx' Explanation of Jacobin Politics," who draws on William Reddy's *The Navigation of Feeling: A Framework for the History of Emotions* (Cambridge: Cambridge University Press, 2001), which also deals with the role of emotions during the French Revolution.

10. I return to this question in chapter 5.

11. Patrice Gueniffey, *La Politique de la Terreur: essai sur la violence révolutionnaire, 1789–94* (Paris: Fayard, 2000), 22. Buchez and Roux used a similar definition to defend their claim that Terrorist methods were justified by circumstances: "The word *terror* designates an ephemeral state; terror is an exceptional means, invoked in certain circumstances against a known danger, means which is then abandoned once the danger has passed," *Histoire parlementaire de la Révolution française* . . . , ed. P. J. B. Buchez and P. C. Roux (Paris: Paulin, 1834–38), 20:v (hereafter cited as *HP*). "Terror is thus sometimes obligatory," the authors conclude (vii). See also R. R. Palmer: "The Terror was born of fear, from the terror in which men already lived," in *Twelve Who Ruled: The Year of the Terror in the French Revolution* (1941; Princeton: Princeton University Press, 1989), 56; George Armstrong Kelly, "Conceptual Sources of the Terror," *Eighteenth-Century Studies* 14, no. 1 (1980): 18–36; Baczko, "Terror before the Terror," 31–32; Wahnich, *Liberté ou la mort*, 25; and Tackett: "[Terror] should also signify the almost panic fear, suspicion and uncertainty that was shared during this time by the revolutionaries themselves," in "La Révolution et la violence," in *La Révolution à l'œuvre*, ed. Jean-Clément Martin (Rennes: Presses universitaires de Rennes, 2005), 216.

12. See Reddy, *Navigation of Feeling*, chap. 6.

The revolutionaries were also far from agreeing on what "terror" meant. For Robespierre, it designated a kind of sublime justice, "prompt, severe, and inflexible," whereas for his friend and fellow Committee member Saint-Just, justice and terror were opposed.[13] By the time the Terror entered into its most radical phase (the so-called Great Terror of June–July 1794), the word had largely disappeared from revolutionary discourse: It does not appear once, for instance, in Couthon's presentation of the law of 22 prairial.[14] These discursive shifts merit attention and may assist us in determining the purpose of the Terror for the Jacobin leaders. But it would be illogical to assert that the law of prairial constituted a radical departure from earlier Terrorist institutions and decrees: The law was presented, after all, as a recapitulation of previous laws, stretching back to December 1792.[15]

As a period label, "the Terror" is a rather misleading term as well. The so-called Jacobin dictatorship was also a time of democratic expansion, civic enterprising, and egalitarianism, during which the foundations for future French institutions were laid.[16] It is precisely these reform efforts, however, that underscore by contrast the violent political repressions of the time. These repressions took many forms: Censorship, ostracization, surveillance, denunciation, and imprisonment were all prominent practices under the New Regime. But it is no doubt the ready recourse to political execution that stands out as the determining feature of the Terror. The other encroachments on individual rights are, if not excusable, then slightly more understandable in a context of civil and international war.

---

13. For Robespierre, see, for instance, the famous statement, "Terror is nothing but prompt, severe, and inflexible justice" (*Rob.*, 10:357); compare with Saint-Just's 8 ventôse an II (26/2/94) report, discussed in chapter 5.

14. See *Réimpression de l'ancien Moniteur, seule histoire authentique et inaltérée de la révolution française depuis la réunion des Etats-généraux jusqu'au consulat* (Paris : H. Plon, 1858–63), 20:694–99 (hereafter cited as *Moniteur*). On the substitution of "justice" for "terror" in the major speeches by members of the *Comité de salut public* of Year II, see Françoise Brunel, *Thermidor* (Brussels: Editions Complexe, 1989), 51; and chapter 5.

15. Article 6, listing all the categories of individuals to be considered "enemies of the people," begins with royalists ("those who sought the return of the monarchy"), whom a December 4, 1792, law had already declared punishable by death (*AP*, 54:351).

16. See, for instance, Marc Bouloiseau, *The Jacobin Republic, 1792–94*, trans. Jonathan Mandelbaum (Cambridge and Paris: Cambridge University Press/Maison des sciences de l'homme, 1983); Isser Woloch, *The New Regime: Transformations of the French Civic Order, 1789–1815* (New York: Norton, 1994); Patrice Higonnet, *Goodness Beyond Virtue: Jacobins During the French Revolution* (Cambridge: Harvard University Press, 1998); Colin Jones, *The Great Nation: France from Louis XV to Napoleon* (New York: Columbia University Press, 2003); and Jean-Pierre Gross, *Fair Shares for All: Jacobin Egalitarianism in Practice* (Cambridge: Cambridge University Press, 2003).

The parallel with the American Revolution—which historians of revolutionary France are fond of drawing, but which remains to be systematically explored—is here highly illuminating, less because of the well-known differences between the two than because of their many similarities. Not only were the American colonists also involved in a brutal military struggle (which, furthermore, took place entirely on their own soil),[17] but they, too, faced a "counterrevolutionary" force in their own midst—the loyalists or "Tories" who opposed independence and continued to serve George III. Though in the minority, loyalists were often found among the rich and powerful (a famous case being Benjamin Franklin's own son), and were deemed sufficiently threatening for Congress to pass a law, on October 6, 1775, recommending the imprisonment of "every person in their respective colonies, whose going at large may, in their opinion, endanger the safety of the colony, or the liberties of America."[18] For historians of the French Revolution, this decree will inevitably call to mind the laws against "suspects" that the National Convention was to pass in 1793. In both cases, suspects were indeed rounded up or subjected to house arrest, and many American loyalists, like the *émigrés* in France, had their property confiscated in violation of their most "natural" rights. But in the American case, this repression did not extend past the moment of danger, when most loyalists were freed and recovered their property. There was an infamous exception to this rule, the 1798 Alien and Sedition Acts, under which political critics of the government (in the hands of the Federalist Party's John Adams) could be and were fined and imprisoned.[19] But even in this clear instance of political repression, the American revolutionaries never adopted policies of political execution, as opposed to their French counterparts: Imprisonment during (and immediately after) the American Revolution was an end in itself, and not the means to a more violent end.[20] Enlightenment political ideals were twisted in many directions

17. For a detailed account of the war, see Don Higginbotham, *The War of American Independence: Military, Attitudes, Politics, and Practice, 1763–89* (New York: Macmillan, 1971).

18. *Journals of the Continental Congress, 1774–89*, ed. Worthington C. Ford et al. (Washington: U.S. Govt., 1904–37), 3:280; this bill is discussed in Harry M. Ward, *The War for Independence and the Transformation of American Society* (London: UCL Press, 1999), 53.

19. See, for instance, James Roger Sharp, *American Politics in the Early Republic: The New Nation in Crisis* (New Haven: Yale University Press, 1995), chap. 8.

20. As Higonnet points out, "in America not a single person . . . was executed for political crimes between 1776 and 1783," *Sister Republics: The Origins of French and American Republicanism* (Cambridge: Harvard University Press, 1988), 2. This parallel with the American Revolution, in my view, challenges Sophie Wahnich's claim that the law of suspects, "rather than worsen violent repression, suspended it. For to be a suspect is not to be accused, and if there is potentially a death sentence, it is differed, indefinitely on occasion" (*Liberté ou la mort*, 58). The Jacobins were most definitely not intent on rounding up suspects to protect them. When

during the Terror, but it is the well-worn path between the Conciergerie and the Place de la Révolution that commands the historian's attention.

What was it about the French experience that led to this prevalence of political executions? This question cuts to the heart of the Terror. Once again, the American comparison may be helpful, if only to cast doubt on some commonly voiced explanations, as many of these explanations rest on factors that were equally prominent during the War of Independence. An obsession with conspiracy plots is often cited as a motivating factor for the Terror, but "paranoid politics" were just as rampant in the American colonies as they were in revolutionary France, and the Continental Congress was not moved to kill those suspected of conspiring.[21] The doctrine of public safety, which pro-revolutionary nineteenth-century historians (following the Jacobins themselves) invoked to justify the Terror decrees, had likewise been a central tenet of the radical Whiggish theories that dominated American political discourse in the 1770s.[22] Finally, the emergence of virulent party politics in the United States (with the Federalist/Republican-Democrat clash) challenged the candid faith that the "general will" would always materialize from the conflict of opinions, causing a disappointment that translated into prophecies of imminent downfall and suspicions of treason on either side of the political aisle—as it did in France—but again, never led to political execution.[23]

Robespierre demanded that a more rigorous law of suspects be imposed, he made the intention behind his proposal clear: "We must not only *exterminate* all the rebels in the Vendée, but also all the rebels against humanity and against the people that are found in France" (speech at the Jacobin club, May 8, 1793; *Rob.*, 9:487, emphasis added). The verb "exterminate" came back repeatedly throughout this speech: "We must exterminate all these vile and base beings" (487); see also, "the Parisian patriots . . . will exterminate them all . . . yes, all the rebels at once" (489); "I have asked the people to make an effort to exterminate the aristocrats who exist everywhere" (490). This last measure, the Jacobin journal tells us, was vigorously applauded. That said, by underscoring this verb, I do not mean to endorse Reynald Sécher's thesis of a Vendéen "geno-cide" (see *Le génocide franco-français, la Vendée-Vengé* [Paris: PUF, 1986], and the discussion of the Vendéen below).

21. As Timothy Tackett acknowledges in "Conspiracy Obsession in a Time of Revolution: French Elites and the Origins of the Terror: 1789–92," *American Historical Review* 105 (2000): 691–713; see also Gordon Wood, *The Creation of the American Republic, 1776–87* (Chapel Hill: University of North Carolina Press, 1969), 40–43. See also, in the French context, Peter R. Campbell, Thomas E. Kaiser, and Marisa Linton, eds., *Conspiracy in the French Revolution* (Manchester: Manchester University Press, 2007).

22. Wood, *Creation of the American Republic*, 63–64.

23. See Bruce Ackerman, *The Failure of the Founding Fathers: Jefferson, Marshall, and the Rise of Presidential Democracy* (Cambridge: Belknap Press of Harvard University Press, 2005); see also Joseph Ellis, *Founding Brothers: The Revolutionary Generation* (New York: Vintage, 2002).

The similarities between these two Revolutions must of course be weighed against the numerous and important differences, and it is these differences (along with the specificities of the French context and chronology) that the present chapter will explore. The particular roles played (a) by the Parisian sections and the *sans-culottes*; (b) by revolutionary bureaucratic practices; and (c) by the counterrevolution in the genesis of the Terror will all be evaluated, but ultimately found wanting as sufficient causes for the Revolution's "death-drive" (no Freudian undertones intended). I argue that the sources for this drive lie instead in two principal differences between the American and French Revolutions: (1) the contemporaneous emergence of the French Republic and the trial of the king, the antirepublican figure par excellence; and (2) the radical vein of natural republicanism particular to French natural right theories (as analyzed in part 1). This historical context and political discourse combined to produce a network of repressive legal concepts, first among which lay the "enemy of humanity," or *hostis humani generis*—an enemy who could be met only with death.

Power to the People?
Popular Violence and State Manipulation

On the face of things, the source of revolutionary violence seems to reside in the crowds that filled the streets of Paris and the pages of French Revolution historiography. Mob lynchings, such as those of Foulon and Berthier de Sauvigny (the *intendant* of Paris) on July 22, 1789, accompanied the revolutionary process from the onset, and calls for increased bloodshed were common in the popular press. The "bloodthirstiness" of the *sans-culottes*, a favorite theme of historians from Burke and Carlyle to Schama, reached its apparent climax during the prison massacres of September 1792, only three months before the National Convention decreed the death sentence for political crimes.[24] A common narrative thus holds that the Convention bowed

---

24. The classic work on the prison massacres remains Pierre Caron, *Massacres de Septembre* (Paris: Maison du livre français, 1935); but see also the documents discussed by George Rudé, in *The Crowd in the French Revolution* (Oxford: Oxford University Press, 1967), that point to a greater involvement on the part of the city and ministerial authorities. The Convention voted on December 4, 1792, that advocating monarchy was henceforth a capital crime (*AP*, 54:351); however, this was largely a political move on the part of the Girondins, aimed at discrediting Philippe Égalité (who sat with the Jacobins); see David P. Jordan, *The King's Trial* (Berkeley: University of California Press, 1979), 75–76. On December 16, the Convention voted that those who sought to dismantle the Republic were punishable by death (*AP*, 55:79); this measure was proposed by Jacques-Alexis Thuriot, a *montagnard*. Both measures were clearly symbolic.

to the pressure of the popular sections, declared that "terror be made the order of the day," and launched a governmental version of the rough justice favored by the radical *peuple*.

This account of the Terror's origins does not necessarily connote a conservative perspective: It was long a staple of Marxist social history, which sought to provide a "bottom-up" interpretation of the Revolution.[25] In an age when revolutionary terrorism was considered a necessary evil, the popular classes were "heroically" made responsible for the Terrorist repressions; historiographically, however, this interpretation served only to displace the question, as it was now the origins of popular violence that demanded an explanation. Recent historians have recognized this necessity and turned to anthropology, religious studies, and psychoanalysis to ground their theories of popular violence.[26]

The interdisciplinary nature of these interpretations complexifies the task of evaluating them, yet one can question their premises on purely historical grounds. Regardless of how or why the Parisian populace manifested its political will or anger through bloody actions, it is not at all clear that the subsequent governmental Terrorist measures were a response or a continuation of popular violence. While the power and importance of the Parisian sections is undeniable (most evidently during the August 10 and May 31–June 2 insurrections), so too was the adroit manipulation of this power by political ringleaders. Such manipulation, furthermore, was patently on display at the two critical junctures in the "bottom-up" narrative of the Terror, in March and in September 1793.

It is to the March decree creating a revolutionary tribunal that historians point as the moment when the National Convention first caved in to popular pressure. For Sophie Wahnich, the most recent advocate of the

---

25. See Albert Soboul's discussion of "la Révolution française vue 'd'en bas,'" in *Mouvement populaire et gouvernement révolutionnaire en l'an II (1793–94)* (Paris: Flammarion, 1973), 12. Soboul is commenting on Georges Lefebvre's 1924 *Les paysans du Nord pendant la Révolution française*, which he describes as a pendulum swing away from the nineteenth-century ideological interpretations (emblematized by Alphonse Aulard's 1901 *Histoire politique*), or "l'histoire de la Révolution française . . . vue 'd'en haut'" (12). More recently, see Daniel Roche, "La violence vue d'en bas. Réflexions sur les moyens de la politique en période révolutionnaire," *Annales ESC* 1 (1989): 47–65.

26. For an anthropological interpretation, see, for instance, Colin Lucas, "Revolutionary Violence, the People and the Terror," in *Terror*, who draws on René Girard's theory of violence; see also Wahnich, *Liberté ou la mort*; for a psychoanalytic interpretation; Lynn Hunt, *The Family Romance of the French Revolution* (Berkeley: University of California Press, 1992); or, more recently, Higonnet, "Terror, Trauma and the 'Young Marx' Explanation of Jacobin Politics."

"bottom-up" theory, this act constituted an attempt to "put a damper on the legitimate violence of the people and give a public, institutional form to vengeance."[27] Voted amidst popular turmoil,[28] the institution of the tribunal was indeed described by Danton as a means to keep the madding crowd at bay:

> Since some in this Assembly have dared to recall those bloody days which make every good citizen shudder, I will say, for my part, that had a tribunal been in existence at that time, the people, on whom the blame for those days has so often and cruelly been placed, would not have bloodied them . . . let us be terrible instead of the people [*soyons terribles pour dispenser le peuple de l'être*].[29]

The specter of the prison massacres is here used to remarkable effect. As the demand for Terror cannot be denied, Danton argues, it is in the Convention's interest to take the lead in the exercise of Terror, so not to be overwhelmed by it. This argument appears indisputable (if historically inexact).[30] Yet never is it mentioned under what circumstances Danton delivered this forceful speech. After a drawn-out debate concerning the right to a jury, the deputies had just risen to leave the Convention for the night, thereby postponing (perhaps indefinitely) the decree on the tribunal. Danton, one of the tribunal's staunchest supporters, then ran to the podium and invoked the specter of the Septembriseurs less as an actual threat than as a scare tactic to cower the Plaine and Girondin deputies into remaining in session and approving it. The latter did not fall for his trick: The Girondins, who had the most to fear from a renewed popular insurrection (as they would discover on May 31), came out vehemently against the measure,

---

27. Wahnich, *Liberté ou la mort*, 63.

28. Riots broke out on February 25 over the high cost of food; on the night of March 9–10, an aborted insurrection briefly created confusion at the Convention.

29. *AP*, 60:62–63. In fact, his historical analogy was faulty, as there *had* been a tribunal in existence at the time of the September massacres. An August 17, 1792, decree created a "tribunal criminel" to judge the Swiss guards defending the Tuileries (*AP*, 48:298). It was precisely because the *sans-culottes* deemed this tribunal to be ineffective that the massacres occurred (as Wahnich herself points out in *Liberté ou la mort*, 40–41).

30. Furet and Richet similarly suggest that "Danton . . . wants to avoid the renewal of the September massacres," *La Révolution française* (Paris: Fayard 1973), 195. On the revolutionary tribunal, see in particular James Logan Godfrey, *Revolutionary Justice: A Study in the Organization and Procedures of the Paris Tribunal, 1793–95* (Chapel Hill: University of North Carolina Press, 1951); Lascoumes et al., *Au nom de l'ordre*, 156–58; and Carla Hesse, "La preuve par la lettre: pratiques juridiques au tribunal révolutionnaire de Paris (1793–1794)," *Annales HSS 3* (1996): 629–42.

branding it "disastrous . . . as it tramples on everything you inscribed in the Declaration of Rights and everything that until now appeared to constitute the unshakeable and untouchable basis of your civil code and criminal legislation."[31] They did not perceive the tribunal as a means for appeasing the *sans-culottes*, but rather (like many future historians) as the institutionalization of the September massacres themselves. Lanjuinais protested against the tribunal in the name of the "events upon which its origin is founded [the prison massacres], and of which it reminds us all."[32]

Rather than channel *popular* anger, moreover, the concept of the revolutionary tribunal is likely to have stemmed from a Jacobin grudge against Girondin ex-ministers. Though the inspiration for the tribunal nominally originated in the Parisian sections, James Godfrey, a preeminent historian of the tribunal, has convincingly argued that the Jacobins probably planted this request.[33] Godfrey calls attention to the fact that already on March 3, at the Jacobin club in Paris, "two of the most ardent Jacobins, Bentabole and Desfieux, demanded the formation of a revolutionary tribunal to judge the former minister and his accomplices."[34] The measure was later presented to the Convention by two leading Montagnards, Jeanbon Saint-André and Jacques-Louis David, and was immediately seconded by the most radical deputies (notably Billaud-Varenne, Carrier, Marat, Prieur de la Marne, and Robespierre), without whose approval the proposal would have petered out.[35] Regardless of whether certain deputies were frightened into voting for the bill by the specter of popular insurrection, the Montagnards themselves do not seem in the least to have been motivated by the fear of popular vengeance. Certainly they shared many beliefs and desires with the radical-

---

31. Lanjuinais, in *AP*, 60:4.

32. The parallel with the September massacres was certainly on everyone's mind. More precise in his historical parallels than Danton, Léonard Bourdon argued, "It is the August 10 tribunal which we must reestablish, so that our brothers fighting on the borders need not worry about the conspiracies and crimes committed by the enemies of the interior" (March 9; *AP*, 60:3).

33. "It is not unlikely that the introduction of this question in the Convention originated in the Jacobin Club and from there found a certain support in a few of the sections of Paris," *Revolutionary Justice*, 6.

34. *Revolutionary Justice*, 6; see also Alphonse Aulard, ed., *La société des Jacobins: recueil de documents pour l'histoire du Club des Jacobins de Paris* (Paris: Librairie Jouaust, 1889–97), 5:64–65. It would not have been the first time that the Jacobins "fabricated" popular demand for their proposals; see Patrice Gueniffey and Ran Halévi, "Clubs and Popular Societies," in *A Critical Dictionary of the French Revolution*, ed. François Furet and Mona Ozouf, trans. Arthur Goldhammer (Cambridge: Belknap Press of Harvard University Press, 1989), 465 (hereafter cited as *CDFR*).

35. See *AP*, 60:3–5, 50–51, 59–70, and 93–95.

ized sections of Paris, but without their critical influence at the Convention, these desiderata would not have become reality.

The "clear-cut" evidence of popular influence on the Convention can also be disputed for a number of other celebrated decrees. One of the most symbolic and adamant demands of the Parisian sections, the creation of a revolutionary army, owed its success largely to the intervention of the Jacobin society, as Richard Cobb acknowledges, and its first Parisian proponent was in fact no other than Robespierre.[36] The campaign to create these armies was spearheaded by the Jacobin club in Paris, and it was largely thanks to a deputation of Jacobins, led by Claude Royer, that the measure passed in the National Convention on September 5, 1793. Once the revolutionary armies truly began to acquire popular support, however, the Committee of Public Safety turned against them, deciding on their demise as early as the end of September.[37]

A similar story can be told regarding the law of suspects, which did not originate from the Parisian sections but from the halls of the National Convention itself. Historians sometimes overlook the fact that the September 17 law essentially recapitulated a decree passed with widespread support six months earlier, on March 21.[38] This law instituted surveillance committees (*comités de surveillance*) in every French *commune* and *section*, and charged them with weeding out "suspects" who might be abetting the counter-revolution.[39] Robespierre had persistently sought to strengthen this initial law, until the Convention finally passed a stricter version on August 12.[40] On the *journée* that subsequently produced the better-known law of suspects,

---

36. *The People's Armies: The "Armées Révolutionnaires," Instruments of the Terror in the Departments, April 1793 to Floréal Year II*, trans. Marianne Elliott (New Haven: Yale University Press, 1987), 21–22.

37. *People's Armies*, 24, 33–35, and 520. The delegation from the Commune also demanded the creation of a revolutionary army that day, but for a very different purpose (see below).

38. Article 2 of the September 17 law refers back to "those who have not justified, in the manner described by the law of last March 21, their means of existence and fulfillment of their civic duties," and article 3 reaffirms the powers of the *comités de surveillance*, created at that time, to draw up "the list of suspect people [*gens suspects*]" (*AP*, 74:304–5). I discuss this law further at the end of the chapter.

39. See Jean Debry's report, presented in the name of the diplomatic committee: *AP*, 60:386–90, esp. 387.

40. Robespierre had already proposed that the Convention arrest all suspects back on May 8, 1793: "I request . . . that all suspects be kept hostage and be arrested" (*Rob.*, 9:481); see also his revealing speech at the Jacobins that evening (quoted above). On August 12, the Convention finally decreed, on Fayau's motion, seconded by Danton, "all suspects are to be arrested" (*AP*, 72:102); this proposition, however, was sent off to the *comité de législation* and only returned on August 31 (see Lascoumes et al., *Au nom de l'ordre*, 158–61). In her analysis of the law of suspects, Wahnich does not mention any of these pre-September decrees.

however, the enactment of this legislation did not even figure among the demands of the Parisian Commune.[41]

In fact, the great irony about the *journée* of September 5 was that, in the first place, it was organized by the Jacobin club and joined by the Parisian sections only in extremis; and second, that the sectional demands were brazenly "recuperated" and ignored by the Convention.[42] The *sans-culottes* wanted bread and demanded Terrorist measures against the merchants and "*les riches*," suspected of hoarding grain.[43] Their other desiderata, such as the creation of a revolutionary army, were of secondary concern and related only to these economic issues.[44] To the extent that the *sans-culottes* formulated concrete political demands, furthermore, these often took the form of requesting that the government implement the Constitution.[45] Essentially, they were demonstrating against *la vie chère*.[46]

---

41. Even the cry made famous that day, "Let Terror be made the order of the day," was not issued by representatives of the Parisian Commune, but by the spokesman for the primary assemblies, Claude Royer, who had gained notoriety at the Jacobin club that August, not in the sections. On this slogan, see Jean-Clément Martin, *Violence et révolution: essai sur la naissance d'un mythe national* (Paris: Seuil, 2006), 186–93, who points out that it was never officially decreed. Michelet called attention to Royer's role in his *Histoire de la Révolution française*, ed. Gérard Walter (Paris: Gallimard/Pléiade, 1952), 2:554; see also Lucien Jaume, *Le discours Jacobin et la démocratie* (Paris: Fayard, 1989), 111–12 and 118–23. Royer had already urged the Convention to adopt terrorist measures on August 12, 1793: "Be terrifying [*Soyez terribles*], but save liberty; surround us with all the power of the people; let them rise together, and the hordes of tyrants dissipate as in a dream before them" (*AP*, 72:101). Danton seconded his motion: "The deputies of the primary assemblies have just advanced the initiative of terror against the enemies of the interior. Let us answer their wish. No, no amnesty to any traitor" (*AP*, 72:102). Of course, the *sans-culottes* had also been employing the language of terror long before; see Albert Soboul, *Les sans-culottes parisiens en l'an II: mouvement populaire et gouvernement révolutionnaire (1793–94)* (Paris: Seuil, 1968), 155–59.

42. For a discussion of the Jacobin role in the September 5 *journée*, see Donald Sutherland, *France 1789–1815: Revolution and Counterrevolution* (New York: Oxford University Press, 1986), 205–8, and his conclusion that "the high-water mark of the *sans-culottes* . . . dissolves into a blur on closer scrutiny. The Jacobins and the commune may have become the spokesmen of the *sans-culottes* on 5 September, they were also fast becoming their masters" (208). Furet also called attention to how the Jacobins repeatedly manipulated popular anger in his article on "Terror" (in *CDFR*).

43. See Soboul, *Mouvement populaire*, 121–22.

44. The *Père Duchesne* demanded the creation of a revolutionary army "to force fat farmers to empty their granaries of wheat, where it is going moldy" (qtd. in Soboul, *Mouvement populaire*, 114).

45. On August 26, the delegation of Femmes-révolutionnaires came to the Jacobin society to demand that the Constitution be implemented (Soboul, *Mouvement populaire*, 109). Leclerc, one of the leaders with Jacques Roux of the *enragés* movement, was demanding similar measures in his *Ami du peuple*.

46. Albert Mathiez, *La vie chère et le mouvement social sous la Terreur* (Paris: Payot, 1927).

And what did they get? As even the Marxist historian Albert Soboul recognizes, almost all of their economic demands were twisted into unrelated governmental actions: "The popular movement was manipulated [*avait été détourné*] toward political objectives."[47] The only economic measure that was declared was the introduction of a *maximum* for bread (more price controls were approved on September 29), which the Convention would do little to enforce; no Terrorist decrees were passed concerning the wealthy class. Most spectacularly, Danton used the occasion to wrestle power *away* from the sections, by limiting their meetings to two per week, on the pretext that they had become dominated by idle aristocrats (poor members would now be paid to attend).[48] The Convention also took advantage of this opportunity to arrest the leading spokesman of the radical *enragés*, Jacques Roux. The Convention did agree to the creation of a revolutionary army, but as we saw, this was as much of a Jacobin as it was a popular idea, and in any case, it was soon to be quelled. Furthermore, the Convention rebutted the Commune's request that the army be outfitted with a tribunal and guillotine, and directed it into battle, not to search for grain hoarders.[49] The traditional "bottom-up" narrative of the Terror's origins thus falters in light of these examples of how the Convention often cherry-picked (when it did not simply ignore) popular demands so as to suit its own agenda.[50]

---

47. *Mouvement populaire*, 126. Rudé reaches a similar conclusion in *The Crowd in the French Revolution*. See also the discussion in Paul Friedland, *Political Actors: Representative Bodies and Theatricality in the Age of the French Revolution* (Ithaca: Cornell University Press, 2002), 287–91. More recently, see Jean-Clément Martin's assessment: "To all the radical proposals put forward by the ultra-revolutionary Parisians, the Convention gives in the least possible," *Violence et révolution*, 190.

48. The sections attempted to have the decree against their permanence reversed on September 17, but were rebuffed.

49. William Doyle, *The Oxford History of the French Revolution* (Oxford: Oxford University Press, 2002), 250–3; see also Mona Ozouf, "Guerre et Terreur dans le discours révolutionnaire: 1792–94," in *L'école de la France: essais sur la révolution, l'utopie, et l'enseignement* (Paris: Gallimard, 1984), 118–22.

50. See again Sutherland: "Some of these measures [passed during the summer] had been anticipated by the militants but just because the demand proceeded there an action does not mean that the Convention was always forced to take measures it regretted. It never gave in to demands for the arrest of the *appelants*, for a general purge of nobles and priests from the armed forces and the civilian administrations, and for confiscatory taxes on the rich" (*France*, 200). This is not to suggest that the people of Paris *never* exerted *any* power on the decisions of the Convention. The contrary is obviously true. It was only after a series of riots, demonstrations, and fears of another *journée* that the Convention grudgingly accepted to institute "maximum" prices on staple supplies; and without the popular insurrection of May 31–June 2, the Girondins might not have been expelled from the Convention. To acknowledge influence in certain areas, however, does not imply influence in all.

Terror by Committee: The Practice of Violence

Since the debate over the exact role of the popular classes in the French Revolution has often doubled as an overt ideological clash, a number of historians have called for greater attention to be paid to social practices in the interpretation of the Terror.[51] Eschewing the political discourses of the Revolution in favor of its practices is a distinctly Tocquevillean gesture, as its practitioners readily acknowledge, yet it does not necessarily lead to a *longue durée* analysis of Old Regime relics in the new French Republic.[52] Indeed, what is perhaps most interesting in the recent scholarship on revolutionary practices is the analysis of pre-Terrorist activities by national and local committees foreshadowing the later mechanisms of the Terror. Patrice Gueniffey, for instance, has traced a political history of the Terror extending back at least to 1791, in which he argues that the antecedents of Terrorist violence are not the outbreaks of popular violence, but rather the government's reactions to these and other events. In particular, he claims that the decrees against the *émigrés* in 1791 already constituted "terror laws," in that they indiscriminately targeted an entire section of the population.[53] But these terror laws were themselves prefigured by the "laws of exception," which the National Assembly had started passing almost as soon as it was formed (beginning with the October 21, 1789, martial law decree). While acknowledging that such exceptional laws are not entirely unusual—indeed, they constitute the very hallmark of sovereignty, as Carl Schmitt famously postulated in *Political Theology*—Gueniffey suggests that in the context of a revolutionary discourse centered (since 1789) on the political principles of the general will and public safety, the exception soon became generalized to the point of arbitrariness. Anne Simonin has further developed the legal genealogy between certain Terror laws and earlier decrees against *émigrés*.[54]

---

51. Carla Hesse argued, for instance, that only such a focus on social practices could truly put an end to the *"guerre idéologique"*; see "La preuve par la lettre," 629–30.

52. On Tocqueville's historiography, see François Furet, *Interpreting the French Revolution*, trans. Elborg Forster (Cambridge/Paris: Cambridge University Press and Editions de la Maison des sciences de l'homme, 1981), 16–28. Gueniffey discusses his own Tocquevillean perspective in *Politique de la Terreur*, 14, 57–62. For a recent assessment, see *Tocqueville and Beyond: Essays on the Old Regime in Honor of David D. Bien*, ed. Robert M. Schwartz and Robert A. Schneider (Newark: University of Delaware Press, 2003); and the review by Keith Baker for *H-France Review* 5 (December 2005), http://h-france.net/vol5reviews/baker.html.

53. *Politique de la Terreur*, 149.

54. See in particular chapter 7, "Le contrat social à l'épreuve de l'exception," which draws heavily on Locke's theory of prerogative, and Gueniffey's definition of Terror as "the univeral and indefinite reign of the arbitrary" (*Politique de la Terreur*, 32). Gueniffey's argument ultimately mirrors Agamben's discussion of exceptionality; see *State of Exception*, trans. Kevin Attell

The French Revolution's descent into Terror can certainly sustain the description of an exception becoming increasingly normalized. During the king's trial, for instance, Robespierre argued that a death sentence for Louis was a "cruel exception to ordinary laws": The king was "the *only* one who can . . . legitimately receive [the death penalty]."[55] A year and a half later, however, Robespierre's ally Couthon presented the infamous law of 22 prairial that essentially made anyone (and everyone) liable for execution. What this apparent normalization of an exception fails to explain, however, is why the exception was an exception to *kill*—and not, say, merely to imprison—in the first place. As Gueniffey's own mentor François Furet recognized, "Situations of extreme national peril do not invariably bring a people to revolutionary Terror."[56] Gueniffey touches on a number of possible reasons for why the Terrorist exception was always death, but falls back on the claim that the Terror was the result of a "revolutionary dynamic."[57]

Revolutionary practices also figure at the forefront of Timothy Tackett's analysis of the origins of the Terror, at the conclusion of his book on the flight to Varennes.[58] Like Gueniffey, Tackett is for the most part dismissive of political interpretations. His previous work had challenged the revisionist claim that the delegates of the Constituent Assembly shared a homogeneous, Rousseauist ideology of the general will.[59] His most recent book extends this critique by arguing that political practices, rather than discourses, were responsible for the Terror. The king's return to Paris triggered the first widespread republican demonstration at the Champs de Mars; this gathering was violently repressed by the Parisian authorities, who declared martial law; this series of events in turn led to the repression of republican and Jacobin leaders, while across the country, more "patriot" officials reacted in kind, censoring and spying on suspect correspondence. For Tackett, these actions

---

(Chicago: University of Chicago Press, 2005). For Schmitt, see *Political Theology*, trans. George Schwab (Cambridge: MIT Press, 1985). Anne Simonin's recent study of *Le déshonneur dans la république: une histoire de l'indignité, 1791–1958* (Paris: Grasset, 2008), which appeared after the present work was in production, further probes the legal genealogy leading from the legislation on *émigrés* to certain terror laws. I return to her interpretations below.

55. December 3, 1792, speech at the Convention (*Rob.*, 9:129–30, my italics).

56. *Interpreting the French Revolution*, 62.

57. At the onset of his study, Gueniffey declares that the Terror was not a "product of ideology," but rather a "product of the revolutionary dynamic and, perhaps, of every revolutionary dynamic" (*Politique de la Terreur*, 14)—a point that renders his detailed analyses of republican and natural right traditions in the genesis of the Terror rather perplexing.

58. *When the King Took Flight* (Cambridge: Harvard University Press, 2003).

59. Timothy Tackett, *Becoming a Revolutionary: The Deputies of the French National Assembly and the Emergence of a Revolutionary Culture (1789–90)* (Princeton: Princeton University Press, 1996).

constitute a clear signal that well before the Terror "officially" began, the repressive practices that came to characterize it were already in place.

One is entitled to ask, however, that since these practices fell short of political execution (the Champs de Mars massacre aside, which was technically authorized by a limited martial law decree), can they really be said to presage the unbridled violence of the Terror? Though they may contradict the spirit and letter of the Declaration of Rights, are these practices fundamentally different from the "patriot" measures taken by the American colonies during their War of Independence? They may represent a worrisome departure from the democratic principles that we take for granted today, but these principles were still relatively unstable in 1791. As Baczko noted, furthermore, the Terror was less a matter of denying the principles enshrined in the 1789 Declaration per se than of denying these principles to certain individuals deemed unworthy of them.[60] Understanding the Terror thus becomes primarily a question of explaining why certain segments of the population saw their rights overruled; and the study of political practices, while critical for comprehending the mechanisms of revolutionary Terror, is unlikely to enlighten us on whom it chose as its victims.

The Revolutionary Dialectic:
The Counterrevolution and Cycles of Violence

One group of French citizens who without a doubt were a principal target of the Terrorist measures was those who openly opposed the Revolution. It was against these "counterrevolutionaries" that the first important legislation was passed that led directly to political execution: the March 19, 1793, decree outlawing the rebels in the Vendée and throughout France. As Donald Greer statistically demonstrated, this law "alone resulted in more executions than all other legislation of the regime."[61] It was used against a wide range of adversaries, notably the Girondins, thereby giving rise to the comprehensible interpretation that the Terror was a reaction to the counterrevolution.

This hypothesis has attracted renewed interest in recent years and has been explored in works by D. M. G. Sutherland, Arno Mayer, David Andress, and

---

60. Backo, "The Terror before the Terror?" in *Terror*, 29.

61. *The Incidence of the Terror during the French Revolution: A Statistical Interpretation* (Cambridge: Harvard University Press, 1935), 14. This decree also created a parallel tribunal system (the military and civil commissions), which would be responsible for far more deaths than the revolutionary tribunal (21).

others. Building on Sutherland's thesis of revolution and counterrevolution as the dialectical (if not diabolical) force of the Revolution, Mayer in particular has drawn attention to the extreme acts of violence perpetrated by both sides of the Vendée war.[62] Carrier's infamous drownings of priests in Nantes, he argues, cannot be analyzed alone; they must be placed within the context of a vicious civil war.[63] Vengeance, for Mayer (as it is, in a somewhat different vein, for Wahnich), was the motivating factor behind the Terrorist measures of repression, in the Vendée as in Paris. Where "ideology" is concerned, Mayer asserts that it is "a poor guide to a revolution's genesis, course, and outcome."[64]

As with popular pressure, it would be absurd to ignore the critical importance of the counterrevolution, particularly as it figured "representatively" in the conspiracy obsessions of the French revolutionaries.[65] But once again, a close examination of the chronology of events and decrees that led up to the Terror poses a serious challenge to this thesis. Admittedly, the circumstances facing the French Republic in the spring of 1793 were dire. On March 1, the commander-in-chief of the Northern front, Dumouriez, suffered a major military setback in Belgium. The coalition armies were suddenly poised to penetrate into France and reach Paris, spelling the death of the republic. The Convention recognized the gravity of the situation on March 8, when Danton, freshly returned from the front, warned of the "malheurs incalculables" that awaited France if Dumouriez were routed: "The annihilation of public finances, the death of 600,000 French citizens could result from it!"[66] The situation became only worse with the news of growing troubles in the West: On March 18, Barère warned the Convention of "troops of openly counter-revolutionary fanatics."[67]

The spring of 1793 presents a clear example of how military troubles could produce a raft of "extraordinary" legislation. It was in March and

---

62. *The Furies: Violence and Terror in the French and Russian Revolutions* (Princeton: Princeton University Press, 2000). A special section of *French Historical Studies*, 24, no. 4 (2001), was dedicated to reviewing Mayer's book; see in particular the articles by David A. Bell and Timothy Tackett (who makes the comparison with Sutherland, whose book *France, 1789–1815,* similarly stresses "the dialectic of revolution-counterrevolution" (219). Sutherland has since reformulated his thesis in *The French Revolution and Empire: The Quest for a Civic Order* [Oxford: Blackwell, 2003]).

63. Civil war and disunity also constitute the main theme of David Andress's history of the Terror, *The Terror: Civil War in the French Revolution* (London: Little, Brown, 2005).

64. *Furies,* 9.

65. See Tackett, "Conspiracy Obsession"; see also Furet, *Interpreting the French Revolution,* 53–63.

66. *AP,* 59:716. On the swift military reversals of February–April 1793, see Furet and Richet, *Révolution française,* 185–89.

67. *AP,* 60:292.

April, after all, that the Convention voted on the revolutionary tribunal, the *hors-la-loi* decree, the surveillance committees, and even the Committee of Public Safety.[68] The deputies had to face both the very real threats of a foreign invasion and widespread resistance throughout the nation to the forced conscription (*levée*) of 300,000 men, decreed on February 23.[69] While it seems hard to deny that these drastic circumstances spurred the Convention to act forcefully, it is far less evident that they dictated the specific content of their legislation. Indeed, what is perhaps most surprising about the spring 1793 laws is that they do *not* constitute a fundamental shift away from the legal philosophy already espoused by many Jacobins and other *conventionnels*. This continuity is most evident in the case of the notorious *hors-la-loi* decree, passed on March 19. At this time, the Convention had yet to learn of General Marcé's devastating defeat that same day in the Vendée, the first sign that the situation in the West was truly critical.[70] There was no indication, in other words, that the Vendée resistance to the *levée* would take the form of a well-organized, counterrevolutionary force. The Convention nonetheless passed one of its most draconian laws.[71]

What is most curious about this law is that it essentially applied a criminal category to the Vendée rebels that had been designed and theorized for another criminal: the king. Indeed, as I examine in the following section, it was around the figure of the king that the concept (and even the terminology) of "outlawry" was first developed and introduced into French legal thought. The punishment that the Vendée rebels were to receive—execution within twenty-four hours, without a trial—was precisely that which the Montagnards had wished to mete out on Louis XVI. The Convention's "reaction" to the Vendée situation, in this regard, was couched in ready-made terms. The challenging military situation may have provided the republican government with a *motive* to act; its specific course of action, however, was not determined by the present circumstances but by a preexisting legal philosophy.

---

68. Mona Ozouf has argued that war and terror only became intrinsically linked in revolutionary discourse in the spring of 1794, but her study, which rests on an analysis of three pivotal moments (September 1792, September 1793, and prairial *an II*), skips over March–April 1793; see "Guerre et Terreur."

69. It was in reaction to the *levée* that the Vendée first erupted, but in this regard it was far from isolated; see Jean-Clément Martin, *La Vendée et la France* (Paris: Seuil, 1987), 28–29.

70. As Martin affirmed, in one of the best studies of the Vendée uprising, until this battle, "there is little thought of defeat among the various commissaries in the West. . . . The situation is therefore not too critical," *Vendée et la France*, 37. Marcé's defeat would become known in Paris on March 23. See also Jacques Godechot, *La contre-révolution* (Paris: PUF, 1996), 230–32; and Martin, *Contre-Révolution, révolution et nation en France, 1789–99* (Paris: Seuil, 1999).

71. Andress acknowledges this chronological discrepancy in *The Terror*, 162.

The *hors-la-loi* decree thus suggests that political violence during the Terror was not simply the product of a counterrevolutionary/revolutionary dialectic of violence, but was in fact rooted in what Mayer and others dismiss as "ideology," or what may more fruitfully be discussed in terms of law. Robespierre called attention to this legal framework in his exhortation to Parisian soldiers heading off to the Vendée:

> You might think that you should be revolting, and giving yourself insurrectionary airs; not at all, it is with the law in one hand [*la loi à la main*] that you must exterminate all our enemies. . . . You will find in the laws everything you need to legally exterminate our enemies.[72]

The law of March 19, to which Robespierre is here referring, functioned as a sort of Terrorist carte blanche: It was the keystone of an ideology of permissiveness, one that did not dictate precise retaliations, but one that seemingly authorized the most violent acts.[73] The political importance of this and subsequent laws resided primarily in the enormous latitude they granted the military commissions, often egged on by zealous *représentants en mission*.[74] The Convention and Committee of Public Safety may have sought at times to curb this latitude (most notably in the cases of Carrier in Nantes and Collot d'Herbois in Lyons), but given the status of the outlaw/rebel, the *représentants* could feel secure that the military commissions were merely

---

72. May 8, 1793, speech on the Vendée at the Jacobin society; *Rob.*, 9:491.

73. Technically, the March 19 law required that all rebels have their identities recorded by a judge and then be officially executed, but their outlaw status was often interpreted differently, as this passage in Hébert's *Père Duchesne* indicates: Antoine-Joseph Gorsas "is an outlaw [*est hors de la loi*], so whoever arrested him had the right to cut him down" (issue no. 295, 7; vol. 9). On the difference between a "Jacobin" and "Cordelier" theory of the enemy, see below.

74. Jean-Clément Martin reached a similar conclusion in his discussion of provincial Terror: "Let us not forget that the crisis is fueled by the institutions themselves. They allowed excesses to occur through imprecise or contradictory laws, by permission given *nolens volens* to repressive organizations of all sorts and by the presence of emissaries with competing authority," *Violence et révolution*, 198. In a recent commentary on his book, Martin emphasized this point even more strongly: The March 19 law, he writes, "'creates' the 'Vendée war' by granting it from the onset a depth that no other concurrent uprising received, to the point of making the 'Vendée' the paradigm of the Counter-Revolution," "Response Essay," in *H-France Forum* 2, no. 2 (2007), http://h-france.net/forum/forumvol2/Martin1Response.html. On the *représentants en mission*, see Michel Biard, *Missionnaires de la République: les représentants du peuple en mission, 1793–95* (Paris: CTHS, 2002). On the repression of Lyons, see Paul Mansfield, "The Repression of Lyon, 1793–94: Origins, Responsibility and Significance," *French History* 2, no. 1 (1988): 74–101.

laying down the law.[75] While the severity of these repressions may have been proportional to the levels of counterrevolutionary atrocities, the March 19 law had *already* removed all legal safeguards protecting defendants.[76] The floodgates of revolutionary violence had already been flung open by this prior decree that placed a swath of French citizens beyond the pale of the law and at the mercy of a whimsical grace.

To Kill a King: Judging by Nature

If, from above the fray, the Terror seems to have been characterized by law-lessness and anarchy, on closer examination its emergence appears to be tied, ironically, to transformations of the law itself. Since Tocqueville, historians have suggested that the severe legislation of the Terror represented a con-tinuity with Old Regime judiciary practices, but this thesis overlooks the radical legal innovations of the Revolution.[77] The *hors-la-loi* category, for in-stance, was not found in any prerevolutionary French criminal code (includ-ing the 1670 *Ordonnance criminelle*). The first recorded use of the expres-sion in French dates back only to 1774: "I am not what they call in England *ex lex*, an outlaw [*hors la loi*]," Beaumarchais wrote in his *Mémoires contre M. Goëzman*.[78] As Beaumarchais's comment indicates, the "outlaw" was a foreign concept, imported from Anglo-Saxon common law.[79] For the revo-

---

75. Hence, for instance, Carrier's great surprise at being recalled and his defense at the time of his trial; see Baczko, *Comment sortir de la Terreur*, 194–254.

76. To draw a parallel with a different American war, the allegedly widespread use of torture by American military interrogators in the "global war on terror" seems to have been the result of a permissive culture, in which soldiers were under the impression that the mistreatment of prisoners was sanctioned by their commanders (who did nothing to dispel this impression). In this case, the legal framework was even looser than during the Terror, but to perceive the willing violations of the Geneva Conventions as mere "practices" by rogue soldiers is to ignore their very clear relation to the administration's belligerent ideology. See Human Rights Watch, "Torture in Iraq," *New York Review of Books* 52 (Nov. 3, 2005): 64–73.

77. On the parallels between Terror laws and the Old Regime concept of "extraordinary jus-tice," see Carla Hesse, "La logique culturelle de la loi révolutionnaire," *Annales HSS* 4 (2002): 915–33.

78. In *Œuvres complètes* (Paris: Burne, 1828), 3:315; text available on ARTFL. On the outlaw category in revolutionary legislation, see in particular Eric de Mari's outstanding disserta-tion, "La mise hors de la loi sous la Révolution française" (PhD diss., Université de Montpellier, 1991). Mari notes a few precedents to the 1793 decree: In July 1791, Barère called for duelists to be declared "ex-loi," which he glossed as "deprived of the protection of the law and of all rights of citizenry" (qtd. 133); in May 1792, Laurent Lecointre demanded that non-juring priests be "déclarés hors-la-loi," but the Assembly did not act on this motion (*AP*, 44:69). The expression, as we will see, was also used during the king's trial.

79. Mari discusses a number of other sources (Greek, Roman, German) for the *hors-la-loi*, before recognizing its close similarity with English "outlawry" (1:67). His ultimate conclusion for why the law was introduced, however, is more anthropological: "All emerging societies will have

lutionaries, however, it quickly became the chief weapon in the arsenal of the Terror: Over three-quarters of the executions that occurred during the Terror were authorized by the March 19 decree.[80] In certain key respects, the legal framework of the Terror clearly parted company with the Old Regime justice system.[81] How and when did this break with earlier French criminal codes occur? As the following section demonstrates, the *hors-la-loi* category first rose to prominence in revolutionary legislation with respect to a specific criminal—the king. It was during his trial that the *conventionnels* eschewed civil forms of prosecution and turned instead to an uncommon body of law, natural right and the "law of nations" (*droit des gens*). Here they found the readymade legal concept of an "enemy of the human race," an enemy who has violated the laws of nature and can never be trusted again in any social or civil context.[82] Accordingly, the only punishment that could be meted out against him was death.

The Law of Nations in the Trial of Louis XVI

Although natural right surfaced repeatedly as the fundamental code authorizing the legal proceedings against the king, historians have paid scant attention to it.[83] Part of the reason for this neglect may stem from a terminological confusion: Many deputies often invoked natural right in terms of *droit des gens*, which, as we saw in the prologue, was widely deemed to be identical to natural right in eighteenth-century France. It was in the name of the law of nations that Saint-Just led his famous charge against the king,

---

recourse to outlawing as its power of radical elimination guarantees the unity and solidarity of the members in the group" (1:62). But Mari misreads Blackstone's discussion of outlawry in the *Commentaries on the Laws of England* (Oxford: Clarendon Press, 1765–68), 4.24, claiming that he rejects it altogether; whereas in fact Blackstone opposes an "antient" (and "inhuman") form of outlawry to a modern, acceptable version; see below, and Mari, *Mise hors de la loi*, 1:67n2.

80. Marc Bouloiseau puts the figure at 78 percent; see *Jacobin Republic*, 211. Donald Greer estimates that in "troubled departments" (those that witnessed over one hundred deaths during the Terror, with the exclusion of Paris), the figure was closer to 93 percent; see *Incidence of the Terror*, table 4, 152–53.

81. It may, however, have perpetuated certain earlier judicial *forms*, as Ted Margadant suggests in his forthcoming work (which I thank him for sharing with me).

82. On the history of this category, see the prologue.

83. Two exceptions are Alison Patrick, *The Men of the First French Republic: Political Alignments in the National Convention of 1792* (Baltimore: Johns Hopkins University Press, 1972); and Mari, "La mise hors de la loi," 1:40–43. Michael Walzer does not so much as mention natural right in his introductory essay to *Regicide and Revolution* (Cambridge: Cambridge University Press, 1974), nor does Mona Ozouf, who claims instead that Saint-Just's famous speech "lacked the logical brilliance with which it was later credited," in "The King's Trial," in *CDFR*, 98; Jean Jaurès ignores natural right arguments in *La mort du roi et la chute de la Gironde*, vol. 5 of *Histoire socialiste de la Révolution française*, ed. Albert Soboul (Paris: Messidor, 1986); and even David Jordan's helpful work, *The King's Trial*, ignores it.

remarking that the Convention "seems to be searching for a law it could use to punish the king," when in fact "the laws we must adopt are to be found in the law of nations [*droit des gens*]." There had been nothing "in the laws of England to try Charles I: he was judged according to the laws of nations."[84] Not only did the *droit des gens* provide legal cover for prosecuting the king; it encouraged the merciless punishment of prisoners whose crimes violated natural right: Louis should be executed as "a barbarian . . . a foreign prisoner of war."[85]

The recommendation that Louis be tried according to the law of nations was not originally a radical Montagnard proposal: It had first been suggested by Jean-Baptiste Maihle, the *rapporteur* for the Committee on Legislation.[86] "Is it only in the new French Code that these laws [against the crimes of a kings] are to be found? Have they not existed at all times and in all places? Are they not as ancient as society?" Maihle asked.[87] This reference to a universally shared set of principles is clearly an allusion to the *ius gentium*, and Maihle's language drew unambiguously from natural right: "Could a people whose rights are . . . founded in nature, could an entire people not have the right to avenge the treachery of an individual . . . to inflict on [him] the punishment reserved for oppressors or brigands?"[88] Not only did natural right constitute a valid jurisprudential reference; its authority trumped all civil forms: "The rights and duties of nature are superior to all institutions," Maihle reminded his colleagues.[89] This same lesson would be emphasized by Robespierre, who scolded the deputies on December 3 for confusing "the rules of civil and positive law with the principles of the law of nations." His friend Camille Desmoulins drove the same point home: "It is in accordance with the law of nations, not civil law, that this trial must proceed. . . . Following the law of nations, Louis XVI was a tyrant, in a state of rebellion against the nation."[90] As we shall see, this argument for prosecuting and executing the king was precisely the same that would soon be used against the Vendée

---

84. "Discours sur le jugement de Louis XVI," November 13, 1792; *SJ*, 378, 380.

85. *SJ*, 381.

86. As Saint-Just himself acknowledged in his November 13 "Discours"; see *SJ*, 380.

87. November 7, 1792; *AP*, 53:278.

88. *AP*, 53:279. The comparison to brigands came back repeatedly; see, for instance, Léonard Bourdon (54:124), Camille Desmoulins (54:175), and Nicolas Hentz (54:208).

89. *AP*, 53:279. See also this characteristic statement by Bonnesœur-Bourginière: "Natural law obligates indistinctly all men, and there is no being on earth who can substract himself from its eternal laws" (54:117).

90. For Robespierre, see *Rob.*, 9:122; for Desmoulins, see *AP*, 54:175; unless otherwise noted, subsequent page references for the trial speeches are to this volume. For other discussions of the *droit des gens*, see notably the speeches by Marc-Antoine Baudot (102), Siméon Bonnesœur-Bourginière (118), and Pierre Delbrel (168).

rebels and later against British prisoners. Like these other "brigands," the king was a "cowardly violator of the rights of nature, the law of nations, the eternal rights of peoples" (Maihle, 279), who must be destroyed.

In fact, though a majority of deputies would reject the radical Montagnard conclusion that the king need not be judged but simply killed, the basic premise that the law of nations provided the legal grounds for trying Louis was widely accepted. Out of a collection of 102 speeches prepared for or delivered on December 3, 68 percent claimed that natural right provided the Convention with the authority to try the king, as opposed to 21 percent who argued that only the Constitution gave the deputies this authority, while the remaining 11 percent defended the king's inviolability (see fig. 1).[91] The 68 percent that recognized natural right were comprised of 23 percent admitting the authority of both natural and constitutional law in the king's trial, and another 14 percent who did not overtly call on natural right but instead invoked the laws of reason and universal justice.[92] Of the remaining 31 percent, 10 percent adhered to the hard-line Montagnard position that natural right authorized not only the trial of the king, but also his immediate execution, whereas 21 percent simply called for Louis to be judged according to the laws of nature (see fig. 2).

Why did this vast majority of deputies abandon constitutional law for the more nebulous constraints of natural right? There was, first, a strong practical reason: Invoking the laws of nature allowed the *conventionnels* to sidestep the thorny issue of the king's inviolability. To invalidate the Constitution, they either needed to reject it for technical reasons (which many did, arguing that since it had not been ratified by the people, it was void),[93] or on legal grounds. In this latter case, only natural right provided the higher legal authority with which to challenge the Constitution's legitimacy. Underpinning the jusnaturalist prosecution of the king, second, was a philosophical argument borrowed from social contract theory. As Robespierre explained, "When a nation is obliged to make use of its right of rebellion [*droit de*

---

91. These 102 speeches are collected in volume 54 of the *Archives parlementaires*, 88–337; they include speeches by most of the prominent deputies in the Convention and were slated to be delivered on December 3. These statistics were compiled with the help of my research assistant, Samantha Leese.

92. Since Roman law, as we saw, the *ius naturale* was believed to be the product of *recta ratio*. This relation was still perceived in the eighteenth century; see, for instance, Boucher d'Argis's article on "droit des gens" ("natural right is the same as the law of nations, both being founded on the natural light of reason," *Encylopédie*, 5:127).

93. See, for instance, Léonard Bourdon's argument that "Louis XVI can only invoke in vain the advantages that this contract seemed to grant him"; "this contract does not really exist, as it was never accepted either by him, or by the people" (126). Similarly, for Desmoulins, the Constitution was just "a contract that he [Louis XVI] was the first to violate" (174).

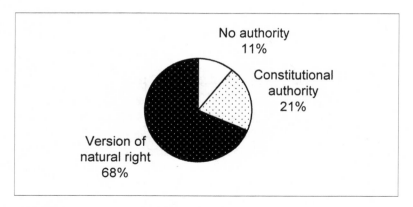

Figure 1   Legal authority for judging the king.

l'insurrection], it returns to a state of nature with respect to the tyrant." If the Constitution was a dead letter, he asked, "What laws replace it?" The answer was evident: "Those of nature."[94] Numerous other deputies were to repeat this same argument: "Louis XVI put us back into a state of nature," declared Michel Azéma, a member of the Committee of Legislation (97); "he placed himself in a state of nature with respect to the nation," echoed Nicolas Hentz (208). Without positive laws, Delbrel claimed, "Louis and every French citizen remain . . . in a pure state of nature, as the rights and laws of nature remain when the laws and positive conventions do not replace them" (168). Among the flurry of decree proposals on the trial proceedings that were debated on December 6, the Convention settled on one by Nicolas-Marie Quinette, who began his report by noting, "during political revolutions, the only positive laws are those of nature" (401).[95]

Despite being the first offender ever to be tried as a "criminal against humanity," in Robespierre's words, the king would ultimately not be ac-

---

94. *Rob.*, 9:123. The idea that Louis had de facto shattered the social contract (or constitution) binding the people to him had already been expressed in the famous Cordeliers petition demanding a republic, after the flight of the king: "But times have changed. This alleged convention between a people and its king no longer exists: Louis has abdicated the throne; from now on Louis is nothing to us, unless he becomes our enemy" (English translation from *The Old Regime and the French Revolution*, ed. Keith Baker [Chicago: University of Chicago Press, 1987], 273).

95. This was not the first time that revolution had been associated with the state of nature. In March 1792, for instance, Maihle himself had used this argument to support an amnesty for the perpetrators of the Glacière massacre in Avignon (*AP*, 40:54). The amnesty debate is discussed in Mary Ashburn Miller, "Violence and Nature in the French Revolutionary Imagination, 1789–94" (PhD diss., Johns Hopkins University, 2008), 95.

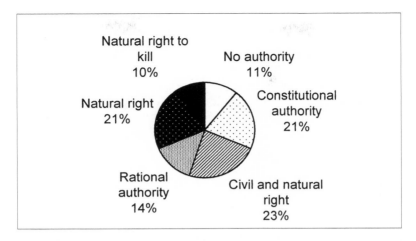

Figure 2 Legal authority for judging the king (detailed).

cused of violating the laws of nature, as the Convention convicted Louis for treason.[96] But the king did provide the Montagnards with an opportunity to draft a legal theory around this real-life case of a natural right transgressor. Even the deputies who believed with Robespierre that capital punishment had no place in civil society agreed that Louis presented a "cruel exception to ordinary laws" and was "the only one who could . . . legitimately receive [the death penalty]."[97] Since the king was in the state of nature with respect to the rest of France, his death could still be authorized by our natural right to punish. In this way, Robespierre remained faithful to his initial abolitionist opinion: "The law of natural justice justifies and approves my action," he had claimed, when I kill someone in the state of nature.[98] The abbé Maury's

96. *Rob.*, 9:130. See Walzer, *Regicide and Revolution*, 68. On the legal background of this indictment, see Hesse, "La logique culturelle de la loi révolutionnaire."

97. Robespierre, December 3, 1792 speech at the Convention; *Rob.*, 9:129–30, my italics. For similar arguments, see Baudot: "I, too, agree that the death penatly shall not dishonor the criminal code of a Republic that respects the rights and duties of man: but . . . a king will always be an exception" (105). Didier Thirion ended his tirade demanding the king's head with a similar suggestion: "Let us then abolish the death penalty, for who else, henceforth, could deserve to be punished like Louis?" (334). See also Quinette, on December 6: "I agree with those who think that this [death] penalty must be erased from our civil legislation; but I will demonstrate in the future that it must be reserved for political crimes, or those that seek to destory liberty. Indeed, a man who has violated all the rights of society should not find asylum among any people" (401).

98. *Rob.*, 7:433. See Goulet, "Robespierre: la peine de mort et la Terreur." Gueniffey also suggests that Robespierre's two views on the death penalty can be resolved; see *Politique de la Terreur*, 301.

satirical response to Robespierre's 1789 speech against the death penalty was prophetic. After August 10, the Mountain was indeed leading France toward the forest of Bondy.

Sovereignty and the State of Nature

By justifying their extraconstitutional proceedings in terms of *droit des gens*, the *conventionnels* ended up presenting a radical interpretation of France's political situation. The Revolution, and particularly the August 10 insurrection, had destroyed the political bonds between the French and their ruler. But what was the "nature" of this state of nature? Clearly France was not in a condition of anarchy or unrestrained individual freedom. The French political structure of *l'an I* even had a name and well-known form: It was a republic. Contrary to the dictates of both classical republicanism and social contract theory, however, this republic was not defined by a new set of fundamental laws, a constitution, or social compact. The king's death, according to Jean-Bon Saint-André, would bring about "the restoration of the *natural order* of societies" (213, my italics). As in Physiocracy (which championed the *Natural and Essential Order of Political Societies*, to quote Le Mercier de la Rivière's title; see chapter 2), many Montagnards seemed to believe that the republic did not need a constitution, given that it was, in Siméon Bonnescœur-Bourginière terms, "the form of government closest to nature" (118). The pressing question thus became, how long would the republic remain without a civil infrastructure to mediate natural right? Was this political state of nature simply a temporary affair (for example, until the Constitution could be implemented or until "peacetime"), or did it represent a new republican ideal, a "natural republic"? Leaving this constitutional matter to be dealt with more fully in chapters 4 and 5, I would emphasize here that much more was at stake than Louis's life during his trial. As Saint-Just reminded his colleagues, "we will establish the republic in the same spirit as we judge the king."[99] The legal discourse employed by the *conventionnels* touched the very foundations of civil society.

Although certain Montagnards embraced the traditional theory of tyrannicide, according to which anyone could kill a tyrant with impunity, the Jacobins by and large insisted on a strict, state monopoly of violence.[100] The recent

---

99. *SJ*, 380.

100. Robespierre made this argument subtly in his December 3 speech to the Convention: "If he [Louis XVI] was saved from the clutches of public anger [on August 10, 1792], it was no doubt only so that his punishment, solemnly ordered by the Convention, would be all the more imposing for the enemies of humanity" (*Rob.*, 9:127). The argument in this paragraph owes much to comments by Robert Morrissey, Paul Cheney, Charly Coleman, and the Modern France Workshop at the University of Chicago.

memory of the September massacres gave the Jacobins additional reasons, if needed, to be fearful of a popular right to execute outlaws. Their insistence on monopolizing justice is seen most clearly in the heated exchange that occurred at the Convention on August 7, 1793, concerning another "tyrant," the English minister William Pitt. A radical delegate, Jacques Garnier, proposed that Pitt be declared an *"ennemi du genre humain,"* further demanding that "everyone have the right to assassinate him." His motion was not seconded and triggered a series of *"violents murmures."* An anonymous delegate responded that "it is dishonorable to suggest that assassination could be authorized by law"; Georges Couthon resolved the situation only by remarking, "I will not second the motion that has been made for you to authorize Pitt's assassination; but I request that you at least solemnly declare Pitt to be the enemy of the human race."[101] The *hostis humani generis* was no *homo sacer*, in the sense that Giorgio Agamben has given this term: "Sacred life may be killed by anyone without committing homicide, but never submitted to sanctioned forms of execution."[102] The Jacobins would have been doubly in disagreement with this style of execution, both in the name of a state monopoly on violence and of the legally sanctioned right to put *ennemis du genre humain* to death: "It is with the law in one hand that you must exterminate all our enemies," as Robespierre insisted.

But how could a sovereign body monopolize the "executive right," or right to punish, if France was in a political state of nature, as the Jacobins also claimed? Had not Locke and most other liberal natural right theorists in the eighteenth century argued that this right lay in the state of nature with every individual? This apparent contradiction disappears, however, if one considers it in the light of Sieyès's theory of natural sovereignty, set forth in *Qu'est-ce que le Tiers état?* (1789). The nation, according to this influential theory, is a unified locus of sovereignty even *before* it contracts into civil society: "The nation exists prior to everything; it is the origin of everything. Its will is always legal. It is the law itself. Prior to the nation and above the nation there is only natural law."[103] Following this logic, the

---

101. *AP*, 70:451. The Convention dutifully proceeded to declare Pitt an *"ennemi du genre humain."*

102. *Homo Sacer: Sovereign Power and Bare Life*, trans. Daniel Heller-Roazen (Stanford: Stanford University Press, 1998), 103; Agamben is in fact referring, in this passage, to Louis's trial (through the lens of Michael Walzer's interpretation).

103. Emmanuel Joseph Sieyès, *What Is the Third Estate?* in *Political Writings*, trans. and ed. Michael Sonenscher (Indianapolis: Hackett, 2003), 136. On Sieyès, see William H. Sewell Jr., *The Rhetoric of Bourgeois Revolution: The Abbé Sieyes and "What Is the Third Estate?"* (Durham: Duke University Press, 1994); Pasquale Pasquino, "The Constitutional Republicanism of Emmanuel Sieyès," in *Invention of Modern Republicanism,* 107–17; and David W. Bates,

154 • CHAPTER THREE

Convention, which represents the nation as it passes from a political state of nature into civil society (but remains in the former until—or unless—it officially contracts), can thus monopolize the executive right of the sovereign since it has already been charged with expressing the sovereign "will."[104] But the nation, though without clear political organization or legal code, is not above the law altogether: It must continue to recognize the laws of nature. While Sieyès's theory of sovereignty assumes an eventual passage out of the state of nature into political society, it resembles in many other aspects the Physiocratic model in which sovereignty also exists naturally, if not in the nation as a whole, then in the *chef de famille* or tribal leader.[105] Ideally, as we shall see in the following chapter, the Jacobins would seek to reduce sovereignty to mere law enforcement, eliminating the need for a legislative power altogether.

From "Ennemi du Genre Humain" to "Hors-la-loi"

The political framework that the Montagnards erected in the course of prosecuting the king carried in its tow the standard injunction against those who violated natural right. The king became the first prisoner of the Revolution to be accused as an "enemy of the human race." Florent Guiot flung the epithet at him by turning the inviolability defense on its head: "A man who claims to have inviolability . . . would cease to belong to the social body: he would be a recognized enemy of the human race" (205). Jean-Bon Saint-André approvingly quoted Saint-Just, then added, "despots [are] enemies of the human race" (213). He was echoed by Marc Vadier, for whom kings were "the eternal enemies of humanity" (336) and the "scourge [*fléau*] of the human race" (334). Others were content with paraphrasing Locke and Jean-Jacques Burlamaqui: "Whoever claims it [the right of the strongest] to kill me is a monster; he is the enemy of

---

Enlightenment Aberrations: Error and Revolution in France (Ithaca: Cornell University Press, 2002), 125–37.

104. As Sieyès puts it, "A body of extraordinary representatives is a surrogate for an assembly of that nation," *What Is the Third Estate?*, 139. Following Grotius (in *The Rights of War and Peace*, 2.20.40; 1021), Blackstone had insisted on the sovereign's sole right to enforce natural right violations; see *Commentaries*, 4.24 (quoted above). Vattel also grants this *ius gladii* to the sovereign alone.

105. As Keith Baker observes, Sieyès's pamphlet "places no emphasis on a social contract as the explicit logical basis of [the nation's] collective being" ("Sovereignty," in *CDFR*, 851). Baker also notes how this position owes more to the Physiocrats than to Rousseau. Sieyès in fact refers to "the natural and essential order of social truths" in his *Vues sur les moyens d'exécution dont les représentans de la France pourront disposer en 1789* ([n.p.], 1789), 46. See the discussion of Quesnay's *Droit naturel* in chapter 2.

humanity," charged Nicolas Hentz, "Every man has the right to destroy this destructive being" (208).

By insisting so repeatedly on the "unnaturalness" of monarchs, the *conventionnels* came close to suggesting that *any* opposition to the French Republic or even to legislation passed by the Convention amounted to a violation of natural right. This conflation of natural and positive law can already be seen in Saint-Just's maiden speech: "The courts are only instituted for citizens," he intoned, but then claimed, "As soon as a man is guilty, he is no longer a citizen [*il sort de la cité*]" (379–80).[106] Such affirmations, often repeated, beg the question of the legal status afforded to the "guilty." If the accusation of guilt is all it takes for an individual to be deemed guilty, then for whom are the courts designed? The evidently ambiguous concept of guilt found here seems to foreshadow the equally ambiguous category of "suspect" (of which more later). But it also reflects the antiprocedural bent of the radical Montagnards, who wished to kill the king and dispense with the trial altogether. This same bent was the driving force behind Robespierre's repeated demands that the revolutionary tribunal's procedure be streamlined so that the "guilty" be sentenced more quickly and certainly.[107] His request would be satisfactorily fulfilled only with the law of 22 prairial, which enacted many provisions first voiced during the king's trial.[108] By that point, of course, the legal system had become little more than a travesty of justice.

Given the clarity and coherence of Jacobin legal thought in other regards, this conflation between two types of criminal, the *hostis humani generis* and the civilian offender, may come as somewhat of a surprise. Surely Saint-Just, Robespierre, and their fellow Montagnards could tell the difference between them? Or might they have had reasons to blur this difference? At least three bear noting. First, as noted above, Jacobin political theory onward from the August 10 insurrection evolved in an increasingly natural-republican direction. In this revision of the Physiocratic *ordre naturel*, the

---

106. A similar idea can also be found in Saint-Just's unpublished treatise, generally known as *De la nature,* but probably meant to be entitled *Du droit social, ou Principes du droit naturel*: The punishment of all crimes, he argued, "concerns the law of nations, for whoever violates the law ceases to be a citizen [*est sorti de la cité*]" (*SJ*, 936). On the proper name of this text, which I discuss further in chapter 4, see Anne Quennedey, "Note philologique sur le manuscrit de Saint-Just faussement intitulé *De la nature*," *AHRF* 351 (2008): 121–49.

107. See in particular his August 11, 12, 25, and 28 speeches; Robespierre's December 28, 1792, speech had already insisted on the necessity for Louis's swift execution (*Rob.*, 9:185).

108. See notably Gueniffey, *Politique de la Terreur*, chap. 10. While I do not subscribe to Gueniffey's overall thesis that "the Terror . . . was the fate, not of the French Revolution, but of every revolution" (226), I find his genealogy of the 22 prairial bill, which traces its origins back to the summer of 1792, quite convincing; see chapter 5.

distinction between natural and civil law ideally tended toward zero. Second, where the justice system was concerned, at least one illustrious eighteenth-century authority, Jean-Jacques Rousseau, had set a precedent for the confusion of natural and civil offenses. As I argue in chapter 1, the *Social Contract* may have rejected the authority of natural right ("this [social] right does not come from nature," 1.1), only to reinscribe it at the very heart of its legal doctrine with the *volonté générale*, which relies on and is structurally identical to the natural "principles" of self-love and compassion. Finally, in an important December 6 speech, Pierre Bourbotte, a Montagnard deputy, pointed out another instance where Rousseau had given civil law the force of natural right. Quoting an author described only as "a man whose memory [is] more revered than Mirabeau's deserves to be" (the latter recently having been discredited by the discovery of his secret correspondence with the king in the *armoire de fer*), Bourbotte read:

> As every offender attacks social law, he becomes by his violation a rebel and traitor to his country. By violating its law, he ceases to be a member of it and even declares war upon it. At this point, the conservation of the State is incompatible with his own, and one of the two must perish. When the guilty party is put to death, it is less as a citizen than as an enemy. The procedure and judgment are the proofs and notification that he broke the social treaty: accordingly, he is no longer a member of the State and must be removed from it; and we have the right to kill, even as an example, one who cannot be allowed to live without risk.[109]

Bourbotte did not bother to cite outright the author or the work from which he was quoting, suggesting that it was all too well known by his audience (if not by his nineteenth-century editors). Whether or not Saint-Just had this passage in mind when composing his own text, Rousseau's authoritative opinion certainly encouraged the punishment of civil violations (attacks on "social laws") according to the harsh strictures of natural right offenses. The legal structure of his argument indeed mirrors the jusnaturalist logic employed by Locke, Burlamaqui, or Vattel in their analyses of the

---

109. *AP*, 54:398; the editors of the *Archives parlementaires* (or of Bourbotte's speech) put only the first sentence in quotes. The reference is to the *Social Contract*, bk. 2, chap. 5, in *Œuvres complètes*, ed. Bernard Gagnebin and Marcel Raymond (Paris: Gallimard/Pléiade, 1959–95), 3:376 (hereafter cited as *JJR*). It is this passage that Camus and Walzer reference in their discussion of Saint-Just, but neither of them (nor to my knowledge anyone else) noticed that it was in fact quoted during the trial.

hostis humani generis. Rousseau thus seems to have bequeathed to the Jacobins a violent and volatile theory of justice, in which *any* criminal offense could potentially deprive the perpetrator of his civilian and natural rights. Under these circumstances, there was hardly any need for due process (even if Rousseau does evoke "procedure"), since the guilty party cannot make demands of a state that has already expelled him.

A further indication that the Montagnards were aware of the hybrid genealogy of their natural-*cum*-civil legal theory can be found in their use of a new term to identify these offenders: *hors-la-loi*. For many deputies, the charge that Louis was an outlaw derived, ironically, from the claim by his defenders that he was inviolable. His constitutional status placed him "beyond all the laws of society," Marc-Antoine Baudot proclaimed, adding that this external position meant that Louis could not "request the protection of the holiest of [laws]," a reference to a future law against capital punishment (105).[110] Michel Azéma came up with a more precise phrase for the king's status: "He is an outlaw [*il est hors la loi*], an *ex legs*."[111] For Azéma, it was the destruction of the social contract that placed Louis *hors la loi* ("Louis XVI put us back into the state of nature"). Baudot's and Azéma's arguments were amalgamated in one of the most damning attacks on royal inviolability, presented by Didier Thirion. The constitutional clause that granted the king immunity from prosecution was "a law that declares him to be beyond the law [*qui le déclare hors de la loi*]" (334), Thirion argued. To be beyond the law (which had been the original, theological signification of *ex lex*) was now to be outside of the law and thus in a state of nature:[112] "If Louis is outside of the law, how could he demand its protection and safety . . . do each of us not regain our natural right to rebuff his attacks and to oppose force with force?" (334). The outlaw category is explicitly glossed here in terms of natural right, as it had been by William Blackstone in his famous

---

110. In his November 7 report for the Committee on Legislation, Maihle had already quoted Rousseau's denunciation of placing "a man above the law" in order to criticize the king's inviolability (*AP*, 53:275).

111. December 3, 1792; *AP*, 54:97. It is telling that Azéma still felt the need to gloss "*hors la loi*" with its Latin translation, underscoring yet again how foreign this legal concept was to French jurisprudence. See Mari, "La mise hors de la loi," 1:40–43. "*Exlex*" was a church Latin term (found notably in 1 Cor. 9:21), often used to signify "above the law," as in Calvin's expression, "Deus legibus solutus est, sed non exlex" (God is free from the law but not above it).

112. Rousseau had made this precise claim in his fragment on *L'état de guerre*: "If the Prince is above the laws he lives in a pure state of nature and does not have to account for his actions to his subjects or to anyone" (*JJR*, 3:603). Although this text would be published only in the nineteenth century, it essentially condenses the Hobbesian theory of absolute sovereignty.

Commentaries on the Laws of England.[113] For good measure, Thirion also emphasized Louis's repeated transgressions against natural right: Kings were "accustomed . . . from father to son, to violate all the laws of humanity" (334). Not only was the king outside of the law; he was "outside of nature [*hors de la nature*]," in Alexandre Deleyre's words (171). To be an outlaw was to be an enemy of the human race.

Outlawing the Nation: Natural Right and Terror Laws

The March 19 decree on *hors-la-loi* thus emerged in the wake of the debates over natural right and the fate of the king. In fact, when Cambacérès presented the decree to the Convention, it was not the first time that the deputies heard such a proposal. A similar bill proposal had been submitted to the Committees on Diplomacy, War, Navy, and Finances on December 24, 1792, that is, in the midst of the king's trial. Drawn up by Jean Debry, this bill would have made an official legal category out of the outlaw: Title 3, article 1, stated that "every individual or group of individuals who assumes or receives a form of authority that was not established by the official delegates of the nation will be declared an outlaw: accordingly, any citizen who does not seek to stop him [*lui courir sus*] will be regarded as an accomplice." The following article provided further instructions: "The National Convention, after three successive debates, separated by at least one day, will formally outlaw the accused who have been denounced, and who cannot be judged by a State court."[114] These measures formalized, in a different context, the hard-line Montagnard attacks on the king. The bill took aim at figures who had usurped authority; it gave citizens the natural right to arrest them; and it stripped the accused of any legal rights. The March 19 decree retained most of these characteristics: It was directed at the "leaders" of the insurrection and not "those men who are more confused [*égarés*] than guilty, and to

---

113. According to Blackstone, "though anciently an outlawed felon was said to have *caput lupinum*, and might be knocked on the head like a wolf, by any one that should meet him; because, having renounced all law, he was to be dealt with as in a state of nature, when every one that should find him might slay him: yet now, to avoid such inhumanity, it is holden that no man is entitled to kill him wantonly or willfully; but in so doing is guilty of murder, unless it happens in the endeavor to apprehend him," *Commentaries on the Laws of England* (Oxford: Clarendon Press, 1765–68), 4.24. It bears noting that this gloss does not reject the notion of outlaw altogether (as Mari suggests), but only the "ancient" practice associated with it. Blackstone's text was translated as *Commentaire sur le code criminel d'Angleterre, traduit de l'anglois de Guillaume Blackstone, . . . par M. l'abbé Coyer, . . .* (Paris: Knapen, 1776); it renders "outlaw" as "*ex loi*" (2:78).

114. *AP*, 55:384. On this bill, see Mari, "La mise hors de la loi," 133.

whom a helping hand must be extended" (although this distinction, as we shall see, would soon fall by the wayside).[115] It did not call on all citizens to *courir sus* the rebels, but set up military commissions to sentence them to death.[116] The role of these commissions, however, was limited to recording the outlaws' identities and then, on the basis of two oral depositions or a written statement, sending them to their deaths. The accused had no legal recourse or appeal. They were to be killed without delay or formalities, as the Montagnards had wanted for the king—"without any other formalities than twenty-three thrusts of a dagger," in Saint-Just's Roman parlance.[117]

The *hors-la-loi* decree did not represent the first time that one of the three revolutionary Assemblies had had recourse to such exceptional measures against civilian enemies: Patrice Gueniffey, as noted above, argued that the laws passed by the Legislative Assembly against *émigrés*, stripping them of their property and even sentencing to death those who returned, must be seen as a first step toward the laws of the Terror.[118] More recently, Anne Simonin has pointed out that the legal forms for judging the *hors-la-loi* (execution within twenty-four hours, after being brought before a military commission) were nearly identical to the law of October 9, 1792, concerning *émigrés* caught in arms (*les armes à la main*).[119] Tellingly, this law also evokes the law of nations in justifying France's right to retaliation (art. 4). But the legal logic behind these different measures does not seem to follow the same tracks. The earlier legislation against *émigrés* found its legal and logical conclusion in the March 28, 1793, law that declared them "civilly dead."[120] While draconian in its own right, this law did not circumvent the

---

115. *AP*, 60:331. This distinction was introduced following complaints by Marat and Delacroix; article 6 called for the indefinite detention of the "confused" rebels, until further notice from the Convention (which arrived on August 1; see below).

116. The expression *courir sus* is somewhat ambiguous. While it clearly indicates a violent action, it does not have the sense of "to kill." See *Trésor de la langue française informatisé*, s.v. "sus," http://atilf.atilf.fr/tlf.htm. As Anne Simonin noted in *Déshonneur dans la république*, a law of June 13–15, 1791, already called upon all citizens to *courir sus* the prince de Condé, should he appear in arms on French soil (223 and 323).

117. *SJ*, 377. In his December 28, 1792, speech, Robespierre insisted on the necessity for a swift execution of Louis's sentence (*Rob.*, 9:185). This requirement would be introduced into the March 19 outlaw decree, article 2; see also article 2 of the March 27 decree on *émigrés* (who, if caught on French soil, will be "judged by a military jury and put to death within 24 hours," *AP*, 60:603).

118. Gueniffey, *Politique de la Terreur*, passim.

119. See Simonin, *Déshonneur dans la république*, 323.

120. See *AP*, 60:643–51. On this concept, see Miranda Frances Spieler, "Empire and Underworld: Guiana in the French Legal Imagination, c. 1789–c. 1870" (PhD diss., Columbia University, 2005), 71–75; and Simonin, *Déshonneur dans la république*, 315–24.

criminal justice system with a separate set of military commissions; it still granted suspects the right to a trial (if not the right to appeal; see article 79). Had the legislation and cultural representations concerning the *émigré* been at the root of the March 19 decree, why did the Convention not simply outlaw the *émigrés* as well? The fact that it chose to apply a different punishment—one that, furthermore, already existed in Old Regime legislation, and only incidentally led to physical death[121]—strongly suggests that the legal logic behind the *émigré* laws derived from a different source, and that, *a fortiori*, the outlaw decree was grounded in more recent developments in revolutionary legislation, particularly the use of natural right in civil prosecution.

The difference between *émigré* legislation and the *hors-la-loi* decree is also evident in the choice of whom to prosecute under the latter. Initially, the outlaw category was used primarily against individuals who, like the king, had usurped authority. On April 3, Dumouriez and his general staff were outlawed;[122] the members of the "popular court" of Marseilles were outlawed on June 19, 1793;[123] Pascal Paoli was declared a "traitor to the French Republic and an outlaw" on July 17;[124] the Girondins were implicitly outlawed on July 28, when the Convention declared them "traitors to the State" and in an "state of rebellion";[125] on August 6, the Committee of public safety had the Convention decree an unlawful Committee of the same name in Bordeaux to be "*hors-la-loi*"; three days later, Couthon imposed an identical punishment on rebel administrators in the Jura;[126] and on September 7, any French citizen who accepted public employment in enemy-occupied territory was made an outlaw.[127] By that summer, however, it was the "brigands" of the Vendée who had come to emblematize the outlaws. In terms of sheer numbers, furthermore, the March 19 decree would certainly fall

---

121. The 1670 *Ordonnance criminelle* declared certain criminals to be "mort civilement" (see title 17, articles 22 and 29).

122. *AP*, 61:303.

123. *AP*, 66:705.

124. *AP*, 69:97. A number of generals and administrators (in the Loire-Inférieure) were also outlawed that day (104), but the Convention reversed itself a day later (129).

125. And thus, by virtue of the March 19 decree, *hors de la loi* (*AP*, 69:631). Ironically, Lanjuinais had attempted to have the Parisian authorities outlawed on June 2, 1793 (65:700), but his motion was rejected.

126. See the decrees on August 6 against officials in Bordeaux (*AP*, 70:376–77) and on August 7 against the *comité de salut public* in the Jura (*AP*, 70:586).

127. *AP*, 73:495. Outlawing would remain a crucial legislative maneuver until the bitter end of the Terror, when Robespierre and his allies were defeated after the Convention declared them *hors-la-loi*.

hardest on peasants and workers in the West, as well in the "Federalist" strongholds of the South.[128]

The outlaw category thus encompassed two apparently heterogeneous groups, usurpers (a variation on tyrants) and brigands. Was there any logic to this grouping, or was the outlaw a makeshift concept, loosely devised to do the *conventionnels'* dirty business? One can detect, in fact, a clear jusnaturalist genealogy behind this linking: The "tyrant" and the "brigand" had been the twin paradigms of the *hostis humani generis*, as evidenced in Grotius and others (see the prologue). Louis himself was described as both during his trial, and other "tyrannical" rulers, such as Pitt, received this epithet as well. (In this latter case, the diabolical roots of this expression were still evident. In the imagery of one popular print, the British minister was portrayed as the Lucifer of the counterrevolution.[129]) The ambivalence of this expression was even evident in *sans-culotte* discourse, as Hébert's *Père Duchesne* testifies: "What is a king or a queen? Are they not what is most impure and wretched on earth? To reign, is that not to be the worst mortal enemy of humanity?"[130] But Hébert did not reserve this dishonorable title for monarchs alone. In an earlier issue, he had declared that "there is no worse enemy of humanity, than one who attempts to spare traitors."[131] Those who sought to curb popular fury were now lumped together with traitors and usurpers themselves. (Danton had similarly exploited this ambiguity when he stirred, and no doubt stunned, the Convention by proclaiming that it should drink "the blood of the enemies of humanity, if we must." It was not at all clear, however, whether he was referring to the British government or to the "traitors to the country," who were destined for the revolutionary tribunal.[132])

---

128. Executions among peasants and the working class would comprise 89 percent of the deaths in the Vendée's judicial Terror (Greer, *Incidence of the Terror*, table 7, 164). Alan Forrest describes how the Vendée was commonly depicted as a land of brigands "unworthy of the name of humanity," in "The Ubiquitous Brigand: The Politics and Language of Repression," in *Popular Resistance in the French Wars: Patriots, Partisans and Land Pirates*, ed. Charles J. Esdaile (London: Palgrave Macmillan, 2005), 37–41.

129. See the print described in the *Catalogue of Pictures, Statues, Busts, Bronzes, Etc., Now Exhibited for Sale at the Great Auction Room, Westminster* (in *Cabinet of Curiosities. . . . to Be Continued* [London, 1795]): "Satan, the enemy of the Human Race, in Pandemonium. A formidable figure with a horrible countenance. It is supposed to be a portrait of Pit [*sic*] himself. There certainly is a strong resemblance" (number 62, 162). The "demonizing of the Other" that defined the Terror can thus be understood literally; see Tackett, "La Révolution et la violence," in *La Révolution à l'œuvre*, 213.

130. *Issue* no. 280 ([Sept.?] 1793), 3–4.

131. Issue no. 278, p. 6 (vol. 8), my italics.

132. Danton's previous sentences reveal an unwillingness to distinguish between them: "You who tire me with your specific complaints, rather than preoccupy yourselves with the safety of

As the Vendée war spun increasingly out of control, in spring-summer 1793, the *hors-la-loi* opposing the republican armies furnished the ultimate proof of this identity between tyrants and brigands: For what were they, after all, if not brigands fighting for a tyrant?[133] The "exceptional" treatment meted out against the "rebel" king—"every king is a rebel," Saint-Just had cautioned—could accordingly be extended to his (or the monarchy's) purported supporters in the West and South, as in Toulon. Tellingly, these other "rebels" were denounced not only for being traitors to the French *patrie*, but also for transgressing the laws of nature. The Vendéens must be killed, Robespierre argued, because they "will eternally conspire against the rights of man and the happiness of all peoples."[134] It was in their "vile and treacherous" nature to oppose the natural rights of man; as "rebels against humanity," they would never change, and only death could put an end to their diabolical villainy.[135] As in Louis's case, the mantle of natural right was bestowed on civil legislation to justify its extreme harshness. This conflation of natural and positive law was further on display when the Convention (on August 1, 1793) finally determined the fate of the lower-class outlaws, whom the March 19 decree had left in limbo.[136] In Barère's words, they, too, were a "race rebelle à faire disparaître," hostile to humanity: "L'humanité ne se plaindra point; c'est faire son bien que d'extirper le mal; c'est être bienfaisant que de punir les rebelles."[137] Twisted as this logic may sound, it in fact

---

the Republic, I repudiate all of you as traitors. I put you all in the same league" (March 10; *AP*, 60:58).

133. It is not uncommon to hear the March 19 decree described as legitimate, to the extent that the Vendée counterrevolutionaries were in open rebellion against the republic. In this regard, it is worth stressing that, as in the case of the king, treason was not the principal reason given by the Jacobin leadership for the necessary extermination of the rebels.

134. Speech at the Jacobin club, May 8, 1793 (*Rob.*, 9:487–88).

135. As Barère would later say, "Only the dead do not come back, but the kings and their slaves are incorrigble: they must disappear" (*HP*, 33:118).

136. On May 10, Danton again proposed that the harsh penalties be restricted to the leaders of the rebellions, and the Convention agreed (*AP*, 64:435), only to reverse itself on August 1.

137. *AP*, 70:91, 101–2. Barère's caution against clemency was itself rooted in Enlightenment theories of justice. Even that most *sensible* of philosophers, Rousseau, for whom compassion was the most natural human impulse, had weighed in against it; see the *Social Contract*, in *JJR*, 3:377; see also the unattributed (and probably invented for the occasion) verse in the *Dernière réponse de J.-J. Rousseau* on his first *Discourse*: "Et le juste au méchant ne sait point pardonner [And the righteous cannot forgive the villain]" (*JJR*, 3:72n). Montesquieu had pointed out the inherent problem with clemency (similarly noting that it was rarely necessary in a republic): "But, some will say, when should we punish? When should we pardon? . . . The Greek emperors forgot that it was not for nothing that they carried a sword," *De l'esprit des lois*, ed. Robert Derathé (Paris: Garnier, 1973), bk. 6, chap. 21; 1:104.

echoed Vattel's stiff pronouncements on the "ennemi du genre-humain": One must disregard his natural right "for the purpose of obliging him to observe [it]."

The revolutionary concept of the *hors-la-loi* can thus be regarded as more of a "rebranding" of the *hostis humani generis* category than as an actual borrowing of an earlier German, English, or Greek version of outlawry.[138] Most significantly, the *hors-la-loi* were not entirely beyond the law, as for these predecessors. They were *hors-la-loi civile*, that is, they were to be denied the protection and rights afforded by positive law (first and foremost, the right to a trial). Though stripped of these rights, however, they did not henceforth reside in an "anomic" zone, to borrow Agamben's expression, since, according to the *conventionnels*, the laws of nature always continued to hold.[139] Rather than the suspension of the law, it was the creation of a parallel legal system that posed the greatest threat to the more liberal justice system established by the Constituent Assembly.

Only "Natural": Becoming a Terrorist

While most accounts situate the beginning of the Terror in September 1793, the "dark machinery of state political Terror"[140] was thus well in place six months prior, before "the Terror" was even proposed as a political goal—a disjunction that will lead us to ask, in chapter 5, what this latter expression may really be said to designate. To be sure, subsequent events, laws, popular uprisings, military campaigns, and political rivalries would prolong the Terror in further, and no doubt unexpected, directions. But these springtime efforts provided a critical foundation for the political violence to come: the legal justification, drawn from one of the most respected and "sacred" sources of revolutionary authority, that could facilitate and authorize subsequent developments.

Identifying spring 1793 as the critical moment for the Terror nonetheless raises a number of questions. For instance, as François Furet queried, if the central institutions were in place by March, why did the number of political executions (both in Paris and nationwide) remain almost negligible until

---

138. My reading of the *hors-la-loi* in this respect departs from Mari's thesis.

139. Even Marie-Antoinette was accused by Fouquier-Tinville at her trial of having "oubli[é] sa qualité de mère et la démarcation prescritte par les loix de la nature"; her alleged incest with her son made her into an *hostis humani generis* as well: *Réquisitoires de Fouquier-Tinville* (Paris: E. Fasquelle, 1911), 32. My thanks to Elena Russo for stressing this point.

140. Jones, *Great Nation*, 471 (in reference to the March 1793 measures).

late winter?[141] Does this not suggest that other political, military, and social events intervened in the meantime to precipitate matters—and if so, would this not mean that they were more important in the history of the Terror? How can we be sure, moreover, that the natural right framework, which presided over the creation of the Terror, remained in place throughout?

I will return in chapter 4 to the question of the temporal slippage between the moment of the Terror's institutional foundation and its bloody implementation, but there are a flurry of reasons why the Terror did not begin with a bang. Until the purge of May 31–June 2, the Convention was embroiled in political infighting between Montagnards and Girondins, which was not conducive to effective governmental action. Militarily, matters were worse, with the Vendée rebels maintaining an upper hand until the battle of Cholet on October 16–17; and the "Federalist" revolt was only brought under control between October 8 (surrender of Lyon) and December 19 (recovery of Toulon).[142] On the political front, the deputies agonized for months over their legal right to create a separate executive (with respect to article 16 of the 1789 *Déclaration*); on August 1, Danton was still urging the Convention to act decisively. The revolutionnaires would have to wait until December 4, 1793 (14 frimaire) for a law that clearly affirmed the Committee of Public Safety's power and authority.[143]

This temporal slippage becomes problematical, however, only if we assume that the *conventionnels* were set on "becoming Terrorists" (to paraphrase Timothy Tackett) from the start. In all likelihood, most deputies did not wish to become Terrorists, and even fewer would have wished to replace positive law altogether with the nebulous constructs of natural right. The "outlaw" category owed its legislative existence only to the deputies' desire to act forcefully against specific and localized threats, such as the *émigrés* or the Vendée rebels. But the scope of this law could not be so easily delimited. Less than ten days after the March 19 decree was passed, Danton successfully demanded that *all* counterrevolutionaries be outlawed ("quiconque a

---

141. In "Terror," in *CDFR*; while arguing that the Terror "had existed since the early summer of 1789" (137), Furet nonetheless affirmed that "the Terror began in March 1793 with the creation of the Revolutionary Tribunal and the first measures of public safety" (143). More recently, Michel Biard similarly situated the beginnings of the Terror in spring 1793; see "Les rouages de la Terreur," in *Les politiques de la Terreur, 1793–1794*, ed. Michel Biard (Rennes: Presses universitaires de Rennes & Société des études robespierristes, 2008), 24.

142. See chapter 4.

143. *AP*, 80:632. See notably Furet, "Revolutionary Government," in *CDFR*, and Hesse, "La logique culturelle de la loi révolutionnaire." The October 10 decree that implicitly suspended the Constitution (see chapter 4) already centralized executive power beneath the Committee of Public Safety.

l'audace d'appeler cette contre-révolution sera mis hors de la loi").[144] The radicalness of this decree, considered significant enough to be formally repealed on 22 Germinal year III (April 11, 1795), is breathtaking.[145] There were no specific criteria provided for determining what it meant precisely to "*appeler cette contre-révolution.*" The passive voice (*sera mis*) disguised the fact that there was no official or formal process for outlawing one or many individuals: Who had this authority?[146] What had originally been construed as an emergency measure was now poised to overthrow the entire system of measured, "enlightened" justice that had been one of the crowning achievements of the Constituent Assembly.[147] In little over a week, the *hors-la-loi* had gone from designating an armed rebel leader to "anyone" who might somehow be construed as opposing the revolution. This slippage, however, does not imply that the *conventionnels* had tasted blood and found it to their liking (the March 19 decree had hardly gone into effect), but rather that, once created, extraordinary legal categories are very difficult to delimit. The temptation to expand their designated targets is hard to resist, particularly in a volatile political situation.[148]

By making natural right the principal authority for arresting and executing enemies of the state, the deputies not only removed essential safeguards against arbitrary condemnations, but they also drastically weakened the process through which positive laws were articulated, and by extension, the institution of civil law per se. Where laws had been meant to express the general will (as stated in article 6 of the 1789 Declaration of Rights), the legislators ultimately transferred authority away from themselves—and through them, from the nation—to "the legislator of the universe" (in Robespierre's words), that is, God or nature. In other words, the laws that the Convention passed in spring 1793 ultimately disempowered the Convention as a lawmaking body. This process was gradual and perhaps not inevitable, but it did assure

144. March 27, 1793; *AP*, 60:605.

145. See Anne Simonin, "An Essay of Political Cartography: The Law of Citizenship under the French Revolution (1793–95)," published online at http://www.crhq.cnrs.fr/images-axe5/tableaux/axe5%20tab-TraducABarnes.pdf.

146. The Convention would formally outlaw certain individuals or groups, but for the vast majority, individuals were simply put to death as outlaws by virtue of the March 19 or March 27 decree. My thanks to Pamela Karlan, Debra Satz, and the Stanford Bungee Lunch group for drawing out the importance of these points.

147. See Shapiro, *Revolutionary Justice in Paris, 1789–90.*

148. In a different, contemporary context, see Michael Ignatieff, *The Lesser Evil: Political Ethics in an Age of Terror* (Princeton: Princeton University Press, 2004); and Bruce Ackerman, *Before the Next Attack: Preserving Civil Liberties in an Age of Terrorism* (New Yaven: Yale University Press, 2007).

that the reign of Terror could progressively sweep up all French citizens in its ever-expanding net. "Who among us will be spared?" Jean Debry ominously asked, when introducing the first law of suspects on March 21.[149] His question was foreboding: Anyone could soon be a *hostis humani generis.*

The following two chapters will also examine the lasting importance of natural right theory during the long months of the Terror. Clearly, the *conventionnels* continued to speak this political language fluently. But was it anything more than a language in the conventional sense? Was it an actual mode of thought, a grammar of ideas, or did it merely provide a discursive veneer for murderous and vengeful passions?[150] As with all studies of revolutionary discourse, these questions raise the difficult issue of distinguishing between rhetoric and substance.[151] The speakers in the National Convention were certainly no strangers to the art of persuasion. Oratory, after all, was taught in the *collèges* and employed by young lawyers to stand out in eighteenth-century courtrooms. Unsurprisingly, they carried this skill into the political assembly halls. As Victor Hugo quipped, "terrorism was Racinian."[152] When historians ponder the role of oratory in revolutionary debates,

149. *AP*, 60:387. This bill was presented as a "report on foreigners" and called for the systematic verification of income to uncover "suspects"; it also created the *comités de surveillance*, which would play a prominent policing role during the Terror. The verification of income recalls prior revolutionary (and even Old Regime) legislation against vagrants, such as the July 5, 1791, decree on "persons without means [*gens sans aveu*]," which employed the same exact language: "Those who refuse to declare [their source of income] will have their identity and address recorded, with the mention of *suspect*" (*AP*, 27:744–745). On the figure of the suspect, see Baczko, "Terror before the Terror," 25–28, who points out that Marat had already introduced the term in July 1789 (27); see also Keith Baker, "Transformations of Classical Republicanism in Eighteenth-Century France," *Journal of Modern History* 73 (2001): 43–47. During the debate over the creation of the *comité de recherches*, in July 1789, Le Chapelier had also described the need for this committee "to receive information about suspects" (*HP*, 2:190).

150. On "political languages" in this cognitive sense, see the introduction.

151. Furet famously warned against "tak[ing] revolutionary discourse at face value," in *Interpreting the French Revolution*, 16. In other studies, he nonetheless recognized that "rhetoric is essential, however, for understanding the forces and passions that determined the relations btween this period and the rest of the Revolution," "Revolutionary Government," in *CDFR*, 554; see also his article on "Terror" in *CDFR*, and the section on Sieyès in *Revolutionary France, 1770–1880.*

152. For Hugo, see the draft for *Quatrevingt-treize* (Paris: Presses Pocket, 1992), 448. See also Hans Ulrich Gumbrecht, *Funktionen parlamentarischer Rhetorik in der Französischen Revolution: Vorstudien zur Entwicklung einer historischen Textpragmatik* (Munich: W. Fink, 1978); Lynn Hunt, "The Rhetoric of Revolution," in *Politics, Culture, and Class in the French Revolution* (Berkeley: University of California Press, 1984); Jean Starobinski, "Eloquence antique, éloquence future: aspects d'un lieu commun d'ancien régime," in *The Political Culture of the Old Regime*, ed. Keith Baker, vol. 1 of *FRCMPC*, 311–30; and the essays by Philippe Roger, Lynn Hunt, and Peter France collected in *Language and Rhetoric of the Revolution*, ed. John Renwick (Edinburgh: Edinburgh University Press, 1990).

however, we tend to forget that truthfulness is not the yardstick with which to measure the success of a rhetorical peroration.[153] What a speaker *believes* is beside the point: It is the speaker's ability to convince his audience that matters. To study rhetoric means to study how a speech is received, not if the speaker's beliefs are genuine (although the *appearance* of sincerity is usually a necessary condition of felicity). The suspicion that a statement is "rhetorical," therefore, should not stop us from weighing it with care. If it manages to sway an audience, then it is substantial, if not substantive.

Language, of course, is not the only factor to weigh when evaluating the reception of an argument. The *conventionnels*, like most politicians, acted in their own interest. They were drawn to arguments that allowed them to obstruct or placate their adversaries, be they on the opposite side of the aisle, in the streets of Paris, or, as the Terror wore on, on the Committee of Public Safety. Fear and intimidation usually prove more persuasive than any flower of rhetoric. But during the first six months of the National Convention's term, the outcome of its heated debates cannot entirely be attributed to external pressures. The great power struggle between the Mountain and the Gironde was in the end a literally "rhetorical" one, hinging as it did on who could persuade the mass of wavering deputies known dismissively as "La Plaine." Even if this struggle was ultimately decided by armed insurrection (with the expulsion of the Girondins on June 2), the Jacobins had already scored a string of legislative victories, beginning with the king's sentencing (and the defeat of the *appel au peuple*). The March decrees instituting the revolutionary tribunal, outlawing rebels, establishing surveillance committees, and (on April 6) creating the dreaded Committee of Public Safety itself, are in this respect all evidence that the Jacobin rhetoric overpowered the objections of the leading Girondin orators in the Convention.[154] Even if it was only rhetoric, it was very successful.

But why was it so successful? While recognizing the complexity and open-endedness of this question, I would submit that the Plain (as well as some Girondins) accepted the natural right logic of the Jacobins for the same

---

153. Aristotle defines rhetoric as the art of "detect[ing] what is persuasive and what is apparently persuasive," contrasting it with dialectic, whose function is to "perceive both the real and the apparent syllogism"; see *The Art of Rhetoric*, trans. H. C. Lawson-Tancred (London: Penguin, 1991), 1.1; 70. In his *Institutio Oratoria*, Quintilian recognized that most scholars considered rhetoric to be "the power to persuade" (*uim persuadendi*), even though he himself preferred to define it as "the art of speaking well" (*bene dicendi scientiam*); 2.15.2–38.

154. In particular Lanjuinais, Gaudet, Fauchet, Vergniaud, and Buzot, who strongly (and at times, rather hysterically) rejected the revolutionary tribunal and the new Committee; see *AP*, 60:3–5, 50–51, 59–70, 93–95 (for the tribunal); and *AP*, 61:123–29, 277–79, 341–43, 373–83 (for the Committee).

reasons that Robespierre and his colleagues had: It constituted the primary political language of liberal reform in the eighteenth century; its keywords furnished the central concepts of Enlightenment political theory.[155] Natural right was not an ideology that needed to be disseminated or imposed onto others: They already shared it. It had been a pillar of the Revolution's legal framework since the 1789 Declaration of Rights. The version of natural right that Saint-Just outlined during the king's trial may have seemed somewhat unusual, but it had a venerable Enlightenment pedigree; if the Jacobins politicized the category of a denatured "enemy of the human race," they did not invent it. Arguments that rested on this category—most notably concerning the *hors-la-loi*—will thus have resonated with deputies, who may not have shared the Jacobins' Manichean interpretation of natural right, but who nonetheless recognized its legal and philosophical authority.

The "naturalness" of the Terror laws and institutions may thus be credited with having facilitated their passage in the Convention and having ensured their execution by the revolutionary commissions and *représentants du people*. Even moderate deputies were drawn in by this discourse: The March 19 decree stemmed from a proposal by the Girondin Lanjuinais, and the same day that Jean Debry (a moderate) sponsored the first law of suspects, he was elected president of the Convention. Constantin-François de Volney, the famous travel writer and member of the Constituent Assembly, published a pamphlet in the spring of 1793 praising natural law as the true and sufficient source of all legislation; one of his closest friends in the Convention was Lanjuinais.[156] Natural right could lead the revolutionaries to become Terrorists in good Enlightenment faith (which, of course, is not to say the Enlightenment inevitably led to the Terror). Many deputies no doubt hoped that the new Constitution would restore their political authority. But here again, the Jacobins triumphed, this time largely through trickery and intimidation, as will be discussed in the following chapter. Despite,

---

155. For this reason, the only other major study of natural right that I am aware of, Florence Gauthier's *Triomphe et mort du droit naturel en Révolution, 1789–1795–1802* (Paris: PUF, 1992), recognizes only its liberal and liberatory functions. Although her book defends an anthropological thesis of political violence, Wahnich nonetheless hints at this natural right framework of the Terror in *Liberté ou la mort*, 83–85. Tocqueville may also have had this genealogy in mind when he claimed that one finds in the Physiocrats "all that is most substantial in the Revolution," *The Old Regime and Revolution*, ed. François Furet and Françoise Mélonio, trans. Alan S. Kahan (Chicago: University of Chicago Press, 1998), 210. Although he does not discuss their natural right theory at great lengths, it constituted a cornerstone of their philosophy, as we saw in the last chapter.

156. On this pamphlet, *La loi naturelle, ou Catéchisme du citoyen français* (Paris: Sallior, 1793), see the following chapter.

or rather in addition to, their clear power grab, the Jacobins still remained committed to reviving "the true golden age," which Billaud-Varenne and his companions were certain had once existed in ancient Egypt and Greece.[157] This pursuit involved pushing natural right to its most radical conclusion, to a point where civil legislation was deemed unnecessary. At this point, however, the "terrors of natural law" would become all too apparent.[158]

---

157. *Les éléments du républicanisme* (n.p., n.d.), 19; this passage is discussed in Mona Ozouf, *Festivals of the French Revolution*, trans. Alan Sheridan (Cambridge: Harvard University Press, 1988), 274–75. On the Egyptian referent in revolutionary culture and ideology, see, for instance, Gilbert Romme's *Rapport sur l'ère de la République* (Paris: Impr. Nationale, n.d. [1793]). I return to this Egyptian golden age in chapters 4 and 5.

158. This expression, somewhat surprisingly, is found in Leo Strauss, *Natural Right and History* (Chicago: University of Chicago, 1948), 237.

＊c CHAPTER FOUR ⊃＊

THE CASE OF THE
MISSING CONSTITUTION
Of Power and Policy

ON APRIL 10, 1793, Robespierre demanded that Brissot, Vergniaud, Gensonné, Gaudet, and "all of Dumouriez's other accomplices" be called before the revolutionary tribunal. It had not taken long for the *conventionnels* to seek to exploit their new institutions for political gain.[1] The Convention balked, but two days later, the Girondins had Marat dragged before the tribunal's bar, only to see him gloriously acquitted on April 24. Was it with this purpose in mind that the Jacobins (and even some Girondin deputies, such as Maximin Isnard) had approved the creation of the *tribunal criminel extraordinaire*?[2] In this context of political recrimination and power struggles, one might wonder whether it is even relevant to recall the natural right foundation of the laws and institutions of the Terror. What could possibly be left of the "Laws of Nature and Nature's God" in a revolutionary tribunal that by June 1794 seemed to mete out death arbitrarily?

More than the facilitating role of natural right in the history of the Terror, these questions highlight the vaster historiographical problem of ascribing any political or ideological agenda whatsoever to revolutionary leaders after September 1792. If the National Convention was merely the scene of a pitched battle between Montagnards and Girondins, and if the Committee of Public Safety was mostly preoccupied with eliminating rival political groups, does this not suggest that power had become an end in itself, and the only end that mattered? There has certainly been a tendency in recent scholarship to discount any "ideological" explanations for the Terror. According to Patrice Gueniffey, for instance, Robespierre's republicanism was merely "a rhetorical artifice, not political," and the Incorruptible had no

---

1. Maximilien Robespierre, *Œuvres de Maximilien Robespierre*, ed. the Société des études robespierristes (Ivry: Phénix éditions, 2000), 9:399, 407 (hereafter cited as *Rob.*). As noted in the previous chapter, the initial impetus for creating this tribunal seems to have come from the Jacobin club in the first place.

2. A number of Girondins would similarly be tracked down that autumn in accordance with the March 19 *hors-la-loi* decree, in favor of which many had voted.

intention of ever establishing a republic, virtuous or other.[3] John Hardman's biography of Robespierre drives this point home, dwelling on details of cronyism, opportunism, and extortion, at the expense of any political agenda.[4] More nuanced, Jean-Clément Martin has brushed a broad portrait of violence during the Revolution, in which "calculation and manipulation" are called on to play starring roles.[5]

There is no reason to challenge many of the insightful conclusions in these and similar works, but their marked opposition to "revisionist" historiography (Martin, for instance, scoffs at any influence of a "dubious Rousseauism"[6]) may have blinded them to a more fundamental question: Why should clear instances of political opportunism preclude the copresence of sincere political beliefs? That the vicious political struggles of 1793–94 did in fact pit groups of like-minded actors against other groups certainly suggests that ideological differences mattered. Evidence of certain opportunistic hacks does not imply that everyone was playing a cynical game. Indeed, a dedicated political commitment tends, if anything, to encourage manipulative procedures; one does not need to peer far back in time to find examples of determined ideologues willing to use any means to stay in power, but also to implement radical agendas. To ask historians to choose between cynical and theoretical concepts of power is a *question mal posée*: The power of ideas can inflame ideas of power.

It is also worth recalling that the Terror was not just a period of bloody murder. As already noted, the *conventionnels* blazed innovative trails in public education, social policy, democratic expansion, economic regulation, and more generally, in republican institutions, with the creation of numerous festivals and other cultural monuments (such as the republican calendar).[7] Victor Hugo's assessment is fairer than most: "Of the 11,210 decrees issued by the Convention, one-third had a political objective, and two-thirds a humane objective."[8] Does this flurry of "humane" activity signify nothing? And if not, is it possible to distinguish between "sincere" republican projects

---

3. *La politique de la Terreur: essai sur la violence révolutionnaire, 1789–94* (Paris: Fayard, 2000), 317.

4. *Robespierre* (Harlow: Pearson Education, 1999).

5. *Violence et révolution: essai sur la naissance d'un mythe national* (Paris: Seuil, 2006), 191.

6. *Violence et révolution*, 181. I return to the revisionist thesis in the last section of this chapter.

7. See, for instance, Isser Woloch, *The New Regime: Transformations of the French Civic Order, 1789–1815* (New York: Norton, 1994); Jean-Pierre Gross, *Fair Shares for All: Jacobin Egalitarianism in Practice* (Cambridge: Cambridge University Press, 2003); and chapter 3.

8. *Quatrevingt-treize* (Paris: Presses Pocket, 1992), 193–94.

and "cynical" republican promises? Anyone familiar with Saint-Just's political treatises—unpublished, and thus difficultly dismissed as rhetorical posturing—knows how important republican culture and *mœurs* were for the Jacobin theorists. Why would one bother with these institutional efforts without some commitment to a republican ideal?

The question that imposes itself, then, is what *did* the Jacobin leaders seek to achieve that seemed worth such a messy political process? This chapter provides part one of an answer (the second part is given in the following chapter), not by distinguishing between crass political maneuvering and lofty political idealism, but rather by insisting on the inseparability of power and policy, the twin faces of politics, during the Terror. I examine more particularly a central event of 1793, the suspension of the Constitution, which is oddly glossed over in histories of the Revolution. I argue that this event should be read as *both* a power grab and an ideological endeavor. It allowed the Jacobins to consolidate their hold on power (and may even have encouraged violent repressions in rebellious departments), but also brought the nation one step closer to realizing the political dream of a natural republic. This political dimension, moreover, can be reconstructed from debates, political pamphlets, and unpublished manuscripts composed *before* the risk of implementing the Constitution even presented itself. Most tellingly, it can be seen in the very Festival designed to celebrate the Constitution, and in which the latter was effaced in favor of natural laws. As Georges Sorel suggested, the men who were responsible for the most spilled blood during the Revolution may have also been those with the strongest desire to restore a golden age.[9]

Chronicle of a Death Foretold: A Jacobin "Conspiracy"

On October 10, 1793, at Saint-Just's request, the Convention suspended the Constitution, ratified exactly two months prior. Or did it? The Convention proclaimed that the "government was revolutionary until peacetime," but the word "constitution" does not appear in any of the fourteen articles of the decree. All the ministries and organs of government were placed under the control of the Committee of public safety (art. 2), but the constitu-

---

9. *Reflections on Violence*, ed. and trans. Jeremy Jennings (Cambridge: Cambridge University Press, 1999), 10. A similar conclusion is reached by Michel Biard in his recent article on "Les rouages de la Terreur": "The dream of an ideal City did indeed coexist in 1793–1794 with the measures taken to defend the real City, which may explain how France could be both generous and violent, arbitrary and legalistic, democratic and intolerant . . . fraternalistic and fratricide," in *Les politiques de la Terreur, 1793–1794*, ed. Michel Biard (Rennes: Presses universitaires de Rennes & Société des études robespierristes, 2008), 24.

tion was never officially suspended, only by *non-dit*. It is granted but one passing mention in Saint-Just's report, whose nonchalant phrasing suggests that the decision to scrap the Constitution was not even in question: "Under the circumstances in which the Republic is today, the Constitution cannot be instituted: it would be the source of its own destruction [*on l'immolerait par elle-même*]."[10]

The principal justification offered for this tacit suspension is also oddly absent from the report. While both its title and the first article of its decree allude directly to France's wartime situation (". . . until peacetime"), the text itself makes virtually no mention of military hostilities, in neither the North, South, nor West.[11] The only "war" to which Saint-Just refers is the struggle against counterrevolutionaries hidden in the midst of Jacobin patriots: "All the enemies of the Republic are to be found in its government," he warns (*SJ*, 522). In fact, as we will see, the military situation was curiously almost never used to justify suspending the Constitution.

What was the true reason, then, for deciding at this particular moment not to implement the Constitution? Missing from the report itself, the Jacobins' rationale was in fact simple and brutal: They did not want to enact the Constitution because doing so would trigger new elections. New elections, so the reasoning went, would bring about a "corrupt" assembly, whereas the Convention, after the June 2 purge, was now "regenerated." A corrupt assembly would lead France back to monarchy, and the Constitution would thus be *immolée par elle-même*, by a nefarious and anonymous "*on*." In plainer language and less speculatively, the Jacobins did not enact the Constitution because they feared they would lose power.

This fear was not new: It can be traced back, in fact, to the purge of the Convention itself and to the "Federalist rebellion" that ensued. Following the expulsion of twenty-nine Girondin deputies, a number of departmental authorities rebelled against this perceived violation of national sovereignty, even going so far (notably in Bordeaux and in the Jura) as to set up parallel "Committees of Public Safety."[12] The Convention moved quickly to outlaw

---

10. "Rapport sur la nécessité de déclarer le gouvernement révolutionnaire jusqu'à la paix," *Œuvres complètes*, ed. Michèle Duval (Paris: Lebovici, 1984), 520–30 (hereafter cited as *SJ*); *Archives parlementaires de 1787 à 1860*, ed. M. J. Mavidal, M. E. Laurent et al. (Paris: Librairie administrative de P. Dupont, 1862–1913), 76:315 (hereafter cited as *AP*).

11. While the Northern front would remain a military threat until spring 1794 (and Toulon would be retaken only on December 18, 1793), the Vendée was not to pose a military threat for much longer. The decisive battle of Cholet took place a week after this speech, on October 17.

12. See Paul R. Hanson, *The Jacobin Republic under Fire: The Federalist Revolt in the French Revolution* (University Park: Pennsylvania State University Press, 2003).

these rebel authorities and, over the summer and fall of 1793, managed largely to crush the rebellion, but continued fears of federalism eventually led to the abolishment of departmental *directoires* or "conseils généraux" on 14 frimaire an II (December 4, 1793).[13]

Even with the military threat under control, however, federalism and counterrevolutionary sentiment continued to pose an electoral danger for the Jacobin authorities. This danger materialized in the form of a conspicuous absence: Why had the Montagnard Constitution been ratified with so few votes against it?[14] At least half of the departments were suspected of harboring anti-Jacobin feelings; was it not odd that these very same departments, some of which were in open insurrection against the Convention (such as Lyon), would vote favorably on a Jacobin proposition, sometimes after a dramatic about-face?[15] Malcolm Crook, and Michelet before him, have suggested that this positive vote may have been motivated by the pressing desire for new elections.[16] If a majority of the country was indeed appalled by the purge of the Convention, then the simplest and most efficient retaliation would be to vote the Montagnards out of office.

This was, in fact, the very threat debated at the Parisian Jacobin club in early August 1793. On August 4, Philippon, a deputy from a commune outside of Lyon, warned the society that "the Lyon aristocrats wish . . . to accept the Constitution in order to federalize [*fédéraliser*] their department at will."[17] This still sounded like the Federalist threat discussed above. But a new danger was voiced that same evening by François Chabot, one of the more radical members of the Convention, who declared that "only

---

13. *AP*, 80:632, §3, art. 6. The first "*directoires de districts*" had been created on December 22, 1789 (*AP*, 10:717).

14. The official tally of 1,784,377 votes for, and 11,531 against, was only made known on August 20; see Malcolm Crook, *Elections in the French Revolution: An Apprenticeship in Democracy, 1789–99* (Cambridge: Cambridge University Press, 1996), 105. As Patrice Gueniffey noted, the referendum saw a significant upsurge in voter participation, although not in regions where the Jacobin Convention was unpopular (with a few exceptions, such as the department of Eure); *Le nombre et la raison: La Révolution française et les élections* (Paris: EHESS, 1993), 247–48.

15. Hanson tells the wonderful story of the Lyonnais primary assembly delegates passing through the camp of the republican army that had come to besiege the town; for this anecdote and the "remarkable turnabout" of the Lyonnais Popular Commission, see *Jacobin Republic under Fire*, 201–3.

16. *Elections in the French Revolution*, 113–15. See also Jules Michelet, *Histoire de la Révolution française* (Paris: Pléiade, 1952), 2:547.

17. Alphonse Aulard, ed., *La société des Jacobins: recueil de documents pour l'histoire du club des Jacobins de Paris* (Paris: Librairie Jouaust, 1897), 5:327; Philippon is identified as a "deputé d'une commune du département de Rhône-et-Loire."

counter-revolutionaries can request the implementation of the Constitution, under the current conditions" (327). Counterrevolutionary voters, he argued,

> accept the Constitution . . . to achieve *another legislature* that they plan to fill with men devoted to their cause. They assume that at the *next* legislative elections, they will nominate Brissotins, royalists, etc. They assume that the Mountain would thus be doomed and that, without any further obstacles, they will pack off to a counter-revolutionary tribunal the patriots who have led the revolution. (328)

These claims were backed up by delegates of the primary assemblies who had gathered in Paris to celebrate the ratification of the Constitution on August 10. Claude Royer, who became their spokesman, hardened Chabot's speculations into an empirical truth: "There is a vast conspiracy underhand," he warned, citing "facts," which he claimed to have been told by delegates from the rebel department of the Jura.[18] Royer then reminded the society of Danton's cautionary advice: "Let us not be fooled by the apparent conversion of those who sought to federalize the Republic." This insistence on potentially dissimulating voters (or delegates) raised an even greater question, one that did not get voiced at the Jacobin society that night: If the so-called Federalists could not be trusted now, could they ever? When would their conversion be complete?

This concern may have been another instance of run-of-the-mill Jacobin paranoia, but it had very tangible consequences. On the very next day (August 11) after the Constitution was ratified with pomp and circumstance, Jean-François Delacroix made the self-evident proposition that, as the Convention's work was now ended, it should dissolve and call for new elections.[19] Robespierre pounced on him: "I have no desire to maintain the current Assembly indefinitely," he insisted, but added that "the insiduous proposal that

---

18. *Discours prononcé dans la Société des Jacobins, le 6 août 1793, l'an second de la République, une et indivisible, par le citoyen Claude ROYER, envoyé de Châlons-sur-Saône, département de Sâone et Loire, à la grande réunion des Français le 10 août* (Paris: Jacobin society, 1793), 3. The Jura delegates were most likely responsible for Lyon's about-turn; see Hanson, *Jacobin Republic under Fire*, 201–3. On Royer, see also Serge Aberdam, "Un aspect du référendum de 1793: Les envoyés du souverain face aux représentants du peuple," in *Révolution et république: L'exception française*, ed. Michel Vovelle (Paris: Kimé, 1994), 221–22.

19. *AP*, 72:39–40. The decree of June 24, 1793, announcing the new Constitution and the referendum, had declared that the Convention would set a date for the primary assemblies to meet once the Constitution had been ratified.

I reject would only result in replacing a regenerated, largely pure assembly, with the deputies of Pitt and Cobourg."[20] Once again, it was not the difficult military situation that was invoked to postpone elections—after all, a national referendum had just been held on the Constitution—but rather Chabot's specter of a counterrevolutionary Assembly. Hébert adopted the same tactic in the *Père Duchesne*: "In order to better destroy the Constitution, they pretended to adopt it," he wrote of the Lyonnais.[21] To save the Constitution, the Convention needed to shelve it. And soon deputies were speaking openly shelving it, as Claude Basire did on August 28: "The simple implementation of constitutional laws, designed for peacetime, would be powerless in the midst of the conspiracies that surround us."[22] Well before the October 10 decree did away with it altogether—in fact, even before it was ratified—the Jacobins had already decided that their Constitution was a dead letter.[23]

But for how long? Although no national elections would be held for another two years, the prospect of future elections always loomed on the horizon.[24] Who was to know if counterrevolutionaries would not avail themselves of this republican institution in order to overthrow the republic (or at least the Jacobins) at some later date? This electoral problem would not disappear merely by virtue of postponing the Convention's inevitable dissolution. Nor would it disappear after the rebellious cities were retaken by force. The threat of secession or of a Federalist redistribution of power could be suppressed with the authority of canons, but the authority of elections could not be silenced by gunfire.

Or could it? With this electoral menace in mind, let us recall one of the most perplexing issues in revolutionary historiography, the savage repression of provincial rebellions during the Terror. What makes this repression so perplexing is that, as a general rule, it occurred *after* the military threat had

---

20. *Rob.*, 10:65. Robespierre was already warning of this danger before the purging of the Girondins: "I have told you that the enemies of the republic that sit in the Convention wish to facilitate the counterrevolution by summoning primary assemblies. This truth is obvious. Numerous departments are already, in a sense, openly counterrevolutionary" (April 17, 1793, speech at the Jacobin society; *Rob.*, 9:445). He repeated such warnings on August 23 (10:77) and October 8 (10:143), two days before Saint-Just presented his report.

21. *Père Duchesne*, 279 ([Aug. 1793]), 4 [vol. 8].

22. *AP*, 73:128.

23. In this respect (as in many others), Jacobin interests were opposed by the Cordeliers, who demanded that the Constitution be enacted; see Françoise Brunel, *Thermidor* (Brussels: Editions Complexe, 1989), 14.

24. The *Acte Constitutionnel* of 1793 called for the new *Corps Législatif* to assemble on July 1, 1794 (art. 41).

passed. Turreau's *colonnes infernales* burned their way through the Vendée in January 1794, three months after the *armée catholique et royale* had first been routed at Cholet. The infamous fusillades of Lyon similarly occurred well after the town had been occupied by the national army (and after a first wave of punitive measures). Was this how the republicans "converted" those suspected of federalism or counterrevolutionary sympathies? Once the Convention had decided, as it did on August 1, that the Vendée peasants were a "rebellious race that must disappear," could they ever be trusted to vote? Would the alleged *aristocrates* of Lyon, who had killed Joseph Chalier, ever elect a Jacobin majority?

It is very difficult to evaluate just how decisive these electoral concerns remained in the minds of the Jacobin authorities. The unevenness of the repressions of provincial rebellions may, however, be a telling indicator: If the Vendée, Lyon, or Toulon were particularly hard hit, certain departments avoided the wrath of the Jacobin republic altogether. This unevenness was far from arbitrary—repressions tended to be harshest where there was the greatest suspicion of counterrevolutionary sentiment—yet the laxity shown to some departments is nonetheless surprising, as Donald Greer remarked long ago.[25] Were there really no counterrevolutionaries whatsoever in the six departments that had zero death sentences during the Terror? These disparities are less surprising, however, when one interprets them from an electoral angle: deputies, after all, were not elected nationally but by departmental assemblies.[26] If enough departments sent anti-Jacobin deputies to a National Assembly (and given the low participation in the elections, it would not even take a "true" majority of voters), they could reverse the course of the Revolution. In this respect, revolutionary and monarchic sovereignty were not the same: When it slipped from the king's hands into those of the National Assembly, in June 1789, national sovereignty had fractured into eighty-three pieces.

Judging from public statements, electoral concerns indeed figured centrally in the rhetoric of the revolutionary government's powers. Saint-Just,

---

25. Greer emphasizes "the extreme variability of the geographic incidence of the Terror," adding that "Revolutionary justice may have struck . . . with the rapidity of lightning; unless we can find an explanation, it was capricious," *The Incidence of the Terror during the French Revolution: A Statistical Interpretation* (Cambridge: Harvard University Press, 1935), 39. On population districting during the Revolution, see Serge Aberdam, *Démographes et démocrates: l'œuvre du Comité de division de la Convention nationale* (Paris: Société des études robespierristes, 2004).

26. On the electoral process, see Gueniffey, *Le nombre et la raison*, and Crook, *Elections in the French Revolution*. See also article 23 of the 1793 Constitution.

for instance, began his famous October 10, 1793, speech by announcing that

> it is time to declare a truth which, henceforth, must never leave the thoughts of those who shall govern: the Republic will only be founded when the will of the sovereign has suppressed the monarchic minority, and rules over it by right of conquest. You need show no restraint against the enemies of the new order, and liberty must triumph at any price.[27]

As Rousseauist as this statement may sound, it also reveals a distinct electoral worry: What if the monarchic minority was not so minor? Had not Robespierre proclaimed a year earlier that "virtue shall always be in a minority on Earth"?[28] As we will see, Saint-Just's April 15 speech on the Constitution also reveals a somewhat unorthodox idea of what constituted "the will of the sovereign," as well as his deep mistrust of direct democracy: "If you are not cautious, in twenty years, the throne will be reestablished by the fluctuations and illusions supplied to the general will," he warned the Convention.[29] An apprehension of direct democracy, in fact, had characterized Jacobin politics ever since the Mountain's opposition to the *appel au people* during the king's trial.[30] In any case, the Jacobins could not do away with elections altogether: hence, Saint-Just's conclusion that the republic could be founded (and elections held) only once the "enemies of the new order" had been eliminated. The vaunted Jacobin ideal of a national, unified general will may ultimately have had more to do with winning elections than with policing political opinions.[31]

It would soon become apparent that the political purges announced in Saint-Just's speech were indeed directed toward departmental authorities and provincial rebels. In a November report on the revolutionary government, Billaud-Varenne stressed that the specter of federalism had not vanished:

---

27. *AP*, 76:313; see also Billaud-Varenne's report, introducing the 14 frimaire an II (December 4, 1793), *AP*, 80:635.

28. December 28, 1792, speech at the Convention (*Rob.*, 9:199). On the Jacobin "minority mentality," see Lucien Jaume, *Le Discours Jacobin et la démocratie* (Paris: Fayard, 1989), 106–8, and Donald Sutherland, *France 1789–1815: Revolution and Counterrevolution* (New York: Oxford University Press, 1986), 194–95.

29. "Discours sur la constitution de la France," April 24, 1793. See also Saint-Just's acknowledgment, in his October 10 report, that "the people [*peuple*] can be wrong," even if "the people are wrong less often than men" (*AP*, 76:313).

30. My thanks to Colin Jones for emphasizing this parallel.

31. On the general will in Jacobin political thought, see below.

The most pressing issue currently facing the nation was still "the crime of the departments."[32] Ever since May 31, 1793, the "secondary authorities" had intentionally distorted or suppressed many of the Convention's laws and decrees, thereby misleading the French people on the true intentions and nature of the Mountain's policies. Billaud-Varenne's prescription for this "crime" was, like Saint-Just's, a strong dose of Terror throughout the land: "We thus require, and you granted it, the sword of Damocles to hover over the whole territory [*sur toute la superficie*]. What do the righteous have to fear!"[33] Even if it was only on a select part of the French *superficie* that the Terror would be felt, it had become clear by the winter of 1793 that Terror and territory were henceforth inseparable.

The non-enactment of the Constitution thus seems to have been intrinsically connected to the political repressions in the departments suspected of political dissent. Viewed from this angle, one could indeed claim that the Jacobins sought to hold on to power "at any price." But does this relatively cynical portrayal tell the whole story? Even Jean-Clément Martin, who has emphasized the manipulative ways of the Montagnards, acknowledges that the fear that the entire Vendée was "gangrened by the counter-revolution or by Federalism . . . helps explain the repressive practices of the *représentants en mission* . . . but it does not explain their intensity" (*Violence et révolution*, 203). If the only motive for devastating rebellious departments was to ensure a future electoral majority, the Jacobin Convention protested too much. There are, after all, simpler and more discreet means for rigging elections. Killing undesirable voters may be brutally effective, but it is not particularly time- or labor-efficient. The severity of the Terror in the provinces raises the same issue discussed in the previous chapter: Why always death? How did capital punishment come to constitute the only acceptable form of defense against counterrevolutionaries? As we already saw, the Convention's reliance on natural right theory may explain the refrain of death sentences in the Terror legislation. But given the indisputable uses of this legislation in the power politics of Years I and II, we must re-pose the question with which this chapter opened: Did natural right merely serve as a cover for the elimination of political enemies? Or did it genuinely serve as a touchstone of Jacobin political thought?

Our investigation of the 1793 Constitution and its sudden disappearance may in fact shed further light on this difficult question. Before the repressions

---

32. "Rapport sur un mode de gouvernement provisoire et révolutionnaire," 28 brumaire an II (November 18, 1793); *AP*, 79:451–57 (454 for quote).

33. *AP*, 79:457, my italics.

in the provinces were even under way (although after the March 19 decree that authorized them was passed), the Jacobin Convention celebrated the newly ratified Constitution with a grand festival. Held on August 10, 1793, the first-year anniversary of the sacking of the Tuileries, this festival offers a fascinating window onto the republican vision the Jacobins sought to promote. Strangely, given the importance of constitutions in classical republicanism, the republic on display that summer day seemed perfectly content to exist independently from any human laws or, for that matter, constitution. It claimed to owe its authority and existence to a different source of right: the laws of nature herself.

The "Festival of Nature": Performing Natural Authority

Even compared to other revolutionary festivals, the *Fête de l'Unité et de l'Indivisibilité de la République* might qualify as the most baroque. Its primary objective, the official ratification of the Constitution, does not even figure in its title, which refers instead to the Jacobin hope for national reconciliation after the May 31–June 2 purge of the Convention and to the ongoing Federalist revolt in the South. The festival also featured some of the most bizarre iconography that the Revolution had yet seen, effectively burying the festival's official purpose beneath layers of symbolism. As Michelet remarked, this purpose took on the appearance of a mere afterthought: "The acceptance of the Constitution, that moving demonstration of French unity in a common thought, only played a secondary part."[34] The entire festival can be read, in fact, as a political sleight-of-hand, intended to make the Constitution disappear into thin air—or rather, to dissolve it into nature.

The first place to glimpse this subterfuge is in the festival's structure and dynamics.[35] Instead of beginning with a tribute to the lawmakers who

---

34. *Histoire de la Révolution française*, 2:537.

35. This festival has received somewhat less attention than others in revolutionary historiography, but is amply discussed in Bronislaw Baczko, *Lumières de l'utopie* (Paris: Payot, 1978); Ronald Paulson, *Representations of Revolution (1789–1820* (New Haven: Yale University Press, 1983); James Billington, *Fire in the Minds of Men* (New York: Basic Books, 1980), 45–50; David Lloyd Dowd, *Pageant-Master of the Republic: Jacques-Louis David and the French Revolution* (1948; repr. ed., Freeport: Libraries, 1969), 110–16; Serge Aberdam, "Un aspect du référendum de 1793, 215–16; Lynn Hunt, *Politics, Culture, and Class in the French Revolution* (Berkeley: University of California Press, 1984), 96–100; and Warren Roberts, *Jacques-Louis David and Jean-Louis Prieur, Revolutionary Artists: The Public, the Populace, and Images of the French Revolution* (Albany: SUNY Press, 2000), 292–96. For an interesting political reading of this festival, see Jaume, *Discours Jacobin,* 118. In the following description I have drawn from two main primary sources: David's *Ordre et marche de la fête de l'unité et de l'indivisibilité de la République* (Paris: Firmin Gourdin, 1793) (also found in *AP,* 70:549–50),

had produced a constitution worthy of Lycurgus, the festival began at the Place de la Bastille, where a Fountain of Regeneration, consisting of a bare-breasted Egyptian nature goddess, had been erected. Four other stations followed. At the second, on the Boulevard Poissonnière, a triumphal arch celebrated the famous *poissardes* women of October 5–6, 1789. The third station was at the Place de la Révolution (presently Concorde), where emblems of royalty were burned beneath a statue of the goddess of Liberty. A Herculean statue of the French *peuple* crushing the monster of federalism constituted the fourth station, at the Place des Invalides. The festival concluded at the Champ de Mars, where the people and deputies swore an eternal oath to the Constitution.

As Lynn Hunt pointed out, the stations in this festival are arranged to recount a miniature (and populist) history of the French Revolution.[36] The Fountain of Regeneration stands at the mythical origin of the Revolution; the second station commemorates an event that took place three months after the storming of the Bastille; the Place de la Révolution is where Louis XVI was executed on January 21, 1793; federalism, the subject of the fourth station, was the latest conspiracy to threaten the Revolution; with the oath of allegiance to the Constitution, the festival's historical narrative coincided with the festival as historic moment in itself. This coincidence may have helped produce what Hunt has termed the "mythical present" of revolutionary festivals, "the instant of creation of the new community, the sacred moment of the new consensus."[37] There may have been more, however, to this myth than present unity, as it extended to the very source of mythical authority: nature.

This other political mythology can also be perceived in the order of the stations. While superficially linear, the structure of the festival was ultimately circular. The Constitution, which appears only in extremis at the last station, is described by the *Procès-verbal de la Convention* as expressing "these eternal truths," taken straight from "the voice and maxims of nature." The Constitution, by extension, was already to be found at the first station, where Nature herself was feted by the deputies. The laws of nature and those inscribed in the Constitution were indeed presented here as one and the same: the *Procès-verbal* evokes, in one breath, "that sacred equality, eternal symbol of creation, first law of nature *and* first law of the Republic" (5, emphasis added). At the end of the festival was its beginning: The fifth station is a

---

and the *Procès-verbal de la Convention nationale: Des monumens, de la marche, et des discours de la fête consacrée à l'inauguration de la Constitution de la République Française, le 10 août 1793* (n.p., n.d.).

36. *Politics, Culture, and Class,* 96.
37. Ibid., 27.

repetition of the first since everything begins and ends in nature. From this perspective, however, the Constitution itself is ultimately redundant. The *Procès-verbal* even refers to the entire festival as "a festival of nature [*la fête de la nature*]."

The substitution of nature for the Constitution was most apparent at the first station, where a very odd ceremony took place. Standing before a Fountain of Regeneration, Hérault de Séchelles (the president of the Convention at the time and main author of the Constitution), offered a cup of "regenerating" water to some of the eighty-six delegates of the primary assemblies. The cup was filled by a stream of water flowing from the Egyptian statue's breasts (see fig. 3).[38] The symbolism of this gesture, evoking (if not mocking) the Catholic communion and the Fountain of Youth, was made clear by one of the (no doubt fictional) statements proffered by an elderly delegate: "I am nearing my tomb; but by pressing this cup to my lips, I feel reborn along with the human race, which is regenerating."[39] But regeneration, in this case, was no longer simply a question of restoring good morals to the French people; it had become a process through which "the human race" returned to its natural form of government, the republic. Hérault de Séchelles explained this process in a short speech delivered on the site:

> It is in your bosom, it is in this sacred source that [the French people] has recovered its rights, that it is regenerated. After having passed through so many centuries of error and servitude, it needed to return to your simple ways in order to recover liberty and equality. O NATURE! Receive the eternal gratitude of the French people for your laws; and may these fertile waters that gush forth from your breasts; may this pure drink that quenched the thirst of the first humans consecrate with this cup of fraternity and equality France's oaths to you today, the finest day that the sun has illuminated since it was suspended in the immensity of space![40]

The political process in which France had been engaged for the previous four years was now reduced entirely to its recovery of natural rights.

38. There is at least one sculptural precedent for this fountain, Bartolomeo Ammannati's *Terra* (1556–61), on display at the Bargello Museum in Florence (previously in the private collection of the Medici grand dukes). This female personification similarly presses her breasts, out of which flows water.

39. *Procès-verbal*, 3. See also Michelet, *Histoire de la Révolution française*, 2:541.

40. *Recueil des six discours prononcés par le président de la Convention nationale, le 10 Août an 2ème de la République* (n.p., n.d.), 1.

Figure 3 Helman (after Monnet), *La fontaine de la Régénération* (1797).
Courtesy of the Bibliothèque Nationale de France.

The Constitution that Hérault himself had penned is here defined merely
as "*your* laws"; it is not the product of learned constitutional jurisprudence, but rather natural "simplicity." The French people had returned, in
fact, to the same stage as the "first humans," an association that the *Procès-
verbal* also emphasized: The ceremony "so augustly recalled and . . . in a
sense brought back the first days of the human race" (3). The Constitution
of 1793 was meant to restore no less than the golden age.

The return of the golden age was indeed the great theme of this festival.
This Virgilian motif (*redeunt Saturnia regna*) had been sufficiently detached
from its earlier monarchic connotations for it to figure prominently in the
festival's rhetoric. Publicola Chaussard, poet and *commissaire national* for
Belgium, alluded to the fourth *Eclogue* in his *Dithyrambe* composed for the
occasion:

> O sainte égalité! ce fut sous ta balance
> Qu'apparut aux mortels le premier âge d'or:
> La terre a ressenti ton heureuse influence,
>   Ces temps recommencent encore.[41]

41. "Oh holy equality! It was under your scales / That the golden age first appeared to
mortals / The earth benefited from your happy influence / Those days start all over," *Dithyrambe sur la fête républicaine du 10 aoust* (n.p., n.d.).

Instead of a new Augustus, this golden age was placed under the aegis
of Astraea, goddess of justice, referred to here through her zodiacal scales
(*"sous ta balance"*).[42] But it wasn't only in poetry that this return to the
golden age was suggested. The festival itself comprised numerous attempts
to materialize, or perform, this restoration of a natural state. First among
these was the statue of Nature herself. Here was no ordinary allegory, not
one of those Cybele's or Ceres's that parade through revolutionary iconography, but the original nature goddess herself, Isis.[43] "The ancients . . . called
Nature . . . *Is-is*," Nicolas de Bonneville reminded his readers in his 1792
treatise on religion and myth.[44] One did not need an antiquarian's erudition
to note this identity: Kant, for instance, refers to Isis as "Mother Nature" in
a famous footnote in the *Critique of Judgement*.[45]

If Isis was different from other allegories, it was because Egypt was different, or more specifically, because Egypt came first. "Greek myths [are only]
an imitation of Egyptian ones," Pernety asserted, echoing Plutarch's claims
in *Isis and Osiris*.[46] And in the beginning, humanity worshipped nature:
"Our fathers rendered a cult to nature whom they called . . . *Isis*."[47] A slew of
antiquarian research favored this Egyptian primacy, associating Egypt with

42. "Balance" is also the French term for the zodiacal sign of Libra, the constellation
that was in the heavens on September 22, 1792 (when the republic was declared). Gilbert
Romme made much of this date—the fall equinox—and even the zodiacal sign under which it
occurred; see his *Rapport sur l'ère de la République* (Paris: Impr. Nationale, n.d. [1793]), 5–6.
In Virgil, of course, Astraea is associated with the constellation Virgo (which precedes Libra in
the zodiac).

43. As the mythologist Dom Pernety wrote: "Many authors have correctly identified her
as the universal Goddess of paganism, honored under different names. Ceres, Juno, the Earth,
Proserpina, Thetis, the Mother Goddess or Cybele, Venus, Diana, Hecate, Rhamnusia, etc., even
Nature are all the same as Isis." See his *Dictionnaire Mytho-Hermétique dans lequel on trouve
les allégories fabuleuses des poëtes, les métaphores, les énigmes, et les termes barbares des philosophes
hermétiques expliqués* (1787; repr. ed., Paris: Denoël, 1972), s.v. "Isis," 178.

44. *De l'esprit des religions* (Paris: Cercle Social, 1792), 20. On Bonneville's religious
theories, see Frank Bowman, *Le Christ romantique* (Geneva: Droz, 1973), 72ff. Bonneville was
one of the founders of the influential Cercle Social; on this society, see Gary Kates, *The "Cercle
Social," the Girondins, and the French Revolution* (Princeton: Princeton University Press, 1985).
To my knowledge, the only historian who has positively identified her as Isis is Simon Schama in
Citizens (New York: Vintage, 1990), 5.

45. See Kant's note on "the famous inscription on the Temple of Isis (Mother Nature),"
Critique of Judgement, trans. J. H. Bernard (New York: Hafner, 1951), §49, 160n44. See also
the *Encyclopédie* entry for "Isis": "The word *Isis* is derived from *Iscia*, and originally signified
the true essence of things, or nature, which (it should be noted) would justify the origins of this
ancient cult, and connect it with the ideas of the wisest philosophers," 8:913.

46. *Dictionnaire Mytho-Hermétique* . . . , s.v. "Fables," 127. Even the *Encyclopédie* entry for
"Egypte" records this primacy: "It was the cradle of pagan superstition, as well as the Sciences
and Arts," 5:434.

47. Bonneville, *De l'esprit des religions*, 20.

the "historical" land of the golden age.[48] By choosing Isis over a Roman or Greek goddess, David, who planned the festival, was thus signaling that the Revolution took its mythical vocation seriously.[49] Enigmatically seated where the process of French regeneration had begun four years before, Isis symbolized less the Enlightenment idea of nature *qua* observable "system"[50] than an antiquarian idea of nature *qua* original order of the world, since lost.[51] As E. H. Gombrich noted in his discussion of the fountain, "the *novus ordo* was somehow a return to the wisdom of the ancients."[52]

More tangibly, the return to the golden age was performed through the refusal to distinguish between *conventionnels*, delegates, and the people during the procession. They all walked together rather than in separate groups.[53] On a rhetorical level, this choice was justified, again, in terms of antiquity: "In this manner the sublime alliance recognized by the citizens of ancient republics between agriculture and legislation was renewed" (*Procès-verbal*, 5). Since Court de Gébelin, the golden age was indeed associated with the *advent* of agriculture (and property), not with its absence; associating it with legislators helped to "naturalize" them as well. On a practical level, the mingling of representatives and people also suggested the abolition of all distinctions and hierarchy; as in the golden age, or Fénelon's Boetica, there were no judges or magistrates, only equals.

---

48. Court de Gébelin singled out Egypt as the home of the golden age in his *Monde primitif considéré dans son génie allégorique et dans les allégories auxquelles conduisit ce génie . . .* (Paris, 1773–81); see chapter 2. According to the abbé Barthélemy, a colony of Egyptian settlers (from Saïs, no less) then brought the golden age to Greece: *Voyage du jeune Anacharsis en Grèce* (1788; repr. ed., Paris: n.p.: 1856), 1:10. For Bonneville, Christianity was simply the latest version of an older Egyptian religion, which the French Revolution would restore.

49. David had received the command for the festival on July 4 (Aberdam, "Un aspect du referendum," 215).

50. See, for instance, the first definition in the *Encyclopédie* entry on "Nature": "*Nature* sometimes signifies the system of the world, the machine of the universe, or the assembly of all creation. *See under* SYSTEM," 11:40. Even before the baron d'Holbach, the expression "*le système de la nature*" was a commonplace phrase in Enlightenment philosophy.

51. For this alternative understanding of nature, see in particular Court de Gébelin's Physiocratic declarations about the "ancient and eternal Order" found in nature, which gave perfection to the original *monde primitif*, but was since lost (*Monde primitif*, 8:xviii); see chapter 2.

52. E. H. Gombrich, "The Dream of Reason: Symbolism in the French Revolution," *British Journal for Eighteenth-Century Studies* 2, no. 3 (1979): 203.

53. This refrain was repeatedly emphasized even before the festival—see, for instance, Claude Royer's speech to the Convention, read on August 8, which stresses the intermingling of Paris and France, the people and their representatives: "The representatives of all the sections of the Republic came to *identify* themselves with the representatives of the sovereign, and revealed to humanity the moving scene of a large family"; see also the *adresse* he then read in the name of the primary assembly delegates: "Paris is no longer in the Republic, but the entire Republic is in Paris; we have only one feeling, we share our souls" (*AP*, 76:518, my italics).

All this symbolism was clearly devised to play a political and propagandist role. The people assembled at the Place de la Bastille that morning undoubtedly had no clue who the woman in the Egyptian headgear represented, or that she differed from the other allegorical goddesses to which they had become accustomed by that time. They were simply told that she was Nature and that she had something to do with a constitution that few of them had probably read. In this regard, however, the fact that the festival's organizers specifically chose an *Egyptian* goddess to indicate that the Constitution codified the laws of nature suggests that they were not simply seeking to provide the *peuple* with a more sensual religion (following the Enlightenment commonplace of a "double doctrine"), but did in fact give credence to the idea that a state based entirely on nature had once existed, and could again.[54]

The blurring of civil distinctions during the procession conveyed a different, if related, political message. If France had now restored the natural order, then *who* exactly was in charge did not really matter. The government no longer needed to derive its authority from the will of the people, but could claim to legislate on the basis of natural right alone. As the latter was universal, those officials presently in charge could do as good a job as anyone else. The *person* of the representative was thus downplayed in favor of an ideal "transparent representation";[55] the Convention could continue "representing" the people, even without new elections.

The naturalization of the Constitution fulfilled a final political function. If the principles on which the Constitution rested were to be found in nature, then swearing to defend it forever gave the deputies a legal loophole. As Royer argued on August 6, the Constitution could still be suspended without any loss of fundamental natural rights: "Neither individuals nor properties will be harmed; the rights of nature will not be violated."[56] It was precisely in this spirit that the Jacobins would act, since the Declaration of Rights, which preceded the "*Acte constitutionnel*," was not considered to be affected by this suspension.[57] Copies of the Declaration remained posted

---

54. As Mona Ozouf suggested: "In destroying history the men of the Revolution were merely retying a broken thread, either with primitive history—a mirror that had not yet distorted nature's features—or with Nature herself, in her primal purity," *Festivals of the French Revolution*, trans. Alan Sheridan (Cambridge: Harvard University Press, 1988), 34. On the "double doctrine" of religion, see Frank Manuel, *The Eighteenth Century Confronts the Gods* (Cambridge: Harvard University Press, 1959). I return to this question in chapter 5.

55. On this concept, see Paul Friedland, *Political Actors: Representative Bodies and Theatricality in the Age of the French Revolution* (Ithaca: Cornell University Press, 2002), 250–53.

56. *Discours prononcé dans la Société des Jacobins*, 6–7.

57. See Bronislaw Baczko, "The Terror Before the Terror?" In *The Terror*, ed. Keith Baker. Vol. 4 of *The French Revolution and the Creation of Modern Political Culture* (Oxford: Pergamon Press, 1987–94), 29.

everywhere throughout *l'an II*, including in the Cordeliers's meeting place, where, with Montesquieuian flair, disgruntled members placed a veil over it in March 1794.[58]

Even if this festival appears largely to have been a Jacobin public relations blitz, its web of symbolism is thus tantalizing. The excessive mythological touches compose a coherent pattern of natural-republican motifs, suggesting that Hérault's statements may constitute more than just posturing. Furthermore, granting that the festival was essentially promotional, what were the Jacobins promoting? Apart from the reference to the Federalist rebellion at the fourth station, the festival was remarkably nonpartisan in tone. One of the stated ambitions of this performance was precisely to win over those primary Assembly delegates who may have been disturbed by the May 31–June 2 purge on the Convention. The Jacobin leaders thus had to make a convincing pitch that they were committed to cementing the republic and guaranteeing political rights for all; but how they chose to make that pitch is highly revealing. This natural-republican narrative grows ever more discernible and clear when resituated within the context of parliamentary debates over the nature of—or even the need for—a constitution.

Conventions, Constitutions, and the Declaration of Rights

The National Convention was obviously not the first French revolutionary assembly charged with drawing up a constitution, but the political framework in which its work had to be accomplished differed enormously from that of its predecessor. In 1789, the National Constituent Assembly was still operating within the institutional context of an established power structure, namely, the monarchy and its attending bureaucracy. The deputies of the Third Estate and the people of Paris had both "rebelled" in their own ways, but the government had not been toppled, as it would be in August 1792 (when even the Legislative Assembly proved largely powerless). This distinction is visible at the political level with the Constituents' claim to be "fixing" the Constitution rather than writing one from scratch.[59]

---

58. Montesquieu famously claimed that "the usage of the freest people that ever lived on earth makes me believe that there are cases where a veil has to be drawn, for a moment, over liberty, as one hides the statues of the gods," *Spirit of the Laws*, trans. Anne M. Cohler, Basia C. Miller, and Harold Stone (Cambridge: Cambridge University Press, 1989), 2.12.19; 204. For the Cordeliers incident, see notably Albert Soboul, *Mouvement populaire et gouvernement révolutionnaire en l'an II (1793–94)* (Paris: Flammarion, 1973), 216.

59. Keith Baker, "Fixing the French Constitution," in *Inventing the French Revolution: Essays on French Political Culture in the Eighteenth Century* (Cambridge: Cambridge University Press, 1990).

The National Convention did not have that option. Indeed, its very name highlights its radically different political status. As Denis Lacorne noted, from the British Convention Parliament of 1689 through to the Philadelphia Convention of 1787, "the 'Convention' does not represent the people as hierarchically distinguished into different social orders, but rather the people as undifferentiated multitude, grasped in its state of nature."[60] Sieyès had made such a claim on behalf of *la nation* (and, by extension, the Third Estate) in his famous 1789 pamphlet: "It is enough for its will to be made known for all positive law to fall silent in its presence, because it is the source and supreme master of all positive law."[61] But if few would have suggested that France, in 1789, was in a political state of nature, this was precisely the argument that many *conventionnels* used against the king during his trial: "Louis XVI put us back into a state of nature."[62] As the expression "state of nature" indicates, the political tradition underpinning this logic came directly from natural right theory. Guillaume-Joseph Saige's *Catéchisme du citoyen*, for instance, described the effect of "despotism" as that of

> annulling the social contract, and consequently, dissolving the body politic. As soon as the conventions that bound it are destroyed by force, every individual recovers his primitive independence; and, master and judge of himself, he is only subject to the eternal laws of nature and can dispose of himself without the consent of his past associates.[63]

---

60. In the case of the constitutional conventions organized by each of the thirteen American colonies at the conclusion of the war, Lacorne further states that "these conventions are properly extraordinary as they symbolize the people's return to a state of nature," *L'invention de la république: le modèle americain* (Paris: Hachette, 1991), 72 and 77. Hannah Arendt also pointed out this political difference: "The rupture between king and parliament . . . threw the whole French nation into a 'state of nature'; it dissolved automatically the political structure of the country as well as the bonds among its inhabitants," *On Revolution* (1963; London: Penguin, 2006), 172. The term "Convention nationale" appears in the August 10, 1792, decree suspending the Legislative Assembly, and Verginaud defines it in terms very reminiscent of Sieyès (see below): "In every National Convention, the people exercises its full sovereignty . . . and when the people exercises its full sovereignty, all other authorities vanish," *AP*, 47:646.

61. *What Is the Third Estate?* in *Political Writings*, trans. and ed. Michael Sonenscher (Indianapolis: Hackett, 2003), 138. Pierre Philippeaux, a *conventionnel* and an ally of Danton, echoed this statement during the Convention's first session: "It is generally recognized that the National Convention, invested with the sovereign power of the people, dissolves all other authorities," September 21, 1792; *AP*, 52:72. See also the distinction between "corps législatif" and "Convention nationale" in the 1793 Acte Constitutionnel, arts. 115–17.

62. Michel Azéma; *AP*, 54:97. See also the similar remarks by Robespierre, Hentz, and Delbrel discussed in chapter 3.

63. *Catéchisme du citoyen* (Geneva: n.p., 1787), 28–29.

"Recovering primitive independence" is undoubtedly *not* what the Jacobins had in mind when they suggested that the king's demise had dissolved France's social bonds. Tellingly, however, one of the very first decrees passed by the National Convention was a declaration that all prior legislation and existing political authorities should be provisionally upheld.[64] What this decree reveals is the implicit sense (or fear) that the law of the land, in theory at least, had been suspended. A number of deputies stated this point directly, albeit in negative terms: Nicolas Quinette (who was soon to argue that in revolutions, "the only positive laws are those of nature"; see chapter 3), warned on September 21 that "there may be . . . some ill-meaning people who would wish it to be known that there is no longer, at this moment, any Constitution, or any laws—which would lead to disorder" (*AP*, 52:72). Claude Basire, a Montagnard, concurred, raising the specter of anarchy: Some could "surmise from this silence that there is no government or laws" (73). If the *conventionnels* could only conceive negatively of such an interpretation of the current political state of France, they nonetheless found it necessary to formally renew existing laws, and chose to do so solely on a provisional basis. In this manner, it was still possible to claim that while the French Republic was not de facto without positive laws, it remained de jure in a political state of nature. The Convention could not even declare France to be a republic since it had already decreed that popular sanction was needed to bring the Constitution into existence.[65] Though a constituent power, it was not vested with sufficient sovereignty to restore the fundamental civil bond.

Given such shaky political foundations, it is surprising that the Convention waited five full months, until February 15, 1793, to begin debating the Constitution it had been summoned to produce. Even then, following the chilly reception that greeted Condorcet's initial proposal, it waited another two months before starting discussions in earnest.[66] But at that moment, the

---

64. September 21, 1792; *AP*, 52:73.

65. *AP*, 52:72. Indeed, contrary to what is commonly claimed, the Convention never officially proclaimed the French Republic on either September 21 or 22: The September 21 decree merely decreed the abolition of royalty (*AP*, 52:74), while the following day, the Convention voted that all official documents, as of September 21, be dated "l'an premier de la République française" (80). On September 25, it unanimously declared that "the French Republic is one and indivisible" (143), in response to concerns about federalism. As with the suspension of the Constitution, the proclamation of the republic was done tacitly.

66. On the context and content of the debates during this period, see Michel Pertué, "Les projets constitutionnels de 1793," in *Révolution et république*, 174–99; Pertué notes how the constitutional endeavors of 1793 do not seem to have sparked much interest outside the Convention (176). See also Marcel Gauchet, *La révolution des droits de l'homme* (Paris: Gallimard, 1989), 209–56; Ladan Boroumand, *La guerre des principes: les assemblées révolutionnaires face*

Jacobins moved immediately (and successfully) to shift attention away from the Constitution and toward the Declaration of Rights that preceded it: "To arrive at this [republican] Constitution, we must begin by proclaiming the eternal rights of humanity," asserted Robespierre (who had eagerly announced a new constitution in the immediate aftermath of the August 10 insurrection).[67] While this move recalled the Constituent Assembly's decision, prompted by Mirabeau, to debate the Declaration of Rights before the Constitution,[68] it also signaled in this new context a strong sense among many Montagnards that the former was the only truly important document. The Constitution, they would argue, could simply be "deduced" from the laws of nature outlined in the Declaration, and could be construed, in this respect, as redundant.

Although Robespierre, in his speeches to the Convention and the Jacobin society, and Saint-Just, in his unpublished manuscripts, insisted most clearly on this redundancy of the Constitution, their position can be seen, in fact, as the logical conclusion of arguments (and hidden tensions) expressed by many Montagnards at the time of Louis's trial. When Robespierre claimed that the true constitution actually lay in the Declaration of Rights ("The Declaration of Rights is the Constitution of all peoples, all other laws being variable by nature, and subordinated to this one"),[69] he was in fact borrowing an expression and argument already used by Marie-Joseph Chénier in a speech against the king:

Now, citizens, let us climb to a more philosophical height, more worthy of the French National Convention; let us rise up to those primordial ideas of justice that nature engraved in the hearts of all

---

aux droits de l'homme et à la souveraineté de la nation, mai 1789– juillet 1794 (Paris: EHESS, 1999), 315–59; and Swenson, *On Jean-Jacques Rousseau,* 220–26.

67. April 15, 1793, speech on the Constitution; *Rob.,* 9:438. The need for a discussion on the Declaration of Rights to take precedence on the debate over the Constitution had also been emphasized by Gilbert Romme, in his report preceding Robespierre's speech: *AP,* 62:120. See Gauchet, *Révolution des droits de l'homme,* 216–20 and 235–40, on Robespierre's constitutional proposal (discussed below). Robespierre's reasoning also rested on the belief that France had a "provisional Constitution," namely, the 1791 Constitution, with the monarchic executive struck out; see Julien Boudon, *Les Jacobins: une traduction des principes de Jean-Jacques Rousseau* (Paris: LGDJ, 2006), 194–95. This exceptional work, which I discovered only after finishing my book, is a gold mine of information and analysis regarding the constitutional, legal, and political debates of the Terror.

68. See Keith Baker, "The Idea of a Declaration of Rights," in *The French Idea of Freedom,* ed. Dale Van Kley (Stanford: Stanford University Press, 1994), 186.

69. May 10, 1793; *Rob.,* 9:507.

men . . . and which have been conserved without change among all people despite forty centuries of hereditary biases and errors. Listen to this natural morality, source of public morality, foundation of every social pact, model of the Declaration of Rights. This is what, during revolutionary movements, fills the interregnum of laws . . . consult this eternal law, this Constitution of all peoples. (*AP*, 54:145)

The need to legitimize the proceedings against the king had led the Jacobins to emphasize the eternal and superior authority of natural right, but also to hypothesize its potential sufficiency. Indeed, an unresolved tension between natural right *qua* "interregnum of laws" and "Constitution of all peoples," the expression favored by Robespierre, runs through Chénier's speech: If the Declaration is already a constitution, who needs a second constitution? Camille Desmoulins's description of the Declaration, also presented during the king's trial, is fraught with a similar tension:

This eternal, invariable code, this provisional code of all societies until they have been organized, until particular laws have been drawn from these general laws [whose] articles, nearly erased by the rust of centuries, the French people have enthusiastically adopted and reestablished in all their purity. (*AP*, 54:176)

While this phrasing implies that the "provisional code" must cede ground to more permanent statutes, the Declaration is nonetheless defined in the same sentence as eternal and unchanging. Moreover, the future constitution is not described as an expression of the general will, but as the recapitulation of an ancient collection of legal "articles . . . erased by the rust of centuries," which sounds remarkably like the "eternal code" encapsulated in the Declaration. Finally, the only reason that France needs a provisional code to try the king, Desmoulins argued, is because "we have [removed ourselves] from nature and the primitive laws of every society" (176), suggesting, again, that a future constitution would need only reaffirm these primitive, natural laws, already stated in the Declaration.

Even if they did not go so far as to suggest that the Declaration could simply take the place of a constitution, the Montagnards seem to have been in agreement that the relation between these two documents must be organic, even deterministic.[70] The Declaration must simply "lay down the

---

70. This assessment is based on a survey of the roughly one hundred constitutional projects (and the relevant debates) collected in the *Archives parlementaires*; see in particular the

principles, from which all we need do is draw conclusions [*poser les principes dont il ne nous reste plus ensuite, qu'à tirer les conséquences*]," Robespierre argued.[71] Following this logic, however, the Constitution was quasi redundant since it was already present *in potentia* in the Declaration. And this quasi redundancy was exactly what many deputies demanded: "You are the authors of the Constitution," François Poultier, a Montagnard deputy, reminded the constitutional committee. "Your text must conform, rigorously conform, with the Declaration of Rights; any project that departs from it is perfidious or the result of total ignorance."[72] Jacques-Michel Coupé, another Montagnard, claimed that the Constitution must simply "generalize all individual principles" already found in the "natural constitution," which is "superior to all political institutions," and of which the *political* constitution is simply "an immediate consequence."[73]

Their colleague, François-Agnès Montgilbert, calling the Declaration "the political gospel of nations," insisted that all the rights of man were in nature (as opposed to having a political or civil origin), and that constitutional laws "are merely their explanation and guarantee . . . they can neither abolish, nor supplement them." The Constitution, much like positive laws in Physiocracy, could only ever "*fixer*," "*garantir*," and "*protéger*" natural rights; the Montesquieuian and Rousseauist axiom that different peoples required different constitutions was thus wrongheaded ("For whom could a government founded on the sacred rights of man not be adequate? Liberty

"Annexes" for April 17 (vol. 62), April 24 (vol. 63), and June 24 (vol. 67). This corpus is certainly not exhaustive, but as Michel Pertué notes, most of the constitutional projects submitted to the "commission des six" in charge of reviewing them have been lost; the *Archives parlementaires* regroup most of the projects that can now be found at the Archives Nationales and the Bibliothèque de l'Assemblée Nationale ("Les projets constitutionnels," 175–76).

71. *Rob.*, 9:436. For a similar argument, see Charles Lambert de Belan's "Plan de Constitution républicaine": "It follows that [natural rights], as principles, must always precede a constitutional project, and that [civil and political rights], as corollaries, can only be arrived at subsequently, as the clear and precise consequence of these principles," *AP*, 62:438. On Robespierre's obsessive references to his *principes,* see David P. Jordan, *The Revolutionary Career of Maximilien Robespierre* (New York: Free Press, 1985); Marisa Linton, "Robespierre's Political Principles," in *Robespierre*, ed. Colin Haydon and William Doyle (Cambridge: Cambridge University Press, 1999); and Jaume, *Discours Jacobin*, 183–87. For an illuminating discussion of Robespierre's natural right ideas that stresses their debt to Pufendorf's *The Rights of Man and of the Citizen*, see Gueniffey, *Politique de la Terreur*, 301–5.

72. *AP*, 67:379. To determine political affiliation, I consulted Françoise Brunel's list of Montagnard deputies ; see "Les députés montagnards," in *Actes du Colloque Girondins et Montagnards*, ed. Albert Soboul (Paris: Société des études robespierristes, 1980), 343–61.

73. "Idées Simples de Constitution," *AP*, 62:276. Coupé began his speech by asserting that "the longest lasting, simplest and happiest Constitution is the one that presents the pure elements of natural principles."

and equality are found in every climate"). As many deputies had during the king's trial, Montgilbert concluded that the republic was the restoration of the natural order of society: "We will only perfect the moral and political state of society if we move closer to nature. . . . The object of a republican Constitution is to bring men closer to nature."[74]

The relation between Robespierre's own constitutional project and his proposed Declaration of Rights is in this regard very telling. His first two constitutional articles simply refer back to the text of the Declaration: "The Constitution guarantees to all the French the everlasting rights of man and of the citizen listed in the preceding declaration," reads the first, while the second adds, "it declares tyrannical and void any legislative or governmental act that violates them" (*Rob.*, 9:508). In fact, this second article is only a repetition of article 18 in Robespierre's Declaration: "Any law that violates the everlasting rights of man is fundamentally unjust and tyrannical; indeed, is not law" (467). In his speech presenting the Constitution, Robespierre informed the deputies that this single article could summarize the entire Constitution (501). Its redundancy was thus both theoretical and real. The final article of the Constitution similarly loops back to the Declaration, in a celebration of its sanctity:

> The Declaration of the Rights of Man and of the Citizen will be placed in the most visible spot wherever the constituted authorities will be in sessions: It will be ceremoniously paraded in every public ceremony; it will be the first object of public instruction. (art. 20, 9:510)

No mention is made here of the Constitution's sacred status. This oversight can be explained only by the very limited role the Constitution plays in Robespierre's republican theory. Its mere twenty articles (compared to the thirty-eight in his Declaration) almost uniquely express "negative" principles, and as a whole, the document is remarkably vague about the actual structure of government: It does not even address the question of elections, the structure of the judiciary, or the organization of national finances.

---

74. "Avis du peuple sur la liberté et l'exercice de ses droits, contenu dans un projet de constitution républicaine," June 24, 1793; *AP*, 67:328–62; 328–30 for quotes. Montgilbert, who voted against the *appel au peuple*, seems to have been mostly sympathetic to the Mountain; his Physiocratic tendencies are also evident in his insistence that property was a natural right (*contra* Rousseau, Mably, and Morelly); see 336. Didier Thorion had posed a similar rhetorical question during the king's trial: "Did we ever have a Constitution, and should we give this name to one that is not founded on the eternal and invariable basis of the rights of man and of the citizen?" *AP*, 54:333.

Had the Convention adopted this constitution, it would not have needed to bother suspending it.

A number of the participants in the constitutional debates of spring 1793 had been members of the National Assembly when it had discussed this same issue, and made pointed references back to that period.[75] The parallel is indeed revealing, particularly where the relationship between Declaration and Constitution is concerned. The Assembly had acknowledged the need for a preliminary Declaration, but not without trepidation; in his report on behalf of the constitutional committee, Jean-Joseph Mounier declared:

> In order to have a good constitution, it must be based on the rights of man, which it obviously defends; to prepare the Constitution, then, we must know the rights which natural justice affords to all individuals, and recall the principles that should provide the basis for every kind of society; every article of the Constitution must be the consequence of one of these principles.[76]

At the same time, Mounier and his Monarchist colleagues were wary about the unwanted consequences that might be drawn from such first principles. This fear was expressed most forcefully by the comte de Lally-Tollendal:

> If with the purest of intentions, we highlight natural rights in a declaration without immediately connecting them with positive rights, think of the advantage we are giving to our detractors . . . yes, let us return to natural right, since it forms the principle of all others; but let us swiftly pass through the intermediary links, and arrive at positive right which attaches us to monarchic government.[77]

Natural right, for the Constituents, could thus set a dangerous precedent; certain civil societies, such as democracy, seemed more easily justifiable in terms of natural right than others, such as monarchy. What would happen, Lally-Tollendal worried, "If certain unstable minds, misunderstanding our principles, if certain perverse souls, willfully misunderstanding them, took them to an extreme"? Robespierre had a ready answer:

---

75. See, for instance, Robespierre's reference in his April 15 speech; *Rob.*, 9:434–35.

76. *AP*, 8:216; July 9, 1789.

77. *AP*, 8:222; July 11, 1789; quoted and discussed in Baker, *Inventing the French Revolution*, 262. Maximin Isnard, a Girondin, would make precisely the same argument in May 1793: "Declaring the rights of man in this fashion, is merely to recognize these rights in a document whose vague text lends itself to any interpretation," *AP*, 64:418.

You have been told that the principles of the Declaration of Rights are approved of in general; but you have also been told that they are liable to be interpreted in different ways. That is a great mistake. These are the principles of justice, of natural right, which no human law can change. How could we possibly apply them falsely?[78]

Whether "excessive" or "correct," the applications to which the Jacobins would put the Declaration of Rights four years later were precisely those feared by Mounier and Lally-Tollendal: In the name of natural right, the Jacobins would repudiate monarchy, execute the king, and institute a republic. But were they really just "applying" the principles of natural right? How could they avoid making the leap from natural to positive laws?

A short text appeared around the time of the 1793 debates over the Constitution that sheds some light on how natural right could be understood to determine all aspects of government. Although its title, *La loi naturelle, ou Catéchisme du citoyen français*, suggests otherwise, this work was not by an author from the upper reaches of the Mountain. It was by Volney, already a celebrated writer in 1793, having won fame for his *Voyage en Égypte et en Syrie* (1787) and for *Les Ruines* (1791); he had also been a member of the Constituent Assembly, where his politics were often aligned with Robespierre's; he later remained friends with Lanjuinais and Garat (who served as minister from October 1792 to August 1793).[79] Upon returning from Corsica to Paris in March 1793, Volney published his treatise on natural right; he served in an official position until later that fall, when he was imprisoned for debts (possibly also for his ties with the Girondins). He benefited from exceptionally favorable treatment during his imprisonment, however, which suggests that he was not viewed as particularly troublesome by the Jacobin authorities.

From an epistemological perspective, Volney's pamphlet constitutes a sort of bridge between the Physiocratic theory of natural right and the proto-*Idéologue* philosophy of his friends Cabanis and Destutt de Tracy.[80] Natural law, he claimed,

---

78. *Rob.*, 6:101; October 5, 1789.

79. On Volney's life, see notably Jean Sibenaler, *Il se faisait appeler Volney: approche biographique de Constantin-François Chassebœuf, 1757–1820* (Maulévrier: Hérault, 1992). According to Sibenaler, *La loi naturelle* was published on July 6, 1793.

80. See Jean Roussel, ed., *L'héritage des lumières: Volney et les idéologues* (Angers: Presses de l'Université d'Angers, 1988); see also Emmet Kennedy, *A "Philosophe" in the Age of Revolution: Destutt de Tracy and the Origins of "Ideology"* (Philadelphia: American Philosophical Society, 1978).

makes men happier and better, since it incorporates everything good and useful from other civil and religious laws, that is to say, it provides their essential moral aspect, which, if removed from these other bodies of law, would turn them into chimerical and fantastic opinions, without any practical use.[81]

Not only does it underpin all other bodies law, but only natural law is "sufficient [*seule suffisante*]"; it is the only complete legal philosophy. This is why "the French have adopted it, and they acclaim it as the most worthy of man, and of God, who issued it" (11). As in Physiocracy (and in most other preceding jusnaturalist theories), God is the author of this natural order,[82] but natural right can determine all aspects of legislation and justice only if one follows "its developments and consequences, a complicated assemblage which demands the knowledge of many facts, and wise reasoning" (14). Past legislators may have been aware of "a few precepts," but "only had a vague notion of the totality" (14), which is why no prior government ever succeeded in implementing the rule of nature. By contrast, for the knowledgeable statesman, "natural law constitutes an exact science" (16). Volney's argument thus foreshadows Tracy's highly deterministic epistemology, in which all "secondary" ideas flow from a "primary truth [*vérité première*]" in a necessary chain of thought.[83]

Whether or not Volney's "ideological" presentation of natural right accurately reflects the Jacobin theory of natural right, it does suggest that the belief in an all-determining law of nature was not simply a utopian fantasy, but was a philosophically acceptable position. It also indicates that even before the Constitution became a political obstacle for the Jacobins, it was already a secondary political consideration: If France was returning to the bosom of Mother Nature or Isis, it was her laws that mattered most. This predilection for natural right also placed the Jacobins at odds with their Gi-

---

81. *La loi naturelle, ou Catéchisme du citoyen français* (Paris: Sallior, 1793), 10.

82. See Le Mercier de la Rivière on "the essential order instituted by God," *L'ordre naturel et essentiel des sociétés politiques*, ed. Edgard Depitre (1767; Paris: Paul Geuthner, 1910), 50. This emphasis on the divine origin of natural law is important for Volney, whose *Ruines* were often read as promoting atheism.

83. "All secondary truths are but the consequences of a *primary truth,* in which they are all implicitly contained," *Mémoire sur la faculté de penser . . .*, ed. Anne and Henry Deneys (Paris: Fayard, 1992), 129. I discuss the *Idéologues'* deterministic epistemology in "The Birth of Ideology from the Spirit of Myth: Georges Sorel among the *Idéologues*," in *The Re-enchantment of the World: Secular Magic in a Rational Age*, ed. Joshua Landy and Michael Saler (Stanford: Stanford University Press, 2009).

rondin colleagues, who sought to reinsert into the constitutional debate a political concept that is often associated with Jacobin political thought—the general will.

Republican by Nature: Saint-Just versus the Girondins

During the 1793 constitutional debates, it was indeed the Girondins who adhered much more closely than their opponents to Rousseauist principles (a point to which I shall return more systematically in the conclusion). Their main objection to the Jacobin sacralization of the Declaration of Rights was that it should not be perceived as the foundation of the Constitution, but rather the other way around. Buzot presented this argument in overtly Rousseauist terms:

> The Declaration of Rights is not exactly the foundation of the Constitution, nor what the previous speaker [Valdruche] called the social contract. The social contract consists of the individual liberty each of us places in society. There you will find the true Declaration of the rights of all the citizens; that is, perhaps, what should form the social contract.[84]

By reversing the relation between the Declaration and the Constitution, Buzot could deemphasize the authoritative role of natural right.[85] Political liberty, for the Girondins, had to be earned; as Rousseau had insisted, there must be some sort of transaction between "individual [natural] liberty" and citizenship. Condorcet had similarly stressed this requirement when presenting his committee's constitutional project to the Convention:[86]

---

84. *AP*, 62:121. Valdruche had in fact argued that "our rights originate in the contract we have dressed; they are born with the social contract, from the nature of the political engagements we have made" (ibid.). See also Jean Debry's defense of a Rousseauist concept of general will (*AP*, 55:381–82; December 24, 1792), and Pierre-C.-F. Daunou's demand that primary assemblies approve every bill (*AP*, 62:352).

85. On the general Girondin wariness of natural right, see Gauchet, *Révolution des droits de l'homme*, 222–26; Florence Gauthier, *Triomphe et mort du droit naturel en Révolution, 1789–1795–1802* (Paris: PUF, 1992), 97; and Lucien Jaume, *Les déclarations des droits de l'homme* (Paris: GF, 1993), 44. For another example, see Maximin Isnard's speech on the Constitution, *AP*, 64:417ff.

86. Insightful discussions of Condorcet's project can be found in Keith Baker, *Condorcet: From Natural Philosophy to Social Mathematics* (Chicago: University of Chicago Press, 1975), 320–26; and Jaume, *Discours Jacobin*, 312–18. As both note, Condorcet's draft did not inspire much enthusiasm.

A Constitution which, founded solely on the principles of reason and justice, guarantees all citizens the full enjoyment of their rights . . . in such a way that the necessity to obey laws, and to submit one's individual will to the general will, does not impede on the sovereignty of the people, the equality between citizens, and the exercise of natural liberty.[87]

As this last phrase indicates, natural right was not entirely written out of this project (which may help explain why it did not solicit much interest among Girondin deputies, either), but it certainly did not underpin the entire edifice. Rational thinking replaced natural sentiments as the touchstone of society: This was a constitution designed for "an enlightened [*éclairé*] people . . . a people whom reason [*les lumières*] has led to freedom" (*AP*, 58:584). For the social mathematician, "the political rights that men have received from nature . . . derive essentially from their quality of sensible beings, who can possess moral ideas and can reason."[88] Nature figures in Condorcet's project only to the extent that it is synonymous with reason; one finds no such elegies of natural right as those that clutter Jacobin speeches. In the *Déclaration des droits* that prefaces his constitutional draft, the emphasis is placed on the "natural, civil, and political rights of men" (58:601), as opposed to their natural rights *tout court*.[89] Rather than a "consequence" of the "principles" of natural right, laws were to be the purest possible expression of the general will: "Never shall the will of the representatives of the people, nor of a group of citizens, impose itself on the general will" (587). Following earlier efforts by François Robert and others, Condorcet sought to square the circle of the general will in a representative democracy.[90]

On April 15 Saint-Just gave the most pointed Jacobin response to Condorcet's proposal. Where Robespierre criticized this project for not relying

---

87. *AP*, 58:583.

88. *AP*, 58:594. On the importance of moral sentiments in Condorcet's philosophy, see also Emma Rothschild, *Economic Sentiments: Adam Smith, Condorcet, and the Enlightenment* (Cambridge: Harvard University Press, 2001).

89. As it would be in the final preamble of the 1793 (Jacobin) Constitution: "The French people, convinced that the ignorance and disdain of the natural rights of man are the only causes of unhappiness in the world . . ." Compare with the 1789 text, which invoked instead the "rights of man." See Gauthier, *Triomphe et mort du droit naturel*.

90. Keith Baker emphasized how Condorcet's project was a statistical or rationalist revision of Rousseau's general will: "Submission to the will of the majority is founded not on the right of the greater will but on the probability of its greater rationality," *Condorcet*, 325. In *Le Républicanisme adapté à la France* (Paris, 1790), François Robert had similarly attempted to adapt representative government to a Rousseauist production of the general will (see chapter 2).

sufficiently on natural right, Saint-Just attacked its reliance on the general will and its overly rational (as opposed to *sensible*) quality.[91] Condorcet's definition of the general will was too "intellectual," Saint-Just protested; it presumed that the people could formulate their wills logically and consciously. Following this arithmetic definition, the general will might end up diverging from the general *weal*: "The general will, purely speculative, would seem to be a mental production, and not to reflect the interests of society. . . . Viewed from this angle, the general will is vitiated [*dépravée*]."[92] For Saint-Just, the true general will could not be determined in this "speculative" (that is, rational) manner since the true general will was simply whatever was best for the people, "the *material* will of the people" (423, my italics). The unspoken implication of this argument was that people could not be trusted (after centuries of corrupting despotism) to act in their own best interest.[93] The corollary of this implication, in turn, was that the people's representatives— provided, of course, that they be good Jacobins—were better placed to determine the general will (or *weal*) for them. In Saint-Just's constitutional draft, the only specific function allotted to the general will is the election of representatives, who in turn have sole responsibility for the creation of laws.[94]

On what authority, however, could representatives claim to legislate in the people's interest, even when they went against their will? Saint-Just based his arguments on a theory of human sociability that mirrors the natural-republican model analyzed in part 1. "I have found the social order to be in the very essence of nature [*dans la nature même des choses*]," he declared; "men from a same society live naturally in peace" (416). This anthropological premise combined beliefs in the natural sociability of humanity as well as in its natural primitive lawfulness, two central features of the golden age myth: "Natural justice among men [is] the principle of their society." Saint-Just historicized this mythical vision by drawing on a Tacitean vision of Germanic forests that is oddly reminiscent of Montesquieu's Troglodyte narrative: "The ancient Franks, the ancient Germans, had almost no magistrates; the people was prince and sovereign at once; but when the people lost their taste for assemblies . . . the prince separated himself from the

91. For a similar critique, see Montgilbert, "Avis du peuple" : "il faut renoncer à parler à l'esprit, [il faut] se tenir tout prêt du cœur, et y réveiller le sentiment naturel . . ." *AP*, 67:328.

92. "Discours sur la constitution de la France," April 15, 1793 (*SJ*, 426). In his May 10 speech on the Constitution, Robespierre similarly equated the general will with "l'intérêt public" (9:508). Jaume compares Saint-Just's speech to Condorcet's in *Discours Jacobin*, 318–23.

93. See the above quote on how "les fluctuations et les illusions offertes à la volonté générale" could bring back the monarchy (*SJ*, 423).

94. Pt. 1, chap. 1, arts. 1 and 4; see *SJ*, 426.

sovereign" (417). The moral of this philosophical *conte* was made clearer in an unpublished treatise (discussed below): "Laws corrupt men."[95] Rather than guiding and preserving virtue, as classical republicanism and the later Montesquieu would have it, positive laws *prevented* us from adhering to the dictates of natural right. The only way to restore the natural and just social order was to recover the "harmony" of original human relations:

> Nothing can be well-regulated if it is not self-propelling and does not obey its own harmony. . . . This principle applies in particular to the natural constitution of empires. Laws only keep evil at bay; innocence and virtue arise independently on earth. (416)

In a speech addressing the future constitution of France, the expression "natural constitution" is remarkable. Was Saint-Just implying that there already existed a constitution for all nations, which guaranteed peaceful relations between citizens? By dissociating virtuous conduct from human legislation, he both departed from the classical-republican insistence on their codependence and hinted that another, non-man-made principle was the authentic source of human justice. The laws passed by representatives could have only a "negative" role for Saint-Just, as David Bates has emphasized;[96] the "positive" dictates of the law must be found in nature alone.

In an unfinished and unpublished political treatise, which Anne Quennedy has convincingly argued should be called *Du droit social ou Principes du droit naturel*, Saint-Just developed this natural-republican theory of justice and society in much greater and fascinating detail, contrasting in particular his own ideas sharply with those of Rousseau:[97]

---

95. *Du droit social*, in *SJ*, 931. See also, in reference to natural man, "he is denatured by the power of the law" (927). Saint-Just had an edition of Montesquieu's *Œuvres* with him in Paris (see below for a more detailed discussion of his readings); most complete work editions in the eighteenth century contained the *Lettres persanes*.

96. On Saint-Just's "negative political theology," see David W. Bates, *Enlightenment Aberrations: Error and Revolution in France* (Ithaca: Cornell University Press, 2002), 161–78.

97. All editions of this text present it as *De la nature, de l'état civil, de la cité, ou les règles de l'indépendance du gouvernement*; for Quennedey's arguments, see "Note philologique sur le manuscrit de Saint-Just faussement intitulé *De la nature*," *AHRF* 351 (2008): 121–49. The various versions of this text (Quennedey counts no fewer than three) are believed to have been written between September 1791 and September 1792; see Miguel Abensour, "Lire Saint-Just," in Saint-Just, *Œuvres complètes*, ed. Anne Kupiec and M. Abensour (Paris: Gallimard, 2004), 25, and for a discussion of this treatise, 25–27; see also his earlier article, "La philosophie politique de Saint-Just," *AHRF* 182 (1966): 1–32 (15), and, for pt. 2, *AHRF* 185 (1966): 341–58. On this treatise and Saint-Just more generally, see also Norman Hampson, *Saint-Just* (Oxford: Blackwell, 1991), 57–73; and Jörg Monar, *Saint-Just: Sohn, Denker und Protagonist der Revolution* (Bonn: Bouvier, 1993), 238–56. On Saint-Just's military activities, see Jean-Pierre Gross, *Saint-Just: sa politique et ses missions* (Paris: Bibliothèque Nationale, 1976).

Laws are the natural relations between things, not relative relations or the effect of the general will. Rousseau says that laws can only express the general will and thus concludes that a legislator is needed. But a legislator can only express nature, not the general will. Moreover, this will can err and the social body should not be oppressed by itself, let alone by others. (*SJ*, 941)

This passage reveals the full extent of Saint-Just's suspicion of popular sovereignty (a suspicion shared, as we have seen, by many Jacobins), and the substitution of natural right for the general will as the foundation of all law. More than a foundation, in fact, the laws of nature constituted the only valid form of legislation, all other laws being a corruption of the natural *état social*: "Since there can be no society which is not founded on nature, the State can only accept the laws of nature. . . . The law is therefore not the expression of will, but of nature" (*SJ*, 950–51). This legal doctrine essentially repeats the Physiocratic demand that "positive legislation consists in the declaration of natural laws."[98]

What sort of constitution or social contract was needed in Saint-Just's natural republic? The answer is simply, if astonishingly, none. As Sylvain Maréchal before him, he berates the revolutionaries for having turned their backs on natural right and imposed a necessarily flawed constitution on the French people:[99]

The republic, according to its conventions, agreed on a political contract establishing power relations between the individual and the whole, and this political contract constitutes the social pact. But what a sign of violence and weakness this was, since it ignores and offends nature! (924)

He counters the objection that societies cannot make do without a social contract by selectively borrowing the conclusion of Rousseau's second *Discourse*: "One might ask: how can a people get by without a contract? I would ask in return, who truly has one? Nations have neither contracts nor

---

98. Quesnay, *Le droit naturel,* in vol. 1 of *Physiocratie, ou Constitution naturelle du gouvernement le plus avantageux au genre humain*, ed. Pierre-Samuel Dupont de Nemours (Paris and Leiden: Merlin, 1768), 35. Compare also with Saint-Just's claim in his *Esprit de la Révolution* that "any political law that is not founded on nature is bad," *SJ*, 318. I discuss below how Saint-Just may have come into contact with Physiocratic thought.

99. If this passage was indeed written before August 1792, the "republic" in question must have been the constitutional, monarchic *res publica* of 1791. But it is not entirely clear whether Saint-Just is referring here to France in particular or to a generic republic.

202 • CHAPTER FOUR

pacts, everywhere it is force that governs them" (929). Finally, in a brilliant inversion that might be considered purely rhetorical, were it not for its clear Physiocratic logic, Saint-Just defines *l'état sauvage* as the political state that is chronologically *posterior* to the implementation of a social contract.[100] Indeed, since "the natural ends where the conventional begins" (922), any society founded by a constitution can only be denatured.

Saint-Just was aware that this political theory could be met with the same Voltairean irony that had greeted Rousseau's celebration of natural man: "I do not wish to send men back into forests," he insisted, "on the contrary, I am recalling them to nature, to the social order; should the sun shine only on wild beasts?" (926). But his political theory was not merely based on the naïve belief in "the complete goodness of human nature," as Miguel Abensour suggested.[101] Like Fénelon and the young Montesquieu before him, he clearly recognized the constant danger of corruption, even in the near-perfect natural State. To fend off this danger and preserve natural virtue, Saint-Just opted for the obvious republican solution: "Institutions protect a free people's government against moral corruption" (967). He developed this republican dimension of the natural State in a later, also unpublished, work known as the "Fragments des *Institutions républicaines*" (from which this last quote is taken). Institutions are described here as an antidote to and replacement for laws:[102]

There are too many laws, and too few civil institutions. . . . Only few laws are needed. Too many laws enslave the people. . . . Whoever gives too many laws to a people is a tyrant. . . . It is not clear how to obey the law, since the law is often nothing but the will of the one who has imposed it. We have the right to resist oppressive laws. (976)

In *Du droit social*, Saint-Just had been tempted by the even more radical proposition that "the best civil law would be that there are none" (940), a sentence that would get crossed out.[103] Acknowledging laws as an ambigu-

---

100. Compare with Court de Gébelin's description of *l'état sauvage* as a result of the disorders caused by humanity's forgetting its *état naturel*, which had been just and harmonious; see chapter 2.

101. See "La philosophie politique de Saint-Just," 347.

102. On this point, see Miguel Abensour, "La théorie des institutions et les relations du législateur et du peuple selon Saint-Just," in *Actes du colloque Saint-Just*, ed. Albert Soboul (Paris: Société des études robespierristes, 1968), 239–90.

103. On Saint-Just's antilegalism and his "maternal" institutions, see Marie-Hélène Huet, *Mourning Glory: The Will of the French Revolution* (Philadelphia: University of Pennsylvania Press, 1997), 84–91.

ous necessity, he placed his hopes in the regenerating and preserving power of republican institutions: Only they could provide "the guarantee for political liberty"; only they "moralize government and civilian life" (966) and stave off both governmental and popular corruption (967). Institutions are the secret catalyst for performing the alchemical operation that endows morals with the guiding force of laws: "If there were morals [*des mœurs*], all would be well; institutions are needed to purify them. That should be our goal; that is all that must be done; everything else will follow on its own" (975–76). Institutions, finally, were independent from governmental corruption; hence, as James Swenson argued, Saint-Just could offer "a theory of civil society" that was entirely "in opposition to the state."[104] By privileging social institutions and enshrining natural right over the general will, Saint-Just attempted to eliminate legislative sovereignty altogether, in accordance with natural republicanism and his own axiom that "one cannot rule innocently [*on ne peut régner innocemment*]."

While he may have had a greater faith than earlier republican theorists in the miraculous virtues of institutions, Saint-Just did not ultimately veer far in this respect from the opinions of Machiavelli, Montesquieu, or Rousseau. As noted in part 1, it was a commonplace of republican theory that solid institutions were required to sustain the state. Saint-Just's republicanism was only heretical in its expulsion of civil and constitutional law, although here as well, as we saw, many strands of eighteenth-century French political thought encouraged such a tabula rasa back to *jus naturale*.

The similarities between Saint-Just's political thought and these earlier currents inevitably lead us to ponder his familiarity with the natural-republican narrative examined in part 1. We may glean some indications from his own written works, both from direct references to Hobbes, Montesquieu, and Rousseau (among others), but also from inscriptions of important cultural events: as Voltaire, Diderot, and Maréchal, Saint-Just praises the Tahitians, for instance, for their proximity to the natural order ("happy land, you are far from my sight and close to my heart!").[105] Very little is

---

104. "Saint-Just and Billaud-Varenne" (paper presented at the annual meeting of the Western Society for French History, Colorado Springs, CO, October 28–29, 2005). I thank the author for sharing this communication with me, and for many illuminating discussions about Saint-Just.

105. See *Esprit de la Révolution et de la Constitution de France* and the reference to "L'outaouais": *SJ*, 326; on Tahiti in natural-republican thought, see chapter 2. Abensour claimed (without textual evidence) that "Saint-Just does not connect primitive society with the golden age, a time of abundance when the distinction between thine and mine was unknown," but the reference to Tahiti suggests otherwise. Abensour also overlooks the politico-legal features closely associated with this myth in eighteenth-century thought, in favor of purely economic ones; see "La philosophie politique de Saint-Just," 15.

known about Saint-Just's studies with the Oratorians in Soissons, but we do know which books were in his possession when he was arrested on 9 thermidor.[106] Along with Montesquieu's *Œuvres*, many of Rousseau's works, and a proto-Rousseauist novel (Mme de Graffigny's *Lettres d'une Péruvienne*), Saint-Just kept with him a copy of Fénelon's *Télémaque*, the quintessential political handbook of the eighteenth century, which also contained the seed of natural republicanism, with its description of the land of Boetica.[107]

He also owned a curious text by Nicolas-Gabriel Clerc (or Leclerc) called *Yu le Grand et Confucius, histoire chinoise*. Unfavorably (and unflatteringly) compared to *Télémaque* by the *Correspondance littéraire*, this philosophical novel is a wordy Physiocratic treatise dressed up as a *chinoiserie*.[108] As the "French Confucius" before him, Clerc declared that natural law was the only authentic foundation for all political order and legislation:[109] "Natural law has served as a model for all laws that are sanctioned by humanity. Hence, all established laws, now and in the future, can and should only be *declarative acts of the primitive law that gave birth to the social order*" (667, emphasis in original). The legislator's role was restricted to being the mouthpiece for the one true legislator, God, Clerc wrote in a passage that foreshadows not only Saint-Just, but also Robespierre: "The Supreme Being is the unique Legislator. . . . God's finger traced his code in indelible characters in the human heart; every man can read it there by means of his reason" (140). Although Clerc was more accepting of the need for positive laws, he, too, insisted that they be kept to a strict minimum (649–50), and that they merely recapitulate "the supreme laws of the natural order" (xiv).

Clerc's opus does not merely express a naïve faith in natural right and the natural goodness of man, but in a natural-republican fashion acknowledges the risks of social corruption: "Even though men are born good, very good even, and that they learn from their own needs and the help they receive

106. For a complete list, see *Œuvres completes*, ed. Kupiec and Abensour, 1194–95. As Abensour observes, the small number of works suggests that this was "the working library of a provincial deputy" and does not represent the full breadth of his studies ("La philosophie politique de Saint-Just," 344n93). That said, one can also assume that these were works of particular importance for him.

107. See chapter 1.

108. See *Yu le Grand et Confucius, histoire chinoise* (Soissons: Ponce Courtois, 1769); this work is briefly discussed in Abensour, "La philosophie politique de Saint-Just," 345–46. See also Friedrich Melchior von Grimm, Denis Diderot, François Raynal et al., *Correspondance littéraire, philosophique et critique . . .* , ed. Maurice Tourneux (1877; repr. ed. Nendeln: Kraus, 1968), 9:19–20.

109. Quesnay's *Tableau économique*, Clerc claimed, constituted the "keystone" of the "natural order" of society (xiv). The final section of *Yu le grand*, entitled "De la politique et des lois," loosely summarizes (without mentioning it) the idiosyncratic narrative of natural right theory developed in Quesnay's own *Droit naturel*, discussed in chapter 2.

THE CASE OF THE MISSING CONSTITUTION

how to provide assistance to one another, it is beyond a doubt that they become evil" (255); "morals are the only culprit" (244), Clerc concludes. His prescription for redressing *mœurs* is similarly republican (while maintaining a Physiocratic insistence on a monarchic "tutelary authority," 634): "The Empire owes its large number of wise and lettered men to these sublime and religious *institutions*" (135, emphasis added). Most important among these institutions is education (100). Rather than laws or a constitution, it is the opportunity of a good education that will transform children into model citizens: "All man needs are lessons in humanity and moral rectitude [*bienséance*]. If these virtues are implanted before disorderly passions take root, their sweetness will replace the latter's frenzy" (280); "a good education is thus the precursor to good morals" (633).

Finally, *Yu le Grand et Confucius* underscores how the natural-republican project for political reform did not shy away from severe pronouncements against those individuals, like tyrants, who "violate the laws of order, the law of nature, the law of nations" (222). Generally Beccarian in his discussion of punishment, Clerc advocated much harsher treatment for the sort of man who could "harden himself to the point of showing no remorse": In that case, "there would be only one solution, the man should be choked [*il faudroit étouffer l'homme*]."[110] These barbarians, like Diderot's *raisonneur violent* and Rousseau's unfeeling reader, were deaf to the voice of nature within them;[111] their nefarious example posed a threat to society and government, making more radical measures necessary (268). If our natural instinct for justice—that "secret of the human heart" (274)—was corrupted, there could be no "social harmony" (633). While statements such as these do not amount to anything resembling a theory of the Terror, they certainly do not provide many restraints against violence.

The eradication of legislative sovereignty through such appeals to the unchanging laws of nature could thus fortify the dream of a depoliticized society, even if it did not necessarily lead to a society without violence or power. The Physiocrats also saw the need for a "tutelary authority" who would ensure that natural right was respected; a benign figure in Le Mercier de la Rivière, this authority was nonetheless granted a "despotic" power to enforce the law. Moreover, he was not elected or chosen in any legitimate way

---

110. *Yu le Grand*, 207. See also the subsequent remark on how "ambition, pride, greed create monsters that society should choke" (263).

111. Clerc explicitly identifies such transgressors as barbarians: "All that is barbarian is what goes against Nature, against the natural law, and the love of order" (viii). Diderot "chokes" his *raisonneur* in the *Encyclopédie* article on "Droit naturel" (5:116); Rousseau's pitiless reader is called "*un homme à étouffer*" in the penultimate paragraph of the *Confessions*.

(apart from hereditary succession). His legitimacy stemmed above all from his own moral rectitude and ability to perceive the laws of nature clearly. The legal despot, in other words, could conceivably morph into a dictatorial power, which punished and terrorized in the name of natural right.

Saint-Just's political thought cannot and should not be reduced to a reworking of Physiocratic ideas in an overtly republican key (even if *Du droit social* still accepted a monarch). In many respects, and no doubts thanks to his revolutionary experience, Saint-Just fused the political languages of liberal natural right and republicanism to an unprecedented degree, resolving tensions and contradictions that haunted his intellectual forebearers, and drafting the first truly comprehensive theory of natural republicanism. While Physiocracy probably did provide him with a crucial anticontractualist narrative, his influences should not be sought only in specific texts or authors since the two political languages from which he primarily drew, as well as the representations that fired his imagination (such as Tahiti, the golden age, or pastoral communities), were widespread in late Enlightenment political culture.

Despite his standing in the National Convention and position on the Committee of Public Safety, one may of course find these political reflections irrelevant when compared with the legally encumbered, constitutionalist (if constitution-less) first French Republic. No doubt it would be a mistake to read *Du droit social* as Saint-Just's last word on all political matters or as the quintessence of Jacobin political thought. What his unpublished treatises do enable us to imagine, however, is a different kind of republic, which for Jacobin believers may have glimmered, mirage-like, on the horizon of the Revolution. This republic-to-come can strike us as ludicrous (not to mention murderous), yet it was not an isolated case in eighteenth-century political thought. As a plausible and, for many, praiseworthy politico-legal theory, it cannot simply be brushed away as a cynical representation, a mere foil for holding onto power. The extent to which Saint-Just and his colleagues on the Committee of Public Safety attempted to implement this project is debatable and will constitute the subject of the following chapter. But we should not forget that as they entered uncharted legal waters after October 1793, the Jacobin leaders may in fact have had their sights on an ideal republic of natural right.

What's Left of the General Will?

Saint-Just's arguments against Condorcet—and the claims in his treatises that natural right, not the general will, was the only valid source for civil society—force us to reconsider long-held assumptions about the central tenets of Jacobin thought. After all, for political historians since Alfred Cobban, in particular those sharing François Furet's interpretation of the Revolution, the general will has been perceived as its very keystone.[112] While this thesis has come under attack from many sides, it has usually been dismissed on methodological, rather than philosophical grounds; it is not the importance of the general will per se, but of political thought altogether that tends to be rejected.[113] But if one accepts the arguments laid out in the previous and present chapters—namely, that a legal philosophy based in natural right presided over the first legislative phase of the Terror (December 1792–March 1793), and that the pursuit of power is not incompatible with a passion for ideas— it is worth questioning the role of Rousseau's hallmark concept in Jacobin thought. What a survey of constitutional proposals by Montagnard *conventionnels*, alongside those of other deputies and citizens, suggests is that, to the extent it was a fixture of Jacobin discourse at all, the general will figured not in its Rousseauist form, but in a version nearly identical to natural right.

To begin with a striking example, the Jacobin leader most closely associated with Rousseau, Robespierre, did not see it fit to mention the general will a single time in his constitutional project.[114] It is only in his earlier draft for a Declaration of Rights that one finds a close equivalent: Article 15 states that "the law is the free and solemn expression of the people's will [*la volonté du peuple*]." However, this substitution of an ambiguous phrase for the more common *volonté générale* (which would ultimately appear in the official Declaration) suggests that this popular will can be interpreted in Saint-Just's manner, that is, as a "material will," or *weal*, to be determined for, rather than by, the people.[115] Subsequent articles insist on the need for laws only to forbid "what is harmful to society," to order "what is useful" (art. 17), and never to violate "the everlasting rights of man" (art. 18)—qualifiers

---

112. See Alfred Cobban, "The Political Ideas of Maximilien Robespierre during the Period of the Convention," *English Historical Review* 61 (1946): 45–80; see also Arendt, *On Revolution*, 65–67, and 175. For Furet, see especially *Interpreting the French Revolution*, and "The Terror," in *A Critical Dictionary of the French Revolution*, ed. François Furet and Mona Ozouf, trans. Arthur Goldhammer (Cambridge: Belknap Press of Harvard University Press, 1989).

113. For a discussion of the historiographical responses to the revisionist historians, see chapter 3. One exception to this trend is Timothy Tackett's work on the Estates General, *Becoming a Revolutionary: The Deputies of the French National Assembly and the Emergence of a Revolutionary Culture (1789–1790)* (Princeton: Princeton University Press, 1996), which uses a more quantitative method to challenge ideological assumptions (but his study does not extend past 1791).

114. See *Rob.*, 9:508–10.

115. *Rob.*, 9:466, and 464–69 for the entire Declaration. For Saint-Just, see his April 15 retort to Condorcet, discussed above.

that an authentic Rousseauist would not have found necessary. In an earlier text, Robespierre had already expressed similar reserves: "I adhere to the will of the majority [*du plus grand nombre*], or to what it is assumed to be," he wrote in the fifth issue of his journal, *Le Défenseur de la Constitution*, adding: "but I only respect justice and truth. . . . Society has the right to demand my loyalty, but not the sacrifice of my reason: that is the eternal law of all reasonable beings" (*Rob.*, 4:145). This insistence on justice, reason, and an eternal law point to a politico-legal theory based on the laws of nature, rather than (strictly speaking) the general will.

In fact, Montagnards voiced some of the harshest criticisms of general will theory in their discussions of the Constitution. The Jacobin society member Jean-Baptiste Pressavin argued,

> to say that the general will voiced by the majority of individuals in a society becomes a sacred law for all its members is to unjustly subject the weakest to the strongest, since the general will can be corrupted enough that it commands what reason prohibits . . . it is unjust to force the minority to renounce the rights men have received from nature and the laws that nature dictates through reason.[116]

Where a majority of *conventionnels* and citizens, as we will see, was happy to appeal to both natural right and the general will as the source of law, Pressavin pointed out the possible contradiction between them, echoing Saint-Just's fears about the corruption of the general will. Article 3 of his constitutional project refers even to "the allegedly general will [*la volonté réputée générale*]," and stresses its limits on the rights of the minority (383). The deputy who first aroused Jacobin suspicions about implementing the Constitution, François Chabot, similarly sought to curtail the authority of the general will, in a lengthy speech to the Convention on May 5, 1793. Only insofar as they were contracting into civil society, he argued, did the people need to obey the general will (misinterpreted here as the will of all): "Every citizen must first sign the social part. . . . Only in this regard can the law be considered the expression of the general will." In all other occasions, "the law has a more august definition," which it receives from "the god of nature." This god expresses himself through the reason of the legislators,

---

116. "Projet de Constitution par le citoyen Pressavin, député de Rhône-et-Loire," *AP*, 67:382. Pressavin voted with the Mountain for the sentencing of the king, although he was later expelled from the Jacobin society; see the entry under his name in Michaud's *Biographie universelle ancienne et moderne* (Paris: Mme C. Desplaces, 1843).

not the general will of society (again confused with universal consent): "Every decree that contradicts this rule cannot be called a law: to do so would sacrilegious, and the assent of a universal will would not justify this profanation." As with Robespierre, the general will is deemed valid only if it corresponds to the dictates of natural right: "The expression of the general will can only constitute a law if it does not depart from the goals of nature and of society."[117] Finally, Chabot's insistence on natural right also derived from a natural-republican premise: "All governments were originally democratic, and the origin of things is never corrupt," he declared, echoing Saint-Just, as well as many Montagnard pronouncements made during the king's trial (see chapter 3).

While no doubt less influential than other Jacobin orators (and soon to be undone by a corruption scandal), Chabot nonetheless revealed the rationale for these reservations, which derived from the same Jacobin uneasiness with direct democracy and even popular sovereignty: "Do not mislead the people, who desire happiness, by an alleged sovereignty [*une prétendue souveraineté*] that they could not possibly want, as it makes them anxious and unhappy," Chabot argued, before dropping a bombshell: "Make the people happy despite themselves [*rendez le peuple heureux malgré lui*], if possible, at the risk of not respecting its sovereignty enough."[118] This insidious argument runs like a leitmotif through Jacobin constitutional theory: The people are not the best judges of their own well-being. Legislators are better placed to determine their happiness, since the principles that they follow "stem from the laws of nature who made everything perfect. . . . Do not offer [the people] any other laws besides those inspired by the first principles of eternal justice." Natural right not only was a more authoritative legislative fount for the Jacobins, but it also provided a cover for pulling the mantle of sovereignty away from the people.

The Jacobin discomfort with the general will made its way into the final ratified version of the 1793 Declaration of Rights. Article 6 of the 1789 Declaration had simply stated: "The Law is the expression of the general will. All citizens have the right to contribute directly, or through their representatives, to its creation. It must be the same for all, whether protecting or punishing." Article 4 of the revised version introduced significant qualifiers:

---

117. *AP*, 64:162. Chabot's speech is discussed in Boroumand, *Guerre des principes*, 338–45.

118. *AP*, 64:171. See also: "We must not tire the people with their sovereignty. . . . This sovereignty should only be invoked if the delegates violate the constitutional laws" (163).

The law is the free and solemn expression of the general will; it is the same for all, whether protecting or punishing; it can only command what is just and useful for society; it can only prohibit what is harmful.

Not only are the French citizens no longer called on explicitly to help formulate the law, but two constraints are placed on the "free expression" of the general will. Already present in Robespierre's draft Declaration, these constraints reveal both a distrust of the people's "fluctuations" (to borrow Saint-Just's term), and a desire to equate the general will with a principle of justice that lies *beyond* society, in natural right—whereas, in orthodox Rousseauism, the general will was itself the only source of justice.

The constitutional debates of spring-summer 1793 may also provide a better means of identifying a Girondin "party line" than some of the other commonly used indicators.[119] By ranking projects and major speeches on the Constitution based on (1) the legal authority of natural right versus the general will, and (2) the preeminence of the Declaration versus the Constitutional Act, and then comparing these results for each deputy with their choice on the three crucial votes during the trial of Louis XVI, a distinct pattern emerges (see table 1).[120] Among the deputies who both expressed skepticism about the place of natural right in civil society, and, conversely, argued that the general will and the Constitution should provide the legal basis for rights and laws, fifteen out of eighteen were Girondins, or voted with them on key votes (essentially the *appel au peuple* and the *sursis*, or suspended sentence).[121] While this sample is admittedly very small, it is matched on the opposite end: Among the deputies who placed the Declaration of Rights above and beyond the Constitution, and privileged natural right over

119. The debate about whether the Girondins constituted a homogenous faction has raged since the nineteenth century; see especially M. J. Sydenham, *The Girondins* (London: Athlone Press, 1961); Alison Patrick, *The Men of the First French Republic: Political Alignments in the National Convention of 1792* (Baltimore: Johns Hopkins University Press, 1972); Soboul, *Girondins et Montagnards*; Frederick A. de Luna, "The 'Girondins' Were Girondins, after All," and Michael S. Lewis-Beck, Anne Hildreth, and Alan B. Spitzer, "Was There a Girondist Faction in the National Convention, 1792–93?" both in *French Historical Studies* 15, no. 3 (1988): 506–18, and 519–36, respectively; and François Furet and Mona Ozouf, eds., *La Gironde et les Girondins* (Paris: Payot, 1991).

120. Not all of the interventions in the debate on the Constitution addressed theoretical points of law; for this reason, the sample is relatively small (thirty-one deputies). Given the comparative and political nature of this table, only constitutional projects by *conventionnels* were considered.

121. Of the remaining three deputies, only one, Jean-Michel Coupé, was associated with the Mountain; another, Jean Debry, protested the expulsion of the Girondins; the third was Anne-Joseph-Arnauld Valdruche.

Table 1. Political Theories of Girondins and Montagnards[a]

Name	NR/ GW	Decl/ Const	*Appel*	Sentence	*Sursis*	AP ref.	Party
Chabot, François	1	3	No	Death	No	67:261	Mont.
Harmand, J.-B.	1	2	No	Banishment	No	62:270	
Oudot, C.-F.	1	1	No	Death, suspended	No	67:362	Mont.
Pressavin, J.-B.	1	2	No	Death	No	67:380	Mont.
Saint-Just	1	2	No	Death	No	[*SJ*]	Mont.
Lambert de Belan, Charles	1	2	Yes	Prison/banishment	Absent	62:434	Gir. vote
Robespierre	1.5	1	No	Death	No	[*Rob.*]	Mont.
Montgilbert, F.-A.	2	1	No	Death, suspended	Yes	67:328–62	
Boissy d'Anglas, F.-A.	2	3	Yes	Prison/banishment	Yes	62:287	Gir. vote
Billaud-Varenne	2.5	1.5	No	Death	No	67:220	Mont.
Pepin, Sylvain	2.5	2	Yes	Prison/banishment	No	63:292–94	
Cappin, Joseph	2.5	2	Yes	Prison/banishment	Yes	64:235–43	Gir. vote
Carnot, Lazare	3	1	No	Death	No	62:335	Mont.
Coupé, J.-M.	3	3	No	Death	No	67:266	Mont.
Debry, Jean	3	3	No	Death	No	63:236–40	
Daunou, P.-C.-F.	3	2	No	Prison/banishment	Yes	62:350	Gir.
Bohan, Alain	3	2	Yes	Death	Yes	67:251	Gir. vote
Bourgois, J.-F.-A.	3	2	Yes	Prison/banishment	Yes	63:259–79	Gir. vote
Guyomar, Pierre	3	2	Yes	Prison/banishment	Yes	63:591–99	Gir.[‡]
Condorcet, N.	3	4	No	Prison	Abstain	58:583ff.	Gir.
Valdruche, A.-J.-A.	4	3	Yes	Death	No	62:121	
Brunel, Ignace	4	1	Yes	Prison/banishment	Yes	67:258	Gir.
Buzot, F.-N.-L.	4	3	Yes	Death suspended	Yes	62:121	Gir.
Faure, P.-J.-D.-G.	4	3	Yes	Prison	Yes	63:279–92	Gir.
Isnard, Maximin	4	3	No	Death	No	64:417–23	Gir.
Durand de Maillane, P.-T.	4	2	Yes	Prison/banishment	Absent	62:374	Gir. vote
Kersaint, A.-G.-S.	4	4	Yes	Prison	Absent	62:420	Gir.
Pénières, J.-A.	4.5	0	No	Death	No	62:477	Gir.[‡]
Albouys, Barth.	5	0	Yes	Prison/banishment	Yes	67:176–79	Gir. vote
Rouzet, J.-M.	5	4	Yes	Prison	Yes	62:485	Gir.
Barailon, J.-F.	5	3	N/a	Prison	Yes	67:187	Gir. vote

[a]Girondin affiliation is based on Jacqueline Chaumié's index in "Les Girondins," and, when marked by a ‡, Claude Perroud's list in *La proscription des Girondins* (Paris: Alcan, 1917). Montagnard affiliation is determined according to Françoise Brunel, "Les députés montagnards"; "Gir. vote" indicates that the deputy voted with the Girondins for the *appel au peuple* and the suspended sentence.

The scale for the "NR/GW" column is based on the following assessment:
1 No mention of general will.
2 Natural rights continue to be freely exercised in society; general will is equated with natural right.
3 Natural rights cohabitate with a Rousseauist idea of the general will.
4 Natural rights are redefined by social contract.
5 No natural rights; all rights derive from social contract.

Similarly, the scale for the "Decl/Const" column:
1 Separate declaration, contains all principles of Constitution.
2 Separate declaration, Constitution provides new rights (equal weight).
3 Declaration is either pro-forma or incorporated into constitution, which is given much more weight.
4 No separate declaration, only a constitution.
0 Unclear.

the general will, eight out of thirteen were either Montagnards, or voted against the Girondin proposals during the king's trial; most tellingly, none were Girondins.[122]

While a large number of Girondins and Montagnards (including some of the leading figures in each camp) can thus be distinguished by their dueling political theories, it is also true that a large number of constitutional projects do not seem to have sensed the philosophical tension between the general will and natural right. The proposal by Joseph Cappin, a moderate deputy from the Gers, asserts, for instance, that "the best of social conventions would grant man the fullest enjoyment of his natural rights," before adding shortly thereafter, "the law can only be the expression of the general will."[123] Boissy d'Anglas's constitutional project affirms the absolute inviolability of natural right in articles 4–6, and then also asserts that the law is "the expression of the general will" in article 9.[124] The two concepts cohabitate with similar ease in the proposal presented by a citizen named Ragonneau, who defines the new government as the "fraternal society of the French, organized and governed according to the following principles of natural right," while article 7 of these aforesaid principles falls back on the same Rousseauist definition of the law.[125] This attitude seems to have been the most common, particularly among the deputies of the *Plaine*.

Ultimately, however, there is nothing altogether strange about these juxtapositions. The 1789 Declaration of Rights, after all, had already claimed to "present . . . the natural, inalienable, and sacred rights of man," amongst which was the definition of law as "the expression of the general will" (art. 6). While this text was itself the result of various compromises,[126] it nonetheless highlights the revolutionaries' difficulty in separating these concepts. And yet this difficulty is not surprising either: Natural right and the general will already overlapped in Rousseau, and had in fact been deemed identical in Diderot's *Encyclopédie* article on "*droit naturel*" (see chapter 1). While it would be inexact to suggest that the Jacobins reverted to a Diderotian conception of the general will (since, in that version, it bears no clear relation to the body politic), there are certainly elements of this noncontractualist

122. The deputy who voted with the Montagnards is Jean-Baptiste Harmand; François-Antoine Montgilbert, whom I did not count, voted against the *appel*, but for the *sursis*.

123. Title 1, arts. 2 and 12; *AP*, 64:236. See also the "Plan de Constitution proposé par J.F.A. Bourgois," *AP*, 63:259–79.

124. "Projet de Constitution pour la République française," *AP*, 62:289.

125. *AP*, 64:252.

126. See Johnson Kent Wright, "National Sovereignty and the General Will: The Political Program of the *Déclaration des droits* of 1789," in *French Idea of Freedom*.

definition that they revived, such as Diderot's idea that whoever "listens only to his particular will is the enemy of the human race."[127] This idea, however, had already been expressed in liberal natural right theory (as described in the prologue), and was merely, if intriguingly, reformulated here in voluntarist language.

The fundamental question concerning the place of the general will in Jacobin political thought is whether this concept was instrumental in motivating or justifying the repressions of the Terror. While it may not exactly have encouraged pluralism, it is not at all clear that the general will was decisive in swelling prisons or packing carts off to the guillotine. As we saw in chapter 3, the severity of revolutionary punishments owed more to natural right notions of a denatured enemy than to Rousseau. This distinct origin is apparent even in instances where a voluntarist discourse is used to defend harsh repression, as in Saint-Just's October 10 report: "Since the French people made its will clear, whatever is opposed to it is not part of the sovereign [*hors le souverain*]; whatever is not part of the sovereign is an enemy."[128] This phrasing, however, clearly demonstrates that Saint-Just is using the language of the general will to convey an idea based on natural right: Rousseau never suggested that those who disagreed with the general will were not part of the sovereign, only that they could be "constrained" to obey the will of the majority. To "force someone to be free" is not a license to kill them.[129]

Jacobin power politics throughout most of 1793, therefore, do not appear to have been driven by an obsession with "*une volonté une*" (the famous phrase from one of Robespierre's diary entries). The disparities between repressive practices in provincial departments, discussed above, cannot be explained by a fanatical desire to ensure ideological purity since surely there would have been a few dissenters and suspects in peaceful areas, as well. The focus on departments exhibiting large-scale "counterrevolutionary" activity indicates a concern with political challenges of a certain demographical magnitude—in other words, a concern that was largely about winning elections.

---

127. *Encyclopédie*, 5:115.

128. *SJ*, 521. He also speaks about "la minorité rebelle" in his 8 ventôse speech; *SJ*, 699.

129. This distinction is much clearer in *Du droit social*, where Saint-Just did not drape his thought in terms of the general will: Whoever breaks the law "will henceforth be the enemy of the sovereign, since at that very moment he will have left the State and engaged in war against the sovereign, and will have clearly *violated nature*," *SJ*, 941, my italics. Quentin Skinner has argued that Rousseau's phrase and concept do not warrant the "totalitarian" interpretation often attributed to them since they reflect mainstream classical-republican values; see "The Republican Idea of Political Liberty," in *Machiavelli and Republicanism*, ed. Gisele Bock, Quentin Skinner, and Maurizio Viroli (Cambridge: Cambridge University Press, 1990).

If the general will was not the cornerstone of Jacobin philosophy, the latter cannot simply be dismissed as rhetorical fluff. What seems in fact to have characterized this philosophy, onward from the king's trial at least, may be expressed in terms of the categories Keith Baker has proposed for analyzing both Old Regime and revolutionary political thought: By establishing natural right as the ultimate legislative and penal authority, the Jacobins substituted a "discourse of reason" for a "discourse of will."[130] While there were philosophical justifications for this substitution, it was also made necessary by the repeated Jacobin resistance to popular sovereignty, be it in the form of the *appel au peuple*, primary assembly consultation, or most simply, after October 10, elections. Replacing a discourse of will with one of reason, moreover, enabled the Jacobins to resolve a difficulty that had haunted the French Revolution since the beginning: How and in whom was the will embodied? Absent the impossible reunion of all French citizens on the Champs-de-Mars, how could the will of the people be adequately expressed? If their will mattered only insomuch as it corresponded to the dictates of nature, this problem disappeared. The Jacobins could remain in power without consulting the people, but by consulting only their minds and hearts.

With each successive report from the Committee of Public Safety after October 10, however, it sounded as though the prospect of elections was becoming progressively more distant. In the context of an open-ended "revolutionary government," the question of political violence, but also of political vision, must be posed anew. What did it mean in practice for a state to exist with few laws and mostly institutions, as Saint-Just had hoped? How could natural right practically replace positive legislation as the only law of the land? It is by approaching the institutions of Year II, chief amongst which the Festival of the Supreme Being and the reformed revolutionary tribunal, from this natural-republican perspective that we may understand how the golden age fantasy acted out at the feet of Isis could swiftly descend into a bloody arena. The legal theory underpinning the natural-republican project of restoring social harmony, after all, had first been invoked to decapitate the king. No one said it could not be put to many uses.

---

130. For a definition of these categories, see the introduction to *Inventing the French Revolution*, and more recently, "Political Languages of the French Revolution," in *The Cambridge History of Eighteenth-Century Political Thought*, ed. Mark Goldie and Robert Wolker (Cambridge: Cambridge University Press, 2006).

THE DESPOTISM OF NATURE

Justice and the Republic-to-Come

WITH THE CONSTITUTION OF 1793 literally "suspended" in an ark of covenant above them, the *conventionnels* must have listened with surprise to claims from the Committee of Public Safety that they needed to start the process of founding the French Republic all over.[1] In a November 1793 report, outlining the structure of the revolutionary government, Billaud-Varenne intimated that the Jacobin Constitution was indeed not good enough, and that the new highly centralized and vigorous executive should "serve as a model for composing [*pour la rédaction*] the organic code of the Constitution." The deputies would have to return to their drawing boards to pen a constitution that brought France even closer to nature: "The best civil Constitution is the one that remains the closest to the processes of nature."[2]

Despite the title of his report, Billaud-Varenne gave no indication of when this future revision would take place. If the revolutionary government (announced on October 10) was provisional, its duration was indefinite. Robespierre's report the following month did not allay any qualms about the open-endedness of Jacobin rule: "Founding the French republic is not child's play," he warned the deputies.[3] His report even conveyed the impression

---

1. On David's motion (on August 11), the Convention decreed that the Constitution, still stored in the ark in which it had been placed on August 10, be displayed above the speaker's bar; see *Archives parlementaires de 1787 à 1860*, ed. M. J. Mavidal et al. (Paris: Librairie administrative de P. Dupont, 1862–1913), 72:31 (hereafter cited as *AP*).

2. "Rapport sur un mode de gouvernement provisoire et révolutionnaire," 28 brumaire an II (November 18, 1793); *AP*, 79:451–57; 453 for quotes. He also decried how "we decreed a republic and are still organized as in a monarchy." On Billaud-Varenne, see notably Lucien Jaume, *Le discours Jacobin et la démocratie* (Paris: Fayard, 1989); John M. Burney, "The Fear of the Executive and the Threat of Conspiracy: Billaud-Varenne's Terrorist Rhetoric in the French Revolution, 1788–94," *French History* 5, no. 2 (1991): 143–63; and Françoise Brunel's introduction to her edition of Billaud-Varenne's 1795 *Principes régénérateurs du système social* (Paris: Publications de la Sorbonne, 1992).

3. "Rapport sur les principes du gouvernement révolutionnaire," 5 nivôse an II (December 25, 1793), *Œuvres de Maximilien Robespierre*, ed. the Société des études robespierristes (Ivry: Phénix éditions, 2000), 10:277 (hereafter cited as *Rob.*). If he nonetheless assured the Convention that "the constitutional ship was not built to remain under wraps" (275), his February 5

that, in his mind, France did not yet enjoy a true republican government: "The goal of constitutional government is to safeguard the Republic; that of revolutionary government is to found it."[4] Apparently, neither the early decrees of September 1792, nor the Constitution of 1793 had sufficed to "found" the French Republic. But what would? Peaceful conditions were not enough: the current wartime situation hardly figured in the Committee's political pronouncements. Saint-Just even unhinged the definition of revolutionary government from war in an April 1794 report: "Revolutionary government does not signify war or conquest."[5] The conditions under which France could exchange its revolutionary government for a constitutional republic were murky at best. At worst, the "twelve who ruled" (or at least some of them) were simply exploiting this indeterminacy to prolong their hold on power for as long as possible.

The ultimate signification of "the Terror," or more specifically of Jacobin political practices and institutions, hangs in the balance of these two alternatives. If the architects of the future French Republic were genuinely seeking to bring about a just form of government, their political actions, while remaining in many respects morally reprehensible, acquire a different meaning than if they merely constituted ploys for staying in office. As noted in the previous chapter, these two objectives need not be mutually exclusive: Even if we do find evidence that the leaders of the revolutionary government had strong intentions of holding elections and relinquishing power, they clearly used political stratagems for eliminating rivals as well. Their abuses of power

---

report on the ultimate goals of the Revolution had even less to say about when or how this ship would set sail (see below). On the revolutionary government, see notably Marc Bouloiseau, *The Jacobin Republic, 1792–94*, trans. Jonathan Mandelbaum (Cambridge and Paris: Cambridge University Press/Maison des sciences de l'homme, 1983); Furet's article on the topic in *A Critical Dictionary of the French Revolution*, ed. François Furet and Mona Ozouf, trans. Arthur Goldhammer (Cambridge: Belknap Press of Harvard University Press, 1989) (hereafter cited as *CDFR*); and also Carla Hesse, "The Law of the Terror," *MLN* 114, no. 4 (1999): 702–18.

4. "Rapport sur les principes du gouvernement révolutionnaire," *Rob.*, 10:274. Robespierre's February "Rapport sur les principes de morale politique . . ." repeatedly stressed the need "to found, to consolidate the Republic" (*Rob.*, 10:354 and 353). See also Saint-Just's February 26 "Rapport sur les personnes incarcérées," on the "establishment of the Republic" (in which a constitution does not figure), as well as his "Rapport sur les factions de l'étranger," delivered ten days later, which calls on the people to "return to nature, to morality, in order to found the Republic"; *Œuvres complètes*, ed. Michèle Duval (Paris: Lebovici, 1984), 703 and 730 (hereafter cited as *SJ*).

5. "Rapport sur la police générale . . ." 26 germinal an II (April 15, 1794), *SJ*, 809; compare with his October 10 report, discussed in chapter 4. Robespierre, in fact, introduced his report on the Festival of the Supreme Being by acknowledging the recent military successes: "The moment when the sound of our victories resonates throughout the universe is the moment when the legislators of the Republic must be vigilant . . . and affirm the principles on which the stability and happiness of the Republic must rest," *Rob.*, 10:443; on this festival, see below.

THE DESPOTISM OF NATURE   •   217

are not in question: It is the positive uses to which they may have put it that are.[6] The point of this evaluation is not to determine, in the old Marxist fashion, whether the revolutionary government was "necessary" or even "good," but rather to comprehend on its own terms what, if anything, it sought to achieve.

This inquiry comes with its share of historiographical limitations and difficulties. It will not produce, to be sure, an exhaustive analysis of "the Terror" as it was experienced and practiced throughout France. Much of what the Convention, and especially the Committee of Public Safety, debated and decreed was simply ignored or selectively interpreted by local administrators and *représentants en mission* alike.[7] Studying the intentions of revolutionary leaders must also inevitably adopt a somewhat counterfactual quality, as the 9 of Thermidor interrupted whatever political processes *conventionnels* were planning, be they republican or not. The principal source of information about this republic-to-come, moreover, is the series of reports presented by the spokesmen of the Committee of Public Safety to the Convention.[8] But this corpus of texts is highly problematic: Its authors are equally concerned with justifying the actions of the Committee as they are with announcing its future course. There are fortunately a few ways of evaluating their claims, one of which is to compare them with the actual institutions that they produced; another is to seek out patterns of coherence among them, as if they formed a single text.

Even this attempt to read through the propagandist tone and material of the reports is complicated by the fact that there was not always a convergence of views among the principal political actors of this period. Saint-Just was allegedly furious at Billaud-Varenne for having formalized the structure of the revolutionary government; Carnot, among others, was markedly tepid

---

6. Most of the recent studies of the Terror discussed in the previous two chapters either explicitly or implicitly conclude that from roughly 1794 onward, the leading figures of the Committee of Public Safety no longer had a clear or coherent political project; see in particular Patrice Gueniffey, *La politique de la Terreur: essai sur la violence révolutionnaire, 1789–94* (Paris: Fayard, 2000); and John Hardman, *Robespierre* (Harlow: Pearson Education, 1999) (for an exception to this trend, see Sophie Wahnich, *La liberté ou la mort: essai sur la Terreur et le terrorisme* [Paris: La Fabrique, 2003]).

7. For this other side of the story, see notably David Andress, *The Terror: Civil War in the French Revolution* (London: Little, Brown, 2005); and Jean-Clément Martin, *Violence et révolution: essai sur la naissance d'un mythe national* (Paris: Seuil, 2006); see also Colin Lucas's classic, *The Structure of the Terror: The Example of Javogues and the Loire* (Oxford: Oxford University Press, 1973).

8. I have also consulted the relevant volumes of Aulard's *Recueil des actes du Comité de salut public*, but few of the documents contained there address larger political issues.

toward the cult of the Supreme Being.[9] Notwithstanding these important differences and personal animosities, however, there was also a surprising consensus, and for a while a tenuous alliance, among the leading members of the Committee of Public Safety responsible for political issues (essentially Robespierre, Saint-Just, and Billaud-Varenne, and to a lesser extent, Couthon and Barère).[10] All insisted on the urgent need for public instruction, "not only in schools, or exclusively for children," but for "all citizens";[11] they sought to achieve this goal through the creation of republican "institutions";[12] they accepted a certain number of economic controls, established the basis of a welfare state, and "recentralized French administration," but did not seriously challenge the right of private property;[13] they agreed that the state, like a revolutionary Goldilocks, had to exhibit a level of judicial severity that was "just right," halfway between the demands of the *modérés* and the *ultra-révolutionnaires*; they consistently expressed their

---

9. According to various sources, Saint-Just, who was away at the front when the bill was proposed (first on 28 brumaire an II [November 18], then again on 14 frimaire [December 4, 1793]), subsequently told Billaud-Varenne, "As soon as it is written down, government ceases to be revolutionary"; see Jean-Pierre Gross, *Saint-Just, sa politique, ses missions* (Paris: Bibliothèque nationale, 1976), 60. For Carnot, see Alphonse Aulard, *Le culte de la raison et le culte de l'Être suprême* (Paris: Alcan, 1904), 287–92. Françoise Brunel has questioned whether the new cult actually caused as much friction as is generally assumed: "L'Être Suprême et les divisions de la Montagne avant Thermidor," in *L'Être Suprême*, ed. Michel Vovelle (Arras: Centre culturel Noroit, 1991), 21–26.

10. See especially R. R. Palmer, *Twelve Who Ruled: The Year of the Terror in the French Revolution* (1941; Princeton: Princeton University Press, 1989).

11. Billaud-Varenne, "Rapport sur la théorie du gouvernement démocratique," 1 floréal an II (April 20, 1794), in *Histoire parlementaire de la Révolution française, ou Journal des assemblées nationales depuis 1789 jusqu'en 1815*, ed. P. J. B. Buchez and P. C. Roux (Paris: Paulin, 1834–38), 32:349; see also, for instance, article 12 of Robespierre's 1793 draft for a *Déclaration des droits*: "Society must encourage by every means possible the progress of public reason, and place instruction within reach of all citizens," *Rob.*, 9:466. This insistence on generalized public instruction is also visible in the manifold projects of the Comité d'instruction publique in the Convention; see R. R. Palmer, *The Improvement of Humanity: Education and the French Revolution* (Princeton: Princeton University Press, 1985); and Mona Ozouf, *L'école de la France: essais sur la révolution, l'utopie, et l'enseignement* (Paris: Gallimard, 1984).

12. See chapter 4 and below.

13. Jeff Horn, *The Path Not Taken: French Industrialization in the Age of Revolution, 1750–1830* (Cambridge: MIT Press, 2006), 127, and chap. 5; see also Jean-Pierre Gross, *Fair Shares for All: Jacobin Egalitarianism in Practice* (Cambridge: Cambridge University Press, 2003). As Thomas Kaiser has observed, private property also underpinned the very economic foundation of the revolutionary economy, the *assignats*; see "Property, Sovereignty, and the Declaration of the Rights of Man, and the Tradition of French Jurisprudence," in *The French Idea of Freedom: The Old Regime and the Declaration of Rights of 1789*, ed. Dale Van Kley (Stanford: Stanford University Press, 1994), 327.

faith in the natural goodness and virtue of the people;[14] and they did not view the implementation of a constitution as the sine qua non of republican government.

These shared values and beliefs were stitched together with the narrative thread of Roman history; the speeches from Year II read as though they were composed with a copy of Livy or Plutarch open on the table. Even Robespierre's vaunted obsession with virtue was a traditional republican concern, as he made clear in his speech on political morality:

> I am talking about the public virtue that worked such prodigies in Greece and Rome, and that should produce far more astonishing ones in republican France; that virtue that is none other than love of the homeland and its laws.[15]

Identifying the overall goal of Jacobin rule to be the "republic of virtue," in this regard, is not particularly helpful: Republics had been defined in terms of "public virtue" for at least three hundred years, most famously by Montesquieu.[16] The numerous points of convergence between

---

14. The most succinct expression of this widespread faith may be Robespierre's claim that "If man was created good by nature, we must bring him back to nature," "Observations générales sur le projet d'instruction publique . . ." *Rob.*, 5:208.

15. "Rapport sur les principes de morale politique," in *Virtue and Terror*, trans. John Howe (London: Verso, 2007), 111; *Rob.*, 10:355. Montesquieu had said as much: "One must note that what I call *virtue* in a republic is love of the homeland, that is, love of equality. It is not a moral virtue or a Christian virtue; it is *political* virtue, and this is the spring that makes republican government move. . . . Therefore, I have called love of the homeland and of equality, *political* virtue," *Spirit of the Laws*, xli. Much of Robespierre's speech on political morality is similarly dedicated to extolling equality in a republic (see, e.g., "the love of the homeland necessarily includes the love of equality," 353; see also 354).

16. In her study on *Rousseau and the Republic of Virtue: The Language of Politics in the French Revolution* (Ithaca: Cornell University Press, 1986), Carol Blum writes that "Montesquieu's theoretical distinction of 1748, that the principle of monarchy was honor, while that of a 'popular government' was virtue, had edged toward the prescriptive in Rousseau's writings of the 1750s and 1760s and become, in 1794, programmatic" (242–43). But there is nothing per se more "programmatic" about Robespierre's theory of virtue than Montesquieu's "theoretical distinction"; the central difference between their conceptions of the republic pertains not to the role of virtue, but to its source (natural, for Robespierre; constitutional, for Montesquieu). It is also worth remembering that the founders of the American Republic similarly insisted on the necessity of virtue among its citizens; as Madison argued in *The Federalist*, "Republican government presupposes the existence of these [positive human] qualities in a higher degree than any other form. Were the pictures which have been drawn by the political jealousy of some among us faithful likenesses of the human character, the inference would be, that there is not sufficient virtue among men for self-government; and that nothing less than the chains of despotism can restrain them from destroying and devouring one another"; Alexander Hamilton, James Madison, and John Jay, *The Federalist Papers*, ed. Isaac Kramnick (London: Penguin, 1987), no. 55, 339.

the oft-quarreling members of the Committee of Public Safety can be recognized for the most part as republican commonplaces. What set them apart from this tradition was their belief that natural right, rather than a constitution, should serve as the foundation for laws and *mœurs*. Robespierre's February 1794 report on the principles of political morality, billed as the Committee's final word on "the goal of the Revolution, and the point where we wish to arrive," proclaimed its purpose simply to be "to fulfill nature's wishes." This process would usher in "the reign of eternal justice," whose laws are not man-made (that is, constitutional), but inherent in uncorrupted, human nature ("engraved . . . in the hearts of all men").[17] If a constitution did figure at all in the Jacobin plans for the republic-to-come—and Billaud-Varenne's April 1794 report on democratic government makes no mention of one—it was only insofar as it reflected the "natural and essential order" of society (to borrow the Physiocratic phrase).[18]

The natural republicanism of the revolutionary leaders during the Terror, I argue in the present chapter, was not just rhetorical window-dressing or abstract philosophy, but played a direct role in the political and cultural transformations of Year II. While the Convention only fulfilled its mandate to found a republic after Thermidor, the Jacobin leadership does not seem to have been arbitrarily postponing its advent. Already in February 1794, members of the Committee of Public Safety began insisting that terror was no longer the "order of the day" and that a more permanent era of justice had (or should have) replaced it. There is a long tradition in republican thought, moreover, of waiting for the proper *moment* to establish republican government. The key criterion, according to republican theorists, was the moral and civic preparedness of the people; fostering this sort of "public virtue" took *institutions*, which enabled citizens to assimilate republican laws and manners.

The principle institutions of Year II can be viewed in precisely this light. The cult of the Supreme Being, I suggest, promoted the idea of a "meta-

---

17. "Rapport sur les principes de morale politique," *Virtue and Terror*, 109–10; *Rob.*, 10:351 and 352. There is only a single mention of a—and not necessarily *the* 1793—constitution in this speech; the Revolution, Robespierre promises, will bring about the "peaceful reign of constitutional laws." He also states that "democracy is a state in which the sovereign people [are] guided by laws which are its own work," *Virtue and Terror*, 111; *Rob.*, 10:353. Both of these claims, however, are premised on the assumption that a virtuous people can only provide itself with a constitution that expresses the dictates of natural right.

18. For Billaud-Varenne, see his April 20, 1794, "Rapport sur la théorie du gouvernement démocratique"; Saint-Just's important report delivered five days earlier is similarly silent on the subject of constitutions (see below), as is Robespierre's "political testament," delivered on 8 thermidor. On the Physiocrats and Jacobins, see chapter 4.

physical panopticon," in the hope that individuals, sensing themselves to be under the constant surveillance of "the god of Nature" (identified with the sun), would obey the laws of nature dictated to them by their consciences. Should they fail to do so, divine justice would assert itself both in this world and the next, through the intermediary of another institution, the revolutionary tribunal, as reformed by the law of 22 prairial (June 10, 1794). This law, presented as the solution "to end the crises of the revolution" (Couthon), brought the tribunal more in line with the military commissions set up (on March 19, 1793) to punish the *hors-la-loi*. The justifications for, and legal thinking behind, the law can in fact be directly traced back even further to arguments put forward during the king's trial. It is thus problematic to present this revamped "institution" (as it is repeatedly called by Couthon) as a sign that the Terror had begun to spin wildly out of the control since it reflects fundamental tenets of the Jacobins' legal thought and natural-republican philosophy. Taken together, these institutions (along with others) force us to reevaluate the historical accuracy and historiographical usefulness of "the Terror" as a lens through which to observe the political transformations of Year II.

Waiting for the Republic: The Revolutionary Government

The revolutionary government was not born under the purest auspices, as we saw in the previous chapter: It was an ad hoc solution to a political quandary, namely, the Jacobin fear of losing their majority in a future National Assembly. While it also reflected a natural-republican indifference to constitutionality—the jusnaturalist Declaration of Rights, after all, remained in force—the perpetual postponement of elections appears to have been motivated primarily by political concerns. If the revolutionary government was indeed a stalling tactic, it would not amount to much more than a de facto dictatorship. Here as well, however, there may have been a "nobler" reason for delaying the establishment of a democratic republic, a reason that had been loudly emphasized by every major republican theorist. This nobler reason can be summed up in three words: Timing is everything. Never was this truer than in the foundation of a republic.

This lesson was perhaps most vigorously defended in one of the classic sources for republicanism, Livy's *History of Rome*. After recounting the fall of the Tarquin kings, Livy began book 2 of his *History* with a lengthy reflection on the appropriateness of Brutus's timing: "It cannot be doubted that Brutus . . . would have done his country the greatest disservice, had he yielded too soon to his passion for liberty." Prior to the rule of Tarquinius Superbus, the Roman people were not sufficiently mature for self-government: "One has but to think of what the populace was like in those early days—a rabble of vagrants, mostly runaways and refugees—and to ask what would have happened if they had suddenly found themselves . . . enjoying complete freedom of action, if not full political rights." They did not yet enjoy "any real sense of community," defined by Livy as "the only true patriotism," which "comes slowly and springs from the heart: it is founded upon respect for the family and love of the soil." Until the people of Rome had developed this patriotic sense—which subsequent republican theorists would call public virtue—it had been best for them to remain under kings: "Premature 'liberty' . . . would have been a disaster."[19]

This reflection on the need for good timing in the foundation of republics did not go unnoticed by Livy's readers. It constitutes a central motif, for instance, in Machiavelli's political thought: "We are successful when our ways are suited to the times and circumstances, and unsuccessful when they are not."[20] Rousseau similarly insisted throughout the *Social Contract* on the importance of timing, in terms very close to Livy's: "For nations . . . there is a time of youth, or maturity if you prefer, that must be awaited before subjecting them to laws." Echoing Machiavelli's injunction to seize the proper *occasione*, Rousseau called attention to the political value of different moments: "The choice of the moment of the founding is one of the surest ways to distinguish the work of a Legislator from that of a Tyrant."[21] This extreme attentiveness to timing was warranted for Rousseau by the momentous task facing the founder of a republic, who must feel capable of changing no less than human nature itself (2.7). If citizens had not been inculcated with a deep sense of public virtue, no republic could survive.

---

19. *Early History of Rome*, trans. Aubrey de Sélincourt (London: Penguin, 1960), 2.1; 105. This lesson is repeated by Rollin, in a passage paraphrasing Livy; see his *Histoire romaine*, in *Œuvres complètes de Rollin* (Paris: Firmin Didot, 1821–25), 13:334–35.

20. *The Prince*, ed. Quentin Skinner (Cambridge: Cambridge University Press, 1998), chap. 25, 85; see also *The Discourses*, trans. L. J. Walker and B. Richardson (London: Penguin, 2003), 1.16; and of course J. G. A. Pocock, *Machiavellian Moment: Florentine Political Thought and the Atlantic Republican Tradition*, 2nd ed. (Princeton: Princeton University Press, 2003).

21. *Social Contract*, 2.8, in *The Collected Writings of Rousseau*, ed. Christopher Kelly, Roger D. Masters, and Peter G. Stillman (Hanover, NH: University Press of New England, 1995), 4:158 and 161 (hereafter cited as *CWR*); *Œuvres complètes, ed.* Bernard Gagnebin and Marcel Raymond (Paris: Gallimard/Pléiade, 1959–95), 3:208 and 212 (hereafter cited as *JJR*). The dangers and importance of the right "moment" were particularly apparent in eighteenth-century literature; see Thomas Kavanagh, *Esthetics of the Moment: Literature and Art in the French Enlightenment* (Philadelphia: University of Pennsylvania Press, 1996).

These same concerns were repeatedly voiced by the French revolutionaries, even before the advent of the republic. An early editorial in Prudhomme's *Révolutions de Paris* emphasized that "the most important and most difficult task in the regeneration of a state is the reestablishment of morals [*des moeurs*]."[22] The revolutionary obsession with "regeneration" became only more pressing during Year II.[23] In a key April 1794 report, hailing the beginning of what the Committee of Public Safety hoped would be a post-factional period, Billaud-Varenne returned to this well-worn theme, giving it a distinctly republican (and Rousseauist) twist:

The establishment of democracy in a nation that languished for so long in chains can be compared to the efforts of nature in the astonishing transition from nothing to existence; an even greater effort, no doubt, than the passing from life into nothingness. One must, so to speak, recreate the people we wish to free.[24]

Despite its cosmic hyperbole, Billaud's foundational narrative stuck closely to a republican script: A people corrupted by despotism could not be expected to become virtuous democratic citizens overnight. In fact, most republican theorists argued that this transformation was close to impossible, save for certain exceptional circumstances, such as revolutions. According to Rousseau,

there sometimes occur during the lifetime of States violent periods when revolutions have the same certain effect on peoples as do certain crises on individuals; when the horror of the past is equivalent to amnesia, and when the State, set afire by civil wars, is reborn so to speak from its ashes and resumes the vigor of youth by escaping from death's clutches.[25]

22. *Révolutions de Paris*, 17 (Nov. 1–7, 1789), 2.

23. See notably Mona Ozouf, *L'homme régénéré: essais sur la Révolution française* (Paris: Gallimard, 1989), and her article on "Regeneration" in *CDFR*; see also David Bell, *The Cult of the Nation in France: Inventing Nationalism, 1680–1800* (Cambridge: Harvard University Press, 2001).

24. "Rapport sur la théorie du gouvernement démocratique," 1 floréal an II (April 20, 1794), *HP*, 32:338. Saint-Just had officially laid to rest the factional struggles between the Jacobins, the Dantonistes, and the Hébertistes on April 15. On Billaud-Varenne's speech, see notably Françoise Brunel, "Institutions civiles et Terreur," *Révolution Française.net, Synthèses* (May 2006), http://revolution-francaise.net/2006/05/21/43-institutions-civiles-et-terreur.

25. *Social Contract*, 2.8; in *CWR*, 4:158, and *JJR*, 3:385. On the concept of "crisis" in classical republicanism, see Keith Baker, "The Political Languages of the French Revolution," in *The*

If France could achieve this magical sort of rebirth (which had already been dramatized at the Fountain of Regeneration in August 1793; see chapter 4), it would be a truly exceptional event, almost worthy, in a republican perspective, of Billaud-Varenne's mythical rhetoric. So exceptional was this event, however, that an even greater attention to its timing was required, as the appropriate conditions might present themselves only once: "Free peoples," Rousseau had warned, "remember this maxim: Freedom can be acquired, but it can never be recovered." Two weeks before the Festival of the Supreme Being, Robespierre suggested that the right moment may be at hand and should not be missed: "The present moment is favorable; but it may be unique." Two months later, and one day before his fall, he warned that it may be too late: "We shall perish for not seizing a moment marked in the history of humanity for the foundation of liberty."[26]

Simply because they hesitated to provide France with fully democratic institutions does not imply, therefore, that the leading members of the Committee of Public Safety had no intention of ever doing so. The alternative interpretations—that they could not, or that they chose not to—fail to account for both this long republican tradition of wariness about timing, and for its corollary, which is the tremendous prestige attached to the successful founding of a republic. "Of all men that are praised, those are praised most who have played the chief part in founding a religion," Machiavelli observed, and then added, "Next come those who have founded either republics or kingdoms," insisting that "the heavens [cannot] afford men a better opportunity of acquiring renown [than through reforming a corrupt city]; nor can men desire anything better than this."[27] For Voltaire, the "legislator of Pennsylvania," William Penn, "could boast that he brought to Earth the vaunted golden age," no small feat indeed, while Rousseau could think of no greater individual than his own *Législateur*.[28] In his discussion of the American founders, Isaac Kramnick noted how this emulation of great lawgivers and founders of republics was similarly encouraged by Plutarch, Bacon, and Hume.[29] Despots and tyrants, on the contrary, were as deserving

---

Cambridge History of Eighteenth-Century Political Thought, ed. Mark Goldie and Robert Wolker (Cambridge: Cambridge University Press, 2006).

26. For the first quote, see "Sur les crimes des rois coalisés contre la France," 7 prairial an II (May 26, 1794), *Rob.*, 10:476; for the second, "Contre les factions nouvelles et les députés corrompus," 8 thermidor (July 26, 1794), *Rob.*, 10:573.

27. *Discourses*, 1.10; 134 and 138.

28. See, respectively, the *Lettres philosophiques*, IV, 38, and *Social Contract*, 2.7.

29. Isaac Kramnick, editor's introduction to *The Federalist Papers*, by Alexander Hamilton, James Madison, and John Jay (London: Penguin, 1987), 72.

of contempt as great legislators were of praise (to paraphrase Machiavelli). The gaze of history and the cult of the *grands hommes*—to whom, in the words inscribed on the Pantheon, *la patrie [est] reconnaissante*—combined to make the foundation of a republic the highest political ambition.[30] Precisely because the prize was so great, however, there was intense pressure not to fail—particularly as failure, in 1794, would have spelled foreign invasion and personal death. The inherent cautiousness of republican theory thus encouraged a quasi-dictatorial interregnum.[31]

Ultimately, the revolutionary government itself may have played only an incidental role in the evolution of the Terror.[32] If the repression of counterrevolutionaries reached its height, in sheer numerical terms, during the winter of 1793–94, this was due in part only to the better efficiency and organization of the republican forces: The decisive battles in the Vendée and South had already taken place that preceding autumn.[33] The underlying laws and institutions of the Terror similarly predated the creation of the revolutionary government, whereas the later law of 22 prairial, I will argue, constituted a step toward the foundation of a natural republic. The "dictatorial" revolutionary government may ironically have done less harm to civic rights than the republican "despotism of nature" that was meant to follow it.

"Let Justice Be the Order of the Day": Ending "the Terror"

If the Committee of Public Safety truly intended to found a republic, they would have sought, in good republican fashion, to lay its moral foundations in the citizenry. One should thus be able to detect evidence that the revolutionary government was transitioning toward republican rule, even

---

30. On "the lessons imparted to us by history, and the examples of all great men," to quote Saint-Just (*SJ*, 813), see Jean-Claude Bonnet, *Naissance du panthéon: essai sur le culte des grands hommes* (Paris: Fayard, 1998).

31. Almost all republican theorists praised the institution of a dictator; see, for instance, Machiavelli, *Discourses*, 1.34; Montesquieu, *De l'esprit des lois*, 1.2.3 and 2.11.16; Mably, "you saw how useful dictatorship was to the Romans," *Des droits et des devoirs*, 355; and Rousseau, *Social Contract*, 4.6. Although the Jacobins repeatedly rejected the charge of dictatorship, they would occasionally accept it in more abstract terms. Saint-Just describes the revolutionary government, for instance, as "the dictatorship of justice," *SJ*, 705. Michelet has an interesting chapter on Saint-Just and dictatorship in his *Histoire de la Révolution française* (bk. 19, chap. 1).

32. Its central role in reorganizing the military, by contrast, seems undeniable, as Palmer already argued in *Twelve Who Ruled*.

33. For an analysis of these numbers, see Donald Greer, *The Incidence of the Terror during the French Revolution: A Statistical Interpretation* (Cambridge: Harvard University Press, 1935); and Furet, "Terror," in *CDFR*. On the civil wars, see chapter 4.

if there are no indications of when exactly this transition would be fully achieved—the propitious moment, presumably, would have to present itself. And there are indeed a number of signs, to be found both in speeches and institutions, that the Committee sought to end the "provisional" state of political affairs, and even to end the Terror. The only problem was that the justice system with which they sought to replace the mechanisms of the Terror was every bit as terrible. The sword of justice was no blunter than the blade of the guillotine.

Robespierre's February 1794 report on political morality had already suggested that "terror" in some form or another was an intrinsic part of every democracy, and not just a temporary means. In his infamous phrase, virtue was powerless without terror; he went on to identify terror with justice itself: "Terror is nothing but prompt, severe, inflexible justice."[34] To some extent, there was a republican precedent for this strange definition: It was through "the fear of the gods," after all, that Numa had established justice in Rome.[35] Gods, or at least the Supreme Being, would indeed constitute the keystone of Robespierre's theory of justice, as we shall see. Even if one glosses over the psychological differences between "terror" and "fear," however, Robespierre departed from classical republicanism by associating virtuous conduct, not just with the respect of the laws, but with a much vaguer adherence to principles of "eternal justice," or natural right.

Perhaps in reaction to the campaign by the *indulgents* to scale back the Terror, and to Desmoulins's nagging attacks in *Le Vieux Cordelier*,[36] the spokesmen of the Committee of Public Safety quickly began to distance themselves from the word (and implications of) "terror" altogether, suggesting that the Revolution had moved beyond the fall 1793 state of crisis and entered a new, more permanent phase, an era of "justice."[37] Three weeks after Robespierre insisted on the complementarity between virtue and

---

34. "Rapport sur les principes de morale politique," *Virtue and Terror*, 115; *Rob.*, 10:357. Jaume also notes how for Robespierre, "according to his speeches, Terror is not foreign to democracy," *Discours Jacobin*, 117.

35. Livy, *Early History of Rome*, 1.19; 54; see also Plutarch, *Plutarch's Lives*, trans. John Dryden and ed. Arthur Hugh Clough (New York: Modern Library, 2001), 1:87; and Rollin, *Histoire romaine*, 13:196–97.

36. On *Le Vieux Cordelier*, see notably Caroline Weber, *Terror and Its Discontents: Suspect Words in Revolutionary France* (Minneapolis: University of Minnesota, 2003).

37. See Marie-Hélène Huet, *Mourning Glory: The Will of the French Revolution* (Philadelphia: University of Pennsylvania Press, 1997), 92–93, who also discusses the Saint-Just report quoted below. One exception is Saint-Just's March 13 "Rapport sur les factions de l'étranger," in which he asks: "What is it that you want, you who do not want terror against malefactors?" *SJ*, 730.

terror, Saint-Just presented the Committee's new views on the relation between terror and justice:

> Justice is more fearsome for the enemies of the Republic than terror alone. How many traitors have eluded terror, which merely speaks, and would not elude justice, which weighs each crime in its hand! Justice condemns the enemies of the people and the allies of tyranny among us to an eternal bondage. Terror lets them envisage an end, since every storm comes to an end, as you know. Justice condemns public servants to righteousness; justice brings happiness to the people and consolidates the new order. Terror is a double-edged sword, which some use to avenge the people, and others to serve tyranny; terror has filled the prisons, but the guilty have gone unpunished; terror has passed liked a storm. Only expect the public to adopt an austere character through the force of institutions; an awful calm always follows the storm, and we are much more indulgent after, than before, terror.[38]

The relative novelty of this realignment can be appreciated by comparing this speech to Saint-Just's own October 10 report, where he had claimed that "we must govern with the blade [*par le fer*] those who cannot be governed by justice" (*SJ*, 521). Four months later, however, terror was now criticized for its lack of endurance ("every storm comes to an end") and its irregularities ("how many traitors eluded terror"). Justice, on the other hand, is an ongoing pursuit that will consolidate "the new order" by virtue of its lasting institutions. Justice is thus the permanent answer to the temporary measures of the Terror, but without any hint of moderation or restraint.[39] The decrees issued by the Committee of Public Safety to representatives *en mission* and other administrators similarly bear witness to this shift in tone, around this

---

38. "Rapport sur les personnes incarcérées," 8 ventôse an II (February 26, 1794), *SJ*, 706.
39. On the emphasis on justice versus terror in spring 1794, see Françoise Brunel, *Thermidor* (Brussels: Editions Complexe, 1989), 51; and Julien Boudon, *Les Jacobins: une traduction des principes de Jean-Jacques Rousseau* (Paris: LGDJ, 2006), 285. Martin also underscored how "the absence in archival sources of any mentions of terror to describe decisions taken by the *conventionnels* in September 1793 as in June 1794 cannot be considered an innocent curiosity . . . the members of the Convention are almost unanimous in refusing 'terror' which they associate with Old Regime practices," "Response Essay," in *H-France Forum*, 2, no. 2 (2007), on *Violence et révolution*, at http://h-france.net/forum/forumvol2/Martin1Response.html. I am not sure that Martin's comment holds for September 1793, but certainly from late February 1794 onward, "terror" is no longer a fashionable term.

precise same period: After February 16, the word "terror" essentially drops out of the Committee's correspondence.[40]

Following the crisis of the factions, the Committee seemed even more eager to put the vocabulary of terror behind it. In his April 15 report, Saint-Just sought to place the burden of the Terror on the shoulders of both the Hébertistes and the *indulgents*: "Consider civil life during the factions. Friendship was no longer known; terror reversed itself against the national representatives and the homeland."[41] Danton's famous slogan, "Let us be terrible instead of the people," is invoked as proof of his aristocratic and terrorist motives.[42] As before, "justice" is summoned to replace "terror," but again, only the names have changed: "Let justice gush out like a river wherever accomplices remain."[43] This injunction, in fact, picks up on a new mantra that Saint-Just had already proposed in his March 13 report on the factions and that brilliantly revised the notorious September declaration: "Let justice and righteousness be the order of the day in the French Republic!"[44] This formula became the new *mot d'ordre* of the postfactional period: Billaud-Varenne used it twice in the report he delivered on April 20 ("you have made justice the order of the day"). As Saint-Just before him, Billaud hammered this theme home, in a series of seven paragraphs that began anaphorically, "*La justice . . .*"[45]

This semantic switch from terror to justice might seem purely "rhetorical," yet it pays to remember that the official "reign of Terror" was itself established by a speech act. Where the September 5 declaration, however, managed to be "felicitious" (in Austin's terminology) without receiv-

---

40. A February 16, 1794, decree, signed by Billaud-Varenne, Barère, and Collot d'Herbois, still argues that "we owe to other peoples an example [of virtuous conduct], and to counter-revolutionaries, terror," whereas two subsequent, unsigned directives (*circulaires*) to popular societies (on February 18) and district administrators (March 11) express similar sentiments, but do not employ that term; see Aulard, *Recueil des actes du Comité de salut public . . .* (Paris: Imprimerie nationale, 1889–1951), 11:183, 252–54 and 642–43, respectively. Perhaps it is no more than a coincidence, but it may be worth noting that Billaud-Varenne left on a mission to Saint-Malo on February 17 (only returning on March 11). I could not find any uses of the word "terror" in this corpus between these dates and 9 thermidor.

41. "Rapport sur la police générale, sur la justice, le commerce, la législation et les crimes des factions," 26 germinal an II (April 15, 1794), presented in the names of both the Committees of Public Safety and General Security; *SJ*, 806–22, 813 for quote. The "Dantonistes" had been dispatched to the guillotine ten days earlier.

42. See *SJ*, 811.

43. *SJ*, 817; see also 818.

44. "Rapport sur les factions de l'étranger," 23 ventôse an II (March 13, 1794), *SJ*, 736.

45. "Rapport sur la théorie du gouvernement démocratique," 1 floréal an II (April 20, 1794), *HP*, 32:338 and 348; for the paragraphs on justice, 340–41.

ing official sanction, as Jean-Clément Martin has recently shown, Saint-Just's March 13 response, though technically approved by the Convention, did not register as a fundamental change:[46] It passed unnoticed not only by historians, but even by the Thermidorians themselves, who moved swiftly to make justice "the order of the day."[47] Still, there was nothing trivial about replacing this original speech act with another since, in all fairness, it could be construed as carrying as much weight (if not more) as its predecessor. Most important, this substitution also suggests that the very question of "ending the Terror," for the Committee of Public Safety, had become moot: For all theoretical purposes, it already had.

To have ended "the Terror" did not imply that the revolutionary government had run its course, but that the Committee was in the process of transitioning the state toward a more stable republic. This intention can be seen in its genuine efforts to replace the hodge-podge of laws and ad hoc institutions that characterized "the Terror" with a more systematic and permanent structure of republican institutions.[48] As Carla Hesse has noted, Billaud-Varenne, beginning in December 1793, spearheaded an attempt to codify the labyrinth of revolutionary legislation; his endeavor was later incorporated into a vaster legislative project, entrusted to Cambacérès, Merlin de Douai, and Couthon, but disrupted by 9 thermidor.[49] Before then, however, the Committee had succeeded in reforming the central judicial institution of the Revolution, the revolutionary tribunal, with the law of 22 prairial, whose introductory report by Couthon tellingly does not mention the word "terror" once. As I argue below, it makes less sense to view this law as the final push of the Terror (or its extension ad infinitum) than as the culmination of a Jacobin theory of justice that predates the revolutionary government. It was also in the spring of 1794 that the Committee pushed through a series of economic measures, most notably Saint-Just's 8 and 13 ventôse decrees, as well as Barère's 22

---

46. See Martin, "La terreur a été et n'a jamais été à l'ordre du jour," *Violence et révolution*, 186; for J. L. Austin, see *How to Do Things with Words* (Cambridge: Harvard University Press, 1975). On studies of performativity in recent revolutionary scholarship, see Keith Baker, "Après la 'culture politique'? De nouveaux courants dans l'approche linguistique," *Dix-huitième siècle* 37 (2005): 243–54.

47. This episode is discussed, without reference to Saint-Just's and Billaud-Varenne's earlier declarations, in Bronislaw Baczko, *Comment sortir de la Terreur: Thermidor et Révolution* (Paris: Gallimard, 1989), 92–93.

48. Most banally, this effort is evident in the continuous emphasis on the need for better institutions. See, for instance, in Billaud-Varenne's April 20 report (among countless other examples): "We need not only to cultivate the mind, but to purify the heart, to propagate republican sentiments. This form of instruction is disseminated by institutions. . . ." (*HP*, 32:348–49).

49. Hesse, "The Law of the Terror," 712.

floréal decree, which were presented as pillars of a future republic: "Our goal is to *establish* a government, in such a manner that brings happiness to the people," Saint-Just announced.[50] Finally, and perhaps most important, the Committee endorsed Robespierre's cult of the Supreme Being, in his eyes the most essential institution of all ("it alone [is] a revolution," he later rhapsodized),[51] and the keystone of his theory of justice.

The Committee's repeated claims that justice, not terror, was now the order of the day were thus matched, at least in part, by their legislative and institutional efforts, many of which were indeed focused on reforming the justice system. Even the redistribution of land was as much a measure against counterrevolutionaries as it was for *les malheureux*, as Saint-Just made clear: "The Revolution has led us to recognize this principle, namely, that whosoever has shown himself to be an enemy of his country cannot own any land."[52] Equality was one of the principal meanings of justice, Robespierre reminded the Convention: "If justice does not reign with absolute authority in the Republic, and if that word does not signify love of equality and the homeland, then liberty is but a vain word!"[53] As it was primarily through institutions such as the Festival of the Supreme Being, among the flurry of others decreed on 18 floréal (May 7, 1794), that the Committee urged the Convention to exchange terror for justice, their commitment to founding a republic may be judged favorably. For most Jacobins, after all, the republic was the sum of its institutions; the day before his downfall, Robespierre was still promising more: "The guarantee of patriotism" was not to be found in a constitution, he claimed, but in "certain political and moral institutions . . . which will be presented to you once the most pressing conspiracies allow the friends of liberty to breathe freely."[54] It is only by taking a closer look at some of these institutions that we may glimpse what the republic-to-come might have resembled.

---

50. For Saint-Just, see his "Rapport sur les personnes incarcérées" (from which the quote is taken; *SJ*, 703, emphasis added), and "Rapport sur le mode d'exécution du décret contre les ennemis de la révolution"; for Barère, see his *Rapport sur les moyens d'extirper la mendicité dans les campagnes, et sur les secours que doit accorder la République aux citoyens indigens* (Paris: Imprimerie Nationale, an II [1794]). On these measures, see notably P. M. Jones "The 'Agrarian Law:' Schemes for Land Redistribution during the French Revolution," *Past and Present* 133 (1991): 96–133; Gross, *Fair Shares for All*; and Brunel, "Institutions civiles et terreur."

51. "Contre les factions nouvelles et les députés corrompus," 8 thermidor, *Rob.*, 10:561.

52. "Rapport sur les personnes incarcérées," *SJ*, 705; see also his "Rapport sur les factions de l'étranger," which similarly associates the two: "If you give land to the poor; if you take it from the villains," *SJ*, 731.

53. "Contre les factions nouvelles et les députés corrompus," 8 thermidor an II (July 26, 1794); *Virtue and Terror*, 139; *Rob.*, 10:575.

54. "Contre les factions nouvelles," *Rob.*, 10:569.

One Republic under the Supreme Being:
The Metaphysical Panopticon

If both laws and institutions, in classical republicanism, shouldered the burden of preserving virtue, it was ultimately thanks to the efforts of a third entity, known in French as *les mœurs*. As the *Révolutions de Paris* article quoted above went on to state, morals "can supplement laws; but laws can never supplement them; a people without morals avoid the laws, if they do not destroy them."[55] From a natural-republican perspective, *mœurs* had an even greater responsibility, as positive laws were drastically marginalized: "The Republic can only depend on nature and on morals," Saint-Just proclaimed in February 1794.[56] Nature fit into this equation as the "physiological" source of human virtue (in the Rousseauist sense of a natural "principle," such as pity), but also as the author of natural laws, which for the Jacobins were meant to replace civil legislation. The relation between *mœurs* and nature was thus symbiotic: Natural human goodness was sustained by a code of conduct, *mœurs*, that itself was determined by the laws of nature. The key role of institutions, therefore, was to ensure that individuals stayed attuned to the dictates of natural right, so that their *mœurs* remained pure and capable of preserving virtue.

This entire operation, however, occurred in an invisible sphere: the human heart and mind. Where civil laws could be instilled through pedagogical exercises, civic instruction, or simply public display, natural laws were "engraved on the heart," and must accordingly be discovered through intuition or emotional intelligence: "Honor the spirit, but trust the heart," Saint-Just recommended.[57] To achieve this goal, he continued, institutions had to penetrate into the hearts and heads of citizens:

> We must focus on creating a public conscience: that is the best police. It is in the people's heads that the public spirit is to be found. . . . Create, therefore, a public conscience, since all hearts equally share the

---

55. *Révolutions de Paris*, XVII, 2. The same idea had been advocated by an American revolutionary, Benjamin Franklin, who chose as the motto of the University of Pennsylvania, *leges sine moribus vanae* ("laws without morals are useless," from Horace's third *Ode*).

56. "Rapport sur les personnes incarcérées," 8 ventôse an II (February 26, 1794); *SJ*, 699–700.

57. I do not mean to deny the central importance the Jacobins placed on public instruction or even "revolutionary catechisms," which relied on rote learning methods. However, their understanding of *justice*—the focus, as we will see, of the cult of the Supreme Being—rested on a more "sentimental" basis for virtue.

sentiment of evil and good, and this conscience draws on the people's inclination toward the general good.[58]

This natural "sentiment of evil and good" was at the core of the Jacobin theory of justice.[59] To ensure that it was properly heard and obeyed, some form of "mind police" was needed; Robespierre found it in the cult of the Supreme Being. The inordinate importance that he and his allies attributed to this cult came from its unique ability to solve the mystery of the golden age: How can natural virtue be preserved in the absence of laws?

Omnia Videt: The Cult of the Supreme Being

The cult of the Supreme Being has been interpreted in a variety of ways, not all of which are mutually exclusive. It was evidently a reaction against the Hébertist cult of Reason, with its seductive female personifications; it was also aimed against the (seemingly small number of) actual atheists among the de-Christianizers, on the grounds, according to Robespierre, that the people need a religion.[60] In this regard, it makes little sense to read the cult in more mystic terms, as the dawn of a "theocratic" era,[61] even if it may have marked an attempt to reconcile disheartened Catholics with revolutionary goals: The first Festival of the Supreme Being was held, after all, on Pentecost. But I would argue that its fundamental purpose was clearly laid out by Robespierre himself, in the 18 floréal (May 7, 1794) report announcing this cult: "The idea of the Supreme Being and the immortality of the soul

---

58. "Rapport sur la police générale, sur la justice . . ." in *SJ*, 811. See also his March 13 report: "Place justice in every heart and justice in every mind in order to safeguard the government," *SJ*, 732.

59. William Reddy, *The Navigation of Feeling: A Framework for the History of Emotions* (Cambridge: Cambridge University Press, 2001), 180.

60. See especially Aulard, *Culte de la raison*; Michel Vovelle, *Révolution et religion: la déchristianisation de l'an II* (Paris: Hachette, 1976); Mona Ozouf, *Festivals and the French Revolution*, trans. Alan Sheridan (Cambridge: Harvard University Press, 1988); Vovelle, ed., *Être Suprême*; and Huet, *Mourning Glory*.

61. See notably Henri Guillemin, *Robespierre: politique et mystique* (Paris: Seuil, 1987); Anne Simonin has applied the adjective "theocratic" to the March–July 1794 period; see *Le déshonneur dans la république: une histoire de l'indignité, 1791–1958* (Paris: Grasset, 2008), 325–27. See also Jean Duprun, "Robespierre, pontife de l'Etre Suprême: note sur les aspects sacrificiels d'une fête (1794)," in *Les fêtes de la Révolution*, ed. Jean Ehrard and Paul Viallaneix (Paris: Société des études robespierristes, 1977), 485–502. These interpretations, in my view, underplay the bluntly pragmatic tenor of Robespierre's 18 floréal report, well illustrated by his repeated quotation of Voltaire's *mot*, "If God did not exist, we would have to invent him," and his claim that "in the eyes of the legislator, truth consists of everything that is useful in the world and good in practice," *Rob.*, 10:452.

incessantly recall men to justice [*un rappel continuel à la justice*]."[62] In this regard, it partook in the general spirit of all republicans institutions, whose goal was always to direct "the passions of men . . . toward justice."[63]

Robespierre's report, however, did not provide many practical indications about how the new cult would redirect human passions; much of the speech is dedicated to other festivals and topics, such as the intellectual relationship between the Enlightenment and the Revolution. A long, famous passage eulogizing Rousseau suggests that the cult of the Supreme Being may in large part have institutionalized the Savoyard Vicar's faith;[64] but even if this were the case, it is not clear why Robespierre perceived the belief in otherworldly divine justice as the silver bullet that could stop the counterrevolution in its tracks. The urgency and great import attached to this institution beg an explanation.[65]

From a classical-republican perspective, this insistence on the need for religion is not unusual:[66] The example of Numa, so dear to Livy, Plutarch, Machiavelli, Rousseau, and many others, comes to mind both for his pragmatic (not to say manipulative) approach, as well as for the efficiency of his moral transformation of Rome. But neither Livy nor his commentators provided much insight into how exactly Numa was able to "impress on the souls" (*descendere ad animos*) of the Romans the fear of the gods (*deorum metum*).[67] A more detailed psychological explanation may be found in an equally famous passage from Cicero, who, as Robespierre noted in his speech, "invoked both the sword of the laws and the lightening of the gods against traitors":

> Therefore let the citizens be persuaded of this at the outset, that the gods are lords and managers of all things . . . that they observe

---

62. "Sur les rapports des idées religieuses et morales avec les principes républicaines, et sur les fêtes nationales," *Rob.*, 10:452.

63. *Rob.*, 10:446; Robespierre had indeed demanded that "all [festivals] be celebrated under the auspices of the Supreme Being, to whom they should all be dedicated," *Rob.*, 10:459.

64. As Aulard, among others, recognized at the beginning of *Culte de la raison*, 1.

65. Saint-Just describes the cult as an "institution" in his "Fragments des *Institutions républicaines*" (see the section entitled "Institutions morales," *SJ*, 984–85), and Robespierre similarly concludes his speech on the Festival of the Supreme Being by describing it as a critical "institution" (*Rob.*, 10:458–59).

66. It was not unusual in natural right theory, either: Pufendorf observes how "those who do not fear God have nothing worse to fear than death, and anyone who had the courage to despise death could make any attempt he pleased against the government," *On the Duty of Man and Citizen According to Natural Law*, trans. Michael Silverthorne, ed. James Tully (Cambridge: Cambridge University Press, 1991), 42–43.

67. See Livy, *Early History*, 54. Machiavelli addresses Roman religion in the *Discorsi*, only to remark on how "great a fear of God . . . there was in this republic," *Discourses*, 1.11; 139.

234 • CHAPTER FIVE

what sort of person each man is, what he does, what he permits himself . . . and that they keep account of the good and the wicked. Minds that are steeped in these beliefs will not be averse to useful and true opinions [*sententia*]. . . . Who could deny that such opinions [*opiniones*] are useful when he understands how many things are secured by oaths, how conducive to safety are the religious guarantees of treaties, how many people have been kept from crime by the fear of punishment?[68]

This fundamental need to create a profound "sense" (*sententia* meaning both opinions or feelings) in citizens about the omnipotence of the gods finds an echo in one of Robespierre's few comments about how the cult of the Supreme Being would concretely benefit justice: The greatest republican achievement, he declared, would be the creation of a moral reflex, "a rapid instinct which, without the slow assistance of reason, would lead [man] to do good and avoid evil." As with Rousseau's pre-rational principle of compassion, this instinct would be rooted in *sensibilité*, not reason, yet it was not entirely natural: A "religious sentiment" was required to instill "in men's souls the idea of a sanction given to moral precepts."[69] The cult of the Supreme Being was thus a republican institution that fortified natural virtue from *within*: It existed entirely "in the people's heads" (Saint-Just's expression) of citizens. The Supreme Being was the mind police inside the mind.

But how could this internalization take place? According to Cicero, the gods are feared because "they *observe* what sort of person each man is." This "observation," of course, really applies only to our *impression* of the gods. It is because our minds are "steeped in these beliefs," chiefly the belief that we are being observed, that we choose to act justly. The fear of divine punishment thus depends on our internalizing the gaze of the gods. Establishing justice in the republic, for Cicero, as well as, I hope to show, for Robespierre, was tantamount to instituting a judicial, if metaphysical, panopticon.

Since Robespierre himself was strategically taciturn on the practical functioning of this cult, we must turn elsewhere for clues. Before attempting to reconstruct its mechanics, let us recall that the concept of a "panopticon,"

---

68. *On the Laws*, 2.15–16, in *On the Commonwealth and On the Laws*, trans. James E. G. Zetzel (Cambridge: Cambridge University Press, 1999), 135. The "*opiniones*" refer to the more rational argument that the universe must be endowed with reason. Robespierre's quote can be found at *Rob.*, 10:453.

69. *Rob.*, 10:452–53.

well known to scholars since Foucault, was not foreign to the revolutionaries either. In 1791, the deputy Jean-Philippe Garran-Coulon (later a member of the Convention as well) presented Bentham's treatise on the panopticon prison to the Legislative Assembly, which decreed its publication.[70] In accordance with the etymology of Bentham's neologism, this text stresses the importance of "the all-seeing eye [*l'œil qui voit tout*]": "In the panopticon the eye is everywhere . . . it can see everyone." The concept of an internalized gaze is also developed: "Were he absent," Bentham notes in reference to the guard, "the impression of his presence is as efficient as his actual presence."[71]

This capacity to "see everyone" was precisely what Robespierre's allies emphasized in their celebrations, defenses, and representations of the cult of the Supreme Being. Claude-François de Payan, a Robespierrist who became *procureur* of the Commune de Paris after Chaumette's fall, addressed the Convention on 25 floréal (May 14, 1794) and spoke of how every good citizen would henceforth feel "incessantly surrounded by a beneficent God, who reads in his heart, sees all his actions, and can wisely distinguish him from the corrupt man," whereas the latter would feel "incessantly surrounded by a powerful and terrifying witness, who sees him, who watches over him, and from whom he cannot escape."[72] This description (particularly the first part) essentially paraphrases the Ciceronian passage quoted above: The gods "observe what sort of person each man is, what he does . . . they keep account of the good and the wicked." But it also underscores how the cult of the Supreme Being was closely tied up with the cult of *sensibilité*: To "read in someone's heart" was the prerogative of both God and the *âme sensible*.[73] This ideal form of communication is essentially what has been

---

70. At the Convention, Garran-Coulon, who voted with the Girondins for the king's sentencing, nonetheless expressed more Montagnard views on the Constitution: "I am astonished that in an assembly composed of righteous, enlightened men, it is possible to doubt that man brings his natural rights with him into society . . . only these [rights] can be proclaimed in a Declaration of the Rights of Man. . . . Is it possible to imagine a society in which these rights could be taken from him and replaced by social rights?" April 17, 1793; *AP*, 62:279.

71. *Panoptique, Mémoire sur un nouveau principe pour construire des maisons d'inspection, et nommément des maisons de forces* (Paris: Imprimerie Nationale, 1791), 35, 8–9. For Foucault, see *Discipline and Punish: The Birth of the Prison*, trans. Alan Sheridan (New York: Vintage, 1995).

72. Qtd. in Aulard, *Culte de l'être suprême*, 285–86; Aulard notes that in his opinion this speech constitutes "the most instructive commentary on the 18 floréal decree," 282.

73. For a few late-eighteenth century literary examples, see Choderlos de Laclos's *Liaisons dangereuses* (Paris: Gallimard, 2003), where Mme de Volanges writes to the Présidente de Tourvel that, "only God can give you absolution when you repent; he reads in our hearts" (letter 32; 84); see also Marmontel's *Bélisaire*, whose eponymous hero claims "I am certain that the Emperor, who is but a man, would never have hurt me, could he have read in my heart like

studied, ever since Jean Starobinski's magisterial thesis on Rousseau, under the heading of "transparency."[74] During the Revolution, it became a judicial, as well as a political problem: Robespierre lamented how "we cannot read in their hearts; we can distinguish between the honest and the conspiring."[75] The cult of the Supreme Being was to be the ultimate religion of *sensibilité*.

The panoptic fantasy invested in this conception of the Supreme Being was particularly evident in the iconography surrounding the cult, which in turn drew on preexisting revolutionary representations of divinity. One of the commonest images of God since the onset of the Revolution was indeed an *eye* surrounded by a triangle.[76] This symbol, of course, was not itself a revolutionary creation: Christian iconography often represented God (or the Trinity) in this form.[77] The theological basis for the eye-synecdoche was straightforward and anticipated Bentham's prison: God sees everything (*deus omnia videt*).[78] As E. H. Gombrich noted, the revolutionaries maintained the Trinitarian symbolism of the divine eye, recasting the triangle as a Masonic leveler.[79] The "panoptic" force of this symbol was reinforced by the use of a disembodied eye as the emblem of various revolutionary groups, most notably the Cordeliers, the committees of surveillance, and even the Committee of Public Safety.[80] By the time of the Festival of the Supreme Being, however, the heavenly eye predominated as the sign of

---

[God]" (178); and Jean-Pierre Claris de Florian's *Numa Pompilius* (Paris: Didot Aîné, 1786), where Léo tells Camille, in a classic moment of *sensibilité*, "You may speak before this friend [Numa]: he knows all our secrets, he can read in my heart as well as I . . ." (285); text available on ARTFL.

74. For Starobinski, see *Jean-Jacques Rousseau: la transparence et l'obstacle* (1957; Paris: Gallimard, 1971). On transparency in revolutionary historiography, see especially Lynn Hunt, *Politics, Culture, and Class in the French Revolution* (Berkeley: University of California Press, 1984), 44–49.

75. Intervention at the Jacobin club, August 14, 1793; *Rob.*, 10:72.

76. See, for instance, the famous representation of the 1789 *Déclaration des droits de l'homme et du citoyen* (fig. 5), in which a divine eye, encased in a triangle, shines above the new tables of the law.

77. This symbol can be seen, for instance, on the façade of the Aachen Cathedral, or in Iacopo Pontormo's *Cena in Emmaus* (1525), in the Uffizi Galleries.

78. See, for instance, Aquinas, *Summa theologia*, ed. Thomas Gornall (Cambridge: Cambridge University Press, 2006), vol. 4 of 61, 1a. 14, 8; 28. In *De l'esprit des religions* (Paris: Cercle Social, 1792), Nicolas de Bonneville suggested that the original etymology for God was "he who sees" (19).

79. E. H. Gombrich, "The Dream of Reason: Symbolism in the French Revolution," *British Journal for Eighteenth-Century Studies* 2, no. 3 (1979): 202.

80. See also Susan Maslan, *Revolutionary Acts: Theater, Democracy, and the French Revolution* (Baltimore: Johns Hopkins University Press, 2005).

Figure 4 *Fête célébrée en l'honneur de l'Etre Suprême* (1794). Courtesy of the Bibliothèque Nationale de France.

l'Être Suprême, as various engravings from that period indicate (see figs. 4 and 7).

Nothing Like the Sun

If the logic underpinning the cult of the Supreme Being merely repeated the traditional Christian notion of an all-seeing, providential God, it remains difficult to understand why Robespierre wagered so much political credit on this institution. Catholic countries, such as Old Regime France, were not exactly havens of virtue before the Revolution; why would the cult of the Supreme Being bring sudden moral rectitude to the nascent French Republic? The similarities between these cults, however, should not blind

238 • CHAPTER FIVE

us to their differences. And what distinguished the revolutionary version was not negligible. Where the Christian God was an abstract, metaphysical entity, the Supreme Being was *naturalized*, gaining both a "real presence" and a "natural" place in revolutionary sensibility. Brilliantly, in accordance with the esthetics of the sublime, it took as its physical form an object that was itself "beyond representation," one of two that "cannot be looked at directly" (as La Rochefoucauld famously opined)—the sun.[81]

As with the eye, the sun had been associated with divine will in revolutionary prints since 1789. Paintings and illustrations often chose to portray key moments in a festival or ceremony when the dark clouds part and sunlight floods the scene. In David's *Oath of La Fayette at the Festival of the Federation*, for instance, a sudden wind accompanies the timely *éclaircie*, suggesting that the whole of nature—clouds, winds, and storms—is echoing the Revolution under way in Paris.[82] This identification of the course of history with the cycles of nature signaled the Revolution's providential calling.[83] Like the revolutionary calendar, which began on the day when "the equality of the days and nights was marked in the heavens" (that is, on the equinox), these representations naturalized, and thereby authorized, the radical political transformations under way.[84]

But the sun also appeared as the explicit symbol (or attribute) of divinity itself, often in conjunction with the other attributes discussed above. The eye of the Supreme Being in the 1789 illustration of the *Déclaration*

---

81. On the sublime in revolutionary representations, rhetoric, and ideology, see especially Huet, *Mourning Glory*, 36–48 (42 for quote), and Weber, *Terror and Its Discontents*; see also Ronald Paulson, *Representations of Revolution (1789–1820)* (New Haven: Yale University Press, 1983). On solar iconography, see notably Jean Starobinski, "Sur quelques symboles de la Révolution française," *NRF* 188, no. 16 (1968): 41–67. La Rochefoucauld's full maxim reads, "Le soleil ni la mort ne se peuvent regarder fixement."

82. This portrait can be viewed at the Musée Carnavalet in Paris. See also Prieur's drawing, engraved by Berthaut, of the *Travaux du Champ-de-Mars pour la [fête de la] Fédération*, the central half of which depicts a shower of light falling onto the Champs-de-Mars; reproduced in Michel Vovelle, *La Révolution française: images et récits* (Paris: Livre club Diderot/Messidor, 1986), 2:110–11.

83. Starobinski, in his article "Sur quelques symboles de la Révolution française," makes a great deal of the Revolution's "solar mythology" but associates it primarily with the victory of the *siècle des lumières* over the darkness of feudalism. But I have found that most engravings identify the sun with divine, rather than human, "enlightenment"; see, for instance, G.-F. Blondel's *Esquisse* portraying the "*celestial* light that appeared thanks to the decrees of the National Assembly" (reproduced in Vovelle, *Révolution française*, 1:299, emphasis added). The Revolution, in this perspective, is fulfilling a natural prophecy, or in Robespierre's words, "fulfilling the wishes of nature."

84. For the quote, see Gilbert Romme's *Rapport sur l'ère de la République* (Paris: Impr. Nationale, n.d. [1793]), 5. For a similar endeavor, see Jean Delormel, *La grande période ou le retour de l'âge d'or* (Paris: Blanchon, 1790), discussed in chapter 2.

des droits de l'homme et du citoyen, for instance, is clearly identified with the sun (see fig. 5), as it would continue to be up through the Festival of the Supreme Being.[85] Where the eye and triangle figured divinity only in an abstract, culturally coded manner, moreover, the sun was a different kind of sign, a tangible, almost "iconic" (in the Peircean sense) representation of heavenly power. The eye of God had to be imagined; the sun could be observed, albeit indirectly, as befitting a sublime object.

By the time of the Festival of the Supreme Being, a number of engravings, in fact, dropped the leveler-triangle symbol altogether, replacing it with a circle (see figs. 6 and 7). In these instances, the identity between the sun and the Supreme Being was made even clearer; in one engraving (fig. 6), a mother points to a sun unadorned of any other attributes to call her child's attention to the existence of the Supreme Being.

This type of solar imagery was not only present in illustrated engravings of the cult, but also figured centrally in David's orchestration of the festival itself, held on 20 prairial (June 8, 1794). The sun played a truly starring role in this celebration. As David's program informs us, the festivities were to begin precisely at daybreak: "Dawn has just announced the day and already the sound of martial music can be heard from all sides."[86] The first activity of the day was placed under the nurturing gaze of the sun: "Upon seeing this beneficent star that enlivens and colors nature, friends, brothers, spouses, children, seniors, and mothers embrace." The sections gathered in the Tuileries gardens; and at noon, when the sun was at its highest, the members of the Convention filed out of the palace, led by Robespierre. At a critical moment in the celebration, mothers were told to grasp their youngest children and present them to the heavens, "in homage to the author of nature" (6–7). The festival concluded, at the Champ de Mars later in the day, with no less than a pledge of allegiance to the sun: In the words of the Committee

---

85. See also Etienne Jeurat's painting, *Jean-Jacques Rousseau et les symboles de la Révolution*, at the Musée Carnavalet, in which light radiates out of a divine eye; reproduced in Vovelle, *Révolution française*, 3:217.

86. *Ordre, marche et cérémonies de la fête de l'Etre Suprême, qui doit être célébrée le 20 prairial, d'après le plan proposé par David* . . . ([Paris]: Lerouge and Berthelot, n.d. [1794]), 1. David's instructions for the August 10, 1793, Festival of Unity and Indivisibility (discussed in chapter 4) were already structured around solar time: "The French who have gathered to celebrate the Festival of Unity and Indivisibility will rise before dawn; the touching scene of their reunion will be illuminated by the first rays of the sun; this beneficent start whose light extends over the entire universe will appear to them as the symbol of truth; they will sing its praise in hymns," *Ordre et marche de la fête de l'unité et de l'indivisibilité de la République* (Paris: Firmin Gourdin, 1793), 2. For a description of this festival, see notably Blum, *Rousseau and the Republic of Virtue*, 250–55, and Huet, *Mourning Glory*, 36–39.

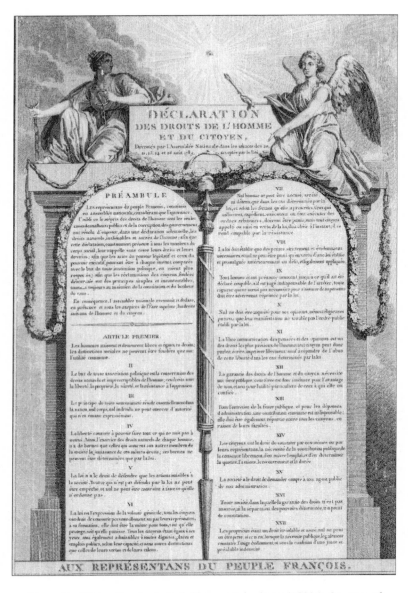

Figure 5 *Déclaration des droits de l'homme et du citoyen* (1789?). Courtesy of the Bibliothèque Nationale de France.

Figure 6 *Le peuple français reconnaît l'Être suprême et l'immortalité de l'âme* (1794). Courtesy of the Bibliothèque Nationale de France.

of Public Safety, "all arms raised, stretched out toward the sky, swear on the sun [*devant le soleil*] to uphold virtue and the Republic."[87]

This strange inscription of a "solar cult" within the cult of the Supreme Being was no doubt lost on most observers and probably disappeared completely in the many provincial enactments of the festival, but it may nonetheless help us understand the role of this institution in directing "the passions of men toward justice."[88] Drawing attention to the sun, for instance, enabled David to distinguish between a revolutionary and a Christian God, as Robespierre had wanted: "The god of nature is not the god of priests!" he had exclaimed in his *floréal* report.[89] The sun was also, following this logic, the

---

87. Qtd. in Aulard, *Culte de la raison*, 328, emphasis added.

88. For this quote, see above. On the provincial festivals, see notably Aulard, *Culte de la raison*, and Michel Vovelle, *La Révolution contre l'Eglise: de la Raison à l'Etre Suprême* (Brussels: Complexe, 1988). At the festival in Bailleul, the Supreme Being was represented by "a sphere . . . that reminded everyone of the miracles of nature"; qtd. in Alain Lottin, "Les manifestations de culte de l'Être Suprême dans le Nord: l'exemple de Bailleul et de Lille," in Vovelle, *Etre Suprême*, 32.

89. *Rob.*, 10:457. Sylvain Maréchal, in attendance that day, concurred: "The God of free men, different from that of priests, smiled through the solar disk on this solemnity," qtd. in Aulard, *Culte de la raison*, 81n2.

Figure 7   *Être suprême, people souverain, République française* (1794). Courtesy of the Bibliothèque Nationale de France.

emblem of nature, a point that suited both the cultural mood and Robespierre's professed deism ("The true priest of the Supreme Being is nature; its temple, the universe . . .").[90] But there may have been a more pragmatic reason for associating, if not identifying, the sun with the Supreme Being. If the goal of this cult was to "incessantly recall men to justice," then the sun was the one natural object that was constantly visible and could thus incarnate the metaphysical panopticon. As farfetched as this idea may sound, it was in fact supported by a collection of antiquarian studies, which suggested that the sun had been worshipped as a God during that enchanting and alluring time that the Jacobins sought to restore: the golden age.

The God of the Golden Age

David had already drawn on antiquarianism to enhance the golden age claims of the Jacobins at the Festival of Unity and Indivisibility, where an Egyptian goddess of nature, Isis, had presided over the first station (see chapter 4). The place of the sun in the Egyptian pantheon had been most

---

90. *Rob.*, 10:457.

emphatically (and most recently) stressed by one of David's colleagues at the National Convention, Charles-François Dupuis. Before the Revolution, Dupuis had been elected to the Royal Academy of Inscriptions and *Belles-lettres*, on the basis of his 1781 *Mémoire sur l'origine des constellations*.[91] This work already presented the thesis for which he would gain fame (with the publication of his magnum opus in 1794, *Origine de tous les cultes, ou Religion universelle*), that all religions were derived from the ancient Egyptian zodiac and that mythological gods, as well as the Christian God, were allegories of the sun.[92] While his thesis, in large part borrowed from book 1 of Macrobius's *Saturnalia*, is often perceived as materialist and reductionist, Dupuis preserved some of the "illuminist" rhetoric about the sun that his predecessor, Court de Gébelin, had already employed: "The Sun [is] the eye of Nature and the source of vision," Court had argued.[93] There was nothing surprising about solar worshipping, he contended in his 1780 *Lettre sur le Dieu Soleil*:

> The entire universe worships you [the sun] under a host of different names. The universality of this cult has nothing to surprise us: the Sun needed only to show itself to receive the admiration and respect of men, who saw in it the King and Father of nature; and even if wise men elevate their minds to the idea of a superior, invisible God, they will still recognize the Sun as his first creation and his most beautiful image.[94]

91. *Mémoire sur l'origine des constellations, et sur l'explication de la fable, par le moyen de l'astronomie* . . . (Paris: Desaint, 1781); this text appeared in the fourth volume of Lalande's *Astronomie* (third edition). On Dupuis's mythological ideas, see Frank Manuel, *Eighteenth Century Confronts the Gods* (Cambridge: Harvard University Press, 1959); and Brian Juden, *Traditions orphiques et tendances mystiques dans le romantisme français (1800–1855)* (1971; Geneva: Slatkine Reprints, 1984); on his life, see the entry in Michaud's *Biographie universelle ancienne et moderne* (Paris: Mme C. Desplaces, 1855), 12:51–55. During the king's trial, Dupuis voted first for imprisonment, then for a suspended sentence; the *Biographie universelle* notes that "due to his colleagues' low esteem of his intelligence, Dupuis could get away with such a bold speech on the king" (12:53n1).

92. On the huge success and late decline of this theory, see Richard Dorson, "The Eclipse of Solar Mythology," *Journal of American Folklore* 68 (1955): 393–416.

93. *Monde primitif considéré dans son génie allégorique et dans les allégories auxquelles conduisit ce génie* . . . (Paris: n.p., 1773–81), 4:43. Court also interprets the name of the Egyptian sungod "Rhé" as meaning "the Eye" (4:42). On Court and this work, see chapter 2.

94. See his *Lettre sur le Dieu Soleil, adressée à MM. Les Auteurs du Journal des Sçavans; par M. Dupuis, Professeur de Rhétorique, Avocat en Parlement, de l'Académie de Rouen* (n.p., n.d.), 2. This opinion was shared by the abbé Barthélemy, who extracted from the "confusing mixture of truth and lies" that was mythology, a single truth: "What power created the universe out of chaos? The infinite being, *pure light*, the source of life . . ." He proceeded to interpret Jupiter

244 • CHAPTER FIVE

As Court before him, Dupuis did not go so far as to deify the sun, which is merely the "most beautiful image" of an invisible God. But the sun occupied a distinct place in this version of the creation; contrary to the teachings of Genesis, it was "his *first* creation."[95] One may detect in this privileging a distant echo of the "theory of the mystical sun," to which Dupuis refers in his *Lettre*, that is, the Swedenborgian belief that the physical sun is connected in the invisible world to the spiritual sun, home and heart of God.[96] The celestial sun, in this system, marked God's presence in this world, encouraging illuminist writers such as Nicolas de Bonneville to suggest, for instance, that Jesus was born on the sun.[97]

No doubt such beliefs were not shared by David, Robespierre, or many (if any) of the *conventionnels*, but they may still help to explain the prominent role of solar imagery in revolutionary culture. The sun was the emblem not only of nature and God, but also of the golden age before priests had corrupted "natural religion"— a common Masonic narrative, which can also be found, for instance, in *The Magic Flute*. These metaphysical associations were often recognized by the philosophes as well. Rousseau's Savoyard Vicar chose the first moments of dawn to divulge his religious ideas and made the capacity to admire the sun one of the two distinguishing qualities of man;[98] this recognition of the sun's divine essence allegedly led Voltaire, late in his life, to regard the sun as an ultimate proof of the existence of God.[99] Even an atheist such as d'Holbach penned an *Hymne au soleil*, in which virtuous shepherds bask in the daylight, debauched courtesans dare go out only at night, and "the villain . . . curses and hates you [the sun]; he hides in his

---

as a solar god: "Jupiter is the most powerful of gods, as he can throw lightening bolts; his court is the most brilliant of all; it is where eternal light resides," *Voyage du jeune Anacharsis en Grèce* (1788; Paris: n.p., 1856), 1:53.

95. Confusing as it may be, Jehovah created light three days before the sun (Gen., 1:3–14).

96. I discuss the influence of Swedenborgianism on solar mythology and physics in "Introduction to the Super-Enlightenment," *The Super-Enlightenment: Daring to Know Too Much*, ed. Edelstein (Oxford: SVEC/Voltaire Foundation, forthcoming). See also Joscelyn Godwin, *The Theosophical Enlightenment* (Albany: SUNY Press, 1994); and, classically, Auguste Viatte, *Les sources occultes du Romantisme: illuminisme—thésophie, 1770–1820* (1927; Paris: Champion, 1979). Dom Pernety published a French translation of Swedenborg, *Les merveilles du ciel et de l'enfer et des terres planétaires et astrales . . .* (Berlin: Decker [the Royal press], 1782).

97. See Viatte, *Sources occultes du Romantisme*, 1:25, for the reference to Bonneville. In a more pagan vein, others, such as Nerval's revolutionary (and perhaps fictional) uncle, would proclaim that the sun really *was* god; see *Aurélia*, in *Œuvres complètes*, ed. Jean Guillaume and Claude Pichois (Paris: Pléiade, 1993), 3:731.

98. *Emile*, in *JJR*, 4:565 and 582, respectively.

99. See the anecdote recounted in Roger Pearson, *Voltaire Almighty: A Life in Pursuit of Freedom* (London: Bloomsbury, 2005), 361–62.

bed to escape from your rays which . . . remind him of crimes he wishes he could forget."[100]

It is not that surprising, then, that the high opinion in which antiquarians and philosophes held solar worshipping was perpetuated during the Revolution. One of the most popular plays of Year II, Sylvain Maréchal's *Le jugement dernier des rois*, stars a castaway French victim of royal tyranny who teaches a tribe of island "savages" to worship a purer God than their local volcano by having them witness the sun rise over the ocean.[101] Around the time Maréchal's play was being staged (October 1793), another major cultural production similarly showcased the central place of the sun in the natural world—the revolutionary calendar. In this instance, the relation between antiquarianism and Jacobin cultural politics is direct, as Dupuis was one of the original three members of Romme's commission and one of the deputies singled out as having "scrupulously examined" the final product.[102] The calendar's debt to Dupuis can be seen in Romme's report, packed as it is with references to Egypt, and largely modeled, by Romme's own admission, on the ancient zodiac: The calendar, he concluded, "is almost entirely modeled on the unfortunately abandoned examples of the most enlightened peoples of Antiquity."[103] Its zodiacal subtext was still apparent in prints of the new calendar months; under one representation of "Messidor" (represented as a reclining, bare-breasted *moissonneuse*) lies the inscription, "The Sun in the sign of Cancer."[104]

---

100. *Hymne au soleil*, 1769, in *Variétés littéraires* (Paris: Xerouet, 1804), 307.

101. *Jugement dernier des rois: prophétie en un acte, en prose* (Paris: C.-F. Patris, an II [1793]), 14–15. On this play's success (the Committee of Public Safety purchased three thousand copies of the text), see Jean-Marie Apostolidès, "Theater and Terror: *Le jugement dernier des rois*," in *Terror and Consensus: Vicissitudes of French Thought*, ed. Jean-Joseph Goux and Philip R. Wood (Stanford: Stanford University Press, 1998), 135–44. I thank the author, also my colleague, for sharing his erudition and interpretations of Maréchal with me.

102. Romme, *Rapport sur l'ère de la République*, 14. See George Gordon Andrews, "Making the Revolutionary Calendar," *American Historical Review* 36 (1931): 10; and Charles C. Gillispie, *Science and Polity in France at the End of the Old Regime* (Princeton: Princeton University Press, 1980), 295.

103. *Rapport sur l'ère de la République*, 14. I discuss Dupuis's influence on the revolutionary calendar in my dissertation, "Restoring the Golden Age: Myths in Revolutionary Culture and Ideology" (PhD diss., University of Pennsylvania, 2004), 154–64. On the revolutionary calendar, see also Bronislaw Baczko, " 'Le temps ouvre un nouveau livre à l'histoire:' L'utopie et le calendrier révolutionnaire," in *Lumières de l'utopie* (Paris: Payot, 1978); Mona Ozouf, "Calendar," in *CDFR*; Caroline Weber, "Freedom's Missed Moment," *Yale French Studies* 101 (2001): 9–31; and Sanja Perovic, "Untamable Time: A Literary and Historical Panorama of the French Revolutionary Calendar (1792–1805)" (PhD diss., Stanford University, 2004).

104. See the engravings by Tresca, after Laffitte, for the revolutionary calendar months (at the Musée Carnavelet), each of which is related to its zodiacal equivalent; in Vovelle, *Révolution*

Since the restoration of nature was the predominant theme of Jacobin speeches and festivals, it is not surprising that David and his helpers would have looked for examples of "natural" institutions in descriptions of golden age societies.[105] While they no doubt could access many of these descriptions from memories of their schooldays, antiquarian sources such as Court de Gébelin (who, according to his biographer, was "considered on equal standing" with Rousseau in the 1780s) were easily accessible and provided an abundance of colorful details about the "ancient and eternal order" of humanity.[106] This emphasis on details may in part have been motivated by a sense that the people needed a palpable religion, yet antiquarians had described ancient religion in terms remarkably similar to the cult of the Supreme Being: The sun priests at Thebes, wrote Court de Gébelin, "worshipped a single God of creation, and . . . in their mysteries taught this dogma, along with that of a life to come."[107]

The *conventionnels* may even have discovered in these antiquarian sources, as one enthusiastic reader claimed to have in 1789, the key to restoring this ancient order. In a text that closely foreshadows the panoptic theory behind the cult of the Supreme Being, the feminist pioneer Olympe de Gouges suggested that it was precisely the belief in the sun's divine nature that had made the golden age possible in the first place. "Follow it [the Supreme Being] throughout nature; raise your eyes to the sky; and never forget [*ne perdez jamais de vue*] that he incessantly watches your actions and that he reads in your souls [*il lit dans vos âmes*]," she wrote in her bizarre and fascinating treatise, *Le bonheur primitif de l'homme*, a cross between a *roman sensible*, a pastoral vignette, and Rousseau's second *Discourse*. In the preceding quote, the Supreme Being was not overtly identified with the sun (even if the expressions "follow it" and "raise your eyes to the sky" would suggest so), but Gouges goes on to consider the great social value of actual solar worship:

> I like to believe, although I could be wrong, that the people who worshipped the sun were not entirely senseless. Is not this star the living soul of all things? Did God not create it to warm and enliven the earth? Has it not been demonstrated that if the sun did not exist,

---

française, 4:218–19. The revolutionary months, which stretch from the 21st of each traditional month to the 20th of the next, indeed correspond to traditional zodiacal periods.

105. For a discussion of such borrowings, notably from Barthélemy, Court de Gébelin, and Florian, see Ozouf, *Festivals and the French Revolution*, 5–7.

106. See Anne-Marie Mercier-Faivre, *Un Supplément à l' "Encyclopédie": le "Monde primitif"* *d'Antoine Court de Gébelin* (Paris: Champion, 1999), 36; and *Monde primitif*, 8:xviii, and *passim*.

107. *Monde primitif*, 8:185.

there would be no life? Is it surprising, then, that men who worshipped the sun were more pure, more faithful to their culture than
all these other peoples who practiced so many strange religions? This
[Sun] God shows himself everywhere and to all; no mortal can avoid
him. Temples are closed to the outside: no criminal is afraid of a God
that we hide. It seems to me that sun worshippers could not have
a guilty thought without immediately rejecting it, when they raised
their eyes to the heavens. . . . In those days, no one would have dared
to commit a crime in the open; whereas today, crimes are proudly
committed in public.[108]

The moral strength of solar worshippers derives both from the sun's privileged place in the universe ("the living soul of all things") and its panoptic
force: "This God shows himself everywhere and to all; no mortal can avoid
him." Once the belief in the sun's divinity had been fully internalized, it
could function as the perfect moral watchdog: all it took to dissuade solar
worshippers from committing a crime was to look up. They needed no other
laws than their natural virtue and their fear of God to act righteously; to
paraphrase Kant, with the sunny sky above them and the natural law within
them, they could do no harm. They had developed, in other words, a version of what Robespierre would later call "a rapid instinct . . . to do good
and avoid evil." Living "virtuously without laws" (*sine lege fidem rectumque*),
they could have inhabited Ovid's golden age.

Robespierre was no friend of Olympe de Gouges, to be sure, and I have
come across no evidence that he (or David) ever read this work.[109] Her
description of the primitive solar cult differs significantly, furthermore,
from the Jacobin cult of the Supreme Being in its omission of otherworldly
punishments or rewards. Nonetheless, her political appropriation of contemporary antiquarian theses provides an interesting point of comparison

108. Olympe de Gouges, *Le bonheur primitif de l'homme, ou les rêveries patriotiques* (Amsterdam, 1789), 15 and 30–31. On Gouges, see notably Joan Wallach Scott, *Only Paradoxes to
Offer: French Feminists and the Rights of Man* (Cambridge: Harvard University Press, 1996),
chap. 1. Her celebration of a solar cult also echoes the praiseful descriptions of the solar Incan
religion in Françoise de Graffigny's *Lettres d'une péruvienne* (1747; Oxford: Voltaire Foundation, 2002). On the idea of worshipping God outdoors, see also Rousseau: "When innocent
and virtuous men enjoyed having Gods as witnesses of their actions, they lived together in the
same huts; but soon becoming evil, they tired of these inconvenient spectators and relegated
them to magnificent Temples," first *Discourse*, in *CWR*, 2:16; *JJR*, 3:22. See also his *Lettre
à d'Alembert*: "Let the sun illuminate your innocent entertainments,"in *CWR*, 10:344; *JJR*,
5:115.

109. On their relations, and Gouges's political views, see notably Janie Vanpée, "Performing
Justice: The Trials of Olympe de Gouges," *Theatre Journal* 51, no. 1 (1999): 47–65.

for understanding related Jacobin efforts. The metaphysical theory of justice she developed on this basis enables us to imagine why Robespierre might have viewed the cult of the Supreme Being as *the* crucial institution in the natural-republican justice system. It was in a speech delivered at the Festival of the Supreme Being, after all, that he expressed his ambitions for the republic in the most overtly millenarian terms: "French republicans," he declared, "it is your duty to purify the earth that they [the tyrants] have soiled, and to bring back justice, whom they banished from here."[110] As Simon Schama remarked, Robespierre spoke on this occasion "as if he were announcing the return of the Ovidian Golden Age."[111] Perhaps there was no "as if." For the citizens of France to become so virtuous as to live *sine lege*, however, the Supreme Being had to be more than an abstract, metaphysical entity. Nature herself, whose laws had presided over both the death of the monarchy and the birth of the republic, also had to preside over the internalization of her laws among French citizens. And what part of nature was better suited to keep watch on the people who had restored "primitive equality" than the most primitive, and hence purest, of all symbols of God, the sun? Only this naturalization of the Supreme Being can explain why the well-worn theological concept of a metaphysical panopticon could suddenly appear as such an urgent and conclusive institution.

There was another, perhaps equally important difference, however, between the Jacobin cult and Christian dogma. Although Robespierre insisted, against the *déchristianiseurs*, on the eternity of the soul and thus on divine justice beyond the grave, neither he nor any other Jacobins (to my knowledge) sought to use the fear of otherworldly torments as a psychological restraint against misconduct. The cult of the Supreme Being was much more a matter of the here and now than the hereafter: The sublime *éclaircies* in revolutionary engravings of the festival reminded viewers that the God of nature intervened in this world, as well as the next (see fig. 8). Virtue, in this regard, was its own reward: A peaceful country, "the joys of a cabin and a fertile plot," were the only delights the Jacobins offered.[112] By the same token, however, they could not let vice go unpunished until the afterworld; it must also receive its due on earth. As Robespierre re-

---

110. *Rob.*, 10:482.

111. Simon Schama, *Citizens* (New York: Vintage, 1990), 834; see also Boudon, *Jacobins*, 667. It was Virgil, in fact, who prophesied in the famous fourth *Eclogue* that the golden age would resume when Astraea, the goddess of justice, returned to Earth from her exile in the constellation Virgo.

112. Saint-Just, "Rapport sur les factions de l'étranger," 23 ventôse an II (March 13, 1794); *SJ*, 729.

Figure 8   Tessier, *Vue du Champ-de-Mars le jour du 20 prairial* (1794).
Courtesy of the Bibliothèque Nationale de France.

minded his audience, Cicero insisted that both "the sword of the laws and
the lightening of the gods" were needed to guarantee justice in the republic. The cult of the Supreme Being could therefore not stand alone. It may
have been the keystone in the array of institutions that the Committee of
Public Safety put forward, but it was not the pillar. That dubious honor
belonged to another institution: the revolutionary tribunal, as reformed by
the law of 22 prairial.

And Justice for All: The Law of 22 Prairial

Two days after the Festival of the Supreme Being, the Convention learned
what Robespierre and his colleagues meant by "recalling justice to earth."
Through the intermediary of Couthon, the Committee of Public Safety presented a decree that denied the accused the right to legal counsel; allowed
the prosecution to introduce "moral" proofs, in the absence of (or in addition to) material evidence; vastly accelerated the entire judicial process;
maintained trial by jury, but handpicked the jurors; and finally, limited
sentencing to the stark choice between acquittal and death.[113] The timing

113. Anne Simonin has recently pointed out that, in practice, many defendants were
acquitted without being entirely cleared of charges; see "Les acquittés de la Grande Terreur:

of its presentation, its severity, and the lack of a clear, immediate motive transformed the law of 22 prairial into a emblem of primal violence. What prompted the Committee to push this piece of legislation through, at this particular time, independently from comprehensive legal reform?[114] Georges Lefebvre's thesis that it was a response to the "assassination" attempts on Collot d'Herbois and Robespierre earlier that month has been convincingly rejected by both Liliane Abdoul-Mellek and Patrice Gueniffey, who point to the much earlier announcements by the Committee of its intention to revise and revamp the tribunal's proceedings.[115] It is similarly difficult to pin the justification for the law on the ongoing war: Couthon hardly mentions the war in his report (even if a number of definitions of the "enemies of the people" do involve military affairs).[116] The question has thus traditionally been framed in terms of why this revision was so harsh: Had the Committee simply reached the point where it faced an "impossibility to ever end the terror"?[117]

Viewed from the perspective of legal precedent, earlier Jacobin judicial arguments, and natural right theory, however, the prairial law appears in a very different light. The reformed revolutionary tribunal can be seen, in fact, as synthesizing the different strains of legal theory that the Jacobins had been advocating ever since the trial of Louis XVI.[118] Rather than constituting a paranoid overreaction to foreign plots, an inevitable escalation of state violence, or a final, provisional push to purge society of counterrevolutionaries, the law arguably sought to establish a central, lasting institution for the republic-to-come. An intransigent judicial order, after all, lay at the heart of

---

réflexions sur l'amitié dans la République," in *Les politiques de la Terreur, 1793–94*, ed. Michel Biard (Rennes: Presses universitaires de Rennes & Société des études robespierristes, 2008), 185.

114. On the comprehensive reform efforts, see Hesse, "The Law of the Terror," and Martin, *Violence et révolution*, 223–36.

115. Robespierre had in fact promised a major overhaul of the tribunal in his 1793 "Christmas" speech on revolutionary government and had been pressing the Convention to reform the tribunal since July 1793; see Liliane Abdoul-Mellek, "D'un choix politique de Robespierre: la Terreur," in *Robespierre: de la nation artésienne à la république et aux nations*, ed. Jean-Pierre Jessenne, Gilles Deregnaucourt, Jean-Pierre Hirsch, and Hervé Leuwers (Lille: Université Charles de Gaulle, 1993), 191–204; and Gueniffey, *Politique de la Terreur*, chap. 10. For Lefebvre, see "Sur la loi du 22 prairial an II," *AHRF* 23 (1951): 225–56.

116. A number of historians have suggested that the law exhibits a "logic of war," but as I argue elsewhere, this thesis is anachronistic and tells the story backward; see "War and Terror: The Law of Nations from Grotius to the French Revolution," *French Historical Studies*, 31, no. 2 (2008): 229–62.

117. See Ozouf, "Guerre et Terreur," in *Ecole de la France*, 124; see also Brunel, *Thermidor*, 44–52.

118. Gueniffey also makes this connection in *Politique de la Terreur*, chap. 10.

Jacobin political theory: "It is said that a vigorous government is oppressive," Saint-Just wrote in his *Institutions républicaines*, "but that is mistaken. . . . Justice is needed in government. A government cannot be considered vigorous and oppressive because it exercises justice, since only evil is being oppressed."[119]

The continuity between the law of 22 prairial and earlier revolutionary legislation is particularly evident with the criminal category at the heart of the new law: the "enemy of the people." In her insightful study of criminality during the Terror, Anne Simonin argued that this category was a new creation, yet as Jean-Clément Martin points out, it had featured in prior revolutionary legislation, notably the 12 germinal (April 1, 1794) decree.[120] Saint-Just had in fact already provided, two weeks earlier, a detailed definition of the "*ennemi du peuple*"—"whoever usurps the power [of the National Convention], whoever threatens its safety or dignity"— and the requisite punishment ("[he] will be put to death").[121] Article 2 of the March 13 decree foreshadows the prairial law by the number of amorphous categories that it groups together: "those who are convicted of having encouraged, *in any possible manner*, the corruption of citizens, or the subversion of authority or of the public spirit in the Republic" (emphasis added).

Most important, this decree also reveals the legal blueprint on which the "enemy of the people" was modeled: Article 8 states that "those who, while accused of conspiring against the Republic, fail to present themselves in court, are outlawed [*sont mis hors la loi*]." Those accused of being enemies of the people were *hors-la-loi* in the making, outlaws over whom lingered a shadow of doubt.[122] The underlying crime (abetting the counterrevolution) was identical, as was the punishment (immediate death); the March 19, 1793, decree, however, only gave the state the authority to outlaw individuals who had engaged in *overt* counterrevolutionary activities (armed insurrection, wearing rebellious insignia, and the like). In cases where this activity was *covert*, and thus required a "conviction" (here: "those who are convicted"), the March 19 decree was silent.

119. *SJ*, 978–79.

120. Simonin, *Déshonneur dans la république*, 301–2, 311; Martin, *Violence et révolution*, 225.

121. "Rapport sur les factions de l'étranger," 23 ventôse an II (March 13, 1794), article 3; *SJ*, 737.

122. While insisting on the novelty of the "enemy of the people" category, Simonin acknowledges that it was "a hybrid category, cobbled together from the categories of the *outlaw* and the one of the *émigrés*," "An Essay of Political Cartography," 5.

The "enemy of the people" category allowed the Committee of Public Safety to close this loophole, granting (with the law of 22 prairial) the accused a brief hearing in order to determine their guilt and occasionally their innocence, after which the guilty were dispatched with the same inflexibility and swiftness as outlaws: "It is less a matter of punishing than of annihilating them," in the words of Couthon's report.[123] In terms of criminal categories, then, the prairial law did not so much constitute a departure from prior revolutionary jurisprudence, but was rather an attempt to codify once and for all the confusing array of legislation on counterrevolutionaries.[124] It took as its model, moreover, the very category that, as shown in chapter 3, first translated into law the natural right theory of the enemy elaborated by the Jacobins during their prosecution of the king; the reformed tribunal, Couthon declared, was directed against the "ferocious and cowardly enemies of humanity," that is, the *hostes humani generis* who, like the king and the *hors-la-loi*, had transgressed the very laws of nature. While the *conventionnels* clearly strove to create a series of distinct criminal categories, as is evident from Simonin's analyses, the underlying legal philosophy for most of these categories was usually the same: as Simonin also argues, they all define the criminal as a "non-subject of the law" (*non-sujet de droit*).[125] Deprived of civil and natural rights (in the plural), such a criminal could nonetheless be prosecuted and executed according to natural right (in the singular). This had, in effect, already been the lesson of Locke, Vattel, and other jusnaturalist writers.

Even the drastic curtailment of due process that the law enacted can be traced back to that primal scene of the republic, the king's trial.[126] Couthon himself drew attention to this parallel in his report. The provision stripping defendants of legal representation, for instance, is justified by the bitter memory of the Convention's decision to grant lawyers for the king: "With

---

123. For Couthon's report, see the *Réimpression de l'ancien Moniteur . . .* (Paris: Plon, 1861), 20:694–97. As with the 23 ventôse decree, the law of 22 prairial can be seen as supplementing, rather than replacing, the March 19 decree; it was thanks to the latter, after all, that the Thermidorians succeeded in toppling Robespierre. Martin argues that the prairial law was in fact less "terrorizing" of the two, as a system of triage committees ensured that fewer individuals were brought before the tribunal: *Violence et révolution*, 224.

124. The goal of the Committee of Public Safety, Couthon declared, was to "summarize in a single law the scattered definitions and measures from a multitude of decrees." The law indeed recapitulates and organizes laws stretching back to 1792: The very first definition of "enemies of the people," "those who will have labored for the restoration of the monarchy" (art. 6), incorporates a law passed on December 4, 1792.

125. See Simonin, *Déshonneur dans la république*, 315.

126. Gueniffey also makes this connection in *Politique de la Terreur*, chap. 10.

this single act, they abjured the republic; the law itself invited citizens to commit crimes, and scandalously consecrated the attacks against the republic; for to defend the cause of the tyrants is to conspire against the republic." Robespierre had criticized this decision in similar terms at the time of the trial;[127] article 16 elliptically ensured that such a "scandalous" act would never occur again.

The demand that the tribunal speed up its proceedings—or that, in Couthon's words, "the deadline for punishing the enemies of the homeland should only be the time needed to identify them"—had similarly been a common Jacobin refrain during the trial. Saint-Just had chastised the Convention for wasting time with procedures, when the deputies should simply stab Louis XVI on the "Senate" floor and be done with it. With greater success, Robespierre had argued for the swift execution of Louis's penalty, and the king was indeed guillotined within twenty-four hours of his sentencing.[128]

Finally, the right to use "moral" proofs in the absence of material ones, while implicitly accepted, was not an issue during the king's trial since evidence of his treasonous correspondence was abundant; but this right, too, was a long-standing Jacobin demand. In a draft decree that Robespierre penned in August 1793, he had argued, "it is both absurd and fatal for the public interest to employ drawn-out legal processes for crimes committed in clear view, where the nation is the accuser and the universe is a witness."[129] This emphasis on a sort of "judicial omniscience" also underpinned, as we have just seen, his rationale for the cult of the Supreme Being.

"System of Terror" or Natural Republic?

It remains somewhat puzzling why the Committee of Public Safety chose to wait so long to reform the tribunal, if dissatisfaction with the expediency and forms of the justice system were so long-standing. Possibly the Committee

---

127. See his December 3, 1792, speech; *Rob.*, 9:125.

128. See his December 28, 1792, speech; *Rob.*, 9:185. Robespierre repeatedly insisted on the need to accelerate the tribunal's proceedings throughout 1793; see in particular his August 11, 12, 25, and 28 speeches.

129. *Rob.*, 10:160; for a similar argument, see his 3 brumaire (October 24, 1793) speech at the Convention, and his 16 germinal (April 5, 1794) speech at the Jacobin society. See also Drouet's intervention at the Convention on September 5, 1793, in which he argued that there should be no need to provide proof of denunciations and that all suspects should simply be executed; see Albert Soboul, *Mouvement populaire et gouvernement révolutionnaire en l'an II (1793–1794)* (Paris: Flammarion, 1973), 126.

had been planning to revamp all revolutionary legislation, and then out of frustration or impatience, decided to focus on counterrevolutionary crimes. Whatever the rationale, the legal principles and restrictions contained in the law of 22 prairial do not belong narrowly to what the Thermidorians would later call "the system of Terror," but express a more general theory of justice that predates the Terror (and its institutions) altogether, as we saw in chapter 3. Rather than an indication that the Committee of Public Safety was unable to "end the Terror," the severity of the law merely obeys the draconian syllogism imposed by natural republicanism: Whoever violates the laws of nature deserves a swift execution, with few (if any) legal forms; the republic has made the laws of nature its own; *ergo*, all threats to the republic must be met with death.

Since it was a commonplace of republican thought, furthermore, that the state was never far from danger (or, as a metaphorically challenged French statesman once put it, "the chariot of the State sails on a volcano [*le char de l'état vogue sur un volcan*]"), it followed that the reformed revolutionary tribunal would not simply be a provisional, temporary measure, like the Commission d'Orange, but an institution that could preserve the republic-to-come from both present and future danger. Labeling the period between 22 prairial and 9 thermidor the "Great Terror," as Françoise Brunel recently observed, is thus deeply misleading.[130] Not only is the word "terror" absent from Couthon's report and the articles of the law, but the reformed tribunal finally realized, together with the cult of the Supreme Being, a Jacobin ideal of justice—to preserve the laws of nature and to punish their transgressions accordingly. On the foundation of these institutions, the natural republic could rise.

If the judicial logic behind the law of 22 prairial did not result from an uncontrollable spiraling of violence, but was already on display in the first months of Year I, we must in conclusion reevaluate the place and importance of "the Terror" in the history of the first republic. The *journées* of September, as noted in chapter 3, did not actually bring about much significant institutional or ideological change. The administrative machinery of the Terror was already in place, with the exception of the revolutionary armies—but the Convention appropriated this *sans-culotte* demand for

130. Brunel, "Institutions civiles et terreur." Greer's comparison, in *Incidence of the Terror*, between the number of deaths during those seven weeks (roughly 1,400 people) and the number of executions that had been performed up until then (a slightly lower number) is similarly misleading. Provincial revolutionary tribunals were fully closed on May 8, 1794, after which all counterrevolutionary suspects were sent to Paris. Hence, the death toll for the Parisian tribunal during the "Great Terror" includes suspects from throughout France.

other means (fighting rebels versus hunting down *accapareurs*), and then promptly began the process of disbanding them. The institutions that the Committee of Public Safety introduced in Year II were similarly conceived of before the Terror became the "order of the day": Saint-Just wrote the bulk of his *Institutions républicaines* during the summer of 1793, and Robespierre had been publicly expounding on the Supreme Being since at least March 1792.[131] The one exception here are the economic measures forced on the Convention in September 1793 and ultimately incorporated into the Committee's republican program with the Ventôse decrees. For the most part, however, the Committee sought, onward from the end of February 1794, to disentangle its institutional reforms from the nebulous demands of "Terror." Its own brand of justice, to be sure, was hardly clement, but it was not forged in the passions of September: It was an intrinsic part of the republican theory that emerged, not without variations and differences, from the debates over the king's punishment. "Might the Terror itself be a 'myth'?" asks Lynn Hunt in a recent review of Martin's *Violence et révolution*.[132] Obviously, as she recognizes, it was not a myth for the combatants on either side of the Vendée conflict, for the thousands of prisoners cooped up in overcrowded depots, or for the provincial committees that carried out (often liberally interpreted) orders from Paris. But from a political and institutional perspective, it is hard to identify what, if anything, "the Terror" designates, which is not also an inherent part of Jacobin republicanism. Even the revolutionary government derives from an electoral problem brought to light in August 1793 (as discussed in chapter 4). The Committee of Public Safety was adept at speaking the language of terror, especially between October 1793 and February 1794, but it is unclear whether the concept held much sway over their actions.

Calling into question "the Terror" as an institutional reality does more than challenge historiographical terminology (what to call the period between September 1793 and July 1794?). It forces us to think differently about the Committee of Public Safety's intentions. Asking how the Jacobins planned on "ending the Terror" may turn out to be another *question mal posée*: As noted above, Billaud-Varenne and Saint-Just indicated early in the spring of 1794 that, for all intents and purposes, the Committee considered "the Terror" to be a thing of the past. Its stated ambition was to found a

---

131. For Robespierre, see Blum, *Rousseau and the Republic of Virtue*, 239. Billaud-Varenne's *Eléments du républicanisme* was similarly written in the summer of 1793.

132. "Review Essay," *H-France Forum*, 2, no. 2 (2007), http://www.h-france.net/forum/forumvol2/HuntOnMartin1.html.

just republic, rooted in nature and preserved by virtuous institutions—and is that not, in part at least, what it attempted to do? It may sound unconscionable today that the post-prairial revolutionary tribunal could approximate anyone's idea of justice, let alone the golden age announced at the Festival of the Supreme Being, but in 1794 there were few republican precedents available. The "natural republic" might not have seemed any crazier to readers of Livy, Fénelon, and Rousseau than the seven-year-old American experiment across the ocean. If the Committee of Public Safety did not have a concrete plan or timetable for the transition of power, it nonetheless seems to have been leading France down a new, radically ambitious republican path. The only thing we can know for certain is that they never reached the end.

CONCLUSION

LEGACIES OF THE TERROR

THERMIDOR LEFT THE DREAM of a Republic of Nature in shambles, although it is unclear whether this republic could have ever been anything but a dream. While the cult of the Supreme Being may have been more popular than is assumed, it is highly doubtful that it could have successfully played the remarkable policing role attributed to it.[1] The law reforming the revolutionary tribunal similarly struck more fear than enthusiasm in the *conventionnels* (who rightly sensed that it increased their own chances of facing Fouquier-Tinville) and was accordingly rescinded three days after Robespierre's execution.[2] Members of the Committee of Public Safety may have fantasized about a republic in which laws were superfluous, yet their correspondence reveals a highly legalistic mentality;[3] meanwhile, the Convention never tired of passing new decrees. On a more philosophical, as well as a more fundamental level, one can also ask if the Jacobin belief in natural right as a moral code intuitively accessible to all was simply (to borrow Bentham's famous phrase) "nonsense on stilts." If the political leaders of Year II recognized, with James Madison, that men were not angels and some government was necessary, their expectations about government's influence on men clearly exposed them to what Alexander Hamilton called "the deceitful dream of a golden age . . . the happy empire of perfect wisdom and perfect virtue."[4]

---

1. On the popularity of this cult, see Michel Vovelle, *La Révolution contre l'Eglise: de la Raison à l'Etre Suprême* (Brussels : Complexe, 1988), 186, and Françoise Brunel, "L'Être Suprême et les divisions de la Montagne avant Thermidor," in Vovelle, *Être Suprême*.

2. See Bronislaw Baczko, *Comment sortir de la Terreur: Thermidor et Révolution* (Paris: Gallimard, 1989), 95.

3. For two typical examples, see the Committee's directive to departmental and district administrators, instructing them how to interpret the law of 14 frimaire; or their letter to national agents reminding them they did not have a right to vote on administrative matters; in Alphonse Aulard, *Recueil des actes du Comité de salut public, avec la correspondance officielle des représentants en mission et le registre du conseil exécutif provisoire* (Paris: Imprimerie nationale, 1899), 12:323–24 and 12:350.

4. See, respectively, *The Federalist Papers*, ed. Isaac Kramnick (London: Penguin, 1987), nos. 51 and 6.

Faulty as they may be, constitutional laws are doubtless a better guarantee of public and civil liberties than the murky principles of natural right.

At the same time, however, natural right did play a critical role in allowing the French Revolution to occur at all. Unlike the American colonists, the French, in 1789, could not appeal to an established Bill of Rights, guaranteeing their political rights and liberties. While a constitutional tradition, albeit a weak one, could be excavated from French history, authoritative references to the past essentially disappeared from the political debate once it seemed that the Estates General would meet according to the "forms of 1614." As Dale Van Kley has shown, the perceived unfairness of placing the Third Estate on par with the nobility and clergy led most "patriotic" pamphleteers to reject historical precedent in favor of universalism, thus announcing the a-historical tenor of the "Declaration of the Rights of Man and of the Citizen."[5] When Burke complained that the subsequent doubling of the Third and the vote by head represented "a great departure from the antient course," he was criticizing a decision approved by the king himself. [6] Well before the momentous formation of a National Assembly or the pronouncement of a Declaration of Rights, the French had excluded the possibility of a Burkean revolution grounded in constitutional lore (as in the American case); some other form of authority thus became necessary to counter the legitimacy of the monarchy.

Natural right was, of course, one of the authorizing languages of the Revolution from its inception. Even before the Estates General convened, Sieyès had recognized the precedence of natural right over all positive forms of legality.[7] And the Declaration of the Rights citizen famously enshrined natural law principles. But the revolutionaries also had other discourses at their disposal, most notably theories of popular sovereignty, legal voluntarism,

---

5. Van Kley, "From the Lessons of French History to Truths for All Times and All People: The Historical Origins of an Anti-historical Declaration," in *The French Idea of Freedom: The Old Regime and the Declaration of Rights of 1789*, ed. Dale Van Kley (Stanford: Stanford University Press, 1994); see also Paul Friedland, *Political Actors: Representative Bodies and Theatricality in the Age of the French Revolution* (Ithaca: Cornell University Press, 2002), chap. 3. My thanks, as always, to David Bell for his precious comments on this passage, and the conclusion in general.

6. *Reflections on the Revolution in France*, ed. L. G. Mitchell (Oxford: Oxford University Press, 1993), 41.

7. See, for instance, "Prior to the nation and above the nation there is only natural law," *What Is the Third Estate?*, in *Political Writings*, trans. and ed. Michael Sonenscher (Indianapolis: Hackett, 2003), 136. See also Pasquale Pasquino, "The Constitutional Republicanism of Emmanuel Sieyès," in *Invention of Modern Republicanism*, ed. Biancamaria Fontana (Cambridge: Cambridge University Press, 1994), 107–17.

and constitutional monarchy (in either its British, Montesquieuian, or Rousseauist flavors). If anything, these theories played a much larger role in shaping political arguments and legislation during the early years of the Revolution. It was only with the fall of the monarchy in August 1792, and then more particularly with the trial of Louis XVI, that natural right became regarded as the enforceable legal code of the Revolution: As Nicolas Quinette summarized in December 1792, "during political revolutions, the only positive laws are those of nature."[8] As I have argued in the preceding chapters, soon it was only the Girondists who, for both expedient and philosophical reasons, clung to a voluntaristic theory of government, based on some version of the general will; the Montagnards, for their part, explicitly rejected what one deputy even scoffed at as "the alleged general will." It was under the aegis of natural right, not the general will, that the Montagnards brought "terror" into the Republic.

It would be a gross oversimplification, however, to suggest that *quatre-vingt-treize* was *la faute à Locke*. The kind of natural right theories expounded by the likes of Gentili, Bacon, Sydney, Pufendorf, Locke, Barbeyrac, Burlamaqui, or Vattel—or, for that matter, Jefferson—are very different from those developed in the National Convention by Montagnard deputies. Their principal difference is precisely the one identified by the Monarchist deputy Lally-Tollendal in 1789: Unmediated by positive legislation, natural right can be "taken to an extreme," and thus can pose a threat to civil government.[9] For the American revolutionaries, natural right merely contributed to authorize their political proceedings and did not dictate their form or content—hence the list of grievances, a traditional and recognized form of dissent, beneath the preamble to the Declaration of Independence. In France, however, natural right theory had evolved over the course of a century to a point where natural laws could be viewed in opposition to positive laws and as self-sufficient. In this version, which received its most sophisticated theoretical expression in Physiocracy, the traditional social contract narrative was scrapped, leaving natural right alone to dictate the laws of society. It was this variant of natural right theory that the Montagnards, unlike their American counterparts, or even the vast majority of French revolutionaries three years prior, employed to sketch their vision of the republic.

---

8. *Archives parlementaires de 1787 à 1860*, ed. M. J. Mavidal et al. (Paris: Librairie administrative de P. Dupont, 1862–1913), 54:401 (hereafter cited as *AP*); see chapter 3.

9. *AP*, 8:222; see chapter 4.

From a Natural Republic to a World Revolution

The danger that unmediated natural right presents to civil society resides, as we saw, in its radical concept of hostility, which is summed up in the phrase the "enemy of the human race." In traditional natural right theories (that is, those that inscribed natural right within the larger framework of a social contract), there was a distinct need for such a concept, as it targeted individuals who lay beyond the law. No tyrant would pass a law making it legal to kill a tyrant, and pirates or "savages" were beyond civil jurisdiction. In this regard, the *hostis humani generis* was an exceptional category created specially for offenses that could not be prosecuted by any other laws than those of nature. Accordingly, retribution for such offenses was particularly harsh: Theorists overwhelmingly agreed that violations against nature should be punished by death. Once natural right became perceived as the only authentic basis of legal authority, however, what began as an exception ran the risk of rapidly expanding to encompass *any* violation. The corollary of this expansion, of course, is that minor and even petty offenses would receive the same harsh punishment as exceptional transgressions.

This line of legal reasoning roughly describes the course of the French revolutionary Terror: in all likelihood, neither the Montagnards nor the Girondins anticipated the widespread use of the exceptional criminal categories the Convention had originally devised for the very few. Indeed, at first it seemed as though only Louis would be the "cruel exception" to the hoped-for abolition of the death penalty. But the will to punish counter-revolutionaries as violators of natural laws gradually extended from the king and his supporters to almost anyone in the world who was hostile to the French Republic. This universalization of the exception may also help explain why the Jacobin republican project seemed bound to collapse. In a speech denouncing the Hébertistes, Saint-Just proclaimed, "the measures that will be presented to you . . . will rid the Republic and the Earth of all accomplices. . . . The war will be continued furiously. No rest until the enemies of the Revolution and the French people have been exterminated!"[10] The foreign plot, a fixture of the revolutionary *mentalité* since 1789, has morphed here into what David Bell has recently analyzed as "total war": The enemy has been

---

10. "Rapport sur les factions de l'étranger," 23 ventôse an II (March 13, 1794), *Œuvres complètes*, ed. Michèle Duval (Paris: Lebovici, 1984), 736 (hereafter cited as *SJ*). See also Robespierre's pronouncement two months later: "So long as this impure race [of counterrevolutionaries] exists, the Republic will be unhappy and precarious," "Sur les crimes des rois coalisés contre la France," 7 prairial an II (May 26, 1794), *Œuvres de Maximilien Robespierre*, ed. the Société des études robespierristes (Ivry: Phénix éditions, 2000), 10:477 (hereafter cited as *Rob.*).

criminalized, and war can only end with his complete annihilation.[11] The struggle for public liberty, moreover, is no longer contained within (or along) the borders of France: The entire earth has become the battlefield on which the fate of the republic will be decided.

While this transformation of the revolutionary cause into a worldwide struggle was largely due to a "redefinition of war,"[12] it proceeded according to the same natural right logic that had dictated the "extermination" of the republic's internal enemies. Barère revealed this continuity in his infamous, if ultimately only symbolic, decree forbidding French soldiers from taking British prisoners.[13] Because the British had a long of history of "barbarous" acts, going back to the Seven Years War, he could invoke, rather than flaunt, the law of nations in justification of his unyielding decree:

There exists . . . between all nations, between all human societies, a sort of natural right known as the law of nations. But it is unknown to the polished [*policés*] savages of Great-Britain; that people is accordingly foreign to Europe, foreign to humanity; it must disappear.[14]

To buttress his case, Barère enumerated the same list of natural right violations elaborated by prerevolutionary jurists and the *conventionnels* themselves. The British were barbarians (*sauvages*), but also "brigands" (112), ruled over by the "the worst of tyrants" (126), and conniving like devils in their "infernal scheming [*infernale manœuvre*]" (124). Such name calling,

11. David A. Bell, *The First Total War: Napoleon's Europe and the Birth of Warfare as We Know It* (Boston: Houghton Mifflin, 2007); see also Jean-Yves Guiomar, *L'invention de la guerre totale: XVIIIᵉ–XXᵉ siècles* (Paris: Le Félin, 2004).

12. Mona Ozouf, "Guerre et Terreur dans le discours révolutionnaire: 1792–94," *L'Ecole de la France: Essais sur la Révolution, l'utopie et l'enseignement* (Paris: Gallimard, 1984), 124.

13. See the law of 7 prairial (May 26, 1794), in *Histoire parlementaire de la Révolution française, ou Journal des assemblées nationales depuis 1789 jusqu'en 1815*, ed. P. J. B. Buchez and P. C. Roux (Paris: Paulin, 1834–38), 33:101–27. On this law, see Sophie Wahnich and Marc Belissa, "Les crimes des Anglais: Trahir le droit," *AHRF* 300 (1995): 241–42; Wahnich, *L'Impossible citoyen: l'étranger dans le discours de la Révolution française* (Paris: Albin Michel, 1997), 243–62; and Michael Rappaport, *Nationality and Citizenship in Revolutionary France: The Treatment of Foreigners 1789–99* (Oxford: Clarendon Press, 2000). I develop the arguments presented here in greater detail in "War and Terror: The Law of Nations from Grotius to the French Revolution," *French Historical Studies* 31, no. 2 (2008): 229–62.

14. *HP*, 30:122; see also 112 and 117. On the French animosity toward England and its place in Terrorist discourse, see David A. Bell, "English Barbarians, French Martyrs," *The Cult of the Nation in France: Inventing Nationalism, 1680–1800* (Cambridge: Harvard University Press, 2001), 78–106. On French perceptions of the Seven Years War, see Edmond Dziembowski, *Un nouveau patriotisme français, 1750–70: la France face à la puissance anglaise à l'époque de la guerre de Sept Ans* (Oxford: Voltaire Foundation, 1998), 59–110.

while indicative of the legal discourse Barère was drawing on, ultimately provided only a rhetorical flourish for his fundamental argument: The English should lose their natural rights because "they shatter every bond of nature with us, whereas we respect the law of nations with them" (117). This was precisely the lesson that Vattel had imparted.

It is thus misleading to describe the relation between war and the Terror, or war and Jacobin republicanism, as the progressive imposition of a military logic onto civilian affairs.[15] The vector between military and civil struggles in fact moved in the opposite direction: The violent exception contained in natural right treatises was first applied against civilian offenders and only later extended to military enemies. At that point, however, the foundation of the French Republic became an impossible task. Its prime obstacle was less the ongoing war itself—it was not simply a matter of waiting until peacetime—than the redefinition of the republic's relation to the world. The French Republic could now only survive if republicanism triumphed everywhere; so long as conspirators were plotting somewhere on Earth, there could be no respite ("*plus de repos*"). Along with total war, Jacobin republicanism had given birth to world revolution.[16]

Of course, the military adventurism of the French Revolution did not end with Thermidor, or even with the Revolution itself, in 1799. As recent scholarship on the Thermidorian and Directory periods has emphasized, the fall of Robespierre and his allies did not in fact mark a fundamental change in the republican thought or governmental policies of the French state.[17] Andrew Jainchill has recently shown, for instance, how the post-Jacobin period of the Revolution perpetuated the classical-republican faith in the power of civic institutions, public instruction, and education as the principal supports of the republic.[18] But there was one aspect of Jacobin thought that was overtly and strenuously rejected: The *conventionnels* of

---

15. This characterization has been made by historians as diverse as Lucien Jaume (in *Le Discours Jacobin et la démocratie* [Paris: Fayard, 1989], 116), Patrice Gueniffey (in *La Politique de la Terreur: essai sur la violence révolutionnaire, 1789–94* [Paris: Fayard, 2000], 65), and Sophie Wahnich (in *La Liberté ou la mort: essai sur la Terreur et le terrorisme* [Paris: La Fabrique, 2003], 68–69). Anne Simonin has more recently described the Terror as a "juridical fiction," in which politicians acted "as if" France were in a state of siege; see *Le déshonneur dans la république: une histoire de l'indignité, 1791–1958* (Paris: Grasset, 2008), 277–80.

16. On this legacy, see especially James H. Billington, *Fire in the Minds of Men: Origins of the Revolutionary Faith* (New York: Basic Books, 1980).

17. See in particular Baczko, *Comment sortir de la Terreur*; Howard G. Brown, *Ending the French Revolution: Violence, Justice, Repression* (Charlottesville: University of Virginia Press, 2006); and Andrew Jainchill, *Rethinking Politics after the Terror: The Republican Origins of French Liberalism* (Ithaca: Cornell University Press, 2008).

18. Jainchill, *Rethinking Politics after the Terror.*

1794–95 refused to grant natural right a foundational or determining role in the new constitutional government. "The Declaration of Rights of year III (1795) broke with natural right, and introduced a different legal theory, that of the rights of man in society," Florence Gauthier has remarked.[19] But where Gauthier views this break as a reactionary retreat from Jacobin social policies, one may instead concur with Mona Ozouf, who suggested that the Thermidorians offer, in this regard, the best starting point for analyzing the Terror.[20] On this topic at least, the Thermidorians seem to have sensed what subsequent historians overlooked, namely, that natural right was not only a progressive, egalitarian legal discourse, but could be used to justify state violence on a vast scale.

Terror and Totalitarianism

Natural right may have lost its privileged, authorizing function after Thermidor, but its legacy was not so easily erased. The *hors-la-loi* decree, which sealed Robespierre's fate at the National Convention, continued to be applied against enemies of the state up until the very end of the Revolution; the deputies of the Conseil des Cinq-Cents sought to outlaw Bonaparte himself on 18 brumaire.[21] The perseverance of this category even after its legal justification had fallen by the wayside points to another troubling aspect about "emergency" legislation: Not only can its scope expand quickly to encompass individuals not targeted by the original law, but its legacy very often outlives the specific moment for which it was designed. Emergency laws have the bad habit of acquiring a form of jurisprudential value, even in the absence of a recognized legal tradition. Already in Roman Antiquity, Sulla's *proscripti* decrees were revived, some forty years later, by Mark Antony, Octavian, and Lepidus.[22] In more recent times, the fate of the

---

19. Gauthier, *Triomphe et mort du droit naturel en Révolution, 1789–1795–1802* (Paris: PUF, 1992), 9.

20. See Ozouf, "The Terror after the Terror: An Immediate History," in *The Terror*, vol. 4 of *The French Revolution and the Creation of Modern Political Culture*, ed. Keith Baker (Oxford: Pergamon Press, 1987).

21. On this incident and the post-Thermidor history of this category, see Eric de Mari, "La Mise hors de la loi sous la Révolution française" (PhD diss., Université de Montpellier, 1991), 1:634–37.

22. See François Hinard, *Les proscriptions de la Rome républicaine* (Rome: École française de Rome, 1985), who notes how "proscription was essentially an exceptional procedure, but it seems to have become integrated in the ordinary system of repression" (5). See also John Henderson, *Fighting for Rome: Poets and Caesars, History, and Civil War* (Cambridge: Cambridge University Press, 1998).

enemy categories created during the French Revolution has been no less successful: The Soviet Union, for instance, gave new legal vigor to the concepts "counterrevolutionary" and "enemy of the people."[23]

The afterlife of these legal categories points to the larger, more controversial, question of a continuity between the Terror and subsequent revolutionary or totalitarian movements. It is clear that the French Revolution, and more particularly its cast of characters, provided the prism through which nineteenth-century revolutionary movements were perceived, both by their actors and their observers. When a young French anarchist, Emile Henry, threw a bomb in the Café Terminus in 1894, an obvious analogy thrust itself on commentators (no doubt encouraged by the centennial anniversary): He was a new Saint-Just.[24] Yet there was also a more concrete continuity between natural republicanism and anarchist politics. As their Jacobin predecessors, many French anarchists predicated their visions of the future on the existence of a natural order. The anarchist Louis Lumet, for instance, predicted that a "red Messiah" would usher in a new age of nature;[25] a similar ideal was expressed by the *Naturiens*, who published a journal between 1894–98 entitled *L'Etat naturel*, edited by Emile Gravelle, following which another member, Alfred Marné, launched a related *Sauvagiste* movement and founded his own journal, *L'Age d'or* (a single issue, 1900).[26] Conversely, these anarchists never wavered in their belief that acts of popular terror were justified in bringing about this "golden age."[27]

---

23. See notably Ilya Zemtsov, *Encyclopedia of Soviet Life* (New Brunswick: Transaction, 1991), 76–77 and 118–21, respectively.

24. See John Merriman, *The Dynamite Club: How a Bombing in Fin-de-Siècle Paris Ignited the Age of Modern Terror* (Boston: Houghton Mifflin, 2009). I am most grateful to the author for drawing my attention to this connection and sharing his wealth of knowledge on French anarchism with me. Merriman further points out in a private correspondence that the Saint-Just parallel had already been used for Théodule Meunier, who participated in the bombing of the Café Very in 1892. See also Ernest A. Vizetelly, *The Anarchists, Their Faith, and Their Record* (London: John Lane, 1911), 161; and George Woodcock, *Anarchism: A History of Libertarian Ideas and Movements* (1962; Toronto: Broadview Press, 2004), 258.

25. Lumet, *Contre ce temps* (Paris: Bibliothèque de l'Association, 1896). See Jessica Wardhaugh, "Between Sabotage and the Sublime: Anarchist Culture in Belle Epoque Paris" (paper presented at the annual meeting of the Society for the Study of French History, Aberystwyth, UK, July 3–4, 2008). My thanks to the author for generously sharing her paper and insights with me.

26. René Bianco, "Répertoire des périodiques anarchistes de langue française: un siècle de presse anarchiste d'expression française, 1880–1983" (PhD diss., Université Aix-Marseille, 1987), 66; this thesis can be consulted online at http://bianco.ficedl.info/. See also Raoul Girardet, *Mythes et mythologies politiques* (Paris: Seuil, 1986), 103.

27. See Alexander McKinley, *Illegitimate Children of Enlightenment: Anarchists and the French Revolution, 1880–1914* (New York: Peter Lang, 2008), 65–69.

If there was one aspect of French revolutionary Terror that did not find favor among *fin-de-siècle* anarchists, it was the central role played by the state. Where the Jacobins insisted on maintaining an official monopoly on violence, the anarchist aim, of course, was to eliminate the state altogether. Even this difference, however, may be somewhat misleading, given the definite "anarchic" streak in the political theories of the leading Jacobins. Natural republicanism, after all, sought to reduce the presence of the state to a bare minimum: "One cannot rule innocently" was Saint-Just's epigraph for his constitutional project of 1793. His visions of simple rustic life ultimately had much in common with the latter-day anarchist dreams of a golden age.

Still, this pastoral dimension of Jacobin thought was grossly overshadowed by the reality of the state's involvement in political repression. Only with the direct critique of the state, first by anarchists, then by socialists and communists, would the natural-republican ideal of an apolitical society become fully incorporated into revolutionary theory. Marx and Engels' well-known prediction that the state would "wither away" was further reinforced by their refusal to predict or describe the type of society that was to follow, leading Lenin to declare, in 1918, "what Socialism will be, we just don't know."[28] Indeed, Georges Sorel has argued that this silence about the postrevolutionary future was arguably one of the great strengths of the Marxist model: Where other utopian writers put forward concrete proposals that could be weighed and criticized, Marx's revolution acquired the power of a "myth" that could not be challenged.[29] According to Sorel, this mythical quality was essential for stirring workers into action, yet it could also serve, from a more Barthesian perspective, to naturalize whatever form of society came next, as the inevitable, successive stage of history. In this regard, history came to serve in Marxism the same authoritative function that nature had for the Jacobins.

In the absence of explicit political models for the future, there is a tendency to fall back on familiar alternatives, and Marx was no exception.

28. Quoted by Melvin J. Lasky, *Utopia and Revolution* (Chicago: University of Chicago Press, 1976), 50. Marx and Engels famously gave only a single description of life after the Revolution, which "makes it possible for me to do one thing today and another tomorrow, to hunt in the morning, fish in the afternoon, rear cattle in the evening, criticise after dinner, just as I have a mind, without ever becoming hunter, fisherman, shepherd, or critic," *The German Ideology*, trans. and ed. C. J. Arthur (New York: International, 1970), 53; this passage is discussed in Lasky, *Utopia and Revolution*, 39; see also Robert C. Tucker, *Philosophy and Myth in Karl Marx* (New Brunswick: Transaction, 2001), 197.

29. See Sorel, *Introduction à l'économie moderne* (1902; Paris: Rivière, 1922), 394–97; *La décomposition du marxisme* (Paris: Rivière, 1908), 54–55; and *Reflections on Violence*, ed. Jeremy Jennings (Cambridge: Cambridge University Press, 1999), 20ff.

Although he warned, in 1844, against "go[ing] back to a fictitious primordial condition as the political economist does," claiming that "[s]uch a primordial condition explains nothing [and] merely pushes the question away into a gray nebulous distance,"[30] he later acknowledged the perennial attraction of the golden age myth:

> A man cannot become a child again, or he becomes childish. But does he not find joy in the child's naiveté, and must he himself not strive to reproduce its truth at a higher stage? . . . Why should not the historic childhood of humanity, its most beautiful unfolding, as a stage never to return, exercise an eternal charm?[31]

The existence of an original, communistic golden age grew increasingly important in Engels' later work. In his notes on the communist *Manifesto*, and then more extensively in *The Origin of Family, Private Property, and the State*, Engels insisted that "village communities were found to be, or to have been the primitive form of society everywhere from India to Ireland."[32] A corollary of this renewed emphasis on "primordial conditions" was the fact that revolution in unindustrialized Russia no longer seemed unthinkable. In their preface to the 1882 Russian edition of the *Manifesto*, Marx and Engels even suggested that "the present Russian common ownership of land [by village communities] may serve as the starting-point for a communist development."[33]

This declaration, of course, was triggered by the remarkable amount of revolutionary activity disrupting Russian politics onward from the assassination of Alexander II in 1881. These terrorist and revolutionary movements often modeled themselves on another familiar precedent, the French Revolution, although not always in the most expected manner. The Socialist-Revolutionary Maria Spiridonova, for instance, who shot the general responsible for repressing a 1905 peasant rebellion in the face, fashioned herself after Charlotte Corday.[34] Concerning any direct political continuities between 1793 and 1917, Martin Malia has argued that the Russian revolu-

---

30. *Economic and Philosophic Manuscripts* (1844), in *The Marx-Engels Reader*, ed. Robert C. Tucker (New York: Norton, 1978), 71.

31. *Grundrisse*, or *Foundations of the Critique of Political Economy* (1857–58), in *Marx-Engels Reader*, 246.

32. Note from 1888 to the *Manifesto of the Communist Party*, in *Marx-Engels Reader*, 473n6. As in *The Origin of Family*, Engels is drawing here on the anthropological works of Lewis Morgan.

33. *Manifesto of the Communist Party*, 472.

34. See Lynn Patyk, *Written in Blood: Revolutionary Terrorism and Russian Literary Culture* (forthcoming). I thank the author for letting me read a draft of her manuscript.

tionaries ultimately rejected the "Western model" of a popular revolution, choosing instead a model in which "the enlightened elite, the bearer of revolutionary 'consciousness,' would bring the idea of socialism to the 'dark' people."[35] And yet, as we saw in chapter 4, the Jacobins themselves were wary of popular rule and portrayed themselves as the privileged interpreters of a natural order. The Marxist laws of history may have replaced the Jacobin laws of nature, yet in both cases revolutionary authority stemmed not from a voluntaristic but from a "rational" source.

In the aftermath of October 1917, it sometimes seemed as though the Bolsheviks were reenacting scenes straight from *l'an I*. As Stephen F. Cohen observed, "Bolsheviks advertised themselves as proletarian Jacobins; a Socialist Revolutionary wondered: 'Who are we but Russian Girondists?' "[36] More pointedly, this unavoidable parallel had direct institutional effects, particularly in the sphere of justice. Almost immediately after seizing power, the Soviets created "people's courts," a practice that Lenin made official on November 22, 1917.[37] Two days later, however, the Bolsheviks also created "revolutionary tribunals," for trying individuals suspected of being "enemies of the people," or for condemning those already outlawed by governmental decree.[38] As one of its official defenders explained, its goal was not to punish "political crimes," but rather to "struggle against counter-revolutionary forces."[39] Again, the parallel with the French Revolution was explicit: Arno

35. Malia, *History's Locomotives: Revolutions and the Making of the Modern World* (New Haven: Yale University Press, 2006), 259; see also Dmitry Shlapentokh, *The French Revolution in Russian Intellectual Life, 1865–1905* (Westport: Praeger, 1996), who defines this elitist model as "Jacobin."

36. Cohen, *Bukharin and the Bolshevik Revolution: A Political Biography, 1888–1938* (New York: Oxford University Press, 1980), 131. See also Arno Mayer: "Sensitized by the Jacobin experience, the Bolshevik leaders were predisposed to . . . terror, considering it immanent to revolutionary practice," *The Furies: Violence and Terror in the French and Russian Revolutions* (Princeton: Princeton University Press, 2000), 252. These reflections on the early Russian Revolution benefited greatly from conversations with Grisha Friedin, Norman Naimark, Lynn Patyk, Dina Moyal, and Simon Ertz.

37. See the "Decree No. 1, On the Courts." As Mary McAuley describes, "[shortly] after the October seizure of power, the district soviet [of Vyborg] decided to create a 'temporary people's court' composed of five judges," *Bread and Justice: State and Society in Petrograd, 1917–1922* (Oxford: Clarendon Press, 1991), 118.

38. See William A. Clark, *Crime and Punishment in Soviet Officialdom: Combating Corruption in the Political Elite, 1965–1990* (New York: M. E. Sharpe, 1993), 12. Mayer recounts how on November 28, "a decree of the Council of People's Commissars, signed by Lenin, outlawed the Kadet party. Designated 'enemies of the people,' its members became 'liable to arrest and trial by the Revolutionary Tribunal,' " *The Furies*, 253.

39. Peter Stuchka (soon to become the People's Commissar for Justice), "The Old and New Court," an article published by *Pravda* in January 1918; reproduced in William G. Rosenberg,

Mayer even notes how Lenin "expressed his confidence that the revolution would find a 'Fouquier-Tinville . . . of staunch proletarian Jacobin' temperament qualified 'to tame the encroaching counterrevolution.' "[40] The revolutionary tribunal worked closely with the Cheka, the Soviet secret police, and yet was regarded as "an integral part of the legal system."[41] Despite the commonplace practice of summary execution by the Cheka, the Soviets ultimately found it more beneficial to have "counterrevolutionaries" and "saboteurs" dispatched by the law, in following with Lenin's emphasis on "revolutionary legality."[42] This practice would become only more exacerbated with the prevalent use of military tribunals to try political cases under Stalin.[43] From the very onset, and in clear imitation of the Jacobins, therefore, the Soviets instituted a dual justice system, one in which the jurisdiction of the "political" tribunals slowly encroached on, and ultimately absorbed, that of criminal justice.

Interestingly, a very similar story can be told with respect to Nazi Germany. One of the earliest Nazi decrees, following Hitler's election to the Chancellery, established a *Volksgerichtshof*, or "People's Court," to try treason cases.[44] This tribunal proved ruthlessly efficient in eliminating political dissidents: roughly 3,000 political suspects were sent before it between 1934 and 1939; most of them were given long prison terms.[45] Although its activity trailed off somewhat in the late 1930s (mostly because of its prior successes), the court became a violently repressive institution under the presidency of Roland Freisler. In 1943 alone, 5,336 defendants received the

ed., *Bolshevik Visions: First Phase of the Cultural Revolution in Soviet Russia* (Ann Arbor: University of Michigan Press, 1990), 188.

40. *The Furies*, 256.

41. See E. H. Carr, "The Origin and Status of the Cheka," *Soviet Studies* 10, no. 1 (1958): 1–11, 5 for quote.

42. See Peter H. Solomon, *Soviet Criminal Justice under Stalin* (Cambridge: Cambridge University Press, 1996), 19.

43. Ibid., 264.

44. This decree was enacted on April 24, 1934; see William Sweet "The Volksgerichtshof: 1934–45," *Journal of Modern History* 46, no. 2 (1974): 314–29; see also Nikolaus Wachsmann, *Hitler's Prisons: Legal Terror in Nazi Germany* (New Haven: Yale University Press, 2004), 117–18; H. W. Koch, *In the Name of the Volk: Political Justice in Hitler's Germany* (New York: St. Martin's Press, 1989); and Alf Lüdtke and Herbert Reinke, "Crime, Police, and the 'Good Order': Germany," in *Crime History and Histories of Crime*, ed. Clive Emsley and Louis A. Knafla (Westport: Greenwood Press, 1996), 123–34. The authoritative German account of the People's Court is Lothar Gruchmann, *Justiz im Dritten Reich, 1933–1940: Anpassung und Unterwerfung in der Ära Gürtner* (Munich: Oldenbourg, 1988).

45. Wachsmann, *Hitler's Prisons*, 117.

death penalty.[46] This sudden acceleration followed Hitler's own devastating criticism of the judiciary at the Reichstag, on April 24, 1942, when he had urged all tribunals to "pass more brutal and less formal sentences"[47]—an imperative reminiscent of the objectives laid out in the 22 prairial decree.

As in the Soviet Union, Nazi political repression thus relied on what Nickolaus Wachsmann has termed "legal terror." Despite the infamous suspension of rights by the so-called "Reichstag Fire Decree" (or *Verordnung des Reichspräsidenten zum Schutz von Volk und Staat*) of February 28, 1933, Nazi Germany did not exist in a purely "anomic" state, as Giorgio Agamben has argued.[48] If the Gestapo and other police bodies could and often did operate beyond the law, the Nazis also found it necessary (and expedient) to institute a parallel legal system, one in which "justice" could be meted out more swiftly and brutally. It was not the absence of the law, but the laws themselves that abetted Nazi terror.

The Soviet and Nazi examples thus point to a pattern of "totalitarian justice" that can be detected in countless other revolutionary processes, and whose basic structure can be traced back to the French Terror, even if it later underwent developments that modified it significantly. This pattern involves the coexistence of two parallel justice systems, one reserved for "ordinary" crimes, the other for political or "counterrevolutionary" ones; these systems are moreover in a state of permanent tension and competition with one another. Over time, the scope of the political justice system tends to expand exponentially, to the point at which any crime can be tried as a crime against the state.[49] While this gross expansion does not necessarily lead to the total demise of the ordinary criminal justice, it does usually undermine, if not eliminate, the legal principles of due process, double jeopardy, the gradation of punishments, trial by jury, and impartial judges.[50] At this point, it may be

---

46. Sweet, "The Volksgerichtshof," 325.

47. Wachsmann, *Hitler's Prisons*, 118, 315, and 214.

48. *State of Exception*, trans. Kevin Attell (Chicago: University of Chicago Press, 2005), 2.

49. In the Nazi case, this *terminus ad quem* was already present in the mind of the jurist responsible for the Volksgerichtshof's general abandonment of legal principles after 1940, Roland Freisler: as Sweet notes, Freisler proposed in 1935 "that every crime should be considered a gradation of 'Volksverrat' (treason against the people)," "The Volksgerichtshof," 316.

50. This description draws on Ernst Fraenkel's account of how in Nazi Germany the "Prerogative State" gradually imposed itself on a "Normative state"; see *The Dual State: A Contribution to the Theory of Dictatorship*, trans. E. A. Shils et al. (New York: Oxford University Press, 1941). As Fraenkel's own understanding of prerogative is indebted to Schmitt's theory of the exception, he tends to deny the existence of any legality in the prosecution of political "crimes" (see, e.g., 50–56). But as William Sweet has observed, "the Volksgericht was an entirely constitutional creation," staffed by "professional jurists," that passed judgment on the basis of pre-Nazi treason laws; the justice minister at the time, Franz Gürtner, even "thought that the

that the rule of law crumbles altogether, as arguably occurred in the German and Russian cases, although never entirely in revolutionary France (witness the nonnegligible level of acquittals even at the height of the "Great Terror"). That said, even when the lawfulness of the political justice system was little more than window-dressing on a kangaroo court, as in Stalin's "Moscow trials," it is noteworthy that in most instances there was in fact some legal foundation for the proceedings, though it might be as wobbly as the law of 22 prairial, article 58 of the Soviet Russian penal code, or paragraph 83 of the German treason law. It was precisely this attention to legality that Hannah Arendt famously identified as one of the hallmarks of "totalitarian lawfulness":

> Far from being "lawless," [totalitarianism] goes to the sources of authority from which positive laws received their ultimate legitimation. . . . [I]t is quite prepared to sacrifice everybody's vital immediate interests to the execution of what it assumes to be the law of History or the law of Nature. Its defiance of positive laws claims to be a higher form of legitimacy. . . . Totalitarian lawfulness pretends to have found a way to establish the rule of justice on earth—something which the legality of positive law could never attain.[51]

Here again the double-edge sword of natural republicanism (or any form of natural politics) is on display: Revolutionaries justify their recourse to draconian laws in the name of a mythical ideal, "the rule of justice on earth." This appeal to "a higher form of justice" may be heartfelt and genuine; neither the Jacobins nor their latter-day anarchist or Soviet emulators were necessarily cynical manipulators of legal rhetoric and logic. As we have seen, myths of a golden age held a powerful sway over *fin-de-siècle* terrorists, as they did over the Montagnards. Dostoyevsky captured the enchantment of such myths in *The Adolescent*, where a dream about "the golden age" kindles socialist passions in a Russian nobleman.[52] Such conversions did not occur

---

Volksgericht's basic mission was to restore unqualified respect to the law." It is only after February 1940, Sweet argues, that the court adopted "prejudicial, inquisitorial legal procedures." See "The Volksgerichtshof," 315–16. Fraenkel's thesis is discussed in Wachsmann, *Hitler's Prisons*, 379–83.

51. Arendt, *The Origins of Totalitariansim* (New York: Harvest, 1968), 461–62.

52. Fyodor Dostoevsky, *The Adolescent* (1875), trans. Richard Pevear and Larissa Volokhonsky (New York: Knopf, 2003), 466–67; on the author's repeated use of this myth (and dream sequence), see Richard Peace, "Dostoyevsky and 'The Golden Age,'" *Dostoyevsky Studies* 3 (1982): 61–78. I discuss this work and topic more generally in "The Birth of Ideology from the Spirit of Myth: Georges Sorel among the *Idéologues*," in *The Re-enchantement of the World: Secular Magic*

only in fiction; the historian G. D. H. Cole has described how he became a socialist upon reading William Morris's *News from Nowhere,* a dream narrative about an arts-and-crafts golden age.[53] Even the Nazis were besotted with mythical fantasies about a "Hyperborean Atlantis," a golden age of technological sophistication, which had once existed in the Arctic Circle.[54] It was not exceptional that Robespierre should announce a coming golden age, two days before sponsoring the law of 22 prairial: It was the beginning of a tradition.

Two Concepts of Exceptionality

In light of this pattern of "totalitarian lawfulness," it may be viewed with alarm that the Bush administration took to describing terrorists in Iraq and elsewhere as "enemies of humanity."[55] A number of officials and scholars even explicitly invoked the early-modern concept of the *hostis humani generis* to argue that the extreme hostility of terrorists should de facto deprive them of certain rights.[56] This category is not entirely foreign to American jurisprudence: A 1980 U.S. court of appeals ruling determined that "for the purposes of civil liability, the torturer has become—like the pirate and the slave trader before him—*hostis humani generis,* an enemy of all mankind."[57] In this context, however, the *hostis* category was used only to establish

---

in a Rational Age, ed. Joshua Landy and Michael Saler (Stanford: Stanford University Press, 2009).

53. "I became a socialist more than fifty years ago when I read *News from Nowhere* as a schoolboy and realised quite suddenly that William Morris had shown me the vision of a society in which it would be a fine and fortunate experience to live," *William Morris as a Socialist* (London: William Morris Society, 1960), 1. Similarly, one of E. P. Thompson's first books was a study of Morris, *William Morris, Romantic to Revolutionary* (London: Lawrence and Wishart, 1955); my thanks to David Bell for pointing out this parallel.

54. See my "Hyperborean Atlantis: Jean-Sylvain Bailly, Madame Blavatsky, and the Nazi Myth," *Studies in Eighteenth-Century Culture* 35 (2006): 267–91.

55. Eleven instances could be found searching the archives at http://www.whitehouse.gov. A typical line by George W. Bush reads: "These militants are not just the enemies of America or the enemies of Iraq, they are the enemies of Islam and they are the enemies of humanity" (October 28, 2005).

56. See notably Douglas R. Burgess Jr.'s widely discussed article, "The Dread Pirate Bin Laden" in *Legal Affairs* (July–August 2005), http://www.legalaffairs.org/issues/July-August-2005/feature_burgess_julaug05.msp; and Joseph McMillan, "Apocalyptic Terrorism: The Case for Preventive Action," *Strategic Forum* 212 (2004), http://www.ndu.edu/inss/strforum/SF212/SF212_Final.pdf. For a critique of the analogy between pirates and terrorists, see Paul A. Silverstein, "The New Barbarians: Piracy and Terrorism on the North African Frontier," *CR: The New Centennial Review* 5, no. 1 (2005): 179–212.

57. *Filartiga v. Pena-Irala,* 630 F.2d, 876, 890 (2d Cir. 1980). Slave trading had already been identified with piracy in the 1926 League of Nations Slavery Convention.

jurisdiction for crimes against humanity committed in foreign countries (in accordance with the Alien Tort Claims Act of 1789). Applying this designation in order to deprive suspected terrorists of rights guaranteed by the Geneva Conventions would thus constitute a radical departure from legal precedent, one that, moreover, uncannily recalls the French revolutionary use of the concept during the Terror.

Faint as it may be, this parallel is deepened by a number of other similarities that make the narrative of the first French Republic read like a cautionary tale for today's "global war on terror." The Department of Homeland Security is certainly no *comité de salut public*, despite their odd synonymy, but the Bush administration's view of democracy as the "natural" form of government does bear considerable resemblance to the Jacobin faith in natural republicanism. As Francis Fukuyama remarked, "The [Iraq] war's supporters seemed to think that democracy was a kind of default condition to which societies reverted once the heavy lifting of coercive regime change occurred, rather than a long-term process of institution-building and reform."[58] In this regard, the Jacobin political leaders had slightly more foresight, as they recognized that the foundation of the French Republic was precisely a "long-term process," even if they, too, regarded democracy as a "default condition," or natural state of human affairs. The similarities between the Bush administration's "democratic globalism" and the Jacobin (and later Marxist) theory of world revolution were bizarrely underscored by the president himself: In his second inaugural address, Bush quoted a passage from Dostoyevsky (probably via James Billington's book of the same title) to describe how American democratizing efforts had lit a "fire in the minds of men"—a line which, in *The Possessed*, refers to a nihilistic revolutionary cause.[59]

---

58. Fukuyama, "After Neoconservatism," *New York Times Magazine*, February 19, 2006. This view of democracy has been described by neoconservative scholars themselves as "neonatural right": James W. Ceaser and Daniel DiSalvo, "A New GOP?" *Public Interest* 157 (2004): 3–17. See also John Yoo, *The Powers of War and Peace: The Constitution and Foreign Affairs after 9/11* (Chicago: University of Chicago Press, 2005), 34–36. Although Leo Strauss's influence on the Bush administration has no doubt been overstated, it bears mentioning that his famous study on *Natural Right and History*, cited by Ceaser and DiSalvo, made natural right theory an object of considerable interest and respect in (neo)conservative circles.

59. Bush's speech read, "By our efforts, we have lit a fire as well—a fire in the minds of men. It warms those who feel its power, it burns those who fight its progress, and one day this untamed fire of freedom will reach the darkest corners of our world"; available at http://www.whitehouse.gov/inaugural/index.html. A number of commentators noted the surprising origin of this phrase. The expression "democratic globalism" is from Charles Krauthammer, "The Neoconservative Convergence," *Commentary* 120 (July 2005): 21–26. David A. Bell commented on the parallel between Jacobin republicanism and neoconservatism in *H-France Reviews* 5, no. 93 (2005), http://www.h-france.net/vol5reviews/bell4.html.

The reemergence of the *hostis humani generis* as a criminal category depriving suspects of legal rights raises a final question about legislating terror. Does branding suspected terrorists "enemies of humanity," or, in the current legalese, "alien unlawful enemy combatants," mark them out as *exceptions* to a norm, or does it create a new norm entirely? This distinction may seem trivial, but given the lasting power of "exceptional" criminal categories, it can have real jurisprudential consequences. At the heart of this question, ultimately, lies a confusion about the nature and meaning of exceptionality. According to Carl Schmitt, to declare an exception, along with being the fundamental act of sovereignty, means to suspend the rule of law in its entirety and to replace constitutional order with a "state of exception."[60] This theory of exceptionality is perpetuated by scholars writing in a Schmittian vein, such as Agamben, who has argued that places like Guantánamo prison exist in an "anomic" space beyond the law.[61] But this characterization overlooks the complex assemblage of legislation that the Bush administration, as well as Congress, have crafted to address these "alien unlawful enemy combatants."[62] This legislation may be faulty, contrary to international conventions, and a violation of traditional standards, yet like it or not, it is the law of the land and will most likely remain on the books and as a legal precedent for the foreseeable future.[63] In the long run, new laws can do more damage than the temporary suspension of laws.

---

60. Schmitt, *Political Theology: Four Essays on the Concept of Sovereignty*, trans. George Schwab (Chicago: University of Chicago Press, 2005).

61. Agamben, *State of Exception*, chap. 1; see also *Homo Sacer: Sovereign Power and Bare Life*, trans. Daniel Heller-Roazen (Stanford: Stanford University Press, 1998).

62. See in particular the Military Commissions Act of 2006, section 7 of which the Supreme Court struck down as unconstitutional on June 12, 2008. In a debate in March 2007 with Neal Katyal on the *NewsHour with Jim Lehrer*, John Yoo made this precise point: Katyal argued that Guantánamo was a "legal black hole," whereas Yoo countered that "American laws do apply," just not constitutional (or international) ones. Before October 2006, he claimed, the prisoners were held under "the laws of war," and after that date, the Military Commissions Act introduced a version of martial law. Transcript available at http://www.pbs.org/newshour/bb/military/jan-june07/guantanamo_03-26.html.

63. This remains the case with the Alien Enemy Act, passed in 1798 during John Adams's presidency. Widely viewed as unconstitutional and deeply flawed, this act was used to round up German males in 1917; to intern Japanese nationals on U.S. soil during World War II; and, most recently, to argue for limiting the judicial rights of "alien enemy combatants." See Robert P. Griffin, "Constitutional Law: Due Process: Right of Alien Enemy to Judicial Review of Deportation Proceeding," *Michigan Law Review* 47 (1949): 404–6. For the Japanese internment, see Peter Irons, *Justice at War: The Story of the Japanese American Internment Cases*, rev. ed. (Seattle: University of Washington Press, 1996); Greg Robinson, *By Order of the President: FDR and the Internment of Japanese Americans* (Cambridge: Harvard University Press, 2001). For the "global war on terror," see Justice Antonin Scalia's dissent to *Hamdi v. Rumsfeld*, 542 U.S. 507 (2004), at footnote 5.

Given that legislation passed in emergency or rushed situations is almost certain to present serious flaws, it is worth considering how the temporary *suspension* of certain existing laws might constitute a lesser constitutional—and possibly also human—evil. Indeed, "declaring the exception" need not be a blanket measure, rescinding the entire rule of law, or substituting a different legal code to civil legislation (natural right for the Jacobins; military law for the Bush administration). The U.S. Constitution, as is well known, offers an example of a targeted, limited form of exceptionality: Article 1, section 9, provides that the writ of habeas corpus may be suspended "in Cases of Rebellion or Invasion [when] the public Safety may require it." During the Civil War, Lincoln notoriously invoked this "Suspension Clause" (even though it is a congressional, not a presidential, prerogative). His decision has not been judged kindly by historians or legal scholars: It was predominantly motivated to facilitate conscription and was accompanied, moreover, by the establishment of military commissions that were granted powers to court-martial and execute civilians.[64] In 1866, the Supreme Court ruled that the suspension of habeas corpus was constitutional (it had since been ratified by Congress), but that these military commissions should not have had jurisdiction over civilian cases, so long as civilian courts were in operation.[65] In other words, the Court distinguished between two kinds of exceptionality: the suspension of a given law (the writ of habeas corpus), which allowed the government to hold suspects without trial; and the substitution of one kind of law for another (martial law for civil legislation). The majority opinion of the Court, penned by Justice David Davis, was particularly critical of this latter form of exceptional justice: "Civil liberty and this kind of martial law cannot endure together; the antagonism is irreconcilable; and, in the conflict, one or the other must perish."[66]

While it may be preferable to the establishment of military commissions, suspending the writ of habeas corpus, one of the most sacrosanct principles of common law, is obviously not a welcome or desirable course of action. Ideally, no laws or rights would need to be suspended, even in emergency situations. But as Bruce Ackerman has recently argued, there is a great likelihood that under such circumstances political pressure will force lawmakers to enact harsher legislation (the Patriot Act of 2001 being a prime example).[67]

---

64. The authoritative account of this episode is Mark Neely, *The Fate of Liberty: Abraham Lincoln and Civil Liberties* (Oxford: Oxford University Press, 1991).

65. *Ex parte Milligan*, 71 U.S. 2 (1866).

66. *Ex parte Milligan*, 71 U.S. at 124–25.

67. Ackerman, *Before the Next Attack: Preserving Civil Liberties in an Age of Terrorism* (New Haven: Yale University Press, 2007).

The best defense of civil liberty may thus be the engineering of "escape valves," on the model of the Suspension Clause, which can ensure that the fabric of constitutional law and jurisprudence does not get ripped apart. Exceptions that are limited in scope and time can guard against the creation of a dangerous, parallel sphere of legality, which, like Lincoln's or the French National Convention's military commissions, run the risk of replacing civil law altogether. Finally, such targeted exceptions can also prevent actions taken in dark times from acquiring the respectability of rightful law. Hardly a defender of civil liberties, Machiavelli nonetheless underscored an essential psychological point about emergency measures when he argued that certain actions, simply by virtue of being necessary, are no less immoral.[68] Precisely because it conveys authority and a sense of impunity, legislation that creates new categories of hostility only encourages abuses and the travesty of justice. On this point, Robespierre was right: It is much more dangerous to wage war with the law, not the sword, in hand.

---

68. See, for instance, *The Prince*, ed. Quentin Skinner (Cambridge: Cambridge University Press, 1998), chap. 8 (with respect to Agathocles).

Primary Sources

Aquinas, Thomas. *Summa Theologiæ*. Volume 4 of 61. Edited by Thomas Gornall. Cambridge: Cambridge University Press, 2006.

Archives parlementaires de 1787 à 1860. 127 vols. Edited by M. J. Mavidal et al. Paris: Librairie administrative de P. Dupont, 1862–. [abbr. *AP*]

Aristotle. *The Politics*. Translated by T. A. Sinclair and Trevor J. Saunders. Harmondsworth: Penguin, 1981.

———. *The Art of Rhetoric*. Translated by H. C. Lawson-Tancred. London: Penguin, 1991.

Aulard, Alphonse, ed. *La société des Jacobins: recueil de documents pour l'histoire du club des Jacobins de Paris*. 6 vols. Paris: Librairie Jouaust, 1889–97.

———. *Recueil des actes du Comité de salut public, avec la correspondance officielle des représentants en mission et le registre du conseil exécutif provisoire*. 29 vols. Paris: Imprimerie nationale, 1889–1951.

Bacon, Francis. *The Works of Francis Bacon*. 10 vols. London: Baynes, 1824.

Bailly, Jean-Sylvain. *Histoire de l'astronomie ancienne, depuis son origine jusqu'à l'établissement de l'école d'Alexandrie*. Paris: De Bure, 1775.

———. *Lettres sur l'origine des sciences et sur celle des peuples d'Asie. Adressées à M. de Voltaire par M. Bailly & précédées de quelques lettres de M. de Voltaire à l'Auteur*. Paris: Debure, 1777.

Baker, Keith, ed. *The Old Regime and the French Revolution*. Chicago: University of Chicago Press, 1987.

Balzac, Jean-Louis Guez de. *Le Prince*. Paris: Du Bray, 1631. [ARTFL]

Barbeyrac, Jean, trans. and ed. *Le droit de la guerre et de la paix*. By Hugo Grotius. Amsterdam : P. de Coup, 1724.

———. *Traité philosophique des loix naturelles*. By Richard Cumberland. Amsterdam: n.p., 1744.

Barère de Vieuzac, Bertrand. *Rapport sur les moyens d'extirper la mendicité dans les campagnes, et sur les secours que doit accorder la République aux citoyens indigens*. Paris: Imprimerie Nationale, an II [1794].

Barthélemy, Jean-Jacques. *Voyage du jeune Anacharsis en Grèce*. 1788. 8 vols. Paris: n.p., 1856.

Bayle, Pierre. *Pensées diverses sur la comète.* 1683. 2 vols. Edited by A. Prat. Paris: Droz, 1939.

Beaumarchais, Pierre Augustin Caron de. *Mémoires contre M. Goëzman.* In *Œuvres complètes.* Paris: Burne, 1828. [ARTFL]

Bentham, Jeremy. *Panoptique, mémoire sur un nouveau principe pour construire des maisons d'inspection, et nommément des maisons de forces.* Translated by Jean-Philippe Garran-Coulon. Paris: Imprimerie Nationale, 1791.

Billaud-Varenne, Jacques-Nicolas. *Les éléments du républicanisme.* Paris: n.p., 1793.

———. *Principes régénérateurs du système social.* 1795. Edited by Françoise Brunel. Paris: Publications de la Sorbonne, 1992.

Blackstone, William. *Commentaries on the Laws of England.* Oxford: Clarendon Press, 1765–68.

———. *Commentaire sur le code criminel d'Angleterre . . .* 2 vols. Translated by Gabriel-François Coyer. Paris: Knapen, 1776.

Bodin, Jean. *Les six livres de la république.* 1576. Paris: Fayard, 1986.

———. *On Sovereignty.* Translated by Julian H. Franklin. Cambridge: Cambridge University Press, 1992.

Bolingbroke, Henry St. John. *Political Writings.* Edited by David Armitage. Cambridge: Cambridge University Press, 1997.

Bonneville, Nicolas de. *De l'esprit des religions.* Paris: Cercle Social, 1792.

Bougainville, Louis Antoine de. *Voyage autour du monde par la frégate du roi "la Boudeuse" et la flûte "l'Étoile" en 1766, 1767, 1768 et 1769.* Paris: Saillant & Nyon, 1771.

———. *Voyage autour du monde.* Edited by Michel Bideaux and Sonia Faessel. Paris: Presses de l'Université de Paris-Sorbonne, 2001.

Buffon, Georges-Louis Leclerc de. *Des époques de la nature.* Paris: Imprimerie Royale, 1778.

Buonarotti, Philippe. *Conspiration pour l'égalité, dite de Babeuf, suivie du procès auquel elle donna lieu, et des pièces justicatives, etc., etc.* 2 vols. Brussels: Libraire Romantique, 1828.

Burke, Edmund. *Reflections on the Revolution in France.* Edited by L. G. Mitchell. Oxford: Oxford University Press, 1993.

Burlamaqui, Jean-Jacques. *Principes du droit naturel.* Geneva: Barrillot, 1747.

———. *Principes du droit politique.* Amsterdam: Zacharie Chatelain, 1751.

Cabinet of Curiosities. . . . to Be Continued. London: n.p., 1795. [ECCO]

Campan, Jeanne-Louise-Henriette. *Mémoires de Madame Campan, première femme de chambre de Marie-Antoinette.* Paris: Mercure, 1988.

Cicero. *On Duties.* Edited by Miriam Tamara Griffin and E. Margaret Atkins. Cambridge: Cambridge University Press, 1991.

———. *On the Commonwealth and On the Laws.* Edited and translated by James E. G. Zetzel. Cambridge: Cambridge University Press, 1999.

Chaussard, Publicola. *Dithyrambe sur la fête républicaine du 10 aoust.* N.p., n.d. [1793]

Chemin-Dupontès, Jean-Baptiste. *Morality of the Sans-Culottes of Every Age, Sex, Country, and Condition; or, The Republican Gospel*. Philadelphia: n.p., 1794. Translation of *Morale des sans-culottes . . .* Paris: n.p., 1793.

Choderlos de Laclos, Pierre. *Liaisons dangereuses*. Paris: Gallimard, 2003.

Clerc, Nicolas Gabriel. *Yu le Grand et Confucius, histoire chinoise*. Soissons: Ponce Courtois, 1769.

Coke, Edward. *The Selected Writings and Speeches of Sir Edward Coke*. Edited by Steve Sheppard. Indianapolis: Liberty Fund, 2003.

Constant, Benjamin. *The Political Writings of Benjamin Constant*. Translated by Biancamaria Fontana. Cambridge: Cambridge University Press, 1988.

Corneille, Pierre. *Œuvres complètes*. Edited by Georges Couthon. Paris: Gallimard/Pléiade, 1980.

Correspondance Politique de l'Europe: Ouvrage Périodique par une Société de Gens de Lettres. Vol 3. Brussels: n.p., 1780.

Court de Gébelin, Antoine. *Monde primitif considéré dans son génie allégorique et dans les allégories auxquelles conduisit ce génie . . .* 9 vols. Paris, 1773–81.

Cumberland, Richard. *De legibus naturæ disquisitio philosophica . . .* London: Flesher, 1672.

Darwin, Erasmus [falsely attributed]. *The Golden Age: The Temple of Nature, or the Origin of Society*. Edited by Donald Reiman. New York: Garland, 1978.

David, Jacques-Louis. *Ordre et marche de la fête de l'unité et de l'indivisibilité de la République*. Paris: Firmin Gourdin, 1793.

———. *Ordre, marche et cérémonies de la fête de l'Etre Suprême, qui doit être célébrée le 20 prairial, d'après le plan proposé par David . . .* [Paris]: Lerouge & Berthelot, n.d. [1794]

Delormel, Jean. *La grande période ou le retour de l'âge d'or*. Paris: Blanchon, 1790.

Demoulins, Camille. *Le Vieux Cordelier*. Edited by M. Mallon. Paris: Ébrard, 1834.

Destutt de Tracy, Antoine-Louis-Claude. *Eléments d'idéologie. I, Idéologie*. Paris: Vve Courcier, 1804.

———. *Mémoire sur la faculté de penser . . .* Edited by Anne and Henry Deneys. Paris: Fayard, 1992.

Diderot, Denis. *Réfutation suivie de l'ouvrage d'Helvétius intitulé "L'Homme."* Vol. 2 of *Œuvres Complètes*. 20 vols. Edited by M. Assézat. Paris: Garnier, 1875. [ARTFL]

———. *Salon de 1767*. Edited by J. Seznec and J. Adhemar. Oxford: Clarendon Press, 1963. [ARTFL]

———. *Political Writings*. Translated and edited by John Hope Mason and Robert Wokler. New York: Cambridge University Press, 1992.

———. *Supplément au voyage de Bougainville*. Paris: Gallimard, 2002.

Diderot, Denis, and Jean-le-Rond d'Alembert, eds. *Encyclopédie, ou Dictionnaire raisonné des sciences, des arts et des métiers*. Paris: Briasson, David, Le Breton, 1751–72. [ARTFL]

Dollier de Casson, François. *History of Montreal, 1640–1672*. Translated and edited by Ralph Flenley. London: J. M. Dent and Sons, 1928.

Dostoevsky, Fyodor. *The Adolescent.* 1875. Translated by Richard Pevear and Larissa Volokhonsky. New York: Knopf, 2003.

Dupuis, Charles-François. *Lettre sur le Dieu Soleil, adressée à MM. Les Auteurs du Journal des Sçavans; par M. Dupuis, Professeur de Rhétorique, Avocat en Parlement, de l'Académie de Rouen.* N.p., n.d. [1780?]

——. *Mémoire sur l'origine des constellations, et sur l'explication de la fable, par le moyen de l'astronomie . . .* Paris: Desaint, 1781.

Fénelon, François de Salignac de la Mothe. *Telemachus, Son of Ulysses.* Translated and edited by Patrick Riley. Cambridge: Cambridge University Press, 1994.

Florian, Jean-Pierre Claris de. *Numa Pompilius.* Paris: Didot Aîné, 1786. [ARTFL]

Fontenelle, Bernard le Bovier de. *De l'origine des fables.* 1724. Edited by J.-R. Carré. Paris: Libraire Félix Alcan, 1932.

Fouquier-Tinville, Antoine-Quentin. *Réquisitoires de Fouquier-Tinville.* Edited by Hector Fleischmann. Paris: Fasquelle, 1911.

Galiani, Ferdinando. *Dialogues sur le commerce des bleds.* London, 1770.

Gentili, Alberico. *De Jure Belli Libri Tres.* 1621. Edited by Thomas Erskine Holland. Oxford: Clarendon, 1877.

——. *De Jure Belli Libri Tres.* Translated by John C. Rolfe. New York: Oceana, 1964.

Godwin, William. *An Enquiry Concerning Political Justice.* 2 vols. Dublin: n.p., 1793.

Gouges, Olympe de. *Le bonheur primitif de l'homme, ou les rêveries patriotiques.* Amsterdam: n.p., 1789.

Graffigny, Françoise de. *Lettres d'une péruvienne.* 1747. Edited by Jonathan Mallinson. Oxford: Voltaire Foundation, 2002.

Graswinckel, Theodor. *Maris liberi vindiciæ: Adversus Petrum baptistam burgum ligustici maritimi dominii assertorem.* The Hague: n.p., 1652.

Grimm, Friedrich Melchior von, Denis Diderot, François Raynal *et al. Correspondance litteraire, philosophique et critique . . .* 1877. Edited by Maurice Tourneux. 16 vols. Nendeln: Kraus, 1968.

Grotius, Hugo. *The Rights of War and Peace.* 1625. Edited by Richard Tuck. 3 vols. Indianapolis: Liberty Fund, 2005.

Hamilton, Alexander, James Madison, and John Jay. *The Federalist Papers.* Edited by Isaac Kramnick. London: Penguin, 1987.

Hébert, Jacques-René. *Le Père Duchesne, 1790–94.* 9 vols. Paris: EDHIS, 1969.

Helvétius, Claude Adrien. *De l'homme, de ses facultés intellectuelles et de son éducation.* 2 vols. London: Société typographique, 1773. [ARTFL]

Hesiod. *The Works and Days.* Translated by Richard Lattimore. Ann Arbor: University of Michigan Press, 1970.

Histoire parlementaire de la Révolution française, ou Journal des assemblées nationales depuis 1789 jusqu'en 1815. 40 vols. Edited by P. J. B. Buchez and P. C. Roux. Paris: Paulin, 1834–38. [abbr. *HP*]

Hobbes, Thomas. *Leviathan.* Edited by C. B. Macpherson. London: Penguin, 1985.

d'Holbach, Paul-Henri-Thiry. *Hymne au soleil.* 1769. In *Variétés littéraires.* Paris: Xerouet, 1804.

———. *La politique naturelle, ou Discours sur les vrais principes du gouvernement.* 2 vols. London: n.p., 1773.

———. *La morale universelle.* Amsterdam: M.-M. Rey, 1776.

———. *Système social ou principes naturels de la morale et de la politique...* 1770. Paris: Fayard, 1994.

Huet, Pierre-Daniel. *Histoire du commerce et de la navigation des anciens.* Brussels: n.p., 1716.

Hugo, Victor. *Quatrevingt-treize.* Paris: Presses Pocket, 1992.

Journals of the Continental Congress, 1774–89. 34 vols. Edited by Worthington C. Ford et al. Washington: U.S. Govt., 1904–37.

Kant, Immanuel. *Critique of Judgement.* Translated by J. H. Bernard. New York: Hafner, 1951.

———. *On History.* Translated and edited by Lewis White Beck. Upper Saddle River, NJ: Prentice Hall, 2001.

Le Mercier de la Rivière, Pierre-Paul. *L'ordre naturel et essentiel des sociétés politiques.* 1767. Edited by Edgard Depitre. Paris: Paul Geuthner, 1910.

Le Trosne, Guillaume-François. *Mémoire sur les vagabonds et sur les mendiants.* Paris: P. G. Simon, 1764.

Livy. *The Early History of Rome.* Translated by Aubrey de Sélincourt. London: Penguin, 1960.

Locke, John. *Two Treatises of Government.* Edited by Peter Laslett. Cambridge: Cambridge University Press, 1988.

———. *Political Essays.* Edited by Mark Goldie. Cambridge: Cambridge University Press, 1997.

Lorris, Guillaume de, and Jean de Meun. *Le roman de la rose.* Edited by Armand Struebel. Paris: Libraire Générale Française, 1992.

Lumet, Louis. *Contre ce temps.* Paris: Bibliothèque de l'Association, 1896.

Mably, Gabriel Bonnot de. *Observations sur la Grèce.* Geneva: Compagnie des Libraires, 1749.

———. *Des droits et des devoirs du citoyen.* (Written in) 1758. Paris: Kell, 1789.

———. *Entretiens de Phocion.* 1763. In *Œuvres complètes.* Paris: Bossange, Masson et Besson, 1797. [ARTFL]

———. *Doutes proposés aux philosophes économistes sur l'ordre naturel et essentiel des sociétés politiques.* The Hague and Paris: Nyon, 1768.

Machiavelli, Niccolò. *The Prince.* Edited by Quentin Skinner. Cambridge: Cambridge University Press, 1998.

———. *The Discourses.* Translated by L. J. Walker and B. Richardson. London: Penguin, 2003.

Manuel d'exorcismes de l'Église. 1626. Charenton: G. V. P., 2000.

Maréchal, Sylvain. *Dieu et les prêtres: fragments d'un poème moral sur Dieu.* 1781. Paris: Patris, an II [1793].

————. *L'Âge d'or, recueil de contes pastoraux; par le Berger Sylvain.* Mitylene (Paris): Guillot, 1782.

————. *Apologues modernes, à l'usage du Dauphin: premières leçons du fils ainé d'un roi.* Brussels: n.p., 1788.

————. *Dame Nature à la barre de l'Assemblée nationale.* Paris: Chez les Marchands de Nouveautés, 1791.

————. *Jugement dernier des rois: prophétie en un acte, en prose.* Paris: C.-F. Patris, an II [1793].

Mariana, Juan de. *The King and the Education of the King.* Translated by George Albert Moore. Washington, DC: Country Dollar Press, 1948.

Marivaux, Pierre de. *La Vie de Marianne.* 1731–41. Paris: Garnier, 1966.

————. *The Virtuous Orphan, or The Life of Marianne, Countess of *****.* Translated by Mary Mitchell Collyer. Edited by William Harlin McBurney and Michael Francis Shugrue. Carbondale: Southern Illinois University Press, 1965.

Marmontel, Jean-François. *Bélisaire.* Edited by Robert Granderoute. Paris: Société des textes français modernes, 1994.

Marx, Karl, and Friedrich Engels. *The Marx-Engels Reader.* Edited by Robert C. Tucker. New York: Norton, 1978.

Mercier, Louis-Sébastien. *Tableau de Paris.* 12 vols. Amsterdam: n.p., 1783–88. [ARTFL]

Meslier, Jean. *Œuvres complètes.* Edited by Jean Deprun, Roland Desné, and Albert Soboul. 3 vols. Paris: Anthropos, 1970–72. [ARTFL]

Mirabeau, Gabriel Riquetti de. *Considérations sur l'ordre de Cincinnatus, ou Imitation d'un pamphlet anglo-américain.* London: J. Johnson, 1784. [ARTFL]

Mirabeau, Victor Riquetti de. *L'ami des hommes, ou traité de la population.* Avignon: n.p., 1756.

Montagne, Michel de. *The Complete Essays.* Translated by Donald M. Frame. Stanford: Stanford University Press, 1958.

————. *Essais.* 3 vols. Paris: Gallimard, 1965.

Montesquieu, Charles de Secondat. *Lettres persanes.* Edited by Laurent Versini. Paris: Flammarion, 1995.

————. *Persian Letters.* Translated by C. J. Betts. Middlesex: Penguin Books, 1973.

————. *Considérations sur les causes de la grandeur des Romains et de leur décadence.* Edited by G. Truc. Paris: Garnier, 1954. [ARTFL]

————. *Considerations on the Causes of the Grandeur and Decadence of the Romans.* Translated by Jehu Baker. New York: D. Appleton, 1889.

————. *De l'esprit des lois.* 2 vols. Edited by Robert Derathé. Paris: Garnier, 1973.

————. *The Spirit of the Laws.* Translated by Anne M. Cohler, Basia C. Miller, and Harold Stone. Cambridge: Cambridge University Press, 1989.

Morelly, Etienne-Gabriel. *Code de la nature, ou Le véritable esprit de ses loix, de tout tems négligé ou méconnu.* Par-tout: Chez le vrai sage, 1755.

Nerval, Gérard de. *Œuvres completes.* 3 vols. Edited by Jean Guillaume and Claude Pichois. Paris: Pléiade, 1993.

Orange, William of. *Apologie or defence of the most noble Prince William.* Delft: n.p., 1581.

Ovid. *Metamorphoses.* Translated by A. D. Melville. Oxford: Oxford University Press, 1998.

Paine, Thomas. *Collected Writings.* New York: Library of America, 1995.

———. *Common Sense.* Mineola: Dover, 1997.

Patrologia Latina, ed. Jacques-Paul Migne. http://pld.chadwyck.com/.

Pernety, Antoine-Joseph. *Dictionnaire Mytho-Hermétique dans lequel on trouve les allégories fabuleuses des poëtes, les métaphores, les énigmes, et les termes barbares des philosophes hermétiques expliqués.* 1787. Paris: Denoël, 1972.

———. *Les merveilles du ciel et de l'enfer et des terres planétaires et astrales . . .* 2 vols. Berlin: Decker [the Royal press], 1782.

Plutarch. *Plutarch's Lives.* Translated by John Dryden. Edited by Arthur Hugh Clough. 2 vols. New York: Modern Library, 2001.

Procès-verbal of the Convention nationale: Des monumens, de la marche, et des discours de la fête consacrée à l'inauguration de la Constitution de la République Française, le 10 août 1793. N.p., n.d. [1793]

Proudhon, Pierre-Joseph. *Qu'est-ce que la propriété?* 1840. Paris: GF, 1966.

———. *What Is Property?* Edited and translated by Donald R. Kelley and Bonnie G. Smith. Cambridge: Cambridge University Press, 1994.

Pufendorf, Samuel von. *The Whole Duty of Man According to the Law of Nature.* 1673. Translated by Andrew Tooke. Edited by Ian Hunter and David Saunders. Indianapolis: Liberty Fund, 2003.

———. *Le droit de la nature et des gens.* Translated by Jean Barbeyrac. Amsterdam: n.p., 1706.

———. *Les devoirs de l'homme et du citoyen.* Translated by Jean Barbeyrac. Amsterdam: H. Schelte, 1707.

———. *On the Duty of Man and Citizen According to Natural Law.* Translated by Michael Silverthorne. Edited by James Tully. Cambridge: Cambridge University Press, 1991.

Quesnay, François. *Le droit naturel.* In vol. 1 of *Physiocratie, ou Constitution naturelle du gouvernement le plus avantageux au genre humain.* 6 vols. Edited by Pierre-Samuel Dupont de Nemours. Paris and Leiden: Merlin, 1768.

Quesnay, François, and Victor Riquetti de Mirabeau. *Traité de la monarchie.* 1757–59. Edited by Gino Longhitano. Paris: L'Harmattan, 1999.

Raynal, Guillaume-Thomas-François. *Philosophical and Political History of the Settlements and Trade of the Europeans in the East and West Indies.* 10 vols. Translated by J. O. Justamond. London: Strahan, 1783.

Recueil des six discours prononcés par le président de la Convention nationale, le 10 Août an 2ème de la République. n.p., n.d. [1793]

Réimpression de l'ancien Moniteur, seule histoire authentique et inaltérée de la révolution française depuis la réunion des Etats-généraux jusqu'au consulat. 31 vols. Paris, H. Plon, 1858–63.

Robert, François. *Le républicanisme adapté à la France*. Vol. 2 of *Aux origines de la République, 1789–92*. 6 vols. Paris: EDHIS, 1991.

Robespierre, Maximilien. *Œuvres de Maximilien Robespierre*. Edited by the Société des études robespierristes. 10 vols. Ivry: Phénix éditions, 2000. [abbr. *Rob.*]

———. *Virtue and Terror*. Translated by John Howe. Introduction by Slavoj Žižek. London: Verso, 2007.

Roland, Marie-Jeanne. *Mémoires de Mme Roland*. 2 vols. Paris: Plon, 1905.

Rollin, Charles. *Histoire ancienne des Égyptiens, des Carthaginois, des Assyriens, des Babyloniens, des Mèdes et des Perses, des Macédoniens, des Grecs*. Vols. 1–12 of *Œuvres complètes de Rollin*. 31 vols. Paris: Firmin Didot, 1821–25.

———. *De la manière d'enseigner et d'étudier les belles-lettres*. 4 vols. Lyon: Rusand, 1819.

Romme, Gilbert. *Rapport sur l'ère de la République*. Paris: Imprimerie Nationale, n.d. [1793]

Rousseau, Jean-Jacques. *Œuvres complètes*. Edited by Bernard Gagnebin and Marcel Raymond. 5 vols. Paris: Gallimard/Pléiade, 1959–95. [abbr. *JJR*]

———. *Jean-Jacques Rousseau, ses amis et ses ennemis* [correspondence]. 2 vols. Edited by G. Streckeisen-Moultou. Paris: Calmann-Levy, 1865.

———. *Emile, or On Education*. Translated by Allan Bloom. New York: Basic Books, 1979.

———. *Les confessions*. Paris: Gallimard, 1973.

———. *Essai sur l'origine des langues*. Paris: Gallimard, 1990.

———. *Les rêveries d'un promeneur solitaire*. Paris: Poche, 1983.

———. *The Collected Writings of Rousseau*. Edited by Christopher Kelly, Roger D. Masters, and Peter G. Stillman. 12 vols. Hanover, NH: University Press of New England, 1995. [abbr. *CWR*]

Royer, Claude. *Discours prononcé dans la Société des Jacobins, le 6 août 1793, l'an second de la République, une et indivisible, par le citoyen Claude ROYER, envoyé de Châlons-sur-Saône, département de Saône et Loire, à la grande réunion des Français le 10 août*. Paris: Jacobin society, 1793.

Rutledge, Jean-Jacques. *Éloge de Montesquieu*. London: n.p., 1786.

Saige, Guillaume-Joseph. *Catéchisme du citoyen*. Geneva: n.p., 1787.

Saint-Just, Louis-Antoine. *Œuvres complètes*. Edited by Michèle Duval. Paris: Lebovici, 1984. [abbr. *SJ*]

———. *Œuvres completes*. Edited by Anne Kupiec and Miguel Abensour. Paris: Gallimard, 2004.

Sidney, Algernon. *Discourses Concerning Government*. London: n.p., 1698.

Sieyès, Emmanuel Joseph. *Vues sur les moyens d'exécution dont les représentans de la France pourront disposer en 1789*. [Paris:] n.p., 1789.

———. *Political Writings*. Translated and edited by Michael Sonenscher. Indianapolis: Hackett, 2003.

Spinoza, Benedict. *Theological-Political Treatise*. Translated and edited by Jonathan Israel and Michael Silverthorne. Cambridge: Cambridge University Press, 2007.

Vattel, Emmerich de. *Le droit des gens, ou Principes de la loi naturelle appliqués à la conduite et aux affaires des nations et des souverains.* 2 vols. London: n.p., 1758.

———. *The Law of Nations, or Principles of the Law of Nature Applied to the Conduct and Affairs of Nations and Sovereigns.* Translated and edited by Joseph Chitty. Philadelphia: T. and J. W. Johnson, 1883.

———. *Mémoires pour servir à l'histoire de notre tems, où l'on déduit historiquement le droit et le fait de la guerre sanglante qui trouble actuellement toute l'Europe . . .* Frankfurt/Leipzig: n.p., 1758.

Vertot, René-Aubert. *Histoire des révolutions arrivées dans le gouvernement de la République romaine.* Paris: F. Barois, 1719.

Vico, Giambattista. *New Science.* Translated by David Marsh. London: Penguin, 1991.

Vitoria, Francisco de. *Political Writings.* Edited and translated by Anthony Pagden and Jeremy Lawrance. Cambridge: Cambridge University Press, 1991.

Volney, Constantin-François Chassebœuf de. *La loi naturelle, ou Catéchisme du citoyen français.* Paris: Sallior, 1793.

———. *Eclaircissements sur divers ouvrages indiqués dans cet ouvrage.* Paris: Fayard, 1989. [ARTFL]

Voltaire, François-Marie Arouet de. *Voltaire électronique.* http://efts.lib.uchicago.edu/efts/VOLTAIRE/.

———. *Œuvres complètes de Voltaire.* 52 vols. Edited by Louis Moland. Paris: Garnier, 1877–85.

———. *Mélanges.* Edited by Jacques van den Heuvel. Paris: Gallimard/Pléiade, 1961.

———. *Lettres philosophiques.* Paris: Flammarion, 1964.

———. *Romans et contes.* Paris: Flammarion, 1966.

———. *Philosophical Dictionary.* Translated and edited by Theodore Besterman. Middlesex: Penguin Books, 1971.

———. *Essai sur les mœurs et l'esprit des nations.* 2 vols. Edited by René Pommeau. Paris: Bordas, 1990.

———. *Candide and Other Stories.* Translated by Roger Pearson. Oxford: Oxford University Press, 1990.

———. *Dictionnaire philosophique.* Paris: Flammarion, 1993.

Wolff, Christian. *Law of Nations Treated According to a Scientific Method [Jus Gentium Methodo Scientifica Pertractatum].* 1749. Translated by Joseph Drake. New York: Oceana/Carnegie Endowment for International Peace, 1964.

Wooton, David, ed. *Divine Right and Democracy: An Anthology of Political Writing in Stuart England.* Indianapolis: Hackett, 2003.

Secondary Sources

Abdoul-Mellek, Liliane. "D'un choix politique de Robespierre: la Terreur." In *Robespierre: de la Nation artésienne à la République et aux Nations,* edited by Jean-Pierre Jessenne, Gilles Deregnaucourt, Jean-Pierre Hirsch, and Hervé Leuwers. Lille: Université Charles de Gaulle, 1993.

Abensour, Miguel. "La philosophie politique de Saint-Just." *AHRF* 182 (1966): 1–32, and *AHRF* 185 (1966): 341–58.

———. "La théorie des institutions et les relations du législateur et du peuple selon Saint-Just." In *Actes du colloque Saint-Just*, edited by Albert Soboul. Paris: Société des études robespierristes, 1968.

Aberdam, Serge. "Un aspect du référendum de 1793: Les envoyés du souverain face aux représentants du peuple." In *Révolution et république: L'exception française*, edited by Michel Vovelle. Paris: Kimé, 1994.

———. *Démographes et démocrates: l'œuvre du Comité de division de la Convention nationale*. Paris: Société des études robespierristes, 2004.

Ackerman, Bruce. *The Failure of the Founding Fathers: Jefferson, Marshall, and the Rise of Presidential Democracy*. Cambridge: Belknap Press of Harvard University Press, 2005.

———. *Before the Next Attack: Preserving Civil Liberties in an Age of Terrorism*. New Haven: Yale University Press, 2007.

Agamben, Giorgio. *Homo Sacer: Sovereign Power and Bare Life*. Translated by Daniel Heller-Roazen. Stanford: Stanford University Press, 1998.

———. *State of Exception*. Translated by Kevin Attell. Chicago: University of Chicago Press, 2005.

Alleau, René. "Epistémologie du mythique et du symbolique dans les discours politiques de la Terreur." In *Mythe et Révolutions*, edited by Yves Chalas. Grenoble: PUG, 1990.

Amar, Akhil Reed. *America's Constitution: A Biography*. New York: Random House, 2005.

Andress, David. *The Terror: Civil War in the French Revolution*. London: Little, Brown, 2005.

———. "Popular Identification with the Convention in the Civil War Summer of 1793." Paper presented at the annual meeting of the Society for the Study of French History, Brighton, UK, July 3, 2006.

Andrews, George Gordon. "Making the Revolutionary Calendar." *American Historical Review* 36 (1931): 515–32.

Anidjar, Gil. *The Jew, the Arab: A History of the Enemy*. Stanford: Stanford University Press, 2003.

———. "Terror Right," *CR: The New Centennial Review* 4, no. 3 (2004): 35–69.

Antheunis, L. *Le conventionnel belge François Robert (1763–1826) et sa femme Louise de Keralio (1758–1882 [i.e., 1822])*. Wetteren: Bracke, 1955.

Apostolidès, Jean-Marie. "La guillotine littéraire." *French Review* 62 (1989): 985–96.

———. "Theater and Terror: *Le jugement dernier des rois*." In *Terror and Consensus: Vicissitudes of French Thought*, edited by Jean-Joseph Goux and Philip R. Wood. Stanford: Stanford University Press, 1998.

Appleby, Joyce. *Liberalism and Republicanism in the Historical Imagination*. Cambridge: Harvard University Press, 1992.

Arendt, Hannah. *The Origins of Totalitariansim*. 1951. New York: Harvest, 1968.

———. *Between Past and Future.* London: Faber and Faber, 1961.

———. *On Revolution.* 1963. London: Penguin, 2006.

Arneil, Barbara. "Trade, Plantations, and Property: John Locke and the Economic Defense of Colonialism." *Journal of the History of Ideas* 55, no. 4 (1994): 591–609.

Aulard, Alphonse. *Le culte de la raison et le culte de l'Être suprême.* Paris: Alcan, 1904.

Austin, J. L. *How to Do Things with Words.* Cambridge: Harvard University Press, 1975.

Baczko, Bronislaw. *Lumières de l'utopie.* Paris: Payot, 1978.

———. *Comment sortir de la Terreur: Thermidor et la Révolution.* Paris: Gallimard, 1989.

———. "The Terror Before the Terror?" In *The Terror*, edited by Keith Baker. Vol. 4 of *The French Revolution and the Creation of Modern Political Culture.* 4 vols. Oxford: Pergamon Press, 1987–94.

Baecque, Antoine de. *The Body Politic: Corporeal Metaphor in Revolutionary France, 1770–1800.* Translated by Charlotte Mandell. Stanford: Stanford University Press, 1997.

———. "Apprivoiser une histoire déchaînée: Dix ans de travaux historiques sur la Terreur (1992–2002)." *Annales: Histoire, Sciences Sociales* 57, no. 4 (2002): 851–65.

Bailyn, Bernard. *The Ideological Origins of the American Revolution.* Cambridge: Belknap Press of Harvard University Press, 1967.

Baker, Keith. *Condorcet: From Natural Philosophy to Social Mathematics.* Chicago: University of Chicago Press, 1975.

———. "Sovereignty." In *A Critical Dictionary of the French Revolution*, edited by François Furet and Mona Ozouf, translated by Arthur Goldhammer. Cambridge: Belknap Press of Harvard University Press, 1989.

———, ed. *The Political Culture of the Old Regime.* Vol. 1 of *The French Revolution and the Creation of Modern Political Culture.* 4 vols. Oxford: Pergamon Press, 1987–94.

———. *Inventing the French Revolution: Essays on French Political Culture in the Eighteenth Century.* Cambridge: Cambridge University Press, 1990.

———. "Enlightenment and the Institution of Society: Notes for a Conceptual History." In *Main Trends in Cultural History*, edited by Willem Melching and Wyger Velema. Amsterdam: Rodopi, 1994.

———. "The Idea of a Declaration of Rights." In *The French Idea of Freedom: The Old Regime and the Declaration of Rights of 1789*, edited by Dale Van Kley. Stanford: Stanford University Press, 1994.

———, ed. *The Terror.* Volume 4 of *The French Revolution and the Creation of Modern Political Culture.* 4 vols. Oxford: Pergamon Press, 1987–94.

———. "Transformations of Classical Republicanism in Eighteenth-Century France." *Journal of Modern History* 73 (2001): 32–53.

———. "Après la 'culture politique'? De nouveaux courants dans l'approche linguistique." *Dix-huitième siècle* 37 (2005): 243–54.

———. Review of Robert M. Schwartz and Robert A. Schneider, eds. *Tocqueville and*

Beyond. Essays on the Old Regime in Honor of David D. Bien. Newark: University of Delaware Press, 2003. *H-France Review* 5, no. 137 (December 2005). http://h-france.net/vol5reviews/baker.html.

———. "Political Languages of the French Revolution." In *The Cambridge History of Eighteenth-Century Political Thought*, edited by Mark Goldie and Robert Wolker. Cambridge: Cambridge University Press, 2006.

Barret-Kriegel, Blandine. *La république incertaine.* Paris: PUF, 1988.

Barthes, Roland. *Mythologies.* 1957. Translated by Annette Lavers. New York: Hill and Wang, 1984.

Bates, David W. *Enlightenment Aberrations: Error and Revolution in France.* Ithaca: Cornell University Press, 2002.

Batz, William G. "The Historical Anthropology of John Locke." *Journal of the History of Ideas* 35, no. 4 (1974): 663–70.

Beales, Derek. "Philosophical Kingship and Enlightened Despotism." In *The Cambridge History of Eighteenth-Century Political Thought*, edited by Mark Goldie and Robert Wolker. Cambridge: Cambridge University Press, 2006.

Bell, David. *Lawyers and Citizens: The Making of a Political Elite in Old Regime France.* New York: Oxford University Press, 1994.

———. *The Cult of the Nation in France: Inventing Nationalism, 1680–1800.* Cambridge: Harvard University Press, 2001.

———. Review. *H-France Reviews* 5, no. 93 (2005). http://www.h-france.net/vol5reviews/bell4.html.

———. *The First Total War: Napoleon's Europe and the Birth of Warfare as We Know It.* Boston: Houghton Mifflin, 2007.

Bénichou, Paul. *Le sacre de l'écrivain, 1750–1830.* Paris: Corti, 1973.

Benrekassa, Georges. "Loi naturelle et loi civile: l'idéologie des Lumières et la prohibition de l'inceste." *Studies on Voltaire and the Eighteenth Century* 87 (1972): 115–44.

Bianco, René. "Répertoire des périodiques anarchistes de langue française: un siècle de presse anarchiste d'expression française, 1880–1983." PhD diss., Université Aix-Marseille, 1987.

Biard, Michel. *Missionnaires de la République: les représentants du peuple en mission, 1793–95.* Paris: CTHS, 2002.

———, ed. *Les politiques de la Terreur, 1793–94.* Rennes: Presses universitaires de Rennes & Société des études robespierristes, 2008.

Billington, James H. *Fire in the Minds of Men: Origins of the Revolutionary Tradition.* New York: Basic Books, 1980.

Blum, Carol. *Rousseau and the Republic of Virtue: The Language of Politics in the French Revolution.* Ithaca: Cornell University Press, 1986.

Bock, Gisele, Quentin Skinner, and Maurizio Viroli, eds. *Machiavelli and Republicanism.* Cambridge: Cambridge University Press, 1990.

Bonnet, Jean-Claude. *Naissance du panthéon: essai sur le culte des grands hommes.* Paris: Fayard, 1998.

Boroumand, Ladan. *La guerre des principes: les assemblées révolutionnaires face aux droits de l'homme et à la souveraineté de la nation, mai 1789–juillet 1794.* Paris: EHESS, 1999.

Boudon, Julien. *Les Jacobins: une traduction des principes de Jean-Jacques Rousseau.* Paris: LGDJ, 2006.

Bouineau, Jacques. *Les toges du pouvoir, ou la révolution de droit antique, 1789–99.* Toulouse: Editions Eché, 1986.

Bouloiseau, Marc. *The Jacobin Republic, 1792–94.* Translated by Jonathan Mandelbaum. Cambridge and Paris: Cambridge University Press/Maison des sciences de l'homme, 1983.

Bourdin, Jean-Claude. "L'effacement de Diderot par Rousseau dans l'article *économie politique* et le *Manuscrit de Genève.*" In *Diderot et Rousseau: un entretien à distance,* edited by Franck Salaün. Paris: Desjonquères, 2006.

Bowman, Frank. *Le Christ romantique.* Geneva: Droz, 1973.

Bradley, Raymond, and Norman Swartz. *Possible Worlds: An Introduction to Logic and Its Philosophy.* Oxford: Blackwell, 1979.

Brett, Annabel S. *Liberty, Right and Nature: Individual Rights in Later Scholastic Thought.* Cambridge: Cambridge University Press, 1997.

Brisson, Jean-Paul. *Rome et l'âge d'or: de Catulle à Ovide, vie et mort d'un mythe.* Paris: La Découverte, 1992.

Brockliss, L. W. B. *French Higher Education in the Seventeenth and Eighteenth Centuries: A Cultural History.* Oxford: Clarendon Press, 1987.

Brown, Howard G. *Ending the French Revolution: Violence, Justice, Repression.* Charlottesville: University of Virginia Press, 2006.

Brunel, Françoise. "Les députés montagnards." In *Actes du Colloque Girondins et Montagnards,* edited by Albert Soboul. Paris: Société des études robespierristes, 1980.

———. *Thermidor.* Brussels: Editions Complexe, 1989.

———. "L'Être Suprême et les divisions de la Montagne avant Thermidor." In *L'Être Suprême,* edited by Michel Vovelle. Arras: Centre culturel Noroit, 1991.

———. "Institutions civiles et Terreur," Révolution Française.net, Synthèses (May 2006). http://revolution-francaise.net/2006/05/21/43-institutions-civiles-et-terreur.

Burgess, Douglas R., Jr. "The Dread Pirate Bin Laden." *Legal Affairs* (July–August 2005). http://www.legalaffairs.org/issues/July-August-2005/feature_burgess_julaug05.msp.

Burney, John M. "The Fear of the Executive and the Threat of Conspiracy: Billaud-Varenne's Terrorist Rhetoric in the French Revolution, 1788–94." *French History* 5, no. 2 (1991): 143–63.

Burns, J. H., and Mark Goldie, eds. *The Cambridge History of Political Thought, 1450–1700.* Cambridge: Cambridge University Press, 1991.

Campbell, Peter R., Thomas E. Kaiser, and Marisa Linton, eds. *Conspiracy in the French Revolution.* Manchester: Manchester University Press, 2007.

Cañizares-Esguerra, Jorge. *Puritan Conquistadors: Iberianizing the Atlantic, 1550–1700.* Stanford: Stanford University Press, 2006.

Carbasse, Jean-Marie. *Histoire du droit pénal et de la justice criminelle.* Paris: PUF, 2000.

Caron, Pierre. *Massacres de Septembre.* Paris: Maison du livre français, 1935.

Carr, E. H. "The Origin and Status of the Cheka." *Soviet Studies* 10, no. 1 (1958): 1–11.

Ceaser, James W., and Daniel DiSalvo. "A New GOP?" *Public Interest* 157 (2004): 3–17.

Chartier, Roger, Dominique Julia, and Marie-Madeleine Compère. *L'Education en France du XVIe au XVIIIe siècle.* Paris: SEDES, 1976.

Chérel, Albert. *Fénelon au 18e siècle en France (1715–1820): son prestige, son influence.* 1917. Geneva: Slatkine Reprints, 1970.

———. *La pensée de Machiavel en France.* Paris: L'Artisan du livre, 1935.

Clark, William A. *Crime and Punishment in Soviet Officialdom: Combating Corruption in the Political Elite, 1965–90.* New York: M. E. Sharpe, 1993.

Cobb, Richard. *The People's Armies: The "Armées Révolutionnaires," Instruments of the Terror in the Departments, April 1793 to Floréal Year II.* Translated by Marianne Elliott. New Haven: Yale University Press, 1987.

Cobban, Alfred. "The Political Ideas of Maximilien Robespierre during the Period of the Convention." *English Historical Review* 61 (1946): 45–80.

Cohen, Stephen F. *Bukharin and the Bolshevik Revolution: A Political Biography, 1888–1938.* New York: Oxford University Press, 1980.

Cole, G. D. H. *Socialist Thought: The Forerunners (1789–1850).* Volume 1 of *A History of Socialist Thought.* London: MacMillan, 1953.

———. *William Morris as a Socialist.* London: William Morris Society, 1960.

Conley, Tom. "The *Essays* and the New World." In *The Cambridge Companion to Montaigne,* edited by Ullrich Langer. Cambridge: Cambridge University Press, 2005.

Cook, Elizabeth Heckendorn. *Epistolary Bodies: Gender and Genre in the Eighteenth-Century Republic of Letters.* Stanford: Stanford University Press, 1996.

Corn, David. "Secret Report: Corruption Is 'Norm' within Iraqi Government." *Nation,* August 30, 2007. http://www.thenation.com/blogs/capitalgames?pid=228339.

Cotta, Sergio. *Montesquieu e la scienza della società.* 1953. New York: Arno Press, 1979.

Courtney, C. P. "Montesquieu and Natural Law." In *Montesquieu's Science of Politics: Essays on the Spirit of Laws,* edited by David W. Carrithers, Michael A. Mosher, and Paul A. Rahe. Lanham: Rowman and Littlefield, 2001.

Crisafulli, Alessandro S. "Montesquieu's Story of the Troglodytes: Its Background, Meaning and Significance." *PMLA* 58, no. 2 (1943): 379–92.

Crocker, Lester. *Rousseau's Social Contract.* Cleveland: Case Western Reserve University Press, 1968.

Crook, Malcolm. *Elections in the French Revolution: An Apprenticeship in Democracy, 1789–99.* Cambridge: Cambridge University Press, 1996.

Curtis, Mark H. "The Alienated Intellectuals of Early Stuart England." *Past and Present* 23 (1962): 25–43.

Curtius, Ernst Robert. *European Literature and the Latin Middle Ages*. Translated by Willard R. Trask. Princeton: Princeton University Press, 1990.

Dahl, Robert. *On Democracy*. New Haven: Yale University Press, 2000.

Darnton, Robert. *The Literary Underground of the Old Regime*. Cambridge: Harvard University Press, 1982.

———. *The Kiss of Lamourette: Reflections in Cultural History*. New York: Norton, 1990.

Daston, Lorraine, and Fernando Vidal, eds. *The Moral Authority of Nature*. Chicago: University of Chicago Press, 2004.

Delaporte, André. *L'idée d'égalité en France au XVIIIe siècle*. Paris: PUF, 1987.

De Luna, Frederick A. "The 'Girondins' Were Girondins, after All." *French Historical Studies* 15, no. 3 (1988): 506–18.

Denby, David. *Sentimental Narrative and the Social Order in France, 1760–1820*. Cambridge: Cambridge University Press, 1994.

Derathé, Robert. *Jean-Jacques Rousseau et la science politique de son temps*. 1950. Paris: Vrin, 1992.

Desan, Philippe. *Montaigne, les Cannibales et les Conquistadores*. Paris: Nizet, 1994.

Desan, Suzanne. "What's after Political Culture? Recent French Revolutionary Historiography." *French Historical Studies* 23 (2000): 163–96.

Desserud, Donald. "Virtue, Commerce and Moderation in the 'Tale of the Troglodytes': Montesquieu's *Persian Letters*." *History of Political Thought* 12 (1991): 605–26.

Dobie, Madeleine. *Foreign Bodies: Gender, Language, and Culture in French Orientalism*. Stanford: Stanford University Press, 2001.

Dommanget, Maurice. *Sylvain Maréchal, l'égalitaire*. Paris: Spartacus, 1950.

Dorson, Richard. "The Eclipse of Solar Mythology." *Journal of American Folklore* 68 (1955): 393–416.

Dowd, David Lloyd. *Pageant-Master of the Republic: Jacques-Louis David and the French Revolution*. 1948. Freeport: Libraries, 1969.

Doyle, William. *The Oxford History of the French Revolution*. Oxford: Oxford University Press, 2002.

Duchet, Michèle. *Anthropologie et histoire au siècle des Lumières*. 1971. Paris: Albin Michel, 1995.

———. *Diderot et "l'Histoire des deux Indes."* Paris: Nizet, 1978.

Dufour, Alfred. "Pufendorf." In *The Cambridge History of Political Thought, 1450–1700*, edited by J. H. Burns and Mark Goldie. Cambridge: Cambridge University Press, 1991.

Dunn, John. *The Political Thought of John Locke*. Cambridge: Cambridge University Press, 1969.

Duprun, Jean. "Robespierre, pontife de l'Etre Suprême: note sur les aspects sacrificiels d'une fête (1794)." In *Les fêtes de la Révolution*, edited by Jean Ehrard and Paul Viallaneix. Paris: Société des études robespierristes, 1977.

Duval, Edwin. "Lessons of the New World: Design and Meaning in Montaigne's 'Des Cannibales' (I:31) and 'Des coches' (III:6)." *Yale French Studies* 64 (1983): 95–112.

Dziembowski, Edmond. *Un nouveau patriotisme français, 1750–70: la France face à la puissance anglaise à l'époque de la guerre de Sept Ans.* Oxford: Voltaire Foundation, 1998.

Echeverria, Durand. *The Maupeou Revolution: A Study in the History of Libertarianism (France, 1770–74).* Baton Rouge: Louisiana State University Press, 1985.

Eco, Umberto. *Lector in Fabula.* Translated by Myriem Bouzaher. Paris: Grasset, 1985.

Edelstein, Dan. "Restoring the Golden Age: Myths in Revolutionary Culture and Ideology." PhD diss., University of Pennsylvania, 2004.

———. "Hyperborean Atlantis: Jean-Sylvain Bailly, Madame Blavatsky, and the Nazi Myth." *Studies in Eighteenth-Century Culture* 35 (2006): 267–91.

———. "*Hostis Humani Generis*: Devils, Natural Right, Terror, and the French Revolution." *Telos* 141 (2007): 57–71.

———. "War and Terror: The Law of Nations from Grotius to the French Revolution." *French Historical Studies* 31, no. 2 (2008): 229–62.

———. "The Birth of Ideology from the Spirit of Myth: Georges Sorel among the *Idéologues.*" In *The Re-enchantement of the World: Secular Magic in a Rational Age*, edited by Joshua Landy and Michael Saler. Stanford: Stanford University Press, 2009.

———. "Introduction to the Super-Enlightenment." In *The Super-Enlightenment: Daring to Know Too Much*, edited by Dan Edelstein. Oxford: SVEC/Voltaire Foundation, 2009.

Edelstein, Dan, and Bettina Lerner. "Editors' Preface: Mythomanies." In *Myth and Modernity*, edited by Edelstein and Lerner. *Yale French Studies* 111 (2007): 1–4.

Ehrard, Jean. *L'idée de la nature en France dans la première moitié du XVIIIᵉ siècle.* Paris: S.E.V.P.E.N., 1963.

———. "La notion de 'loi(s) fondamentale(s)' dans l'œuvre et la pensée de Montesquieu." In *Montesquieu en 2005*, edited by Catherine Volpilhac-Auger. *SVEC* 5. Oxford: Voltaire Foundation, 2005.

Eigeldinger, Marc. *Jean-Jacques Rousseau: univers mythique et cohérence.* Neuchâtel: Baconnière, 1978.

Ellis, Harold. *Boulainvilliers and the French Monarchy: Aristocratic Politics in Early Eighteenth-Century France.* Ithaca: Cornell University Press, 1988.

Ellis, Joseph. *Founding Brothers: The Revolutionary Generation.* New York: Vintage, 2002.

Elslande, Jean-Pierre van. *L'imaginaire pastoral du XVIIᵉ siècle: 1600–1650.* Paris: PUF, 1999.

Faessel, Sonia. *Vision des îles: Tahiti et l'imaginaire européen, du mythe à son exploitation littéraire (XVIIIᵉ–XXᵉ).* Paris: L'Harmattan, 2005.

Fontana, Biancamaria, ed. *The Invention of the Modern Republic.* Cambridge: Cambridge University Press, 1994.

Ford, Franklin L. *Political Murder: From Tyrannicide to Terrorism.* Cambridge: Harvard University Press, 1985.

Forrest, Alan. "The Ubiquitous Brigand: The Politics and Language of Repression." In *Popular Resistance in the French Wars: Patriots, Partisans and Land Pirates,* edited by Charles J. Esdaile. London: Palgrave Macmillan, 2005.

Foucault, Michel. *Discipline and Punish: The Birth of the Prison.* Translated by Alan Sheridan. New York: Vintage, 1995.

Fox-Genovese, Elizabeth. *The Origins of Physiocracy: Economic Revolution and Social Order in Eighteenth-Century France.* Ithaca: Cornell University Press, 1976.

Fraenkel, Ernest. *The Dual State: A Contribution to the Theory of Dictatorship.* Translated by E. A. Shils et al. New York: Oxford University Press, 1941.

France, Peter. *Rhetoric and Truth in France: Descartes to Diderot.* Oxford: Clarendon Press, 1972.

François Quesnay et la Physiocratie. 2 vols. Paris: Institut national d'études démographiques, 1958.

Friedland, Paul. *Political Actors: Representative Bodies and Theatricality in the Age of the French Revolution.* Ithaca: Cornell University Press, 2002.

Fukuyama, Francis. "After Neoconservatism." *New York Times Magazine.* February 19, 2006.

Furet, François. *Interpreting the French Revolution.* Translated by Elborg Forster. Cambridge/Paris: Cambridge University Press and Editions de la Maison des sciences de l'homme, 1981.

———. "Revolutionary Government" and "Terror." In *A Critical Dictionary of the French Revolution,* edited by François Furet and Mona Ozouf, translated by Arthur Goldhammer. Cambridge: Belknap Press of Harvard University Press, 1989.

Furet, François, and Denis Richet. *La Révolution française.* Paris: Fayard 1973.

Furet, François, and Mona Ozouf, eds. *A Critical Dictionary of the French Revolution.* Translated by Arthur Goldhammer. Cambridge: Belknap Press of Harvard University Press, 1989.

———. *La Gironde et les Girondins.* Paris: Payot, 1991.

———. *Le siècle de l'avènement républicain.* Paris: Gallimard, 1993.

Garrett, Clarke. *Respectable Folly: Millenarians and the French Revolution in France and England.* Baltimore: Johns Hopkins Press, 1975.

Gauchet, Marcel. *La révolution des droits de l'homme.* Paris: Gallimard, 1989.

Gauthier, Florence. *Triomphe et mort du droit naturel en Révolution, 1789–1795–1802.* Paris: PUF, 1992.

Gay, Peter. *The Enlightenment: An Interpretation.* 2 vols. New York: Knopf, 1966–69.

———. *Voltaire's Politics: The Poet as Realist.* 2nd ed. New Haven: Yale University Press, 1988.

Gelbart, Nina. "Last Letters and Revolutionary Self-Fashioning." Paper presented at the annual meeting of the Western Society for French History, Long Beach, CA, October 19–21, 2006.

van Gelderen, Martin, and Quentin Skinner, eds. *Republicanism: A Shared European Heritage*. 2 vols. Cambridge: Cambridge University Press, 2002.

Gillispie, Charles C. *Science and Polity in France at the End of the Old Regime*. Princeton: Princeton University Press, 1980.

Girardet, Raoul. *Mythes et mythologies politiques*. Paris: Seuil, 1986.

Godechot, Jacques. *La contre-révolution*. Paris: PUF, 1996.

Godfrey, James Logan. *Revolutionary Justice: A Study in the Organization and Procedures of the Paris Tribunal, 1793–95*. Chapel Hill: University of North Carolina Press, 1951.

Godwin, Joscelyn. *The Theosophical Enlightenment*. Albany: SUNY Press, 1994.

Gojosso, Eric. *Le concept de la république en France (XVIe–XVIIIe siècle)*. Marseilles: Presses Universitaires d'Aix-Marseille, 1998.

Goldie, Mark, and Robert Wolker, eds. *The Cambridge History of Eighteenth-Century Political Thought*. Cambridge: Cambridge University Press, 2006. [abbr. *CHECPT*]

Gombrich, E. H. "The Dream of Reason: Symbolism in the French Revolution." *British Journal for Eighteenth-Century Studies* 2, no. 3 (1979): 188–204.

Goodman, Dena. *Criticism in Action: Enlightenment Experiments in Political Writing*. Ithaca: Cornell University Press, 1989.

———. *The Republic of Letters: A Cultural History of the French Enlightenment*. Ithaca: Cornell University Press, 1994.

Gordon, Daniel. *Citizens without Sovereignty: Equality and Sociability in French Thought, 1670–1789*. Princeton: Princeton University Press, 1994.

Goulemot, Jean-Marie. "Du républicanisme et de l'idée républicaine." In *Le siècle de l'avènement républicain*, edited by François Furet and Mona Ozouf. Paris: Gallimard, 1993.

Goulet, Jacques. "Robespierre: la peine de mort et la Terreur." *AHRF* 244 (1981): 219–38, and *AHRF* 251 (1983): 38–64.

Greer, Donald. *The Incidence of the Terror during the French Revolution: A Statistical Interpretation*. Cambridge: Harvard University Press, 1935.

Grell, Chantal. *Le dix-huitième siècle et l'antiquité en France, 1680–1789*. 2 vols. Oxford: SVEC/Voltaire Foundation, 1995.

Grell, Chantal, and Christian Michel, eds. *Primitivisme et mythes des origines dans la France des Lumières, 1680–1820*. Paris: Presses de l'Université de Paris-Sorbonne, 1989.

Griffin, Robert P. "Constitutional Law: Due Process: Right of Alien Enemy to Judicial Review of Deportation Proceeding." *Michigan Law Review* 47 (1949): 404–6.

Grosrichard, Alain. *La structure du sérail: la fiction du despotisme asiatique dans l'Occident classique*. Paris: Seuil, 1979.

Gross, Jean-Pierre. *Saint-Just: sa politique et ses missions.* Paris: Bibliothèque Nationale, 1976.

———. *Fair Shares for All: Jacobin Egalitarianism in Practice.* Cambridge: Cambridge University Press, 2003.

Gruchmann, Lothar. *Justiz im Dritten Reich, 1933–40: Anpassung und Unterwerfung in der Ära Gürtner.* Munich: Oldenbourg, 1988.

Gueniffey, Patrice. "Cordeliers et girondins: la préhistoire de la république?" In *Siècle de l'avènement républicain,* edited by François Furet and Mona Ozouf. Paris: Gallimard, 1993.

———. *Le nombre et la raison: La Révolution française et les élections.* Paris: EHESS, 1993.

———. *La politique de la Terreur: essai sur la violence révolutionnaire, 1789–94.* Paris: Fayard, 2000.

Gueniffey, Patrice, and Ran Halévi. "Clubs and Popular Societies." In *A Critical Dictionary of the French Revolution,* edited by François Furet and Mona Ozouf, translated by Arthur Goldhammer. Cambridge: Belknap Press of Harvard University Press, 1989.

Guerci, Luciano. *Libertà degli antichi e libertà dei moderni: Sparta, Atene e i "philosophes" nella Francia del Settecento.* Naples: Guida, 1979.

Guilhaumou, Jacques. " 'La terreur à l'ordre du jour': un parcours en révolution (1793–94)." *Révolution Française.net* (January 2007). http://revolution-francaise .net/2007/01/06/94-la-terreur-a-lordre-du-jour-un-parcours-en-revolution-juillet-1793-mars-1794.

Guillemin, Henri. *Robespierre: politique et mystique.* Paris: Seuil, 1987.

Guiomar, Jean-Yves. *L'invention de la guerre totale: XVIIIᵉ–XXᵉ siècles.* Paris: Le Félin, 2004.

Gumbrecht, Hans Ulrich. *Funktionen parlamentarischer Rhetorik in der Französischen Revolution: Vorstudien zur Entwicklung einer historischen Textpragmatik.* Munich: W. Fink, 1978.

Haakonssen, Knud. *Natural Law and Moral Philosophy: From Grotius to the Scottish Enlightenment.* Cambridge: Cambridge University Press, 1996.

Haillant, Marguerite. *Culture et imagination dans les œuvres de Fénelon "ad usum Delphini."* Paris: Belles Lettres, 1983.

Hammersley, Rachel. "English Republicanism in Revolutionary France: The Case of the Cordelier Club." *Journal of British Studies* 43 (2004): 464–81.

———. *French Revolutionaries and English Republicans: The Cordeliers Club, 1790–94.* Rochester, NY: Boydell Press, 2005.

Hampson, Norman. *Saint-Just.* Oxford: Blackwell, 1991.

Hampton, Timothy. *Writing from History: The Rhetoric of Exemplarity in Renaissance Literature.* Ithaca: Cornell University Press, 1990.

Hanson, Paul R. *The Jacobin Republic under Fire: The Federalist Revolt in the French Revolution.* University Park: Pennsylvania State University Press, 2003.

Hardman, John. *Robespierre.* Harlow: Pearson Education, 1999.

Harth, Erica. *Ideology and Culture in Seventeenth-Century France.* Ithaca: Cornell University Press, 1983.

Hartz, Louis. *The Liberal Tradition in America: An Interpretation of American Political Thought since the Revolution.* New York: Harcourt, Brace, 1955.

Heffernan, James, ed. *Representing the French Revolution.* Hanover, NH: University Press of New England, 1992.

Hénaff, Marcel. "Supplement to Diderot's Dream." In *The Libertine Reader,* edited by Michel Feher. New York: Zone Books, 1997.

Henderson, John. *Fighting for Rome: Poets and Caesars, History, and Civil War.* Cambridge: Cambridge University Press, 1998.

Hesse, Carla. "La preuve par la lettre: pratiques juridiques au tribunal révolutionnaire de Paris (1793–94)." *Annales: Histoire, Sciences Sociales* 3 (1996): 629–42.

———. "The Law of the Terror." *MLN* 114, no. 4 (1999): 702–18.

———. "La logique culturelle de la loi révolutionnaire." *Annales: Histoire, Sciences Sociales* 4 (2002): 915–33.

Higginbotham, Don. *The War of American Independence: Military, Attitudes, Politics, and Practice, 1763–89.* New York: Macmillan, 1971.

Higonnet, Patrice. *Sister Republics: The Origins of French and American Republicanism.* Cambridge: Harvard University Press, 1988.

———. *Goodness beyond Virtue: Jacobins during the French Revolution.* Cambridge: Harvard University Press, 1998.

———. "Terror, Trauma and the 'Young Marx' Explanation of Jacobin Politics." *Past and Present* 191 (2006): 121–64.

Hinard, François. *Les proscriptions de la Rome républicaine.* Rome: École française de Rome, 1985.

Hochstrasser, T. J. *Natural Law Theories in the Early Enlightenment.* Cambridge: Cambridge University Press, 2000.

———. "Physiocracy and the Politics of *Laissez-Faire.*" In *The Cambridge History of Eighteenth-Century Political Thought,* edited by Mark Goldie and Robert Wolker. Cambridge: Cambridge University Press, 2006.

Hoffmann, Stanley. *The State of War.* New York: Praeger, 1965.

Hont, Istvan. "The Early Enlightenment Debate on Commerce and Luxury." In *The Cambridge History of Eighteenth-Century Political Thought,* edited by Mark Goldie and Robert Wolker. Cambridge: Cambridge University Press, 2006.

Horn, Jeff. *The Path Not Taken: French Industrialization in the Age of Revolution, 1750–1830.* Cambridge: MIT Press, 2006.

Huet, Marie-Hélène. *Mourning Glory: The Will of the French Revolution.* Philadelphia: University of Pennsylvania Press, 1997.

Hulliung, Mark. *Montesquieu and the Old Regime.* Berkeley: University of California Press, 1976.

———. *The Autocritique of the Enlightenment.* Cambridge: Harvard University Press, 1994.

Human Rights Watch. "Torture in Iraq." *New York Review of Books*, November 3, 2005, 64–73.

Hunt, Lynn. *Politics, Culture, and Class in the French Revolution.* Berkeley: University of California Press, 1984.

———. *The Family Romance of the French Revolution.* Berkeley: University of California Press, 1992.

———. *Inventing Human Rights: A History.* New York: Norton, 2007.

———. "Review Essay [on Jean-Clément Martin's *Violence et révolution*]." *H-France Forum* 2, no. 2 (2007). http://www.h-france.net/forum/forumvol2/HuntOnMartin1.html.

Hutchinson, Ross. *Locke in France, 1688–1734.* In *Studies in Voltaire and the Eighteenth-Century.* Oxford: Voltaire Foundation, 1991.

Ignatieff, Michael. *The Lesser Evil: Political Ethics in an Age of Terror.* Princeton: Princeton University Press, 2004.

Imbruglia, Gerolamo. "From Utopia to Republicanism: The Case of Diderot." In *The Invention of the Modern Republic*, edited by Biancamaria Fontana. Cambridge: Cambridge University Press, 1994.

Irons, Peter. *Justice at War: The Story of the Japanese American Internment Cases.* Rev. ed. Seattle: University of Washington Press, 1996.

Israel, Jonathan. *Enlightenment Contested: Philosophy, Modernity, and the Emancipation of Man, 1670–1752.* Oxford: Oxford University Press, 2006.

Jacob, Margaret C. *Living the Enlightenment: Freemasonry and Politics in Eighteenth-Century Europe.* Oxford: Oxford University Press, 1991.

Jainchill, Andrew. *Rethinking Politics after the Terror: The Republican Origins of French Liberalism.* Ithaca: Cornell University Press, 2008.

Jameson, Frederick. *The Political Unconscious: Narrative as Socially Symbolic Act.* Ithaca: Cornell University Press, 1981.

Jaume, Lucien. *Le discours Jacobin et la démocratie.* Paris: Fayard, 1989.

———. *Les déclarations des droits de l'homme.* Paris: GF, 1993.

Jaurès, Jean. *La mort du roi et la chute de la Gironde.* Volume 5 of *Histoire socialiste de la Révolution française*, edited by Albert Soboul. 6 vols. Paris: Messidor, 1986.

Johnston, David. "The Jurists." In *The Cambridge History of Greek and Roman Political Thought*, edited by Christopher Rowe and Malcolm Schofield. Cambridge: Cambridge University Press, 2000.

Jones, Colin. *The Great Nation: France from Louis XV to Napoleon.* London: Penguin, 2002.

Jones, Gareth Stedman. "Kant, the French Revolution, and the Republic." In *Invention of Modern Republicanism*, edited by Biancamaria Fontana. Cambridge: Cambridge University Press, 1994.

Jones, P. M. "The 'Agrarian Law': Schemes for Land Redistribution during the French Revolution." *Past and Present* 133 (1991): 96–133.

Jordan, David P. *The King's Trial.* Berkeley: University of California Press, 1979.

———. *The Revolutionary Career of Maximilien Robespierre.* New York: Free Press, 1985.

Juden, Brian. *Traditions orphiques et tendances mystiques dans le romantisme français (1800–55).* 1971. Geneva: Slatkine Reprints, 1984.

Kahn, Victoria. *Rhetoric, Prudence, and Skepticism in the Renaissance.* Ithaca: Cornell University Press, 1985.

———. *Wayward Contracts: The Crisis of Political Obligation in England, 1640–74.* Princeton: Princeton University Press, 2004.

Kaiser, Thomas E. "Property, Sovereignty, and the Delaration of the Rights of Man, and the Tradition of French Jurisprudence." In *The French Idea of Freedom: The Old Regime and the Declaration of Rights of 1789*, edited by Dale Van Kley. Stanford: Stanford University Press, 1994.

Kaplan, Steven L. *Bread, Politics, and Political Economy in the Reign of Louis XV.* 2 vols. The Hague: M. Nijhoff, 1976.

———. "The Famine Plot Persuasion in Eighteenth-Century France." *Transactions of the American Philosophical Society* 72, no. 3 (1992): 1–83.

Kapp, Volker. *Télémaque de Fénelon: la signification d'une œuvre littéraire à la fin du siècle classique.* Tübingen and Paris: G. Narr & J.-M. Place, 1982.

Kates, Gary. *The "Cercle Social," the Girondins, and the French Revolution.* Princeton: Princeton University Press, 1985.

Kavanagh, Thomas. *Writing the Truth: Authority and Desire in Rousseau.* Berkeley: University of California Press, 1987.

———. *Esthetics of the Moment: Literature and Art in the French Enlightenment.* Philadelphia: University of Pennsylvania Press, 1996.

———. "Rousseau's *The Levite of Ephrahim.*" In *The Cambridge Campanion to Rousseau*, edited by Patrick Riley. Cambridge: Cambridge University Press, 2001.

Keohane, Nannerl O. *Philosophy and the State in France: From the Renaissance to the Enlightenment.* Princeton: Princeton University Press, 1980.

Kelley, Donald R. *Foundations of Modern Historical Scholarship: Language, Law, and History in the French Renaissance.* New York: Columbia University Press, 1970.

Kelly, Christopher. *Rousseau as Author: Consecrating One's Life to the Truth.* Chicago: University of Chicago, 2003.

Kelly, George Armstrong. "Conceptual Sources of the Terror." *Eighteenth-Century Studies* 14, no. 1 (1980): 18–36.

Kemp, Anthony. *The Estrangement of the Past: A Study in the Origins of Modern Historical Consciousness.* New York: Oxford University Press, 1991.

Kennedy, Emmet. *A "Philosophe" in the Age of Revolution: Destutt de Tracy and the Origins of "Ideology."* Philadelphia: American Philosophical Society, 1978.

Koch, H. W. *In the Name of the Volk: Political Justice in Hitler's Germany.* New York: St. Martin's Press, 1989.

Kors, Alan Charles. *D'Holbach's Coterie: An Enlightenment in Paris.* Princeton: Princeton University Press, 1976.

Koselleck, Reinhart. *Critique and Crisis: Enlightenment and the Pathogenesis of Modern Society.* Cambridge: MIT Press, 1988.

———. *Future Past: On the Semantics of Historical Time.* Translated by Keith Tribe. New York: Columbia University Press, 2004.

Kramnick, Isaac. *Bolingbroke and His Circle: The Politics of Nostalgia in the Age of Walpole.* Cambridge: Harvard University Press, 1968.

Krauthammer, Charles. "The Neoconservative Convergence." *Commentary* 120 (July 2005): 21–26.

Lacorne, Denis. *L'invention de la république: le modèle americain.* Paris: Hachette, 1991.

Larrère, Catherine. *L'invention de l'économie au xviiie siècle: du droit naturel à la physiocratie.* Paris: PUF, 1992.

Lascoumes, Pierre, Pierrette Poncela, and Pierre Lenoël. *Au nom de l'ordre: Une histoire politique du code pénal.* Paris: Hachette, 1989.

Lasky, Melvin J. *Utopia and Revolution.* Chicago: University of Chicago Press, 1976.

Lefebvre, Georges. "Sur la loi du 22 prairial an II." *AHRF* 23 (1951): 225–56.

Lestringant, Frank. "The Philosopher's Breviary: Jean de Léry in the Enlightenment." *Representations* 33 (1991): 200–11.

Levi-Malvano, Ettore. *Montesquieu e Machiavelli.* Paris: Honoré Champion, 1912.

Levin, Harry. *The Myth of the Golden Age in the Renaissance.* Bloomington: Indiana University Press, 1969.

Lewis-Beck, Michael S., Anne Hildreth, and Alan B. Spitzer. "Was There a Girondist Faction in the National Convention, 1792–93?" *French Historical Studies* 15, no. 3 (1988): 519–36.

Lilti, Antoine. *Le Monde des salons: sociabilité et mondanité à Paris au XVIIIe siècle.* Paris: Fayard, 2005.

Linton, Marisa. "Robespierre's Political Principles." In *Robespierre*, edited by Colin Haydon and William Doyle. Cambridge: Cambridge University Press, 1999.

———. *The Politics of Virtue in Enlightenment France.* New York: Palgrave, 2001.

Lowenthal, David. "Montesquieu and the Classics: Republican Government in the *Spirit of the Laws*." In *Ancients and Moderns: Essays on the Tradition of Political Philosophy in Honor of Leo Strauss*, edited by Joseph Crospey. New York: Basic Books, 1964.

Lucas, Colin. *The Structure of the Terror: The Example of Javogues and the Loire.* Oxford: Oxford University Press, 1973.

———. "Revolutionary Violence, the People, and the Terror." In *The Terror*, edited by Keith Baker. Volume 4 of *The French Revolution and the Creation of Modern Political Culture.* 4 vols. Oxford: Pergamon Press, 1987–94.

Lüdtke, Alf, and Herbert Reinke. "Crime, Police, and the 'Good Order:' Germany." In *Crime History and Histories of Crime*, edited by Clive Emsley and Louis A. Knafla. Westport: Greenwood Press, 1996.

Lutaud, Olivier. *Des révolutions d'Angleterre à la Révolution française: le tyrannicide et "Killing No Murder."* The Hague: Nijhoff, 1973.

Malcom, Noel. *Aspects of Hobbes*. Oxford: Oxford University Press, 2002.

Malia, Martin, *History's Locomotives: Revolutions and the Making of the Modern World*. New Haven: Yale University Press, 2006.

Manent, Pierre. *An Intellectual History of Liberalism*. Translated by Rebecca Balinski. Princeton: Princeton University Press, 1994.

Mansfield, Paul. "The Repression of Lyon, 1793–94: Origins, Responsibility, and Significance." *French History* 2, no. 1 (1988): 74–101.

Manuel, Frank. *The Eighteenth Century Confronts the Gods*. Cambridge: Harvard University Press, 1959.

Manuel, Frank, and P. Fritzie. *Utopian Thought in the Western World*. Cambridge: Harvard University Press, 1979.

Marchi, Dudley M. "Montaigne and the New World: The Cannibalism of Cultural Production." *Modern Language Studies* 23, no. 4 (1993): 35–54.

Mari, Eric de. "La mise hors de la loi sous la Révolution française." 2 vols. PhD diss., Université de Montpellier, 1991.

Markley, Robert. " 'Land Enough in the World': Locke's Golden Age and the Infinite Extension of 'Use.' " *South Atlantic Quarterly* 98, no. 4 (1999): 817–37.

Marouby, Christian. *Utopie et primitivisme: Essai sur l'imaginaire anthropologique à l'âge classique*. Paris: Seuil, 1990.

Martin, Jean-Clément. *La Vendée et la France*. Paris: Seuil, 1987.

———. *Contre-Révolution, révolution et nation en France, 1789–99*. Paris: Seuil, 1999.

———. *Violence et révolution: essai sur la naissance d'un mythe national*. Paris: Seuil, 2006.

———. "Response Essay." In *H-France Forum* 2, no. 2 (2007). http://h-france.net/forum/forumvol2/Martin1Response.html.

Maslan, Susan. *Revolutionary Acts: Theater, Democracy, and the French Revolution*. Baltimore: Johns Hopkins University Press, 2005.

Masters, Roger. *The Political Philosophy of Rousseau*. Princeton: Princeton University Press, 1968.

Mathiez, Albert. *La vie chère et le mouvement social sous la Terreur*. Paris: Payot, 1927.

Mattingly, H. "Virgil's Golden Age: Sixth *Aeneid* and Fourth *Eclogue*." *Classical Review* 48, no. 5 (1934): 161–65.

Mauzi, Robert. *L'idée du bonheur au XVIIIᵉ siècle*. Paris: Armand Colin, 1960.

Mayer, Arno. *The Furies: Violence and Terror in the French and Russian Revolutions*. Princeton: Princeton University Press, 2000.

McAuley, Mary. *Bread and Justice: State and Society in Petrograd, 1917–22*. Oxford: Clarendon Press, 1991.

McDonald, Christie. *The Dialogue of Writing: Essays in Eighteenth-Century Literature*. Waterloo: Wilfrid Laurier University Press, 1984.

McKinley, Alexander. *Illegitimate Children of Enlightenment: Anarchists and the French Revolution, 1880–1914*. New York: Peter Lang, 2008.

McMillan, Joseph. "Apocalyptic Terrorism: The Case for Preventive Action." *Strategic*

Forum 212 (2004). http://www.ndu.edu/inss/strforum/SF212/SF212_Final
.pdf.

Mellor, Ronald. "Tacitus, Academic Politics, and Regicide in the Reign of Charles I:
The Tragedy of Dr. Isaac Dorislaus." *International Journal of the Classical Tradition* 11, no. 2 (2004): 153–93.

Mercier-Faivre, Anne-Marie. *Un Supplément à l' "Encyclopédie": Le "Monde Primitif"
d'Antoine Court de Gébelin.* Paris: Champion, 1999.

Merriman, John. *The Dynamite Club: How a Bombing in Fin-de-Siècle Paris Ignited
the Age of Modern Terror.* New York: Houghton Mifflin, 2009.

Michaud, J. F. *Biographie universelle ancienne et moderne.* 45 vols. Paris: Mme C.
Desplaces, 1843–65.

Michelet, Jules. *Histoire de la Révolution française.* 2 vols. Edited by Gérard Walter.
Paris: Gallimard/Pléiade, 1952.

Miller, Mary Ashburn. "Violence and Nature in the French Revolutionary Imagination, 1789–94." PhD diss., Johns Hopkins University, 2008.

Mitchell, P. C. "An Underlying Theme in *La Princesse de Babylone.*" *Studies on Voltaire
and the Eighteenth Century* 137 (1975): 31–45.

Monar, Jörg. *Saint-Just: Sohn, Denker und Protagonist der Revolution.* Bonn: Bouvier,
1993.

Monnier, Raymonde. "Républicanisme et révolution française." *French Historical Studies* 26, no. 1 (2003): 87–118.

———. *Républicanisme, patriotisme et Révolution française.* Paris: L'Harmattan, 2005.

Morel, Henri. "Le poids de l'antiquité sur la Révolution française." In *L'influence
de l'Antiquité sur la pensée politique européenne.* Aix: Presses universitaires d'Aix-
Marseille, 1996.

Mulier, E. Haitsma. *The Myth of Venice and Dutch Republican Thought in the Seventeenth Century.* Translated by Gerard T. Moran. Assen: Van Gorcum, 1980.

Mullan, John. *Sentiment and Sociability: The Language of Feeling in the Eighteenth
Century.* New York: Oxford University Press, 1988.

Muthu, Sankar. *Enlightenment against Empire.* Princeton: Princeton University Press,
2003.

Neely, Mark. *The Fate of Liberty: Abraham Lincoln and Civil Liberties.* Oxford: Oxford University Press, 1991.

Neff, Stephen C. *War and the Law of Nations: A General History.* Cambridge: Cambridge University Press, 2005.

Neill, Thomas P. "Quesnay and Physiocracy." *Journal of the History of Ideas* 9, no. 2
(1948): 153–73.

Nelson, Eric. *The Greek Tradition in Republican Thought.* Cambridge: Cambridge
University Press, 2004.

Nicolet, Claude. *L'idée républicaine en France.* Paris: Gallimard, 1982.

Nora, Pierre. "Republic." In *A Critical Dictionary of the French Revolution,* edited by
François Furet and Mona Ozouf, translated by Arthur Goldhammer. Cambridge:
Belknap Press of Harvard University Press, 1989.

Ozouf, Mona. *L'école de la France: essais sur la révolution, l'utopie, et l'enseignement.* Paris: Gallimard, 1984.

———. *Festivals of the French Revolution.* Translated by Alan Sheridan. Cambridge: Harvard University Press, 1988.

———. *L'homme régénéré: essais sur la Révolution française.* Paris: Gallimard, 1989.

———. "The King's Trial." In *A Critical Dictionary of the French Revolution,* edited by François Furet and Mona Ozouf, translated by Arthur Goldhammer. Cambridge: Belknap Press of Harvard University Press, 1989.

———. "The Terror after the Terror: An Immediate History." In *The Terror,* edited by Keith Baker. Volume 4 of *The French Revolution and the Creation of Modern Political Culture.* 4 vols. Oxford: Pergamon Press, 1987–94.

Pagden, Anthony. *The Fall of Natural Man: The American Indian and the Origins of Comparative Ethnology.* Cambridge: Cambridge University Press, 1987.

———, ed. *The Languages of Political Theory in Early-Modern Europe.* Cambridge: Cambridge University Press, 1987.

———. *Lords of All the World: Ideologies of Empire in Spain, Britain, and France, c. 1500–c. 1800.* New Haven: Yale University Press, 1995.

Palmer, R. R. *Twelve Who Ruled: The Year of the Terror in the French Revolution.* 1941. Princeton: Princeton University Press, 1989.

———. *The Improvement of Humanity: Education and the French Revolution.* Princeton: Princeton University Press, 1985.

Parker, Harold. *The Cult of Antiquity and the French Revolutionaries: A Study in the Development of the Revolutionary Spirit.* Chicago: University of Chicago Press, 1937.

Pasquino, Pasquale. "The Constitutional Republicanism of Emmanuel Sieyès." In *Invention of Modern Republicanism,* edited by Biancamaria Fontana. Cambridge: Cambridge University Press, 1994.

Patrick, Alison. *The Men of the First French Republic: Political Alignments in the National Convention of 1792.* Baltimore: Johns Hopkins University Press, 1972.

Patyk, Lynn. *Written in Blood: Revolutionary Terrorism and Russian Literary Culture,* forthcoming.

Paulson, Ronald. *Representations of Revolution (1789–1820).* New Haven: Yale University Press, 1983.

Pavel, Thomas. *Fictional Worlds.* Cambridge: Harvard University Press, 1986.

Peace, Richard. "Dostoyevsky and 'The Golden Age.'" *Dostoyevsky Studies* 3 (1982): 61–78.

Pearson, Roger. *The Fables of Reason: A Study of Voltaire's "Contes Philosophiques."* Oxford: Oxford University Press, 1993.

———. *Voltaire Almighty: A Life in Pursuit of Freedom.* London: Bloomsbury, 2005.

Pellerin, Pascale. "Le *Code de la nature* ou l'histoire d'un procès intenté à Diderot." *SVEC* 1 (2003): 105–17.

Perovic, Sanja. "Untamable Time: A Literary and Historical Panorama of the French Revolutionary Calendar (1792–1805)." PhD diss., Stanford University, 2004.

Pertué, Michel. "La Révolution française et l'abolition de la peine de mort." *AHRF* 251 (1983): 14–37.

———. "Les projets constitutionnels de 1793." In *Révolution et république: L'exception française*, edited by Michel Vovelle. Paris: Kimé, 1994.

Petrey, Sandy ed. *The French Revolution 1789–1989: Two Hundred Years of Rethinking*. Lubbock: Texas Tech University Press, 1989.

Pocock, J. G. A. *Barbarism and Religion*. 4 vols. Cambridge: Cambridge University Press, 1999–2008.

———. *The Machiavellian Moment: Florentine Political Thought and the Atlantic Republican Tradition*. 2nd ed. Princeton: Princeton University Press, 2003.

Poirier, Jacques, ed. *L'âge d'or*. Dijon: Figures libres, 1996.

Popkin, Jeremy. "Not Over After All: The French Revolution's Third Century." *Journal of Modern History* 74 (2002): 801–21.

Porset, Charles. *Les Philalèthes et les convents de Paris. Une politique de la folie*. Paris: Champion, 1996.

Putnam, Robert D., with Robert Leonardi and Raffaella Y. Nanetti. *Making Democracy Work: Civic Traditions in Modern Italy*. Princeton: Princeton University Press, 1994.

Ragon de Bettignies, J.-M. *Orthodoxie maçonnique, suivie de la Maçonnerie occulte . . .* Paris: Dentu, 1853.

Rahe, Paul A. *Republics Ancient and Modern: Classical Republicanism and the American Revolution*. Chapel Hill: University of North Carolina Press, 1992.

Rappaport, Michael. *Nationality and Citizenship in Revolutionary France: The Treatment of Foreigners, 1789–99*. Oxford: Clarendon Press, 2000.

Raskolnikoff, Mouza. "L'adoration' des Romains sous la Révolution française et la réaction de Volney et des Idéologues." In *Des anciens et des modernes*. Paris: Publications de la Sorbonne, 1990.

Rawls, John. *A Theory of Justice*. Rev. ed. Cambridge: Belknap Press of Harvard University Press, 1999.

Reddy, William. *The Navigation of Feeling: A Framework for the History of Emotions*. Cambridge: Cambridge University Press, 2001.

Renwick, John, ed. *Language and Rhetoric of the Revolution*. Edinburgh: Edinburgh University Press, 1990.

Richter, Melvin. *The Political Theory of Montesquieu*. Cambridge: Cambridge University Press, 1977.

———. "The Comparative Study of Regimes and Societies." In *The Cambridge History of Eighteenth-Century Political Thought*, edited by Mark Goldie and Robert Wolker. Cambridge: Cambridge University Press, 2006.

Riley, Patrick. *The General Will before Rousseau: The Transformation of the Divine into the Civic*. Princeton: Princeton University Press, 1986.

———, ed. *The Cambridge Companion to Rousseau*. Cambridge: Cambridge University Press, 2001.

———. "The Social Contract and Its Critics." In *The Cambridge History of Eighteenth-*

Century Political Thought, edited by Mark Goldie and Robert Wolker. Cambridge: Cambridge University Press, 2006.

——. "Fénelon's 'Republican' Monarchism in *Telemachus*." In *Monarchisms in the Age of Enlightenment: Liberty, Patriotism, and the Common Good*, edited by Hans Blom, John Christian Laursen, and Luisa Simonutti. Toronto: University of Toronto Press, 2007.

Riskin, Jessica. *Science in the Age of Sensibility*. Chicago: University of Chicago Press, 2002.

Robbins, Caroline. *The Eighteenth-Century Commonwealthman*. Cambridge: Harvard University Press, 1959.

Roberts, Warren. *Jacques-Louis David and Jean-Louis Prieur, Revolutionary Artists: The Public, the Populace, and Images of the French Revolution*. Albany: SUNY Press, 2000.

Robertson, Geoffrey. *The Tyrannicide Brief: The Story of the Man Who Sent Charles I to the Scaffold*. New York: Pantheon, 2006.

Robinson, Greg. *By Order of the President: FDR and the Internment of Japanese Americans*. Cambridge: Harvard University Press, 2001.

Roche, Daniel. "La violence vue d'en bas. Réflexions sur les moyens de la politique en période révolutionnaire." *Annales ESC* 1 (1989): 47–65.

Rodgers, Daniel T. "Republicanism: The Career of a Concept." *Journal of American History* 79, no. 1 (1992): 11–38.

Ronen, Ruth. *Possible Worlds in Literary Theory*. Cambridge: Cambridge University Press, 1994.

Rose, R. B. *Gracchus Babeuf: The First Revolutionary Communist*. Stanford: Stanford University Press, 1978.

Rosenberg, William G., ed. *Bolshevik Visions: First Phase of the Cultural Revolution in Soviet Russia*. Ann Arbor: University of Michigan Press, 1990.

Rosenblatt, Helena. *Rousseau and Geneva: From the First Discourse to the Social Contract, 1749–62*. Cambridge: Cambridge University Press, 1997.

Rothbard, Murray. "The Political Thought of Etienne de la Boétie." Introduction to Etienne de la Boétie. In *The Politics of Obedience: The Discourse of Voluntary Servitude*, translated by Harry Kurz. New York: Free Editions, 1975.

Rothkrug, Lionel. *Opposition to Louis XIV: The Political and Social Origins of the French Enlightenment*. Princeton: Princeton University Press, 1965.

Rothschild, Emma. *Economic Sentiments: Condorcet, Adam Smith, and the Enlightenment*. Cambridge: Harvard University Press, 2001.

Roussel, Jean, ed. *L'héritage des lumières: Volney et les ideologues*. Angers: Presses de l'Université d'Angers, 1988.

Rubin, Alfred. *The Law of Piracy*. Newport: Naval War College Press, 1989.

Rudé, George. *The Crowd in the French Revolution*. Oxford: Oxford University Press, 1967.

Rufi, Enrico. *Le rêve laïque de Louis-Sébastien Mercier, entre littérature et politique*. *SVEC* 326. Oxford: Voltaire Foundation, 1995.

Russo, Elena. "The Youth of Moral Life: The Virtue of the Ancients." In *Montesquieu and the Spirit of Modernity*, edited by David W. Carrithers and Patrick Coleman. *SVEC* 9. Oxford: Voltaire Foundation, 2002.

———. *Styles of Enlightenment: Taste, Politics, and Authorship in Eighteenth-Century France*. Baltimore: Johns Hopkins University Press, 2007.

Sandel, Michael. *Democracy's Discontent: America in Search of a Public Philosophy*. Cambridge: Belknap Press of Harvard University Press, 1996.

Schaefer, David Lewis. "Of Cannibals and Kings: Montaigne's Egalitarianism." *Review of Politics* 43, no. 1 (1981): 43–74.

Schaeffer, Jean-Marie. *Pourquoi la fiction?* Paris: Seuil, 1999.

Schama, Simon. *Citizens*. New York: Vintage, 1990.

Schaub, Diana. *Erotic Liberalism: Women and Revolution in Montesquieu's "Persian Letters."* Lanham: Rowman and Littlefield, 1995.

Schmitt, Carl. *The "Nomos" of the Earth in the International Law of the "Jus Publicum Europaeum."* Translated and edited by G. L. Ulmen. New York: Telos Press, 2003.

———. *Political Theology: Four Chapters on the Concept of Sovereignty*. 1922. Translated by George Schwab. Chicago: University of Chicago Press, 2005.

Schwab, George. "Enemy or Foe: A Conflict of Modern Politics." *Telos* 72 (1987): 194–201.

Schwab, Raymond. *The Oriental Renaissance: Europe's Rediscovery of India and the East, 1680–1880*. Translated by Gene Patterson-Black and Victor Reinking. New York: Columbia University Press, 1984.

Schwartz, Robert M., and Robert A. Schneider, eds. *Tocqueville and Beyond: Essays on the Old Regime in Honor of David D. Bien*. Newark: University of Delaware Press, 2003.

Scott, Joan Wallach. *Only Paradoxes to Offer: French Feminists and the Rights of Man*. Cambridge: Harvard University Press, 1996.

Scubla, Lucien. "Est-il possible de mettre la loi au dessus de l'homme? Sur la philosophie politique de Jean-Jacques Rousseau." In Jean-Pierre Dupuy, *Introduction aux sciences sociales: logique des phénomènes collectifs*. Paris: Ellipses, 1992.

Sécher, Reynald. *Le génocide franco-français, la Vendée-Vengé*. Paris: PUF, 1986.

Seliger, Martin. "Locke's Natural Law and the Foundation of Politics." *Journal of the History of Ideas* 24, no. 3 (1963): 337–54.

Sewell, William H., Jr. *The Rhetoric of Bourgeois Revolution: The Abbé Sieyes and "What Is the Third Estate?"* Durham: Duke University Press, 1994.

———. *Logics of History: Social Theory and Social Transformation*. Chicago: University of Chicago Press, 2005.

Shackleton, Robert. *Montesquieu: A Critical Biography*. Oxford: Oxford University Press, 1970.

———. "Montesquieu and Machiavelli: A Reappraisal." *Comparative Literature Studies* 1 (1964): 1–13.

Shapiro, Barry. *Revolutionary Justice in Paris, 1789–90*. Cambridge: Cambridge University Press, 1993.

Sharp, James Roger. *American Politics in the Early Republic: The New Nation in Crisis*. New Haven: Yale University Press, 1995.

Shklar, Judith. *Men and Citizens: A Study of Rousseau's Social Theory*. Cambridge: Cambridge University Press, 1969.

———. "Montesquieu and the New Republicanism." In *Machiavelli and Republicanism*, edited by Gisele Bock, Quentin Skinner, and Maurizio Viroli. Cambridge: Cambridge University Press, 1990.

Shlapentokh, Dmitry. *The French Revolution in Russian Intellectual Life, 1865–1905*. Westport: Praeger, 1996.

Shovlin, John. *The Political Economy of Virtue: Luxury, Patriotism, and the Origins of the French Revolution*. Ithaca: Cornell University Press, 2006.

Sibenaler, Jean. *Il se faisait appeler Volney: approche biographique de Constantin-François Chassebœuf, 1757–1820*. Maulévrier: Hérault, 1992.

Silverstein, Paul A. "The New Barbarians: Piracy and Terrorism on the North African Frontier." *CR: The New Centennial Review* 5, no. 1 (2005): 179–212.

Simonin, Anne. "An Essay of Political Cartography: The Law of Citizenship under the French Revolution (1793–95)." http://www.crhq.cnrs.fr/images-axe5/tableaux/axe5%20tab-TraducABarnes.pdf.

———. "Les acquittés de la Grande Terreur: réflexions sur l'amitié dans la République." In *Les politiques de la Terreur, 1793–94*, edited by Michel Biard. Rennes: Presses universitaires de Rennes & Société des études robespierristes, 2008.

———. *Le déshonneur dans la république: une histoire de l'indignité, 1791–58*. Paris: Grasset, 2008.

Singer, Brian. *Society, Theory, and the French Revolution: Studies in the Revolutionary Imaginary*. Basingstoke: Macmillan, 1986.

Skinner, Quentin. "The Republican Idea of Political Liberty." In *Machiavelli and Republicanism*, edited by Gisele Bock, Quentin Skinner, and Maurizio Viroli. Cambridge: Cambridge University Press, 1990.

———. "A Third Concept of Liberty." *Proceedings of the British Academy* 117 (2002): 237–68.

Smith, Jay M. *Nobility Reimagined: The Patriotic Nation in Eighteenth-Century France*. Ithaca: Cornell University Press, 2005.

Soboul, Albert, ed. *Actes du colloque Saint-Just*. Paris: Société des études robespierristes, 1968.

———. *Les sans-culottes parisiens en l'an II: mouvement populaire et gouvernement révolutionnaire (1793–94)*. Paris: Seuil, 1968.

———. *Mouvement populaire et gouvernement révolutionnaire en l'an II (1793–94)*. Paris: Flammarion, 1973.

———. "Utopie et Révolution française." In volume 1 of *Histoire générale du socialisme*, edited by Jacques Droz. 4 vols. Paris: PUF, 1979.

Soll, Jacob. *Publishing "The Prince": History, Reading, and the Birth of Political Criticism*. Ann Arbor: University of Michigan Press, 2005.

Solomon, Peter H. *Soviet Criminal Justice under Stalin*. Cambridge: Cambridge University Press, 1996.

Sonenscher, Michael. *Work and Wages: Natural Law, Politics, and the Eighteenth-Century French Trades.* Cambridge: Cambridge University Press, 1989.

———. "Physiocracy as Theodicy," *History of Political Thought* 23, no. 2 (2002): 326–39.

———. "Republicanism, State Finances and the Emergence of Commercial Society in Eighteenth-Century France—or from Royal to Ancient Republicanism and Back." In *Republicanism: A Shared European Heritage,* edited by Martin van Gelderen and Quentin Skinner. 2 vols. Cambridge: Cambridge University Press, 2002.

———. "Property, Community, and Citizenship." In *The Cambridge History of Eighteenth-Century Political Thought,* edited by Mark Goldie and Robert Wolker. Cambridge: Cambridge University Press, 2006.

———. *Before the Deluge: Public Debt, Inequality, and the Intellectual Origins of the French Revolution.* Princeton: Princeton University Press, 2007.

Sorel, Georges. *Introduction à l'économie moderne.* 1902. Paris: Rivière, 1922.

———. *La décomposition du marxisme.* Paris: Rivière, 1908.

———. *Reflections on Violence.* Edited and translated by Jeremy Jennings. Cambridge: Cambridge University Press, 1999.

Spang, Rebecca L. "Paradigms and Paranoia: How Modern Is the French Revolution?" *American Historical Review* 108 (2003): 119–47.

Spieler, Miranda Frances. "Empire and Underworld: Guiana in the French Legal Imagination, c. 1789–c. 1870." PhD diss., Columbia University, 2005.

Spitz, Jean-Fabien. *La liberté politique.* Paris: PUF, 1995.

Starkey, David J., Els van Eyck van Heslinga, and J. A. de Moor. *Pirates and Privateers: New Perspectives on the War on Trade in the Eighteenth and Nineteenth Centuries.* Exeter: Exeter University Press, 1997.

Starobinski, Jean. *Jean-Jacques Rousseau: la transparence et l'obstacle.* 1957. Paris: Gallimard, 1971.

———. "Sur quelques symboles de la Révolution française." *NRF* 188, no. 16 (1968): 41–67.

———. *Le remède dans le mal: critique et légitimation de l'artifice à l'âge des Lumières.* Paris: Gallimard, 1989.

———. "Eloquence antique, éloquence future: aspects d'un lieu commun d'ancien régime." In *The Political Culture of the Old Regime,* edited by Keith Baker, volume 1 of *The French Revolution and the Creation of Modern Political Culture.* 4 vols. Oxford: Pergamon Press, 1987–94.

———. "L'inclinaison de l'axe du globe." In Jean-Jacques Rousseau, *Essai sur l'origine des langues.* Paris: Gallimard, 1990.

Starr, Chester G. "Virgil's Acceptance of Octavian." *American Journal of Philology* 76, no. 1 (1955): 34–46.

Stora-Lamarre, Annie. *La république des faibles: les origines intellectuelles du droit républicain, 1870–1914.* Paris: Armand Colin, 2005.

Strauss, Leo. *Natural Right and History.* Chicago: University of Chicago Press, 1948.

Strugnell, Anthony. *Diderot's Politics: A Study of the Evolution of Diderot's Political Thought after the "Encyclopédie."* The Hague: Martinus Nijhoff, 1973.

Sunstein, Cass. *Republic.com*. Princeton: Princeton University Press, 2002.

Sutherland, Donald. *France 1789–1815: Revolution and Counterrevolution*. New York: Oxford University Press, 1986.

———. *The French Revolution and Empire: The Quest for a Civic Order*. Oxford: Blackwell, 2003.

Sweet, William. "The Volksgerichtshof: 1934–45." *Journal of Modern History* 46, no. 2 (1974): 314–29.

Swenson, James. *On Jean-Jacques Rousseau Considered as One of the First Authors of the Revolution*. Stanford: Stanford University Press, 2000.

———. "Saint-Just and Billaud-Varenne." Paper presented at the annual meeting of the Western Society for French History, Colorado Springs, CO, October 28–29, 2005.

Sydenham, M. J. *The Girondins*. London: Athlone Press, 1961.

Symcox, Geoffrey. *The Crisis of French Sea Power: From the "Guerre d'Escadre" to the "Guerre de Course."* The Hague: Nijhoff, 1974.

Tackett, Timothy. *Becoming a Revolutionary: The Deputies of the French National Assembly and the Emergence of a Revolutionary Culture (1789–90)*. Princeton: Princeton University Press, 1996.

———. "Conspiracy Obsession in a Time of Revolution: French Elites and the Origins of the Terror: 1789–92." *American Historical Review* 105 (2000): 691–713.

———. "Interpreting the Terror." *French Historical Studies* 24 (2001): 569–78.

———. *When the King Took Flight*. Cambridge: Harvard University Press, 2003.

———. "La Révolution et la violence." In *La Révolution à l'œuvre*, edited by Jean-Clément Martin. Rennes: Presses universitaires de Rennes, 2005.

Tai, Emily Sohmer. "Marking Water: Piracy and Property in the Pre-Modern West." Paper presented at "Seascapes, Littoral Cultures, and Trans-Oceanic Exchanges," Library of Congress, Washington, DC, February 12–15, 2003. http://www.historycooperative.org/proceedings/seascapes/tai.html, n9.

Tierney, Brian. *The Idea of Natural Rights: Studies on Natural Rights, Natural Law, and Church Law, 1150–1625*. Atlanta: Scholars Press, 1997.

Tilly, Charles. *Democracy*. Cambridge: Cambridge University Press, 2007.

Tocqueville, Alexis de. *Democracy in America*. 1835. Translated by George Lawrence. New York: HarperCollins, 1969.

———. *The Old Regime and Revolution*. 1856. Edited by François Furet and Françoise Mélonio, translated by Alan S. Kahan. Chicago: University of Chicago Press, 1998.

Tonnesson, K. D. "The Babouvists: From Utopian to Practical Socialism." *Past and Present* 22 (1962): 60–76.

Tournon, André. "Justice and the Law: On the Reverse Side of the Essays." In *The Cambridge Companion to Montaigne*, edited by Ullrich Langer. Cambridge: Cambridge University Press, 2005.

Tuck, Richard. *Natural Rights Theories: Their Origins and Development*. Cambridge: Cambridge University Press, 1981.

———. *The Rights of War and Peace: Political Thought and the International Order from Grotius to Kant.* Oxford: Oxford University Press, 1999.

Tucker, Robert C. *Philosophy and Myth in Karl Marx.* 3rd ed. New Brunswick, NJ: Transaction, 2001.

Turchetti, Mario. *Tyrannie et tyrannicide de l'Antiquité à nos jours.* Paris: PUF, 2001.

Van Den Abbeele, Georges. "Utopian Sexuality and its Discontents: Exoticism and Colonialism in the *Supplément au voyage de Bougainville.*" *L'Esprit créateur* 24 (1984): 43–52.

Van Kley, Dale. *The Damiens Affair and the Unraveling of the Ancien Régime, 1750–70.* Princeton: Princeton University Press, 1984.

———. "From the Lessons of French History to Truths for All Times and All People: The Historical Origins of an Anti-historical Declaration." In *The French Idea of Freedom: The Old Regime and the Declaration of Rights of 1789,* edited by Dale Van Kley. Stanford: Stanford University Press, 1994.

Vanpée, Janie. "Performing Justice: The Trials of Olympe de Gouges." *Theatre Journal* 51, no. 1 (1999): 47–65.

Vartanian, Aram. "Eroticism and Politics in the *Lettres persanes.*" *Romanic Review* 60 (1969): 23–33.

Venturi, Franco. *Utopia and Reform in the Enlightenment.* Cambridge: Cambridge University Press, 1971.

———. *The End of the Old Regime in Europe, 1776–89.* 2 vols. Translated by R. Burr Litchfield. Princeton: Princeton University Press, 1991.

Vernant, Jean-Pierre. *Mythe et pensée chez les Grecs.* Paris: Maspero, 1965.

Viatte, Auguste. *Les sources occultes du Romantisme: illuminisme—thésophie, 1770–1820.* 1927. 2 vols. Paris: Champion, 1979.

Vicenti, Luc. *Jean-Jacques Rousseau: l'individu et la république.* Paris: Kimé, 2001.

Vila, Anne. *Enlightenment and Pathology: Sensibility in the Literature and Medicine of Eighteenth-Century France.* Baltimore: Johns Hopkins University Press, 1998.

Vizetelly, Ernest A. *The Anarchists, Their Faith and Their Record.* London: John Lane, 1911.

Vovelle, Michel. *Révolution et religion: la déchristianisation de l'an II.* Paris: Hachette, 1976.

———. *La Révolution française: images et récits.* 5 vols. Paris: Livre club Diderot/ Messidor, 1986.

———. *La Révolution contre l'Eglise: de la Raison à l'Etre Suprême.* Brussels: Complexe, 1988.

———, ed. *L'Être Suprême.* Arras: Centre culturel Noroit, 1991.

———, ed. *Révolution et république: l'exception française.* Paris: Kimé, 1994.

Wachsmann, Nikolaus. *Hitler's Prisons: Legal Terror in Nazi Germany.* New Haven: Yale University Press, 2004.

Waddicor, Mark H. *Montesquieu and the Philosophy of Natural Law.* The Hague: Nijhoff, 1970.

Wagner, Nicolas. *Morelly, le méconnu des lumières.* Paris: Klincksieck, 1978.

Wahnich, Sophie. *La liberté ou la mort: essai sur la Terreur et le terrorisme.* Paris: La Fabrique, 2003.

Wahnich, Sophie, and Marc Belissa. "Les crimes des Anglais: trahir le droit." *AHRF* 300 (1995): 233–48.

Walzer, Michael, ed. *Regicide and Revolution.* Cambridge: Cambridge University Press, 1974.

Ward, Harry M. *The War for Independence and the Transformation of American Society.* London: UCL Press, 1999.

Wardhaugh, Jessica. "Between Sabotage and the Sublime: Anarchist Culture in Belle Epoque Paris." Paper presented at the annual meeting of the Society for the Study of French History, Aberystwyth, UK, July 3–4, 2008.

Waswo, Richard. "The Formation of Natural Law to Justify Colonialism, 1539–1689." *New Literary History* 27, no. 4 (1996): 743–59.

Weber, Caroline. "Freedom's Missed Moment." *Yale French Studies* 101 (2001): 9–31.

———. *Terror and Its Discontents: Suspect Words in Revolutionary France.* Minneapolis: University of Minnesota, 2003.

Weulersse, Georges. *Le mouvement physiocratique en France de 1756 à 1770.* 2 vols. Paris: Alcan, 1910.

Wills, Garry. *Inventing America: Jefferson's Declaration of Independence.* Garden City, NJ: Doubleday, 1978.

Winterer, Caroline. *The Mirror of Antiquity: American Women and the Classical Tradition, 1750–1900.* Ithaca: Cornell University Press, 2007.

Whatley, Janet. "Un retour secret vers la forêt: The Problem of Privacy and Order in Diderot's Tahiti." *Kentucky Romance Quarterly* 24 (1977): 199–208.

Whatmore, Richard. *Republicanism and the French Revolution: An Intellectual History of Jean-Baptiste Say's Political Economy.* Oxford: Oxford University Press, 2000.

White, Hayden. *Metahistory: The Historical Imagination in Nineteenth-Century Europe.* Baltimore: Johns Hopkins University Press, 1975.

Wolker, Robert. "The Influence of Diderot on the Political Theory of Rousseau: Two Aspects of a Relationship." In *Studies on Voltaire and the Eighteenth Century.* Oxford: Voltaire Foundation, 1975.

———, ed. *Rousseau and Liberty.* Manchester: Manchester University Press, 1995.

Woloch, Isser. *The New Regime: Transformations of the French Civic Order, 1789–1815.* New York: Norton, 1994.

Wolpe, Hans. *Raynal et sa machine de guerre: "L'Histoire des deux Indes" et ses perfectionnements.* Stanford: Stanford University Press, 1957.

Wood, Gordon. *The Creation of the American Republic, 1776–87.* Chapel Hill: University of North Carolina Press, 1969.

Woodcock, George. *Anarchism: A History of Libertarian Ideas and Movements.* 1962. Toronto: Broadview Press, 2004.

Wright, Johnson Kent. "National Sovereignty and the General Will: The Political Program of the *Déclaration des droits* of 1789." In *The French Idea of Freedom: The Old Regime and the Declaration of Rights of 1789*, edited by Dale Van Kley. Stanford: Stanford University Press, 1994.

———. *A Classical Republican in Eighteenth-Century France: The Political Thought of Mably*. Stanford: Stanford University Press, 1997.

———. "The Idea of a Republican Constitution in Old Regime France." In *Republicanism: A Shared European Heritage*, edited by Martin van Gelderen and Quentin Skinner. 2 vols. Cambridge: Cambridge University Press, 2002.

———. "Républicanisme et lumières." In *Dictionnaire critique de la République*, edited by Vincent Duclert and Christophe Prochasson. Paris: Flammarion, 2002.

———. "The Montesquieuian Moment: Republicanism in *De l'Esprit des lois*." Paper presented at the annual meeting of the Western Society for French History, Albuquerque, NM, November 7–10, 2007.

Yalom, Marilyn. *Blood Sisters: The French Revolution in Women's Memory*. New York: Basic Books, 1993.

Yates, Frances A. *Astraea: The Imperial Theme in the Sixteenth Century*. London: Routledge and K. Paul, 1975.

Yeazell, Ruth Bernard. *Harems of the Mind: Passages of Western Art and Literature*. New Haven: Yale University Press, 2000.

Yoo, John. *The Powers of War and Peace: The Constitution and Foreign Affairs after 9/11*. Chicago: University of Chicago Press, 2005.

Zakaria, Fareed. *The Future of Freedom: Illiberal Democracy at Home and Abroad*. New York: Norton, 2007.

Zemtsov, Ilya. *Encyclopedia of Soviet Life*. New Brunswick, NJ: Transaction, 1991.

Zuckert, Michael P. *Natural Rights and the New Republicanism*. Princeton: Princeton University Press, 1994.

———. *The Natural Rights Republic: Studies in the Foundation of the American Political Tradition*. Notre Dame: University of Notre Dame Press, 1996.

des gens), 69n78; *De l'esprit des lois
(On the Spirit of the Laws)*, 9, 62,
68–71, 187n58, 219n15, 219n16;
on importance of ancient laws
and institutions in a republic, 70;
Lettres persanes (Persian Letters),
11, 62–68, 84, 96n36, 97, 103,
199–200; opposition to clemency, 162n137; and public virtue,
70n84, 219, 219n16; *Temple de
Gnide*, 64, 113; theory of republicanism, 62–68, 70n80, 71; *Traité
des devoirs*, 63n61
Montgilbert, François-Agnès, 192–93,
212n122
More, Thomas: *Utopia*, 58
Morelly, Etienne-Gabriel: *Code de la
nature*, 112
Morris, William: *News from Nowhere*,
271
Mounier, Jean-Joseph, 194
Mountain (Montagnards): anti-
proceduralism, 155; attack on Louis
XVI as *ennemi du genre humain*,
18, 25, 144, 252; and Constitution of 1793, 22; and execution
of king, 149, 158, 159; focus on
Declaration of Rights rather than
Constitution, 152, 190–93; and
general will theory, 21, 208, 259;
and *hors-la-loi*, 157–58; opposition
to *appel au people*, 178; political
theories of, 210–12; prosecution of
Louis XVI, 4, 19, 144, 149, 151,
154–58, 159; republican philosophy, 19; and revolutionary tribunal,
136–37; struggle against Girondins, 167; and theory of tyrannicide, 152. *See also* Jacobins

Nantes, drownings of priests in, 143
National Constituent Assembly: laws
of exception, 140, 151; and penal

code reform, 127; and preliminary
Declaration, 190; 1789 martial law
decree, 140; 1791 decrees against
émigrés, 140, 159
National Convention, 4, 17; abolishment of departmental *directoires*,
174; conflation of natural and
positive law, 155, 162–63; creation
of revolutionary army, 139;
creation of revolutionary tribunal,
134–37; and death sentence for
political crimes, 133–34; declaration that existing laws and
authorities be provisionally upheld,
189; draconian laws, 20; economic
measures of September 1793, 255;
8 and 13 ventôse decrees, 229;
hors-la-loi decree, 144–45; infighting between Montagnards and
Girondins, 164, 170; justification
of Louis XVI's trial proceedings in
droit des gens, 152; law of suspects,
131, 137; laws of March–April
1793, 144; and legal authority
for judging the king, 149–51;
manipulation of popular demands,
139; and natural right, 149–52,
165; outlawing of rebel authorities, 19, 173–74; passing of laws
that disempowered Convention as
lawmaking body, 165–66; primacy
of laws of nature, 163; purge of
May 31–June 2, 1793, 21, 164,
173, 180, 187; reaction to Vendée war, 144; role of oratory in
revolutionary debates, 166–67;
September 21 decree (abolition of
royalty), 189n65
National Convention, and 1793 Constitution: debates of spring–
summer 1793, 210–14; delay in
constitutional debate, 189; drafting of Constitution, 187–97;

Made in the USA
San Bernardino, CA
26 March 2017